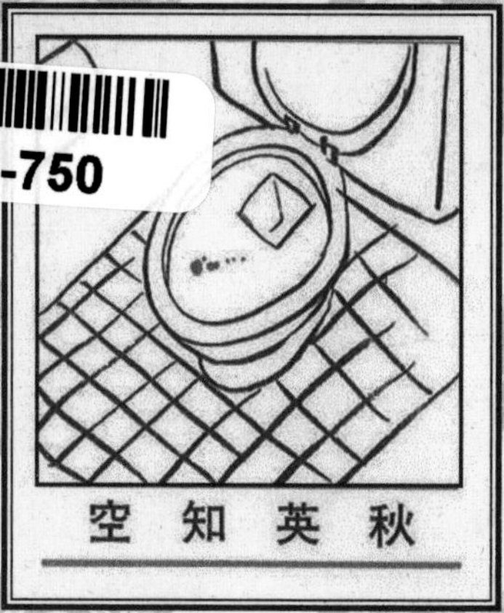
空知英秋

<u>Hideaki Sorachi</u>

In the previous volume, I asked readers for tips on treating hemorrhoids. I've received so many letters prescribing so many different treatments that I can't tell which ones are good and which aren't. But I've learned one thing—there are still "samurai" in this rotten world who won't leave a guy in the lurch. Yes, I'm talking about all of you.

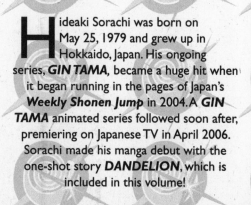

Hideaki Sorachi was born on May 25, 1979 and grew up in Hokkaido, Japan. His ongoing series, ***GIN TAMA***, became a huge hit when it began running in the pages of Japan's ***Weekly Shonen Jump*** in 2004. A ***GIN TAMA*** animated series followed soon after, premiering on Japanese TV in April 2006. Sorachi made his manga debut with the one-shot story ***DANDELION***, which is included in this volume!

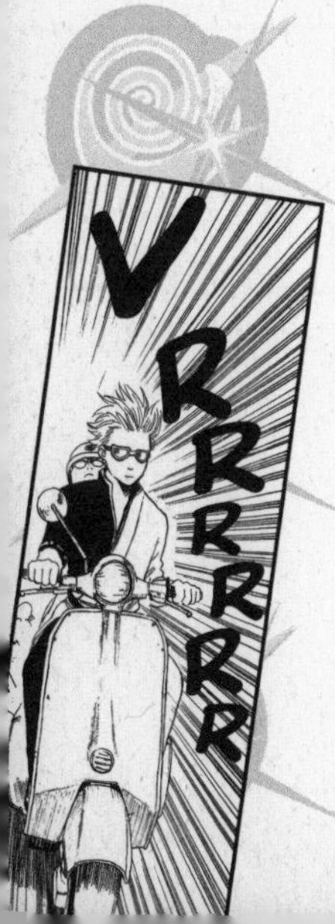
VRRRRRR

GIN TAMA VOL. 12
The SHONEN JUMP ADVANCED Manga Edition

STORY & ART BY HIDEAKI SORACHI

Translation/Kyoko Shapiro, Honyaku Center Inc.
English Adaptation/Lance Caselman
Touch-up Art & Lettering/Avril Averill
Cover Design/Izumi Evers
Interior Design/Ronnie Casson
Editor/Mike Montesa

Editor in Chief, Books/Alvin Lu
Editor in Chief, Magazines/Marc Weidenbaum
VP, Publishing Licensing/Rika Inouye
VP, Sales & Product Marketing/Gonzalo Ferreyra
VP, Creative/Linda Espinosa
Publisher/Hyoe Narita

Printed in the U.S.A.

Published by VIZ Media, LLC
P.O. Box 77010
San Francisco, CA 94107

SHONEN JUMP ADVANCED Manga Edition
10 9 8 7 6 5 4 3 2 1
First printing, May 2009

RATED T+ FOR OLDER TEEN

PARENTAL ADVISORY
GIN TAMA is rated T+ for Older Teen and is recommended for ages 16 and up. It contains suggestive situations.
ratings.viz.com

viz media
www.viz.com

THE WORLD'S MOST CUTTING-EDGE MANGA
SHONEN JUMP ADVANCED
www.shonenjump.com

gest

Shortest Way

STORY & ART BY
HIDEAKI SORACHI

GIN TAMA

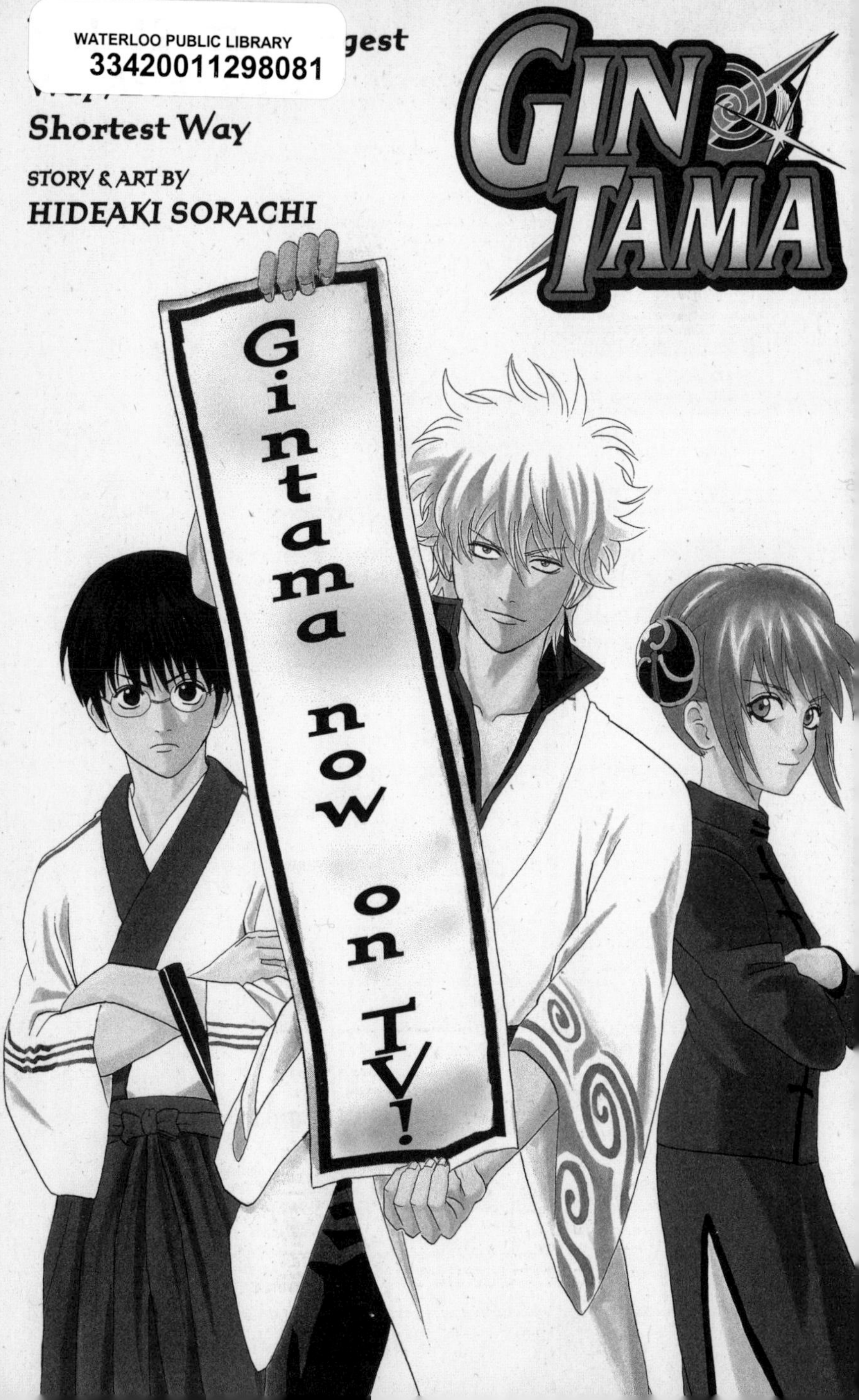
Gintama now on TV!

Cast of Characters

Yorozuya Members

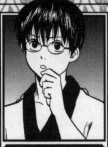

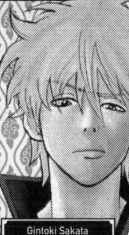

Gintoki Sakata

The hero of our story. If he doesn't eat something sweet periodically he gets cranky—really cranky. He boasts a powerful sword arm, but he's one step away from diabetes. A former member of the exclusionist faction that seeks to expel the space aliens and protect the nation.

Shinpachi Shimura

Works under Gintoki in an attempt to learn about the samurai spirit, but has often come to regret his decision recently. President of the Tsu Terakado Fan Club.

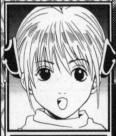

Kagura

A member of the "Yato Clan," the most powerful warrior race in the universe. Her voracious appetite and alien worldview lead frequently to laughter…and sometimes contusions.

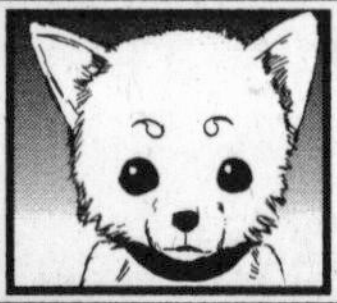

Sadaharu

A giant space creature turned office pet. Likes to bite people (especially Gin).

Shinsengumi Members

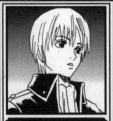

Okita

The Shinsengumi's most formidable swordsman. Behind a façade of amiability, he tirelessly schemes to eliminate Hijikata and usurp his position.

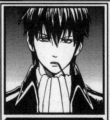

Hijikata

Vice-Chief of the Shinsengumi, Edo's elite counter-terrorist police unit. His air of detached cool transforms into hot rage the instant he draws his sword…or when someone disparages mayonnaise.

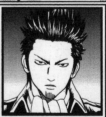

Kondo

The trusted chief of the Shinsengumi (and the remorseless stalker of Shinpachi's older sister Otae).

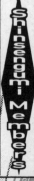

Other Characters

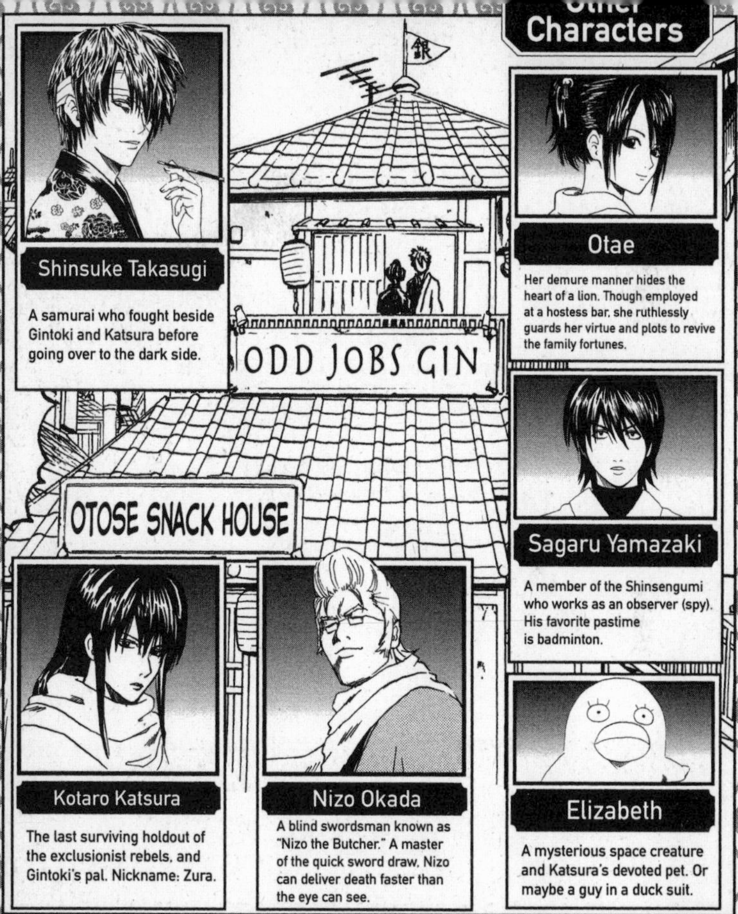
Shinsuke Takasugi
A samurai who fought beside Gintoki and Katsura before going over to the dark side.
Otae
Her demure manner hides the heart of a lion. Though employed at a hostess bar, she ruthlessly guards her virtue and plots to revive the family fortunes.
ODD JOBS GIN
Sagaru Yamazaki
A member of the Shinsengumi who works as an observer (spy). His favorite pastime is badminton.
OTOSE SNACK HOUSE
Kotaro Katsura
The last surviving holdout of the exclusionist rebels, and Gintoki's pal. Nickname: Zura.
Nizo Okada
A blind swordsman known as "Nizo the Butcher." A master of the quick sword draw, Nizo can deliver death faster than the eye can see.
Elizabeth
A mysterious space creature and Katsura's devoted pet. Or maybe a guy in a duck suit.

The story thus far

In an alternate-universe Edo (Tokyo), extraterrestrials land in Japan and the new government issues an order outlawing swords. The samurai, who have reached the pinnacle of power and prosperity, fall into rapid decline.

Twenty years hence, only one samurai has managed to hold onto his fighting spirit: a somewhat eccentric fellow named Gintoki "Odd Jobs Gin" Sakata. A lover of sweets and near diabetic, our hero sets up shop as a *yorozuya*—an expert at managing trouble and handling the oddest of jobs.

Joining Gin in his business is Shinpachi Shimura, whose sister Gin saved from the clutches of nefarious debt collectors. After a series of unusual events, the trio meets a powerful alien named Kagura, who becomes—after some arm-twisting—a part-time team member.

Shinpachi is conned by a girl with cat ears. Then Gin gets blown up while helping a "fast girl" deliver her packages and ends up in the care of a beautiful nurse/assassin. Now to stop Shinsuke Takasugi and his henchmen from destroying Edo with the demonic sword Benizakura, Gin attacks!

WHAT THIS MANGA'S FULL OF
vol. 12

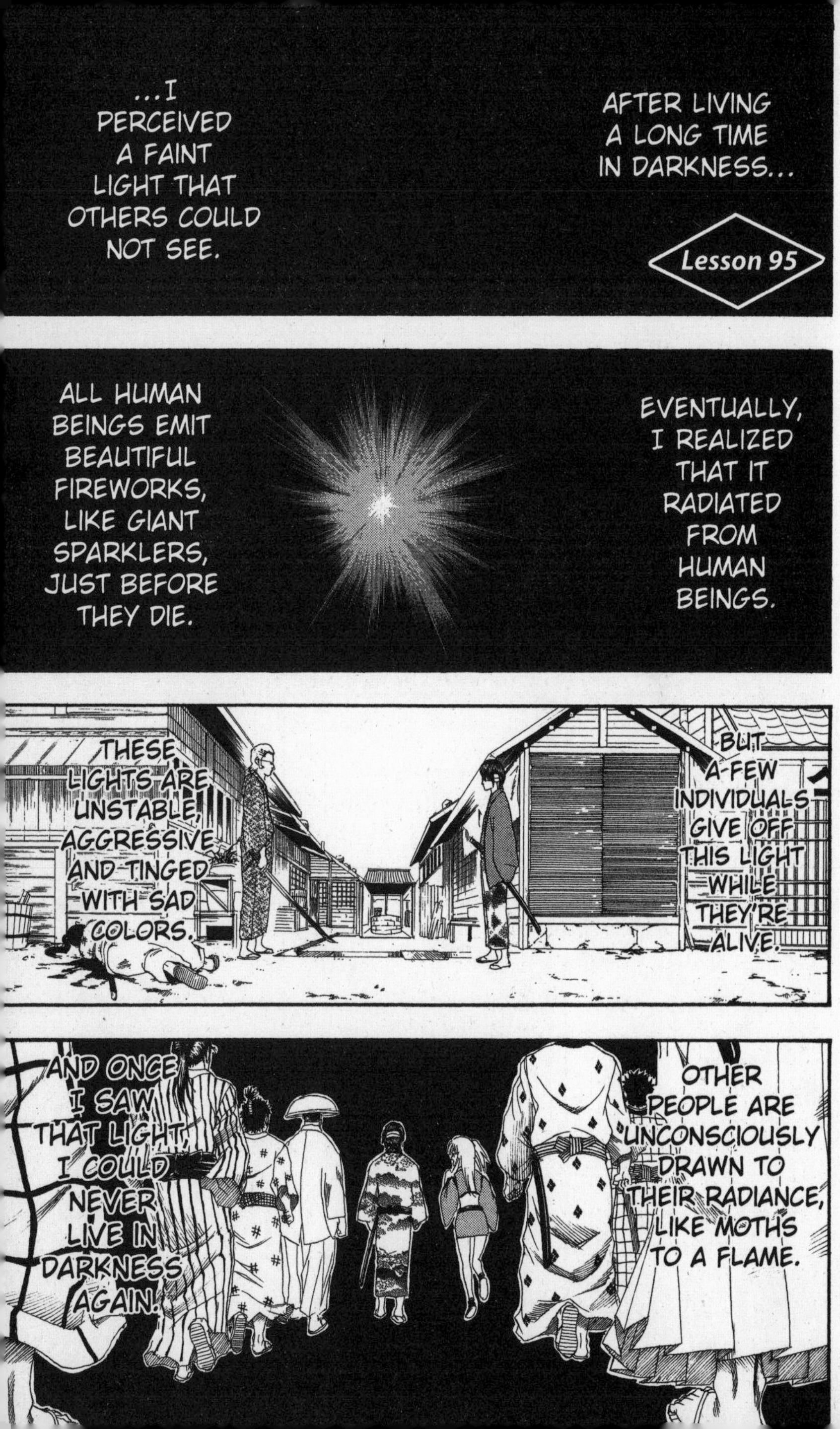
AFTER LIVING A LONG TIME IN DARKNESS...
Lesson 95
...I PERCEIVED A FAINT LIGHT THAT OTHERS COULD NOT SEE.
EVENTUALLY, I REALIZED THAT IT RADIATED FROM HUMAN BEINGS.
ALL HUMAN BEINGS EMIT BEAUTIFUL FIREWORKS, LIKE GIANT SPARKLERS, JUST BEFORE THEY DIE.
BUT A FEW INDIVIDUALS GIVE OFF THIS LIGHT WHILE THEY'RE ALIVE.
THESE LIGHTS ARE UNSTABLE, AGGRESSIVE AND TINGED WITH SAD COLORS.
OTHER PEOPLE ARE UNCONSCIOUSLY DRAWN TO THEIR RADIANCE, LIKE MOTHS TO A FLAME.
AND ONCE I SAW THAT LIGHT, I COULD NEVER LIVE IN DARKNESS AGAIN.

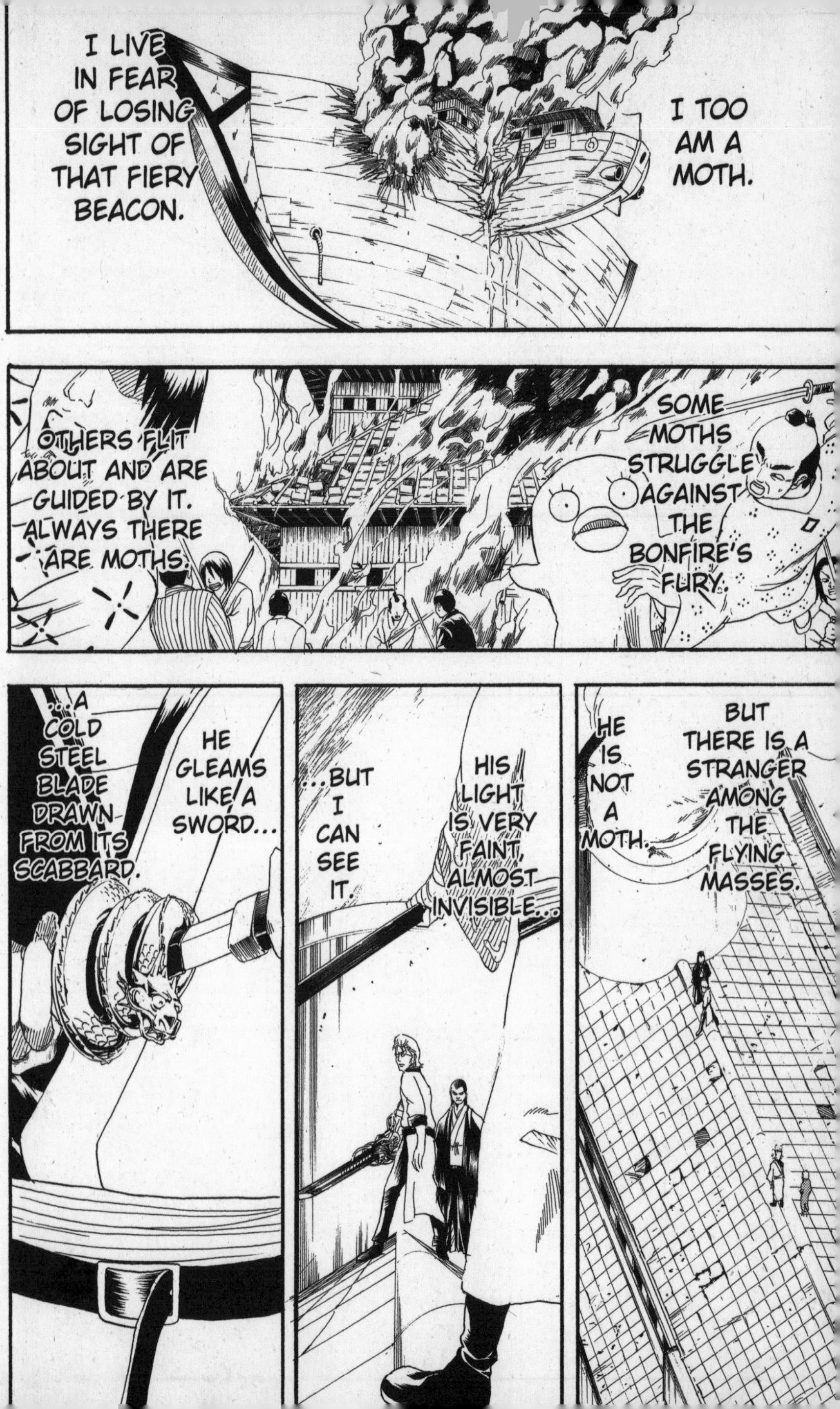
I TOO AM A MOTH.
I LIVE IN FEAR OF LOSING SIGHT OF THAT FIERY BEACON.
SOME MOTHS STRUGGLE AGAINST THE BONFIRE'S FURY.
OTHERS FLIT ABOUT AND ARE GUIDED BY IT. ALWAYS THERE ARE MOTHS.
BUT THERE IS A STRANGER AMONG THE FLYING MASSES.
HE IS NOT A MOTH.
HIS LIGHT IS VERY FAINT, ALMOST INVISIBLE...
...BUT I CAN SEE IT.
HE GLEAMS LIKE A SWORD...
...A COLD STEEL BLADE DRAWN FROM ITS SCABBARD.

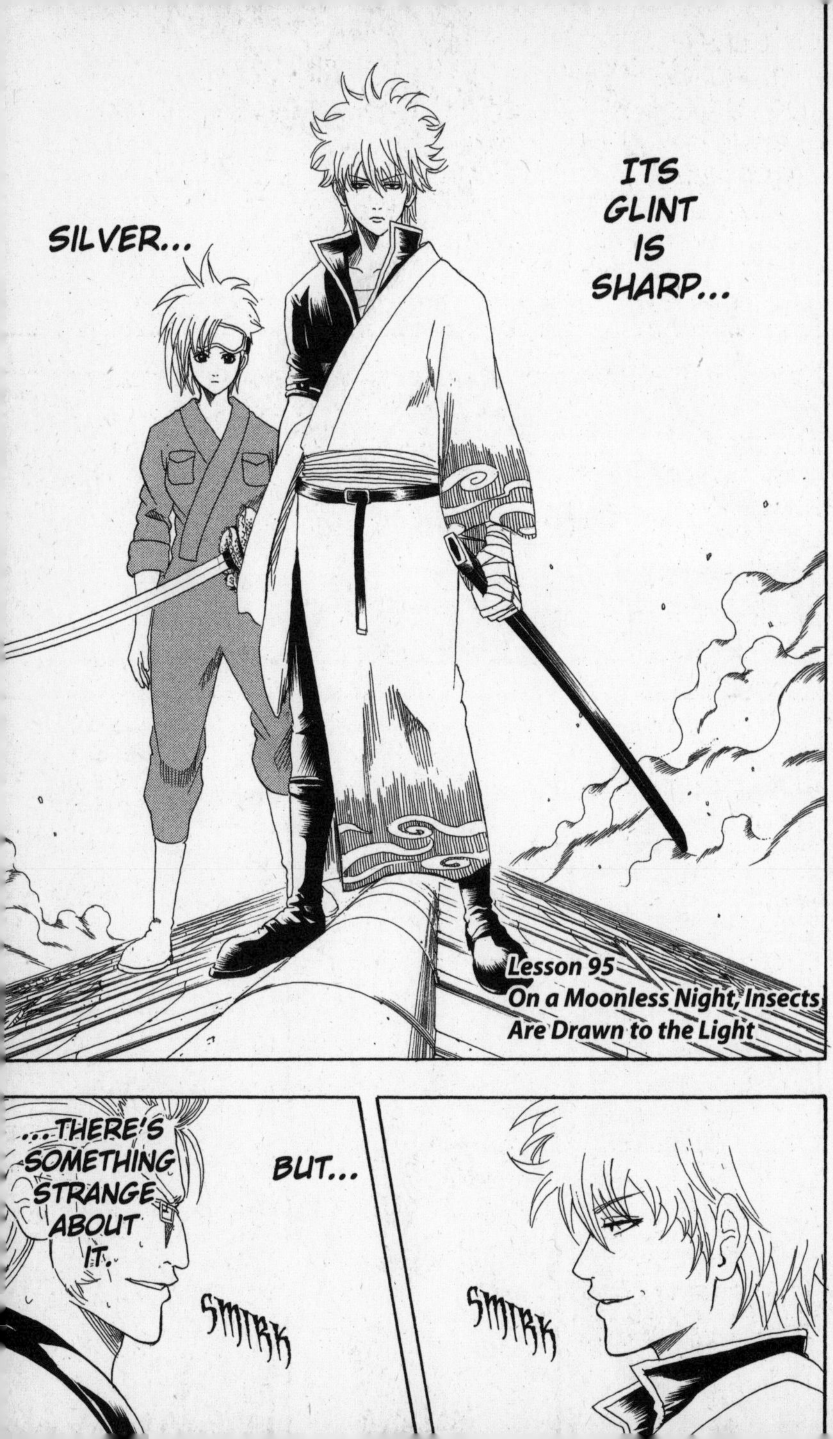
ITS GLINT IS SHARP...
SILVER...
Lesson 95
On a Moonless Night, Insects Are Drawn to the Light
SMIRK
BUT...
...THERE'S SOMETHING STRANGE ABOUT IT.
SMIRK

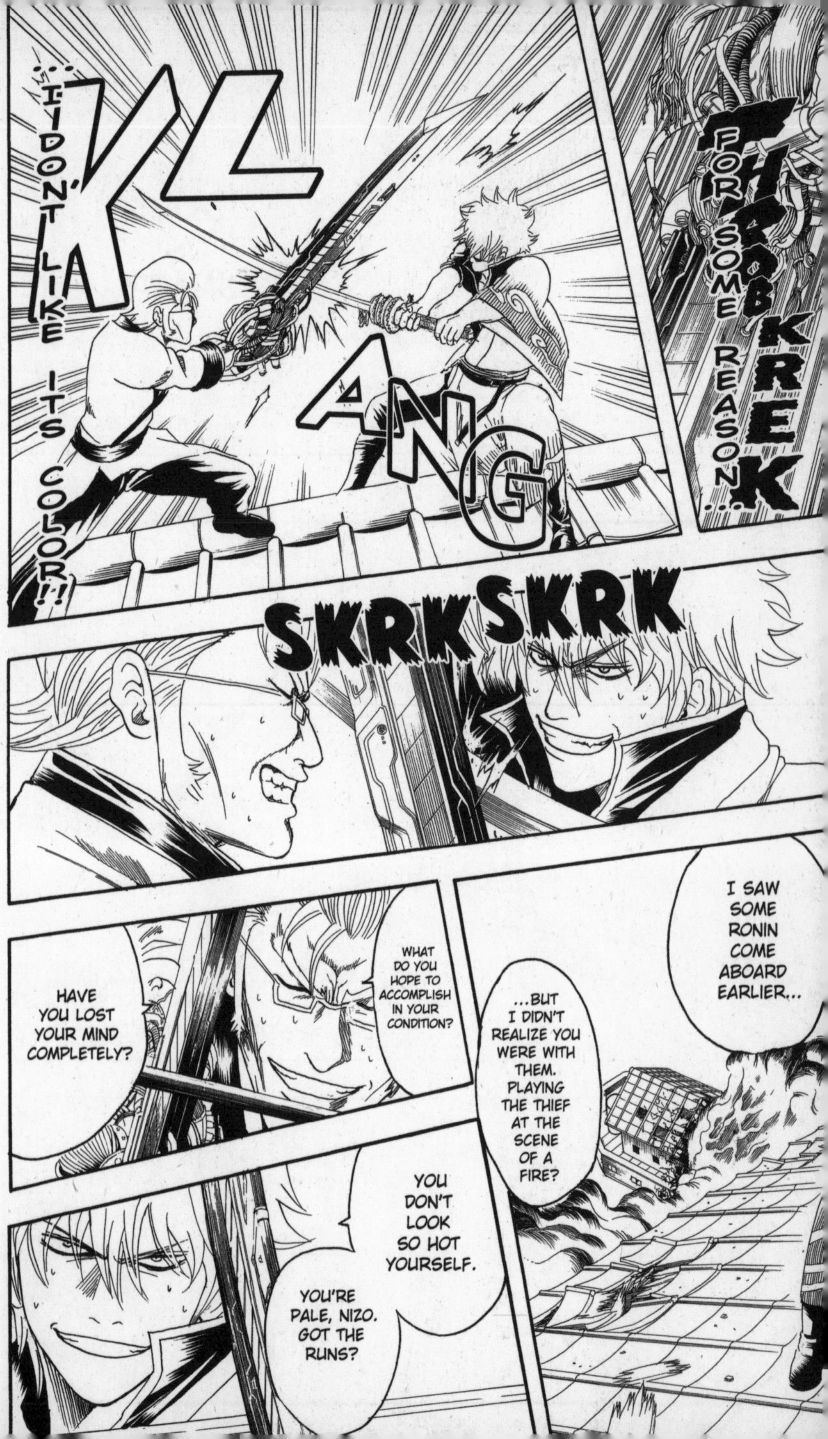
KREK
FOR SOME REASON...
KLANG
...I DON'T LIKE ITS COLOR!!
SKRKSKRK
I SAW SOME RONIN COME ABOARD EARLIER...
...BUT I DIDN'T REALIZE YOU WERE WITH THEM. PLAYING THE THIEF AT THE SCENE OF A FIRE?
WHAT DO YOU HOPE TO ACCOMPLISH IN YOUR CONDITION?
HAVE YOU LOST YOUR MIND COMPLETELY?
YOU DON'T LOOK SO HOT YOURSELF.
YOU'RE PALE, NIZO. GOT THE RUNS?

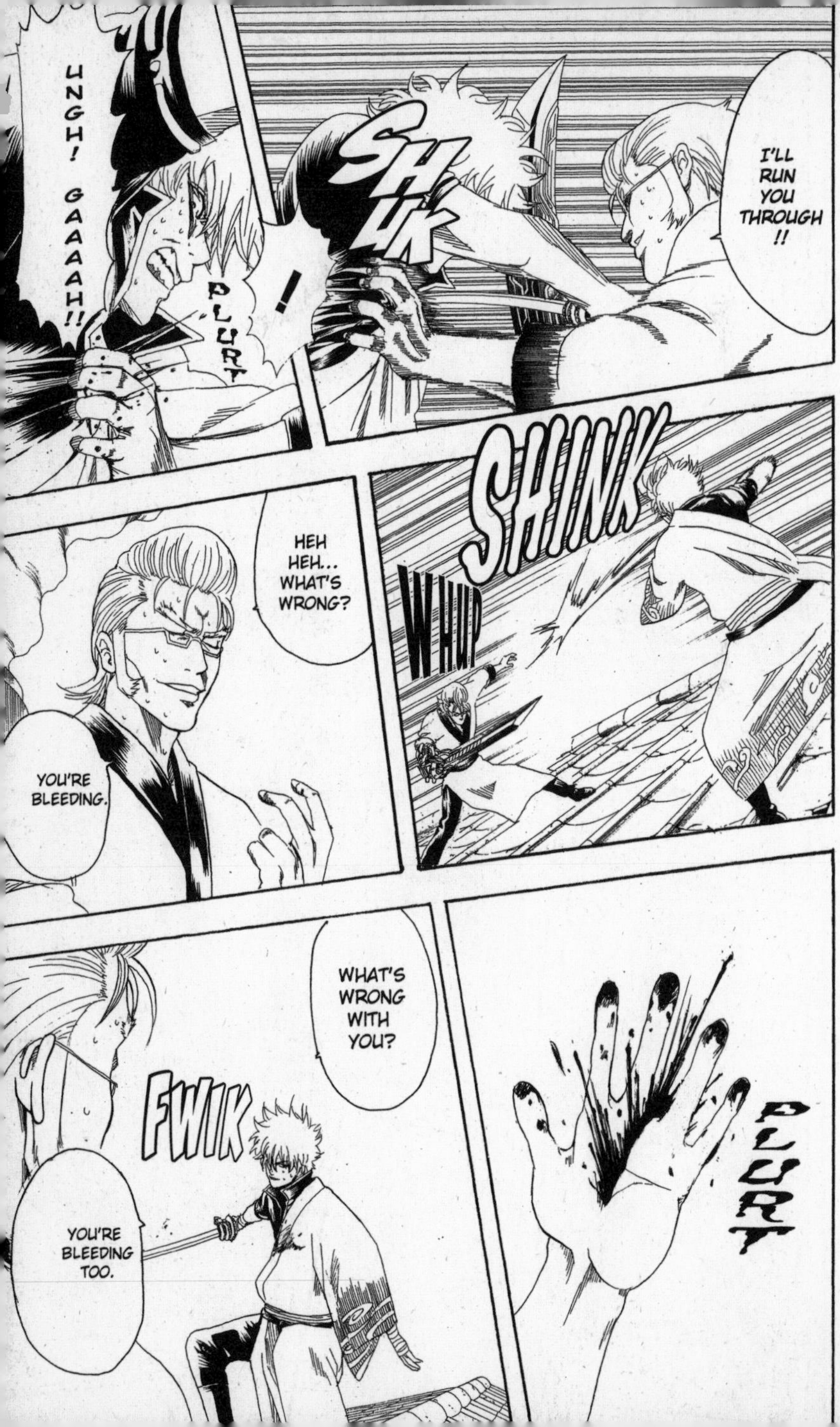
I'LL RUN YOU THROUGH !!
SHUK
!
UNGH! GAAAAAH!!
PLURT
SHINK
WHUP
HEH HEH... WHAT'S WRONG?
YOU'RE BLEEDING.
PLURT
WHAT'S WRONG WITH YOU?
FWIK
YOU'RE BLEEDING TOO.

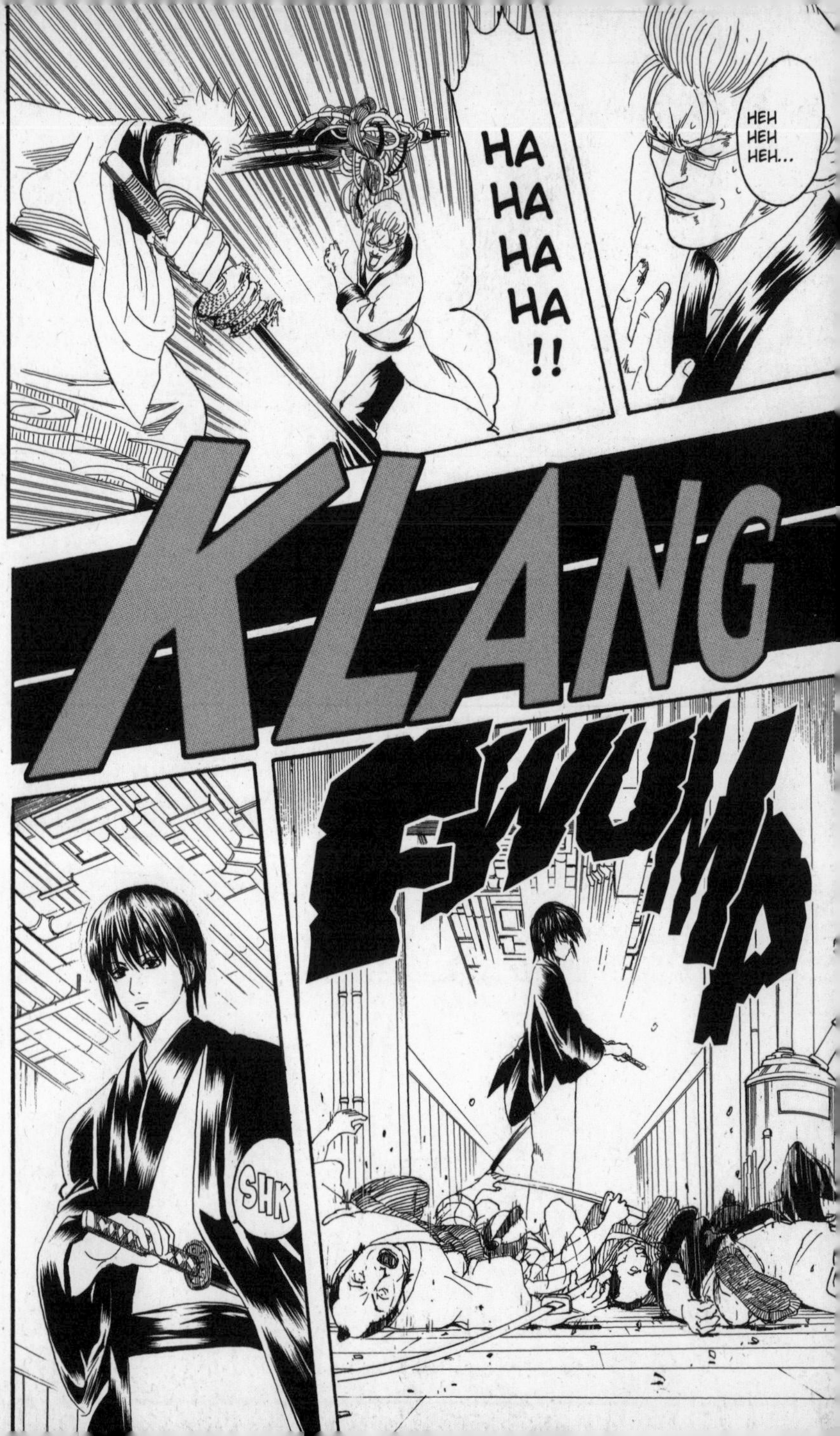

HEH HEH HEH...
HA HA HA HA HA !!
KLANG
FWUMP
SHK

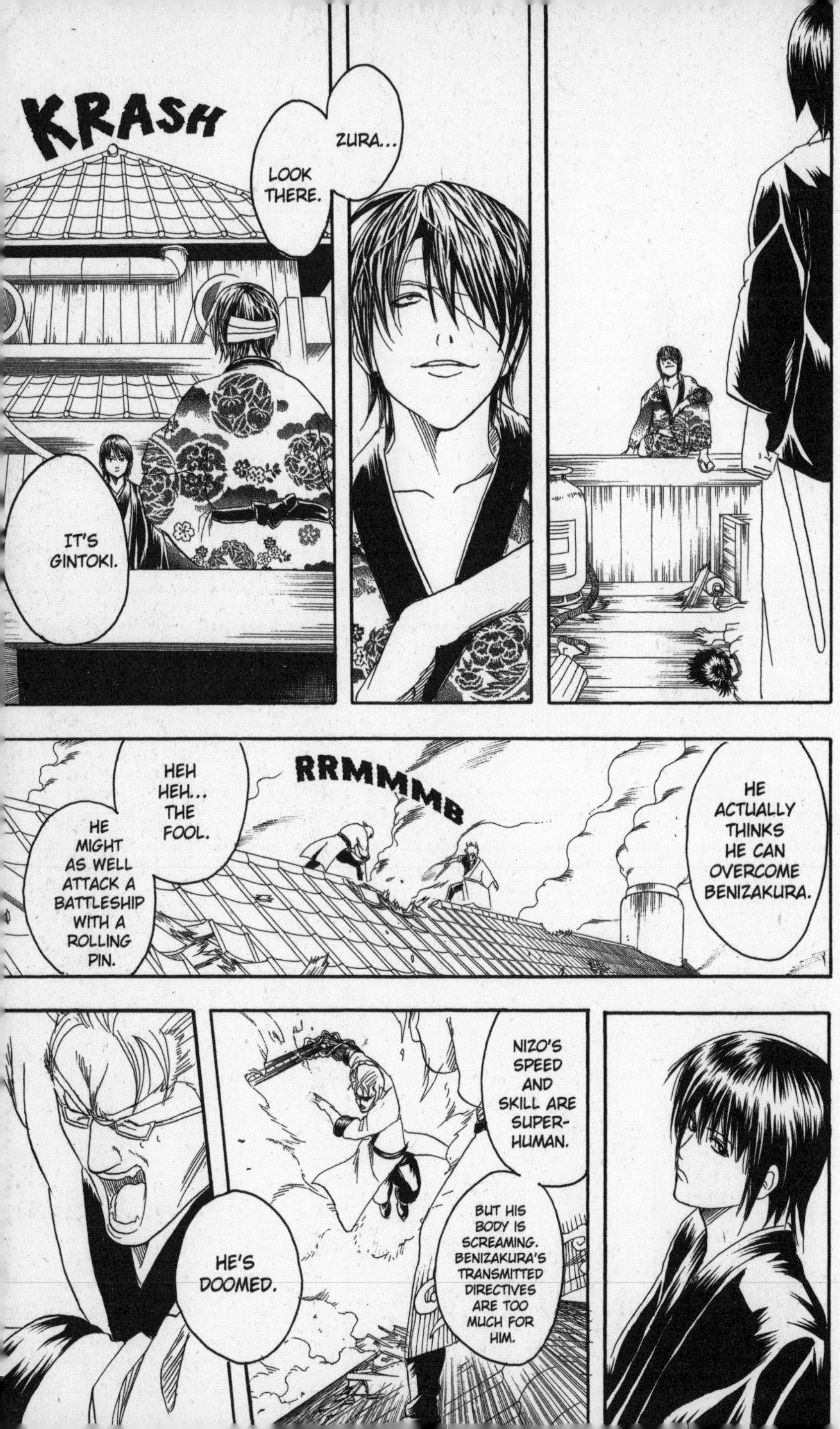
ZURA... LOOK THERE.
KRASH
IT'S GINTOKI.
HE ACTUALLY THINKS HE CAN OVERCOME BENIZAKURA.
RRMMMMB
HEH HEH... THE FOOL.
HE MIGHT AS WELL ATTACK A BATTLESHIP WITH A ROLLING PIN.
NIZO'S SPEED AND SKILL ARE SUPER-HUMAN.
BUT HIS BODY IS SCREAMING. BENIZAKURA'S TRANSMITTED DIRECTIVES ARE TOO MUCH FOR HIM.
HE'S DOOMED.

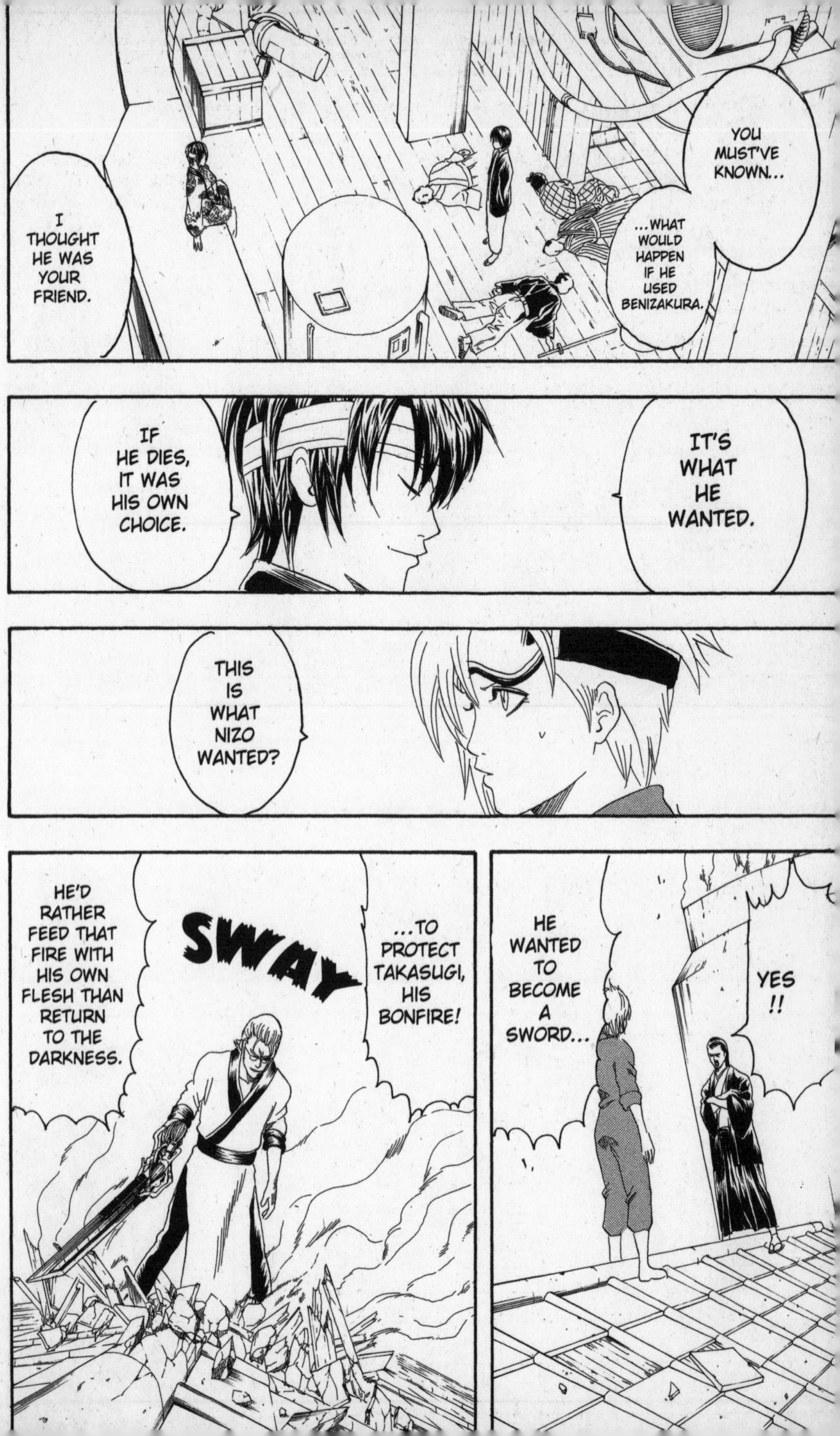
YOU MUST'VE KNOWN...
...WHAT WOULD HAPPEN IF HE USED BENIZAKURA.
I THOUGHT HE WAS YOUR FRIEND.
IT'S WHAT HE WANTED.
IF HE DIES, IT WAS HIS OWN CHOICE.
THIS IS WHAT NIZO WANTED?
YES!!
HE WANTED TO BECOME A SWORD...
...TO PROTECT TAKASUGI, HIS BONFIRE!
SWAY
HE'D RATHER FEED THAT FIRE WITH HIS OWN FLESH THAN RETURN TO THE DARKNESS.

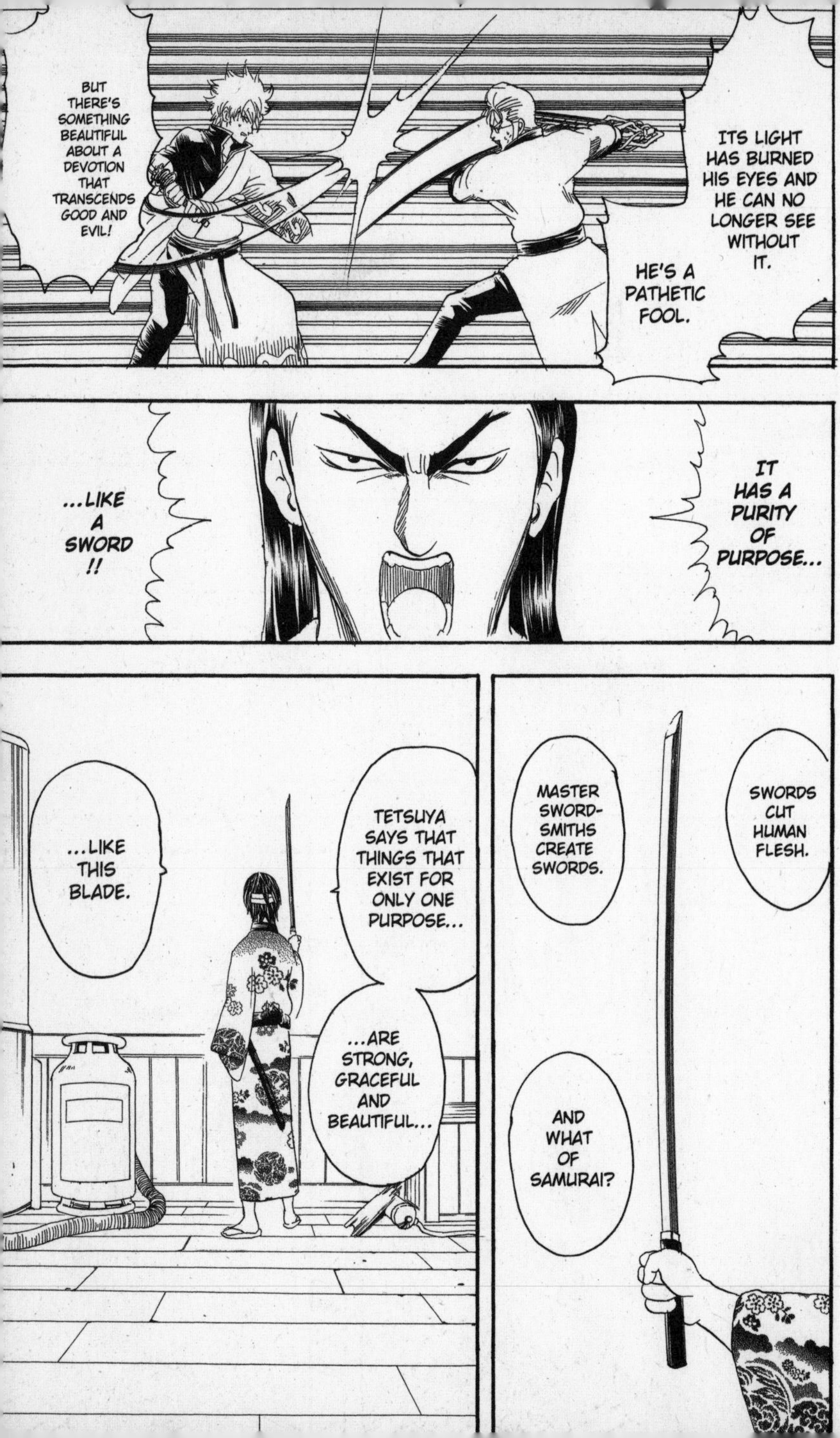
ITS LIGHT HAS BURNED HIS EYES AND HE CAN NO LONGER SEE WITHOUT IT.
HE'S A PATHETIC FOOL.
BUT THERE'S SOMETHING BEAUTIFUL ABOUT A DEVOTION THAT TRANSCENDS GOOD AND EVIL!
IT HAS A PURITY OF PURPOSE...
...LIKE A SWORD!!
SWORDS CUT HUMAN FLESH.
MASTER SWORD-SMITHS CREATE SWORDS.
AND WHAT OF SAMURAI?
TETSUYA SAYS THAT THINGS THAT EXIST FOR ONLY ONE PURPOSE...
...ARE STRONG, GRACEFUL AND BEAUTIFUL...
...LIKE THIS BLADE.

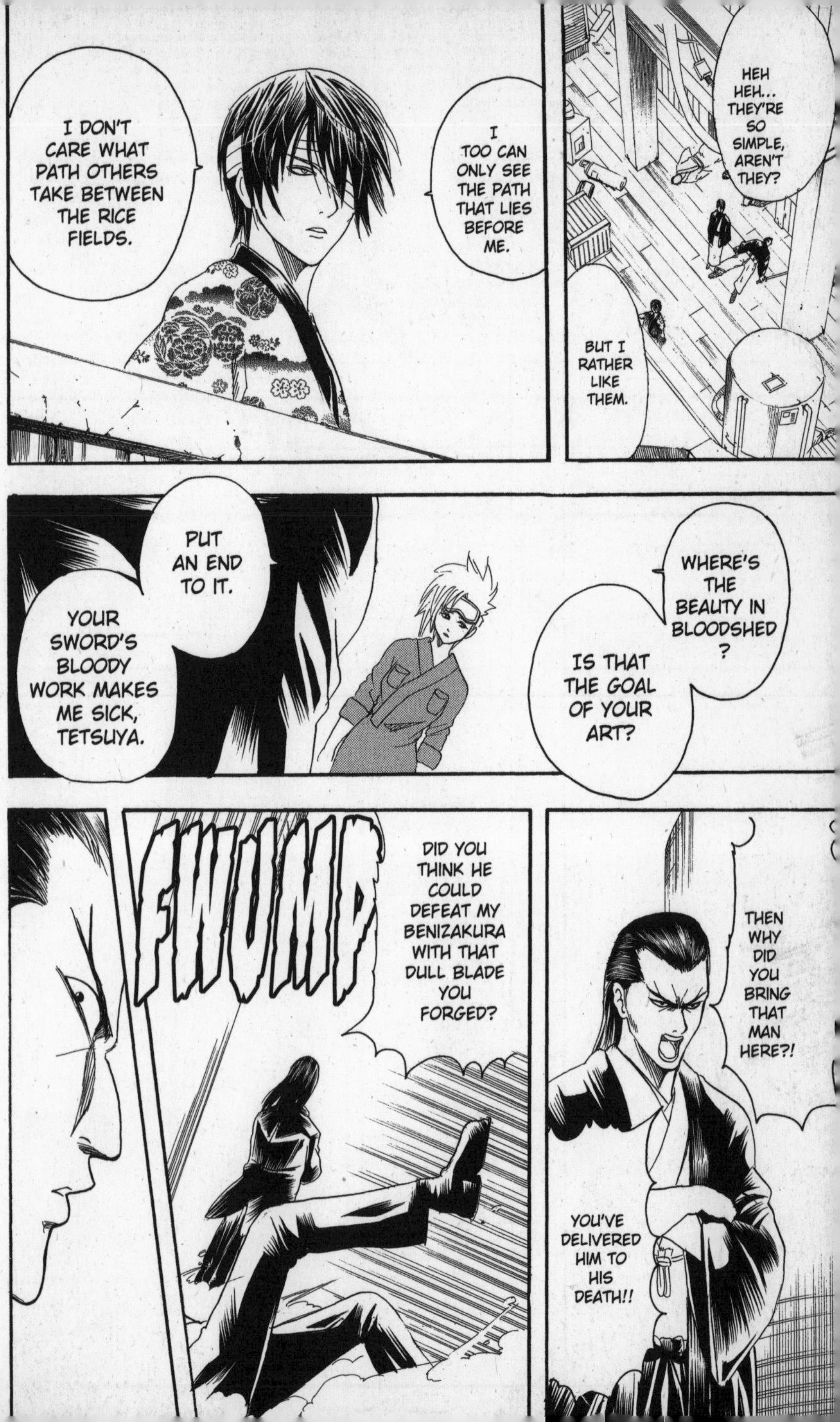
HEH HEH... THEY'RE SO SIMPLE, AREN'T THEY?
BUT I RATHER LIKE THEM.
I TOO CAN ONLY SEE THE PATH THAT LIES BEFORE ME.
I DON'T CARE WHAT PATH OTHERS TAKE BETWEEN THE RICE FIELDS.
WHERE'S THE BEAUTY IN BLOODSHED?
IS THAT THE GOAL OF YOUR ART?
PUT AN END TO IT.
YOUR SWORD'S BLOODY WORK MAKES ME SICK, TETSUYA.
THEN WHY DID YOU BRING THAT MAN HERE?!
YOU'VE DELIVERED HIM TO HIS DEATH!!
DID YOU THINK HE COULD DEFEAT MY BENIZAKURA WITH THAT DULL BLADE YOU FORGED?
FWUMP

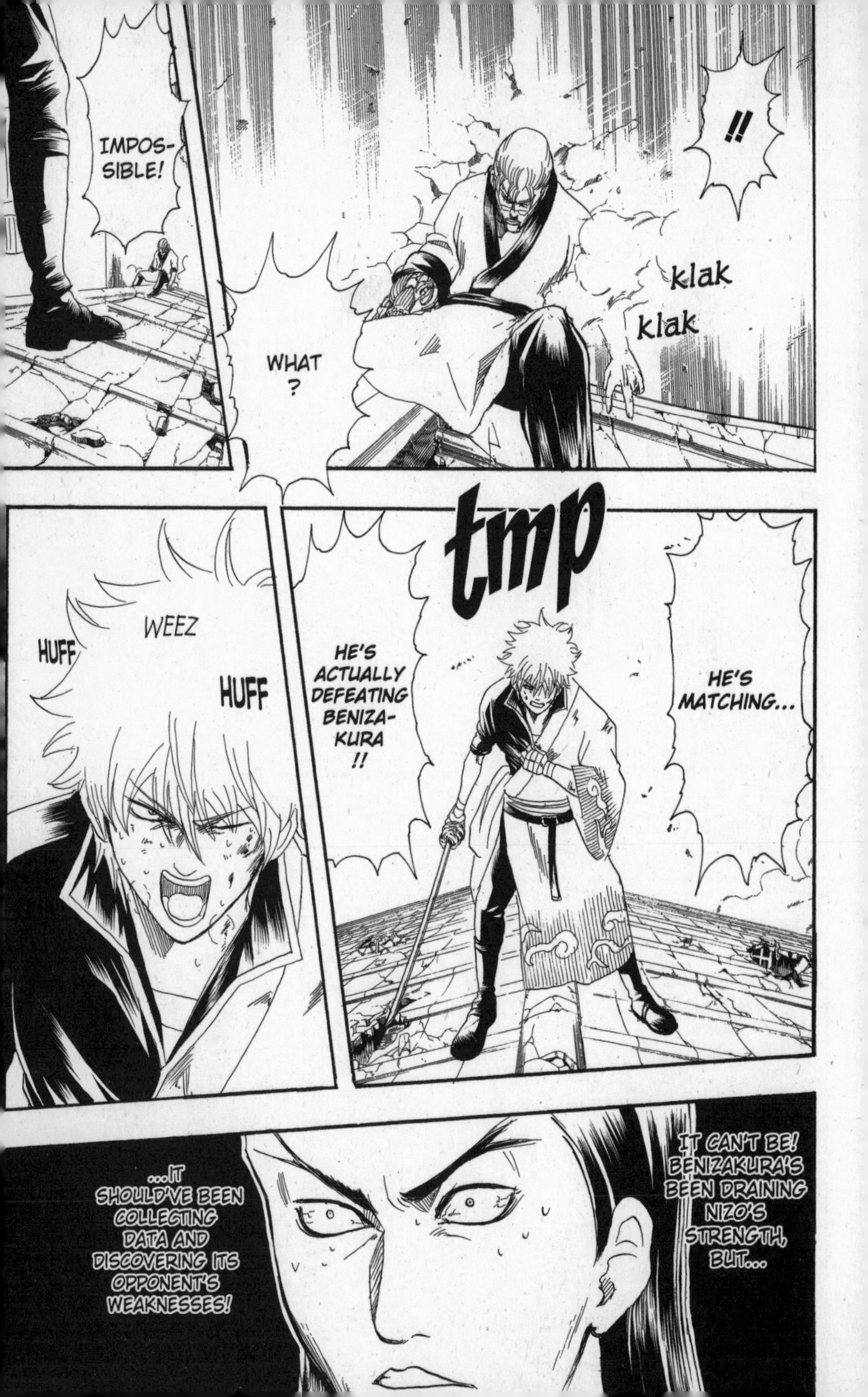
!!
klak
klak
WHAT ?
IMPOSSIBLE!
tmp
HE'S MATCHING...
HE'S ACTUALLY DEFEATING BENIZAKURA !!
HUFF
WEEZ
HUFF
IT CAN'T BE! BENIZAKURA'S BEEN DRAINING NIZO'S STRENGTH, BUT...
...IT SHOULD'VE BEEN COLLECTING DATA AND DISCOVERING ITS OPPONENT'S WEAKNESSES!

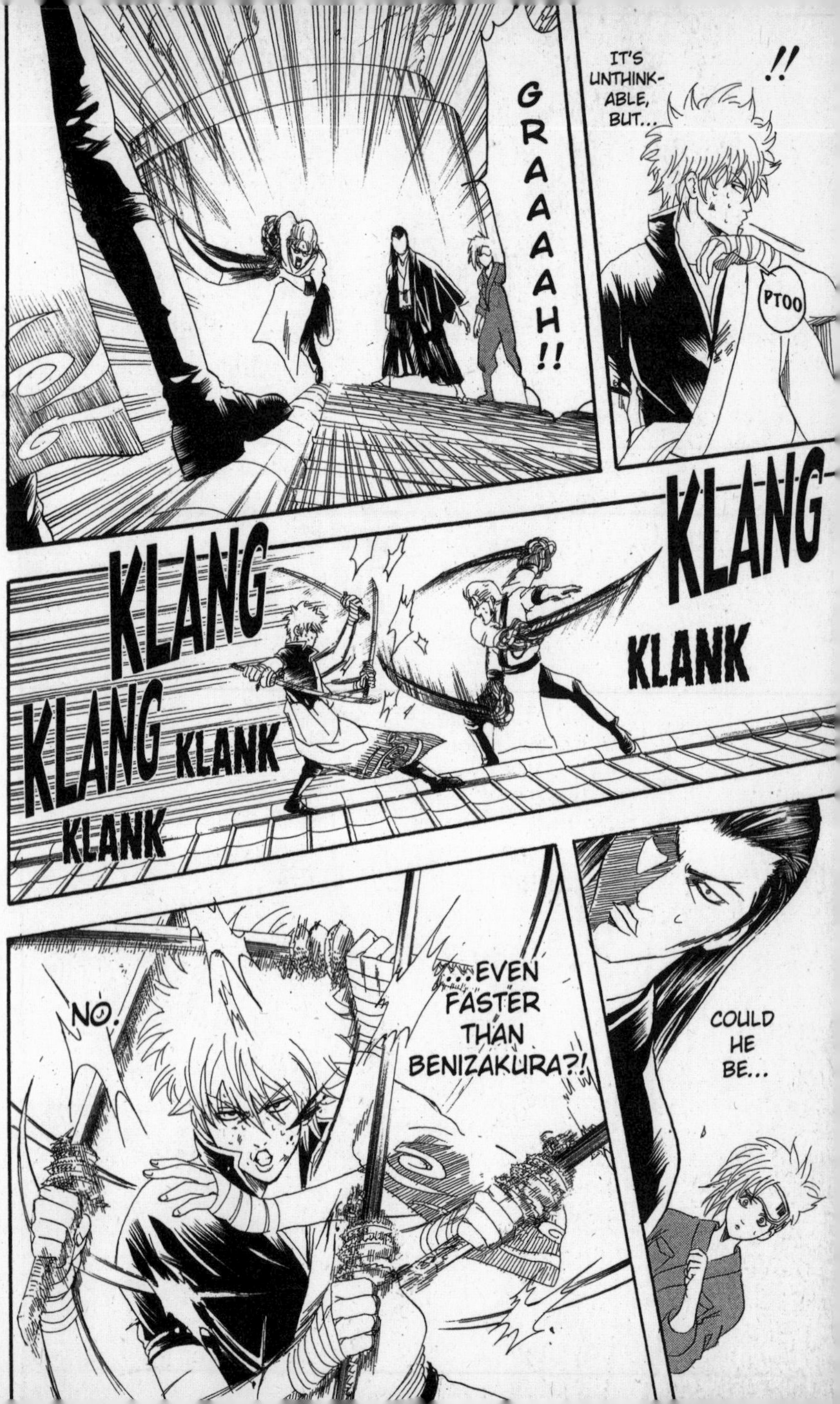
IT'S UNTHINKABLE, BUT...
!!
PTOO
GRAAAAAH!!
KLANG
KLANK
KLANG
KLANG KLANK
KLANK
COULD HE BE...
...EVEN FASTER THAN BENIZAKURA?!
NO.

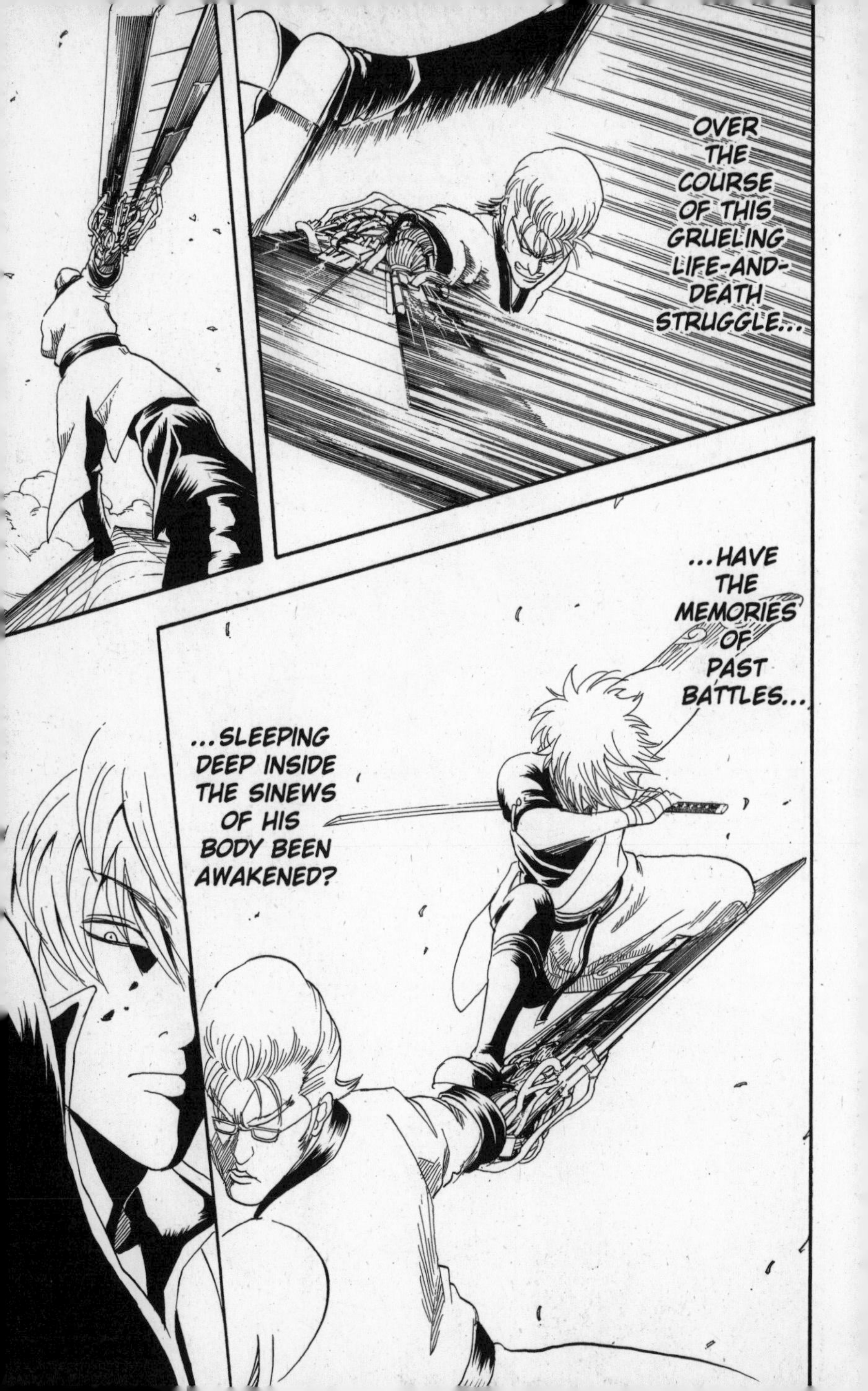

OVER THE COURSE OF THIS GRUELING LIFE-AND-DEATH STRUGGLE...
...HAVE THE MEMORIES OF PAST BATTLES...
...SLEEPING DEEP INSIDE THE SINEWS OF HIS BODY BEEN AWAKENED?

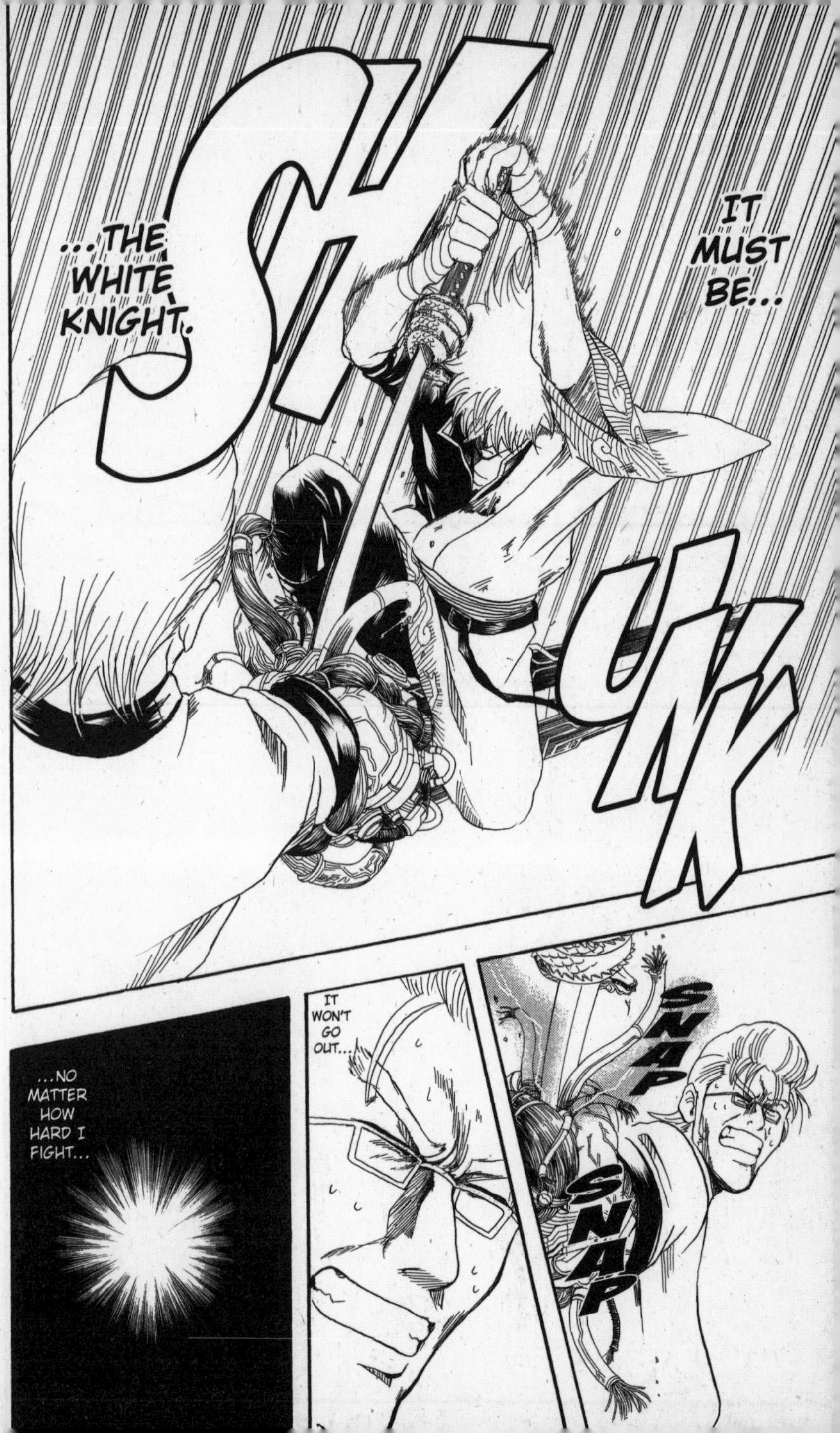
IT MUST BE...
...THE WHITE KNIGHT.
SH
UNK
SNAP
SNAP
IT WON'T GO OUT...
...NO MATTER HOW HARD I FIGHT...

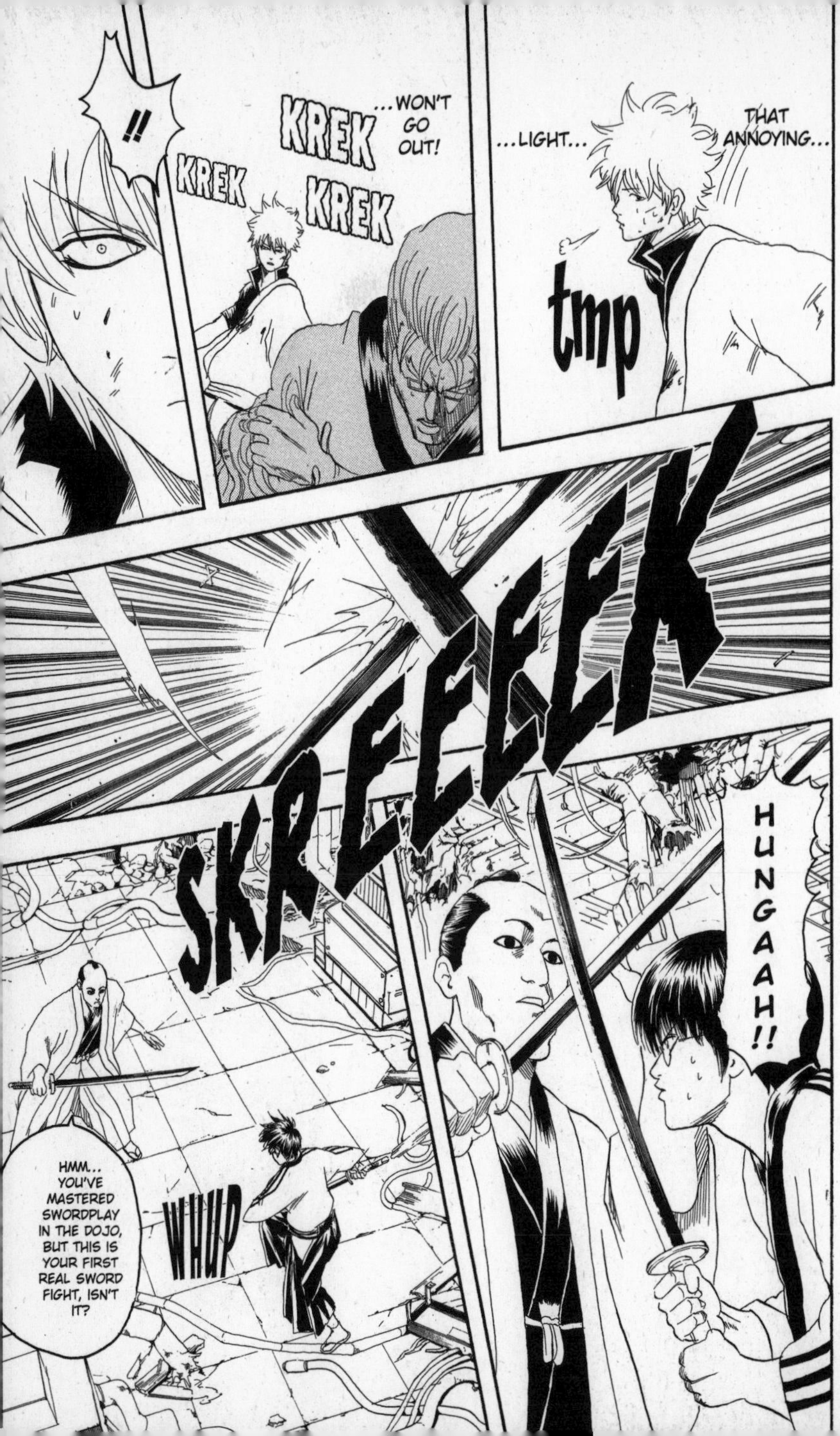
THAT ANNOYING...
...LIGHT...
tmp
...WON'T GO OUT!
KREK
KREK
KREK
!!
SKREEEEK
HUNGAAH!!
HMM... YOU'VE MASTERED SWORDPLAY IN THE DOJO, BUT THIS IS YOUR FIRST REAL SWORD FIGHT, ISN'T IT?
WHUP

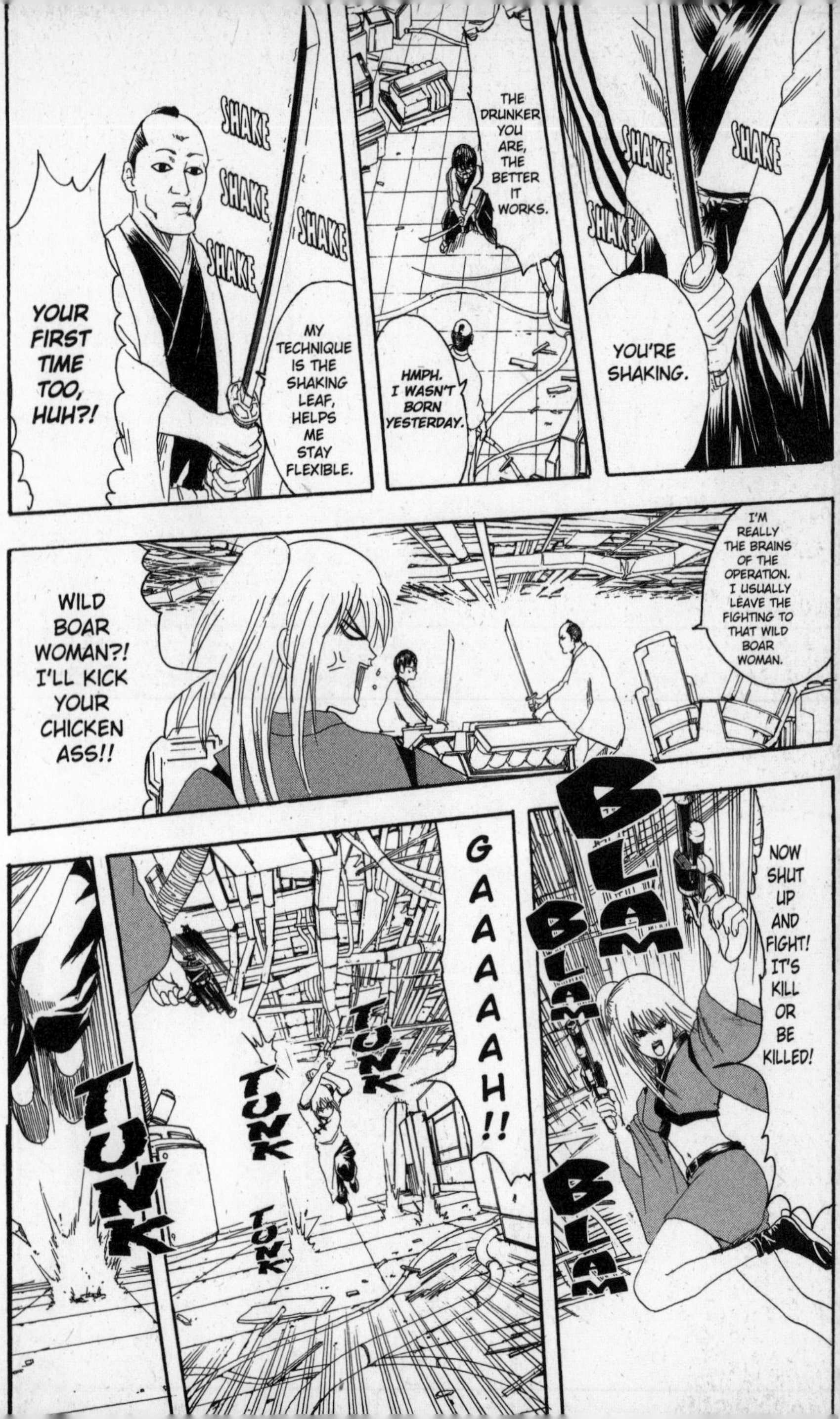
SHAKE
SHAKE
YOU'RE SHAKING.
THE DRUNKER YOU ARE, THE BETTER IT WORKS.
HMPH. I WASN'T BORN YESTERDAY.
SHAKE
SHAKE
SHAKE
SHAKE
MY TECHNIQUE IS THE SHAKING LEAF, HELPS ME STAY FLEXIBLE.
YOUR FIRST TIME TOO, HUH?!
I'M REALLY THE BRAINS OF THE OPERATION. I USUALLY LEAVE THE FIGHTING TO THAT WILD BOAR WOMAN.
WILD BOAR WOMAN?! I'LL KICK YOUR CHICKEN ASS!!
BLAM
BLAM
NOW SHUT UP AND FIGHT! IT'S KILL OR BE KILLED!
BLAM
GAAAAAAH!!
TUNK
TUNK
TUNK
TUNK

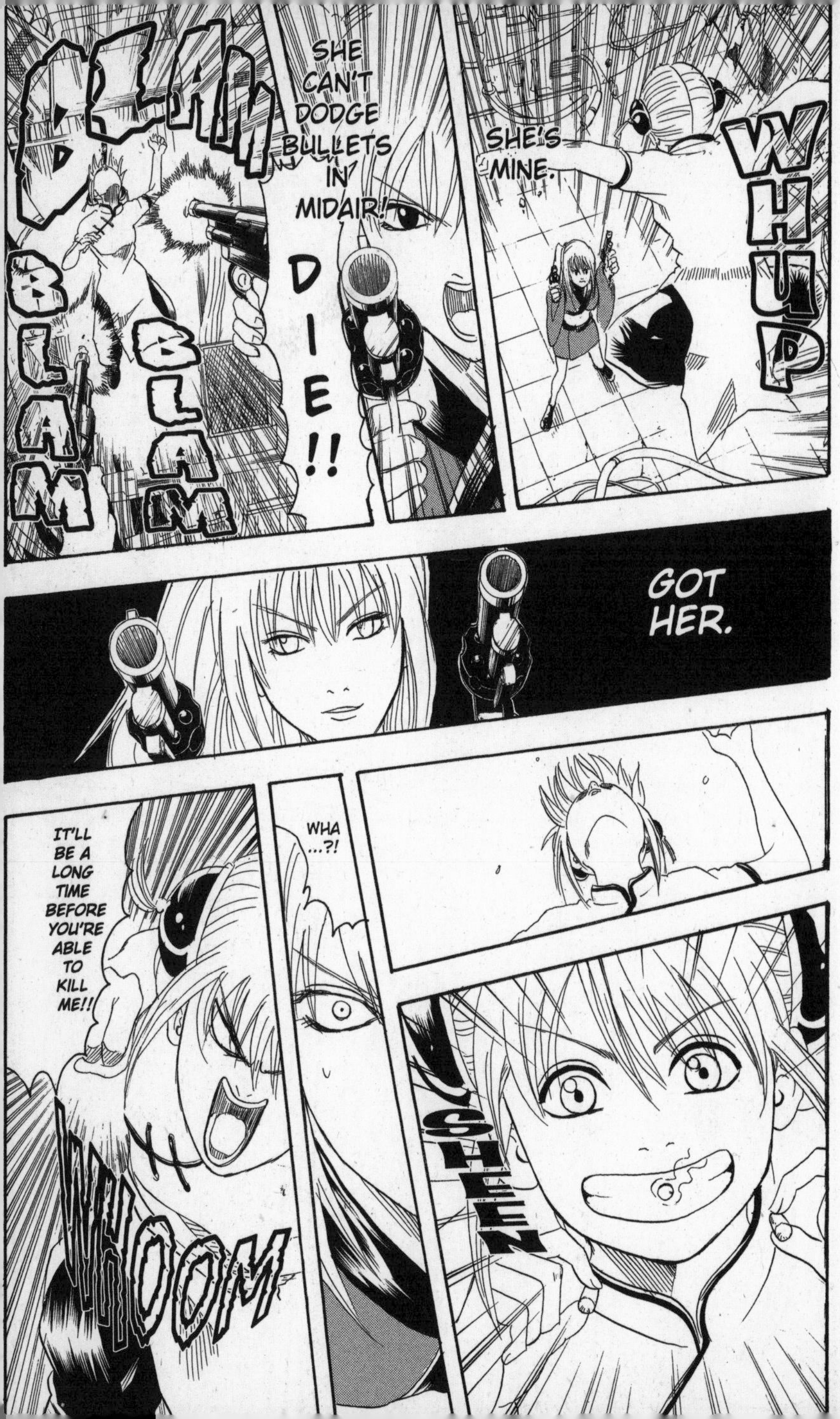
WHUP
SHE'S MINE.
SHE CAN'T DODGE BULLETS IN MIDAIR!
DIE!!
CLAM
BLAM
BLAM
GOT HER.
SHEEN
WHA ...?!
IT'LL BE A LONG TIME BEFORE YOU'RE ABLE TO KILL ME!!
WHOOM

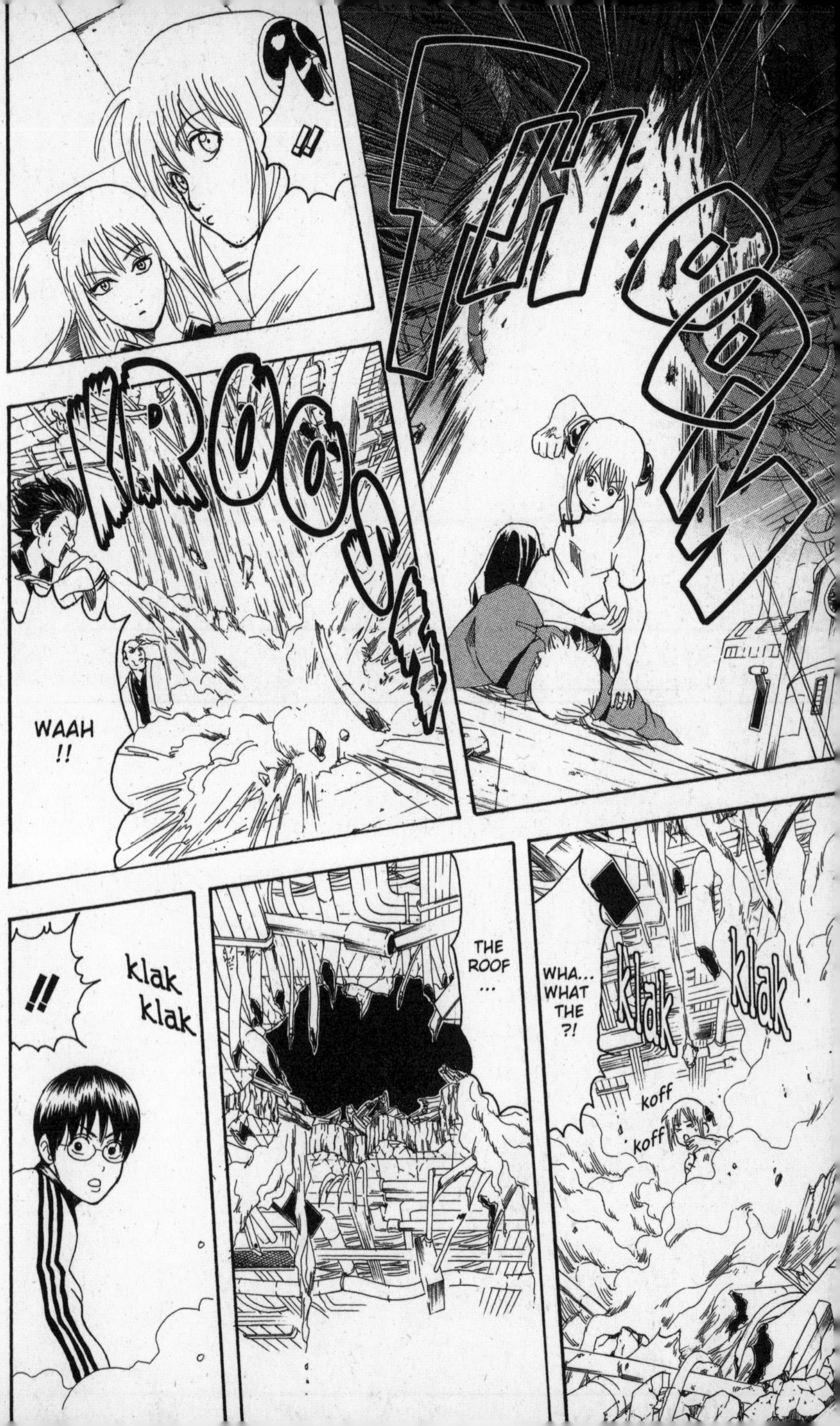
THOOM
!!
KROOSH
WAAH !!
WHA... WHAT THE ?!
klak
klak
koff
koff
THE ROOF ...
!!
klak klak

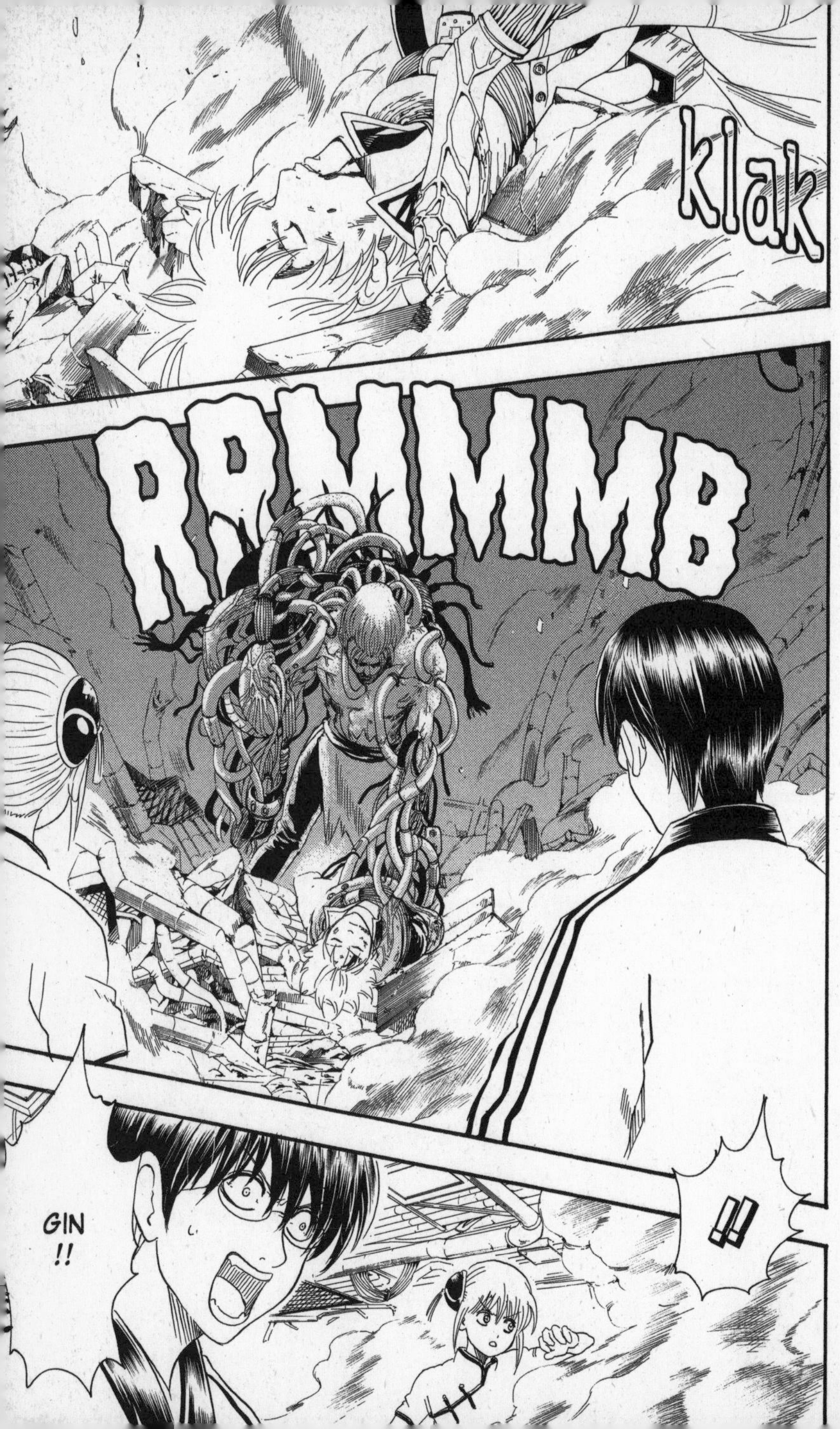
klak
RMMMB
!!
GIN !!

Thank you for purchasing **Gin Tama** volume 12. For those of you who are reading this book on the day it hit the stores, the **Gin Tama** anime debuts tonight, so please watch it instead of whatever you usually watch. I'll thank you in advance. The other day, I visited the animation studio because I wanted to see the voice actors at work, but my editor misread the schedule, so I only got to see Katoken singing the Katoken Samba. I didn't get to see the other voice actors, but I still said, "Wow! All the voices match so well!" But I think they'll all work well for their roles. Well, I really don't know anything about them. I also had a brief conversation with Mr. Sugita, who voices Gin. I'd met him twice before, but we'd never really had a chance to talk. This time, for some reason, we ended up chatting about Masashi Tashiro. Why? We should have talked about the anime! But I think this laid-back man will be perfect for the part of Gin. I also saw the director and other staff members, but 80% of our conversation was about smut. The last time I saw them, they'd been talking about hostess bars. But since they have hot fighting spirits as well as dirty minds, I'm sure the result will be a wonderful anime.

Help!!

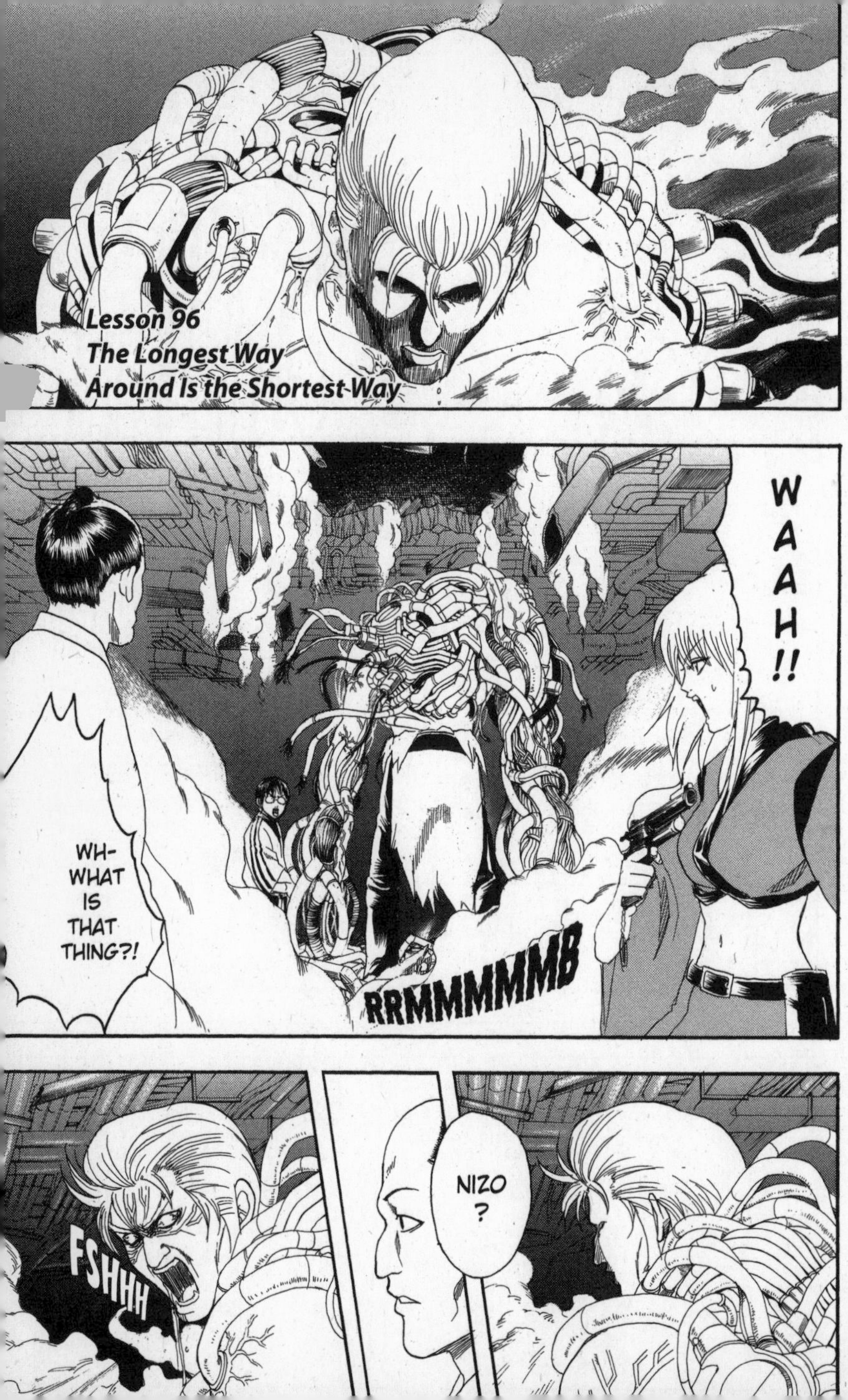
Lesson 96
The Longest Way
Around Is the Shortest Way
WAAAH!!
RRMMMMMMB
WH-WHAT IS THAT THING?!
NIZO?
FSHHH

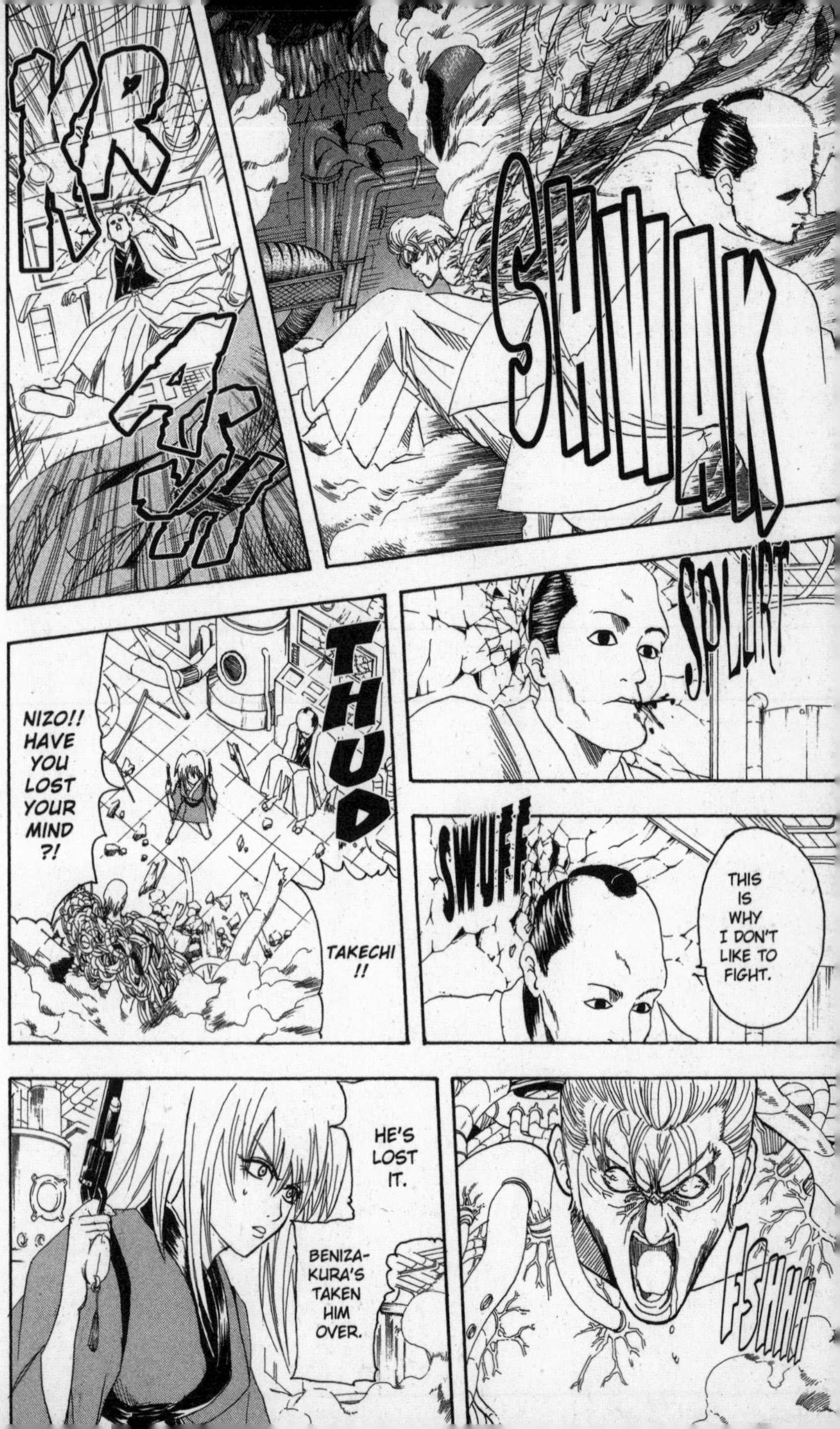
SHWAK
KRASH
SPLURT
SWUFF
THIS IS WHY I DON'T LIKE TO FIGHT.
THUD
NIZO!! HAVE YOU LOST YOUR MIND?!
TAKECHI!!
HE'S LOST IT.
BENIZA-KURA'S TAKEN HIM OVER.

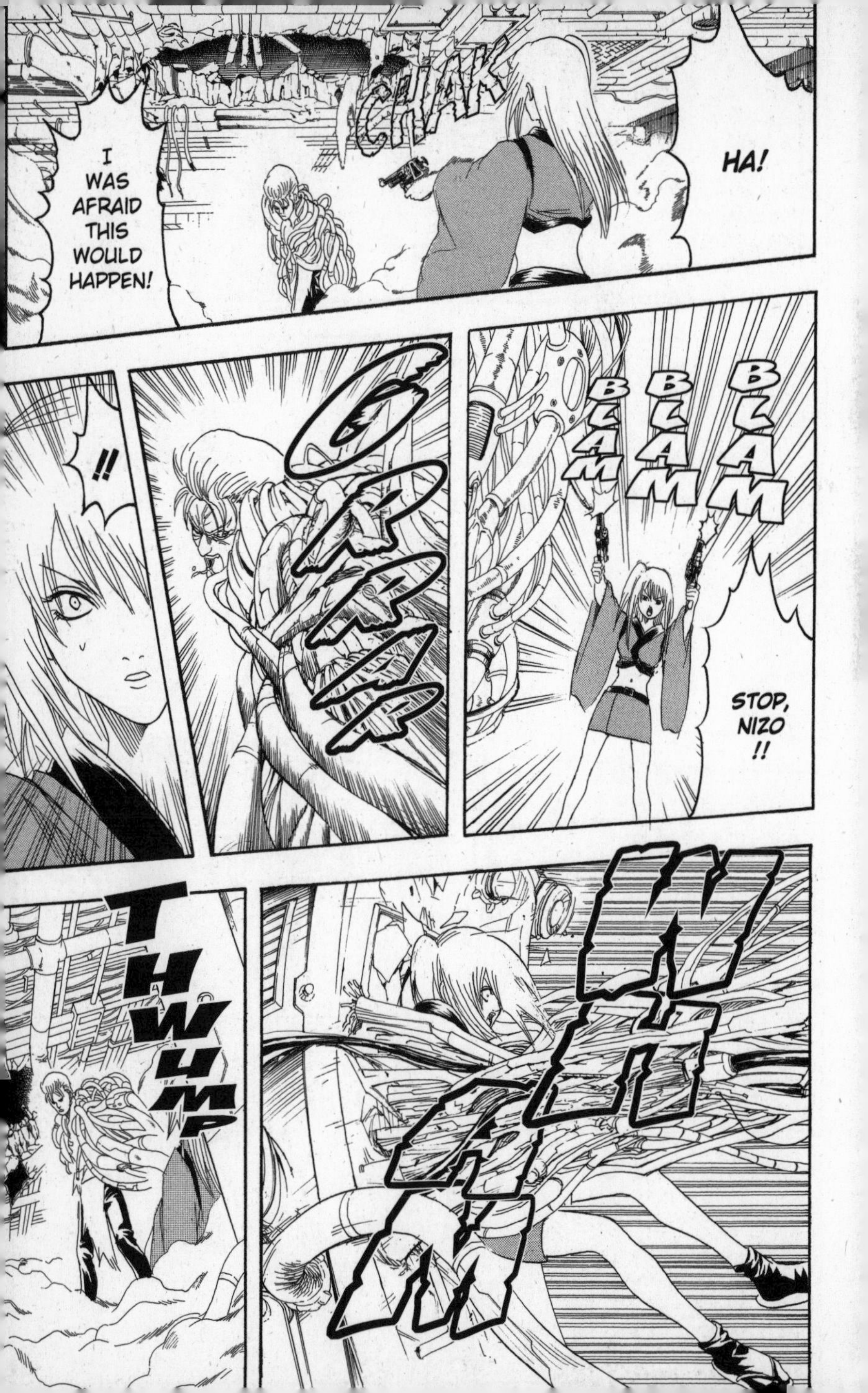
CHAK
HA!
I WAS AFRAID THIS WOULD HAPPEN!
BLAM BLAM BLAM
STOP, NIZO!!
!!
WHAM
THWUMP

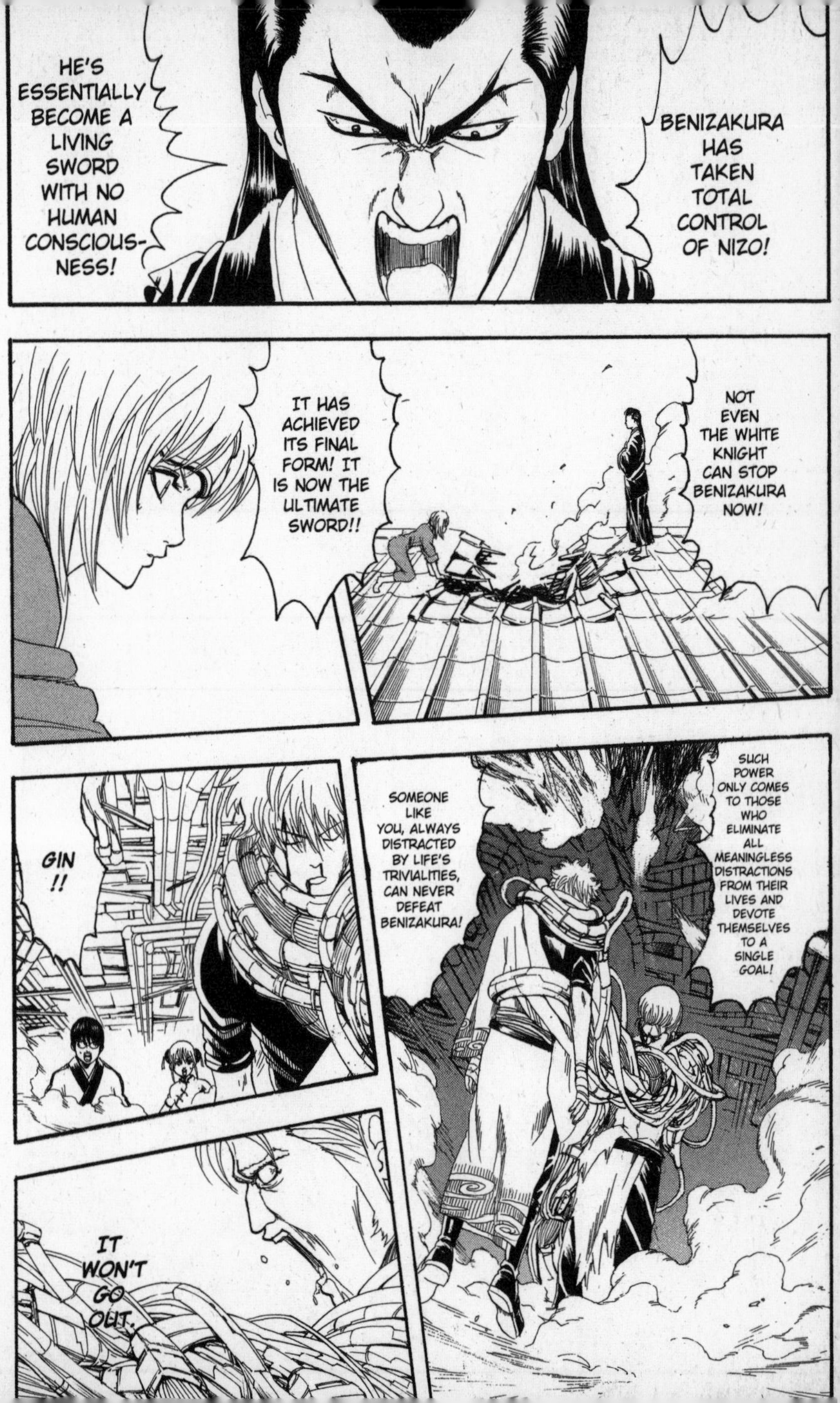
BENIZAKURA HAS TAKEN TOTAL CONTROL OF NIZO!
HE'S ESSENTIALLY BECOME A LIVING SWORD WITH NO HUMAN CONSCIOUS-NESS!
NOT EVEN THE WHITE KNIGHT CAN STOP BENIZAKURA NOW!
IT HAS ACHIEVED ITS FINAL FORM! IT IS NOW THE ULTIMATE SWORD!!
SUCH POWER ONLY COMES TO THOSE WHO ELIMINATE ALL MEANINGLESS DISTRACTIONS FROM THEIR LIVES AND DEVOTE THEMSELVES TO A SINGLE GOAL!
SOMEONE LIKE YOU, ALWAYS DISTRACTED BY LIFE'S TRIVIALITIES, CAN NEVER DEFEAT BENIZAKURA!
GIN !!
IT WON'T GO OUT.

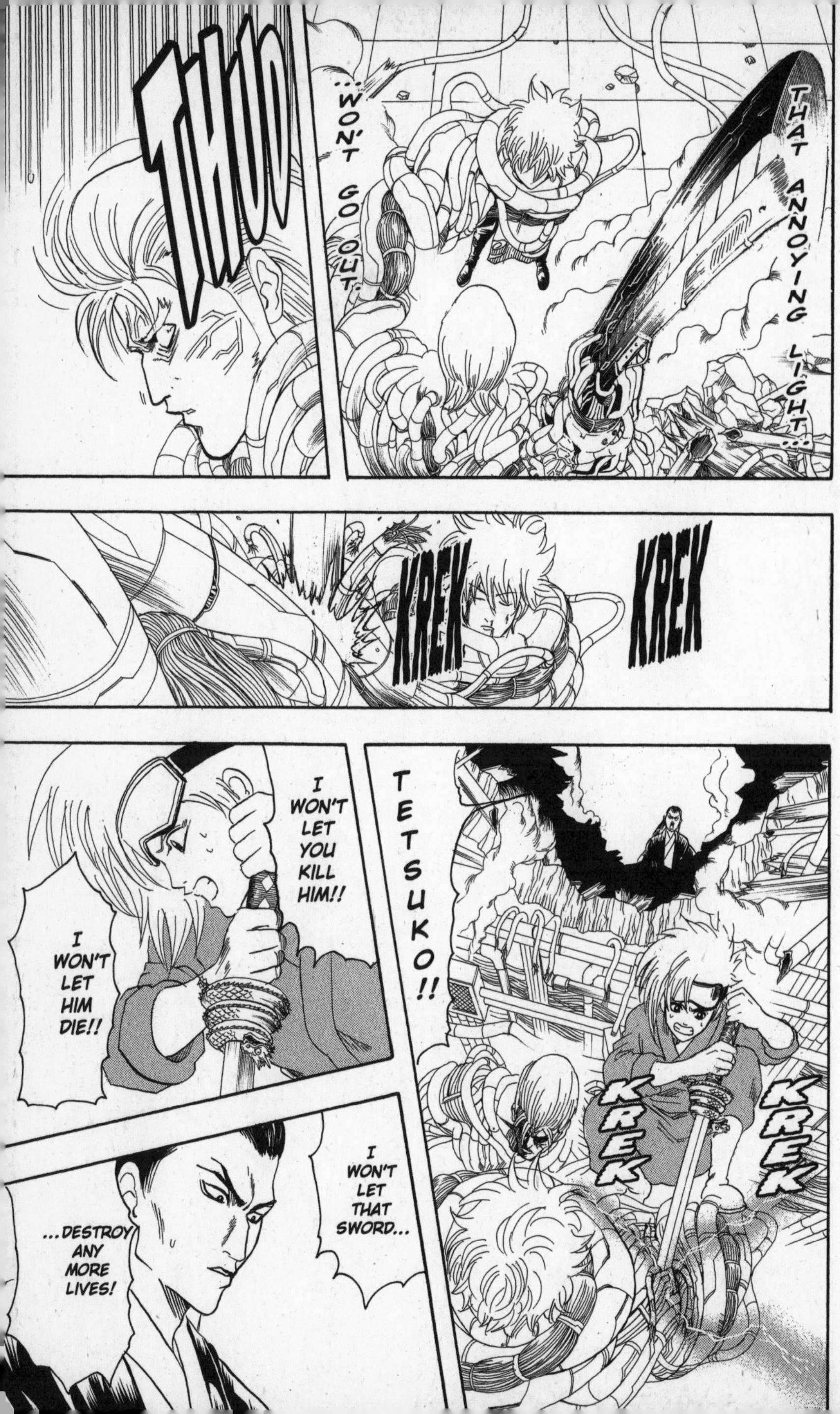
THAT ANNOYING LIGHT...
...WON'T GO OUT.
THUD
KREK
KREK
TETSUKO!!
KREK
KREK
I WON'T LET YOU KILL HIM!!
I WON'T LET HIM DIE!!
I WON'T LET THAT SWORD...
...DESTROY ANY MORE LIVES!

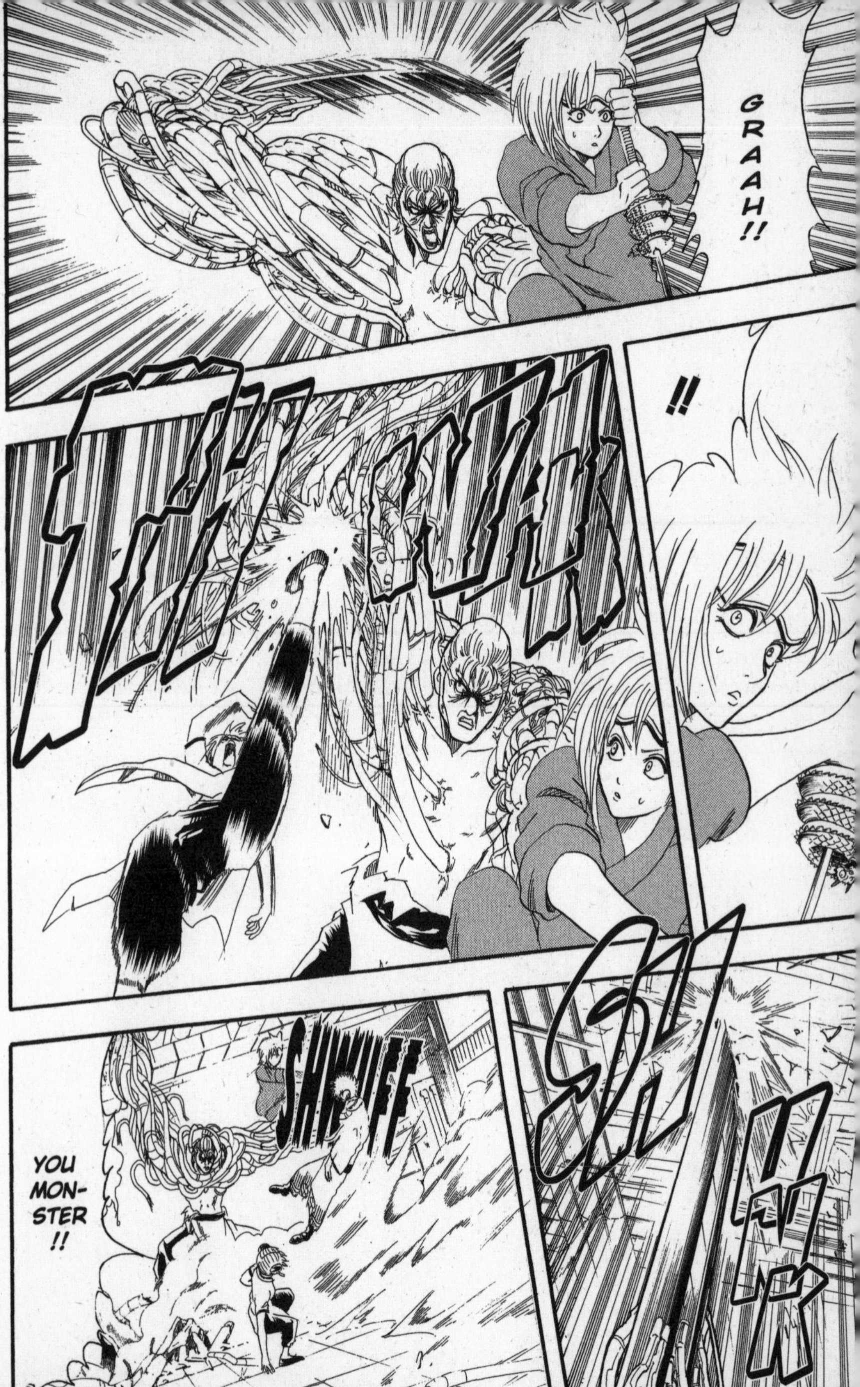
GRAAH!!
!!
THWACK
SHNK
SHWIFF
YOU MONSTER!!

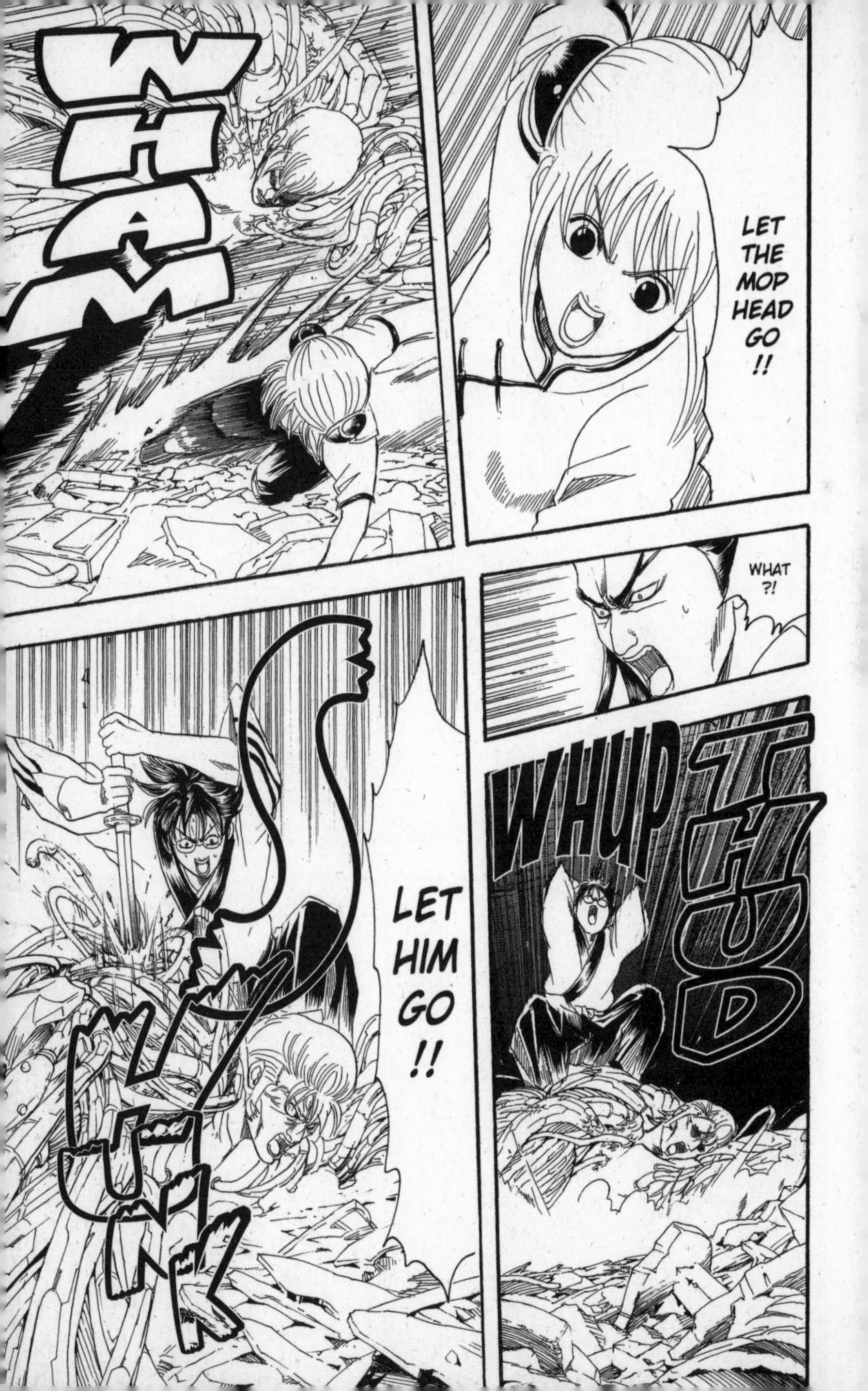
LET THE MOP HEAD GO !!
WHAM
WHAT ?!
WHUP
THUD
LET HIM GO !!
WHUNK

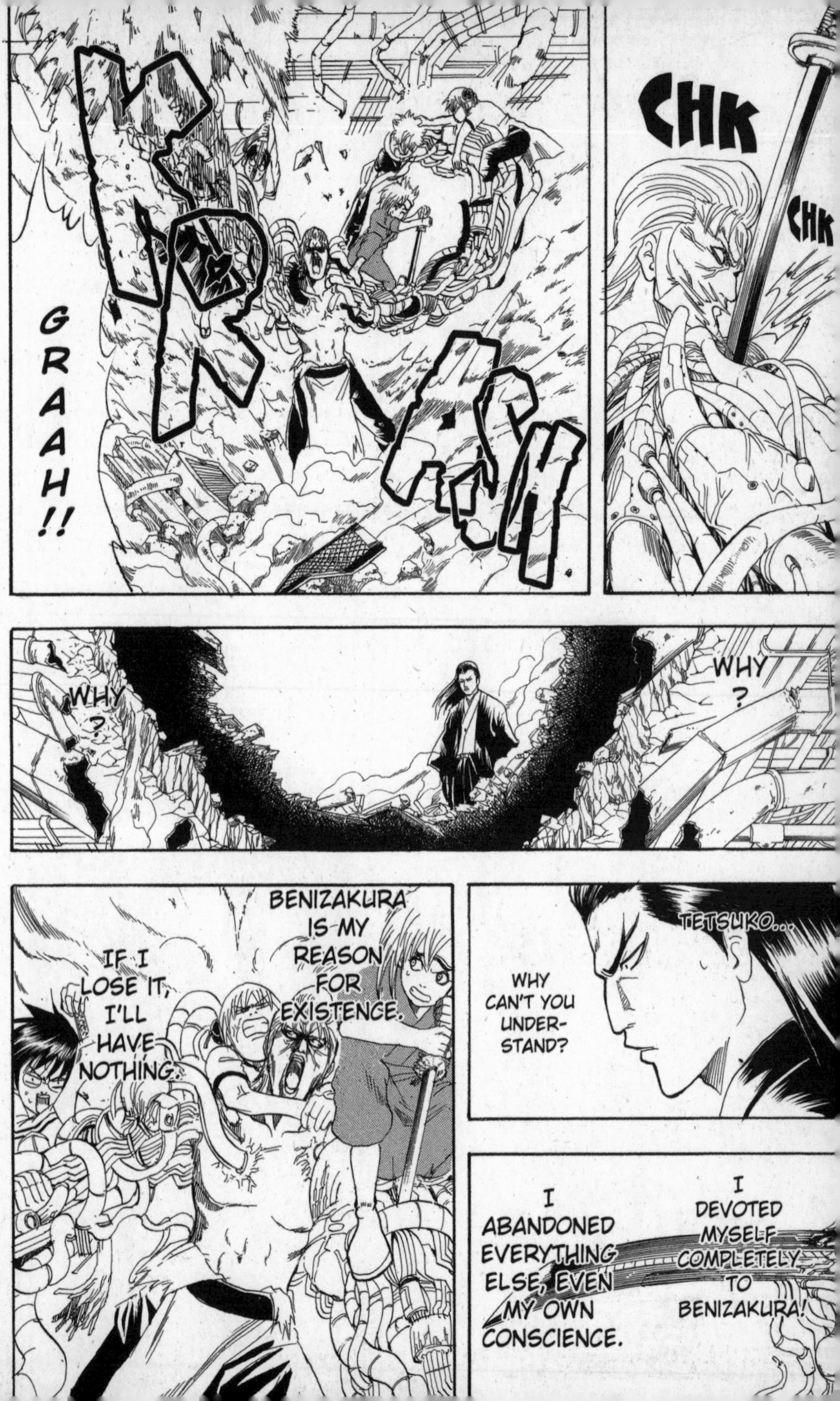
CHK
CHK
GRAAAH!!
WHY?
WHY?
TETSUKO...
WHY CAN'T YOU UNDERSTAND?
I DEVOTED MYSELF COMPLETELY TO BENIZAKURA!
I ABANDONED EVERYTHING ELSE, EVEN MY OWN CONSCIENCE.
BENIZAKURA IS MY REASON FOR EXISTENCE.
IF I LOSE IT, I'LL HAVE NOTHING.

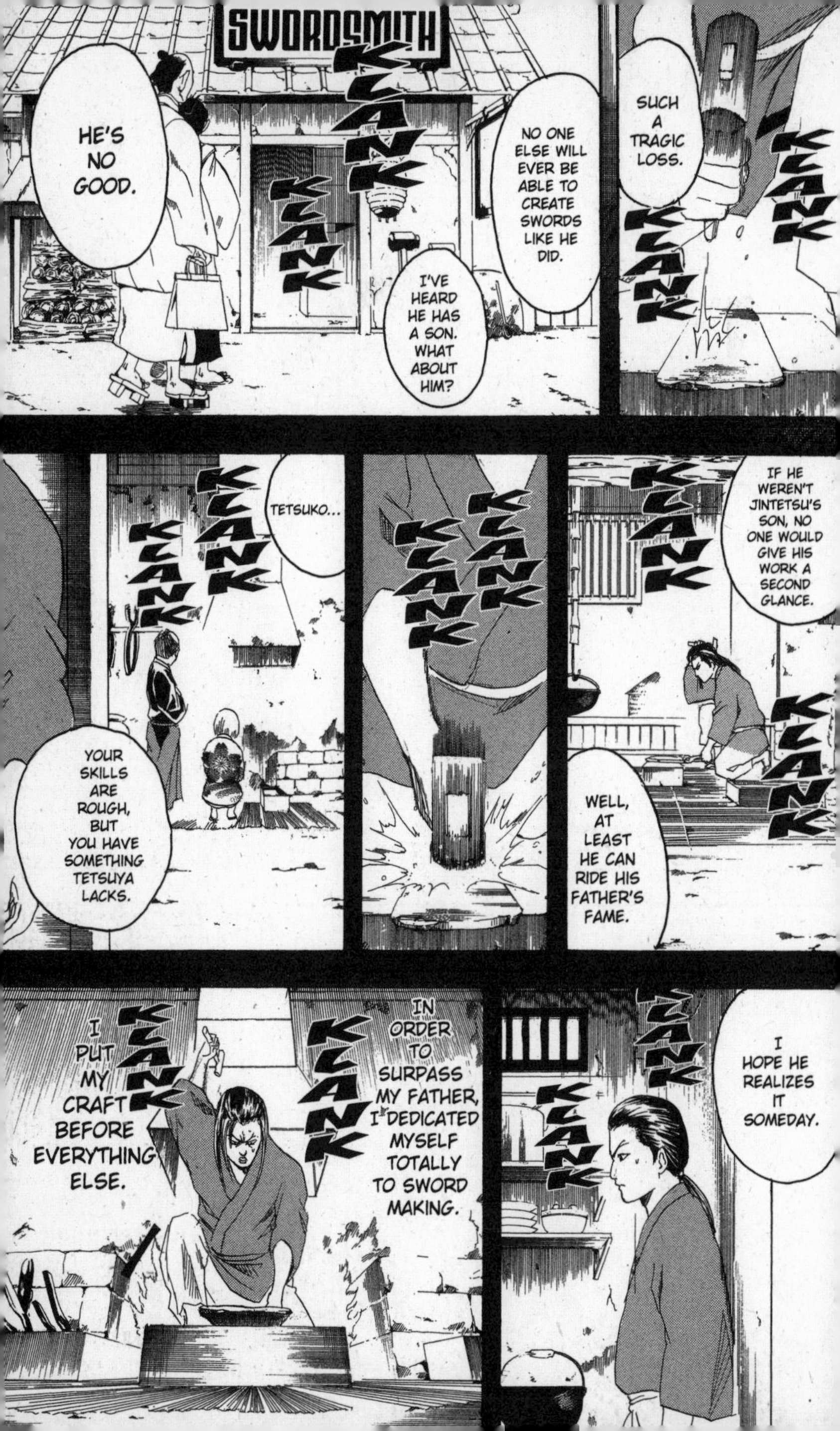
SUCH A TRAGIC LOSS.
KLANK
KLANK
NO ONE ELSE WILL EVER BE ABLE TO CREATE SWORDS LIKE HE DID.
I'VE HEARD HE HAS A SON. WHAT ABOUT HIM?
SWORDSMITH
KLANK
KLANK
HE'S NO GOOD.
IF HE WEREN'T JINTETSU'S SON, NO ONE WOULD GIVE HIS WORK A SECOND GLANCE.
KLANK
KLANK
WELL, AT LEAST HE CAN RIDE HIS FATHER'S FAME.
KLANK
KLANK
TETSUKO...
KLANK
KLANK
YOUR SKILLS ARE ROUGH, BUT YOU HAVE SOMETHING TETSUYA LACKS.
I HOPE HE REALIZES IT SOMEDAY.
KLANK
KLANK
IN ORDER TO SURPASS MY FATHER, I DEDICATED MYSELF TOTALLY TO SWORD MAKING.
KLANK
KLANK
I PUT MY CRAFT BEFORE EVERYTHING ELSE.

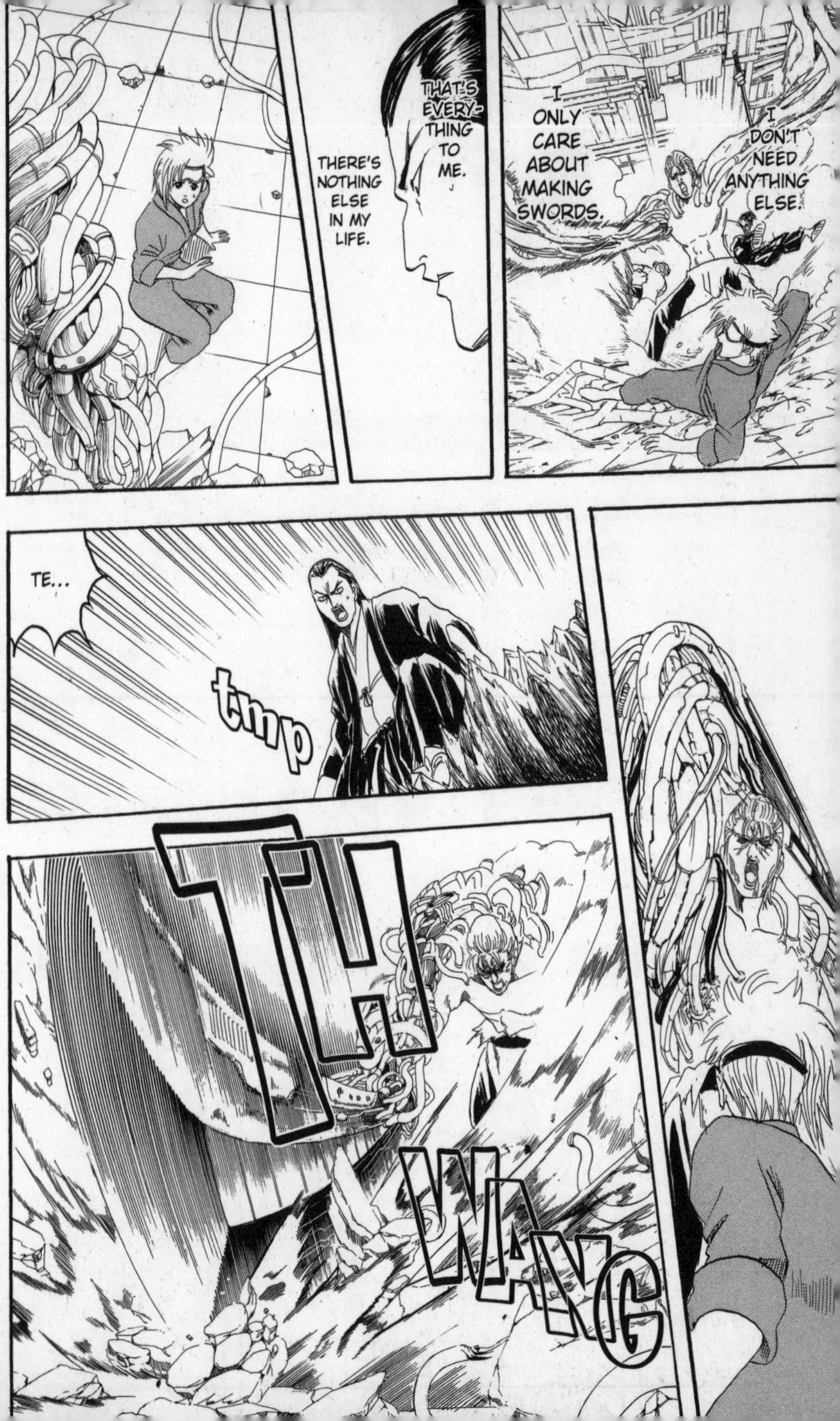
I ONLY CARE ABOUT MAKING SWORDS.
I DON'T NEED ANYTHING ELSE.
THAT'S EVERYTHING TO ME.
THERE'S NOTHING ELSE IN MY LIFE.
TE...
tmp
THWANG

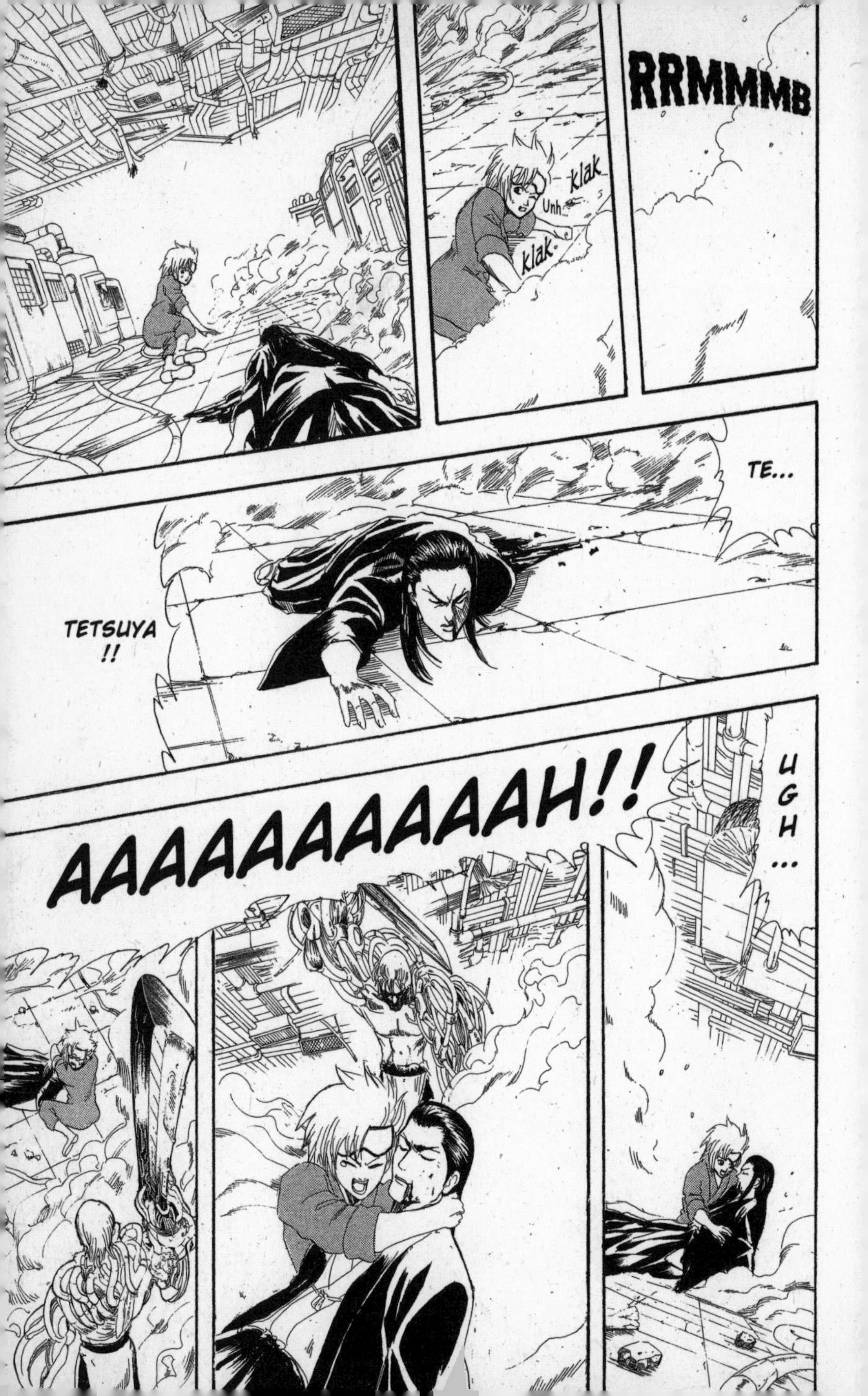
RRMMMB
klak
Unh...
klak
TE...
TETSUYA !!
UGH...
AAAAAAAAAH!!

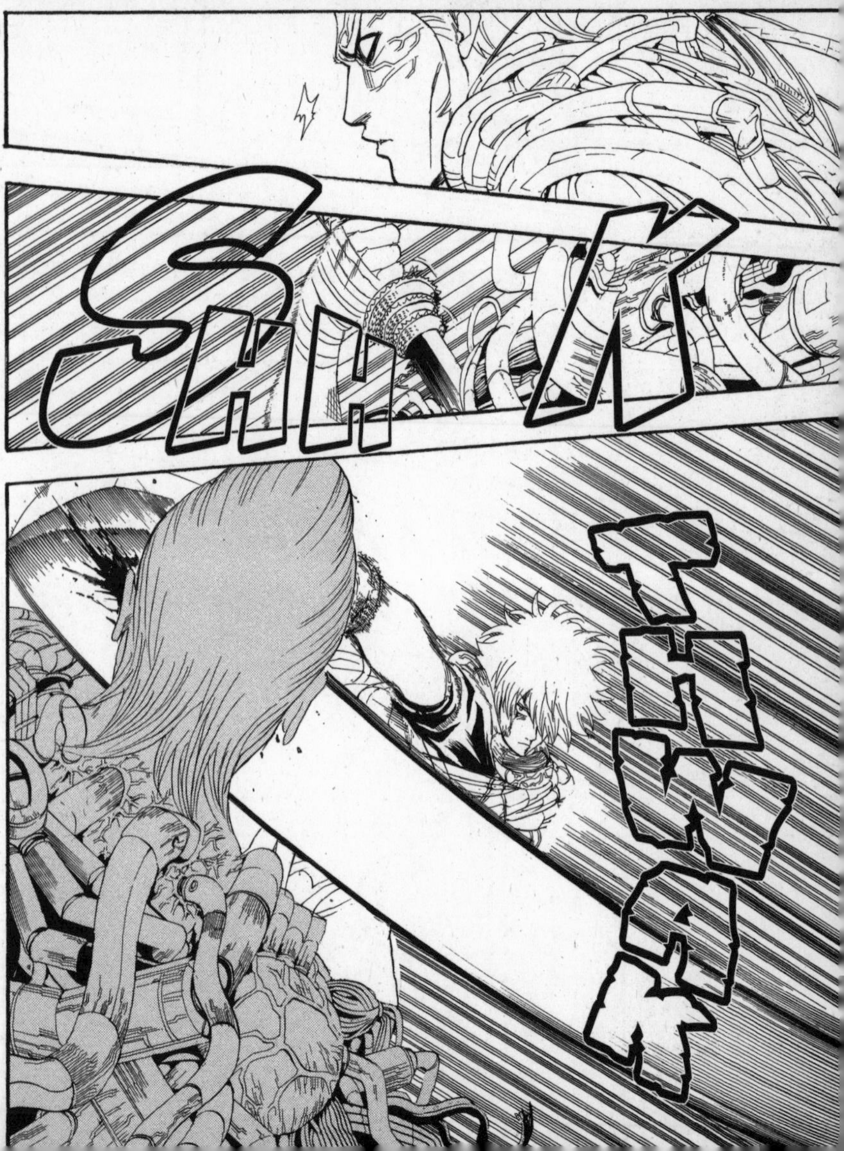
SHHK
THUNK

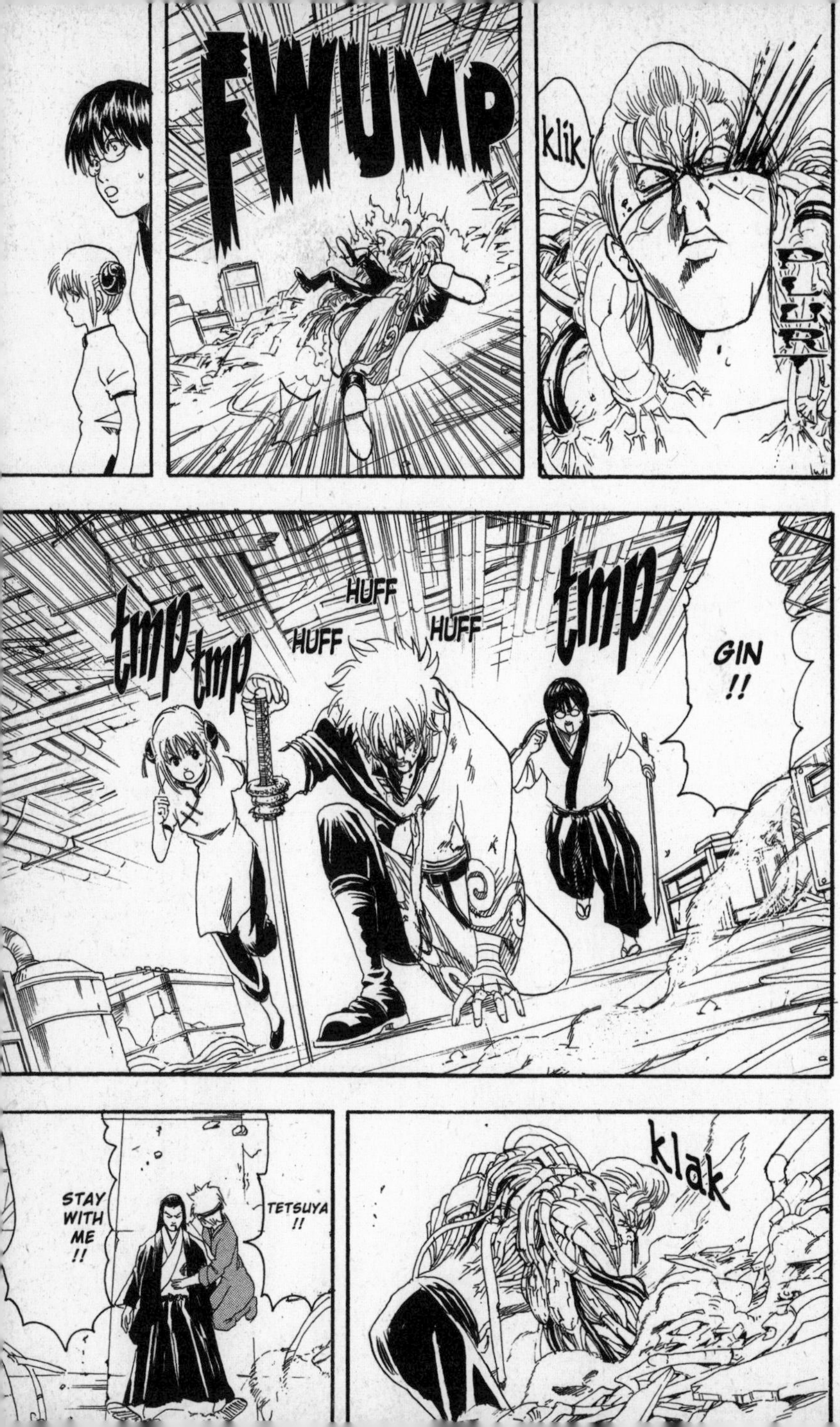
klik
PLURT
FWUMP
GIN !!
tmp
HUFF
HUFF
HUFF
tmp tmp
klak
TETSUYA !!
STAY WITH ME !!

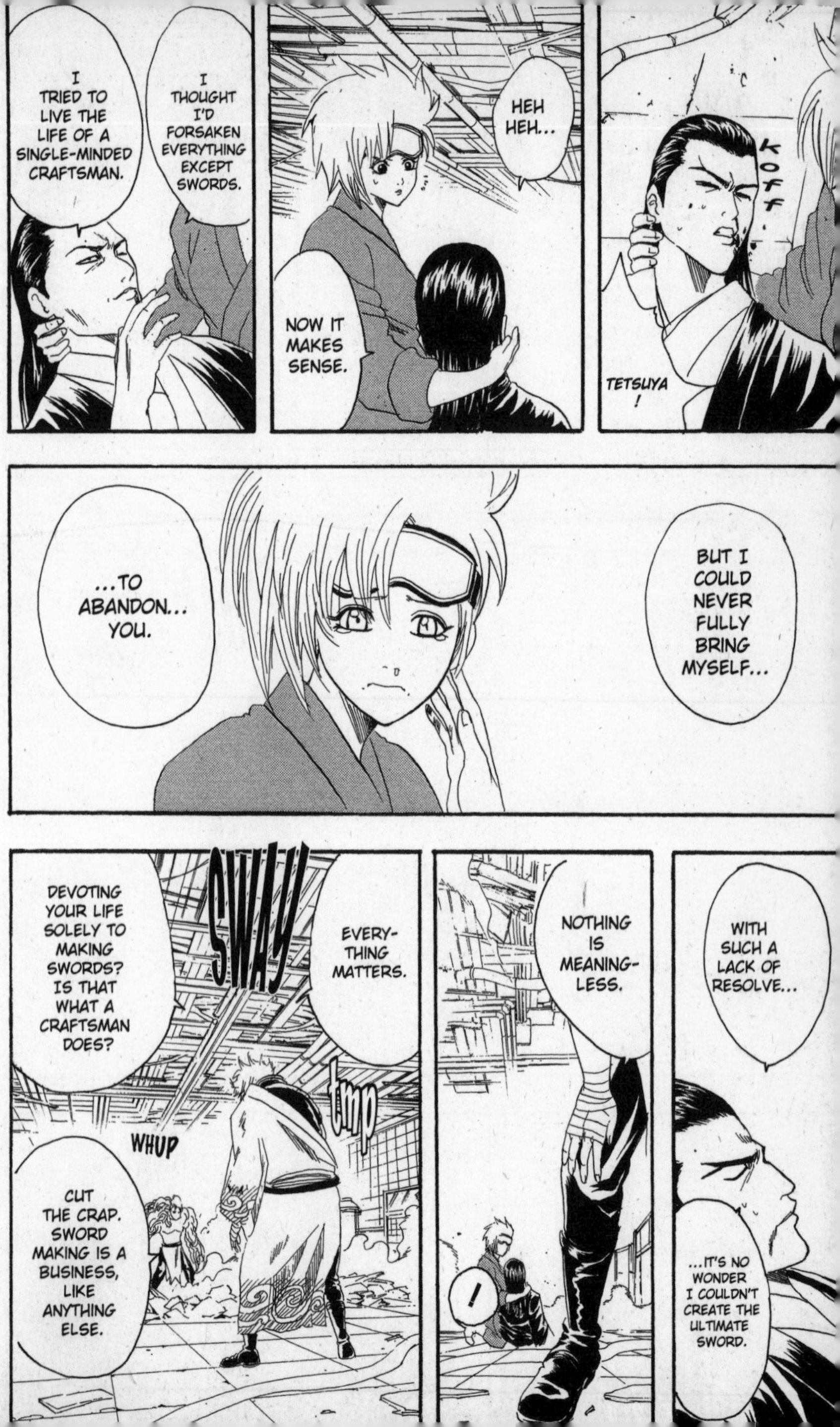
KOFF
TETSUYA!
HEH HEH...
NOW IT MAKES SENSE.
I THOUGHT I'D FORSAKEN EVERYTHING EXCEPT SWORDS.
I TRIED TO LIVE THE LIFE OF A SINGLE-MINDED CRAFTSMAN.
BUT I COULD NEVER FULLY BRING MYSELF...
...TO ABANDON... YOU.
WITH SUCH A LACK OF RESOLVE...
...IT'S NO WONDER I COULDN'T CREATE THE ULTIMATE SWORD.
NOTHING IS MEANING-LESS.
!
SWAY
EVERY-THING MATTERS.
DEVOTING YOUR LIFE SOLELY TO MAKING SWORDS? IS THAT WHAT A CRAFTSMAN DOES?
tmp
WHUP
CUT THE CRAP. SWORD MAKING IS A BUSINESS, LIKE ANYTHING ELSE.

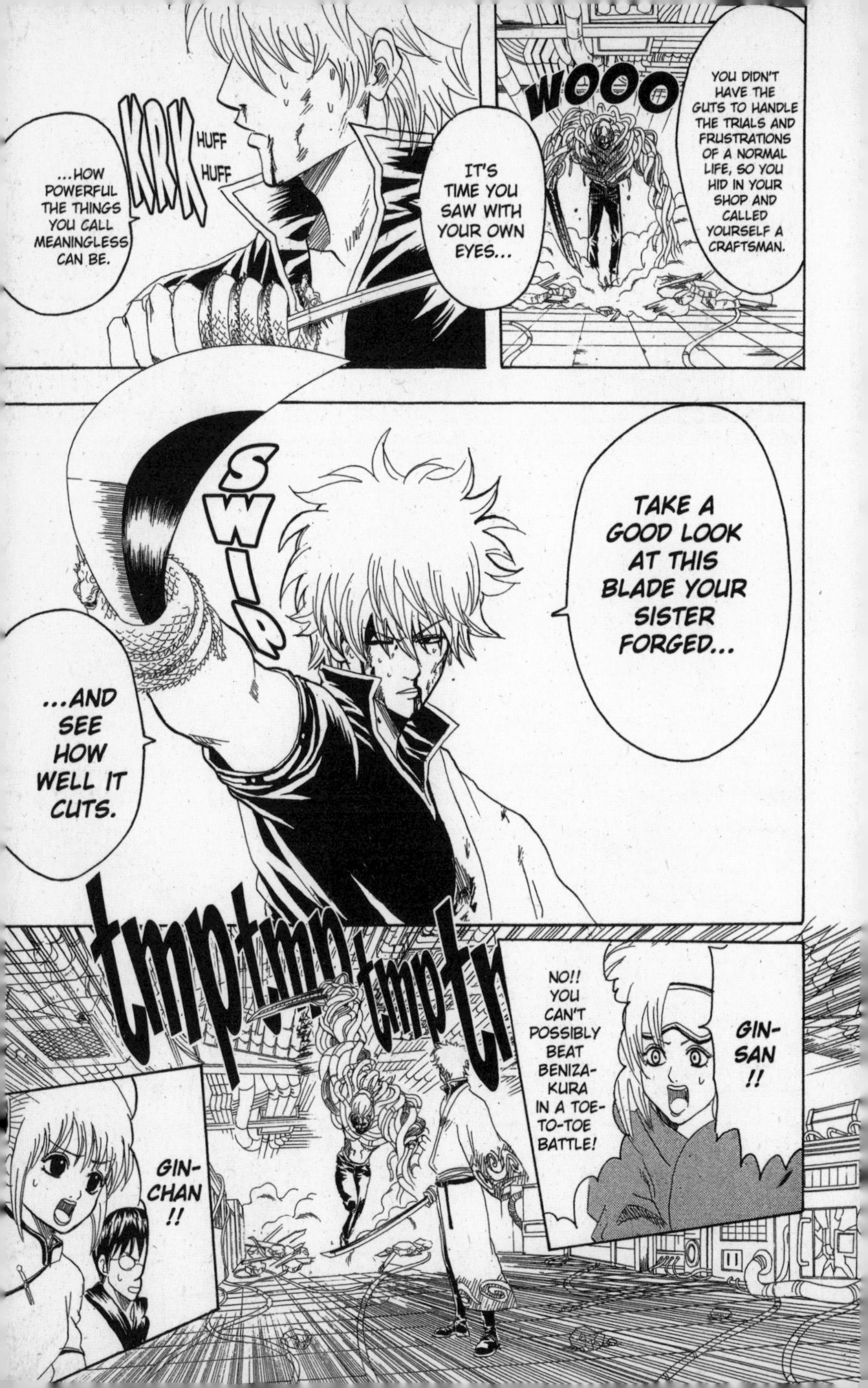
WOOO
YOU DIDN'T HAVE THE GUTS TO HANDLE THE TRIALS AND FRUSTRATIONS OF A NORMAL LIFE, SO YOU HID IN YOUR SHOP AND CALLED YOURSELF A CRAFTSMAN.
IT'S TIME YOU SAW WITH YOUR OWN EYES...
HUFF HUFF
KRK
...HOW POWERFUL THE THINGS YOU CALL MEANINGLESS CAN BE.
TAKE A GOOD LOOK AT THIS BLADE YOUR SISTER FORGED...
SWIP
...AND SEE HOW WELL IT CUTS.
GIN-SAN!!
NO!! YOU CAN'T POSSIBLY BEAT BENIZAKURA IN A TOE-TO-TOE BATTLE!
tmptmp tmp
GIN-CHAN!!

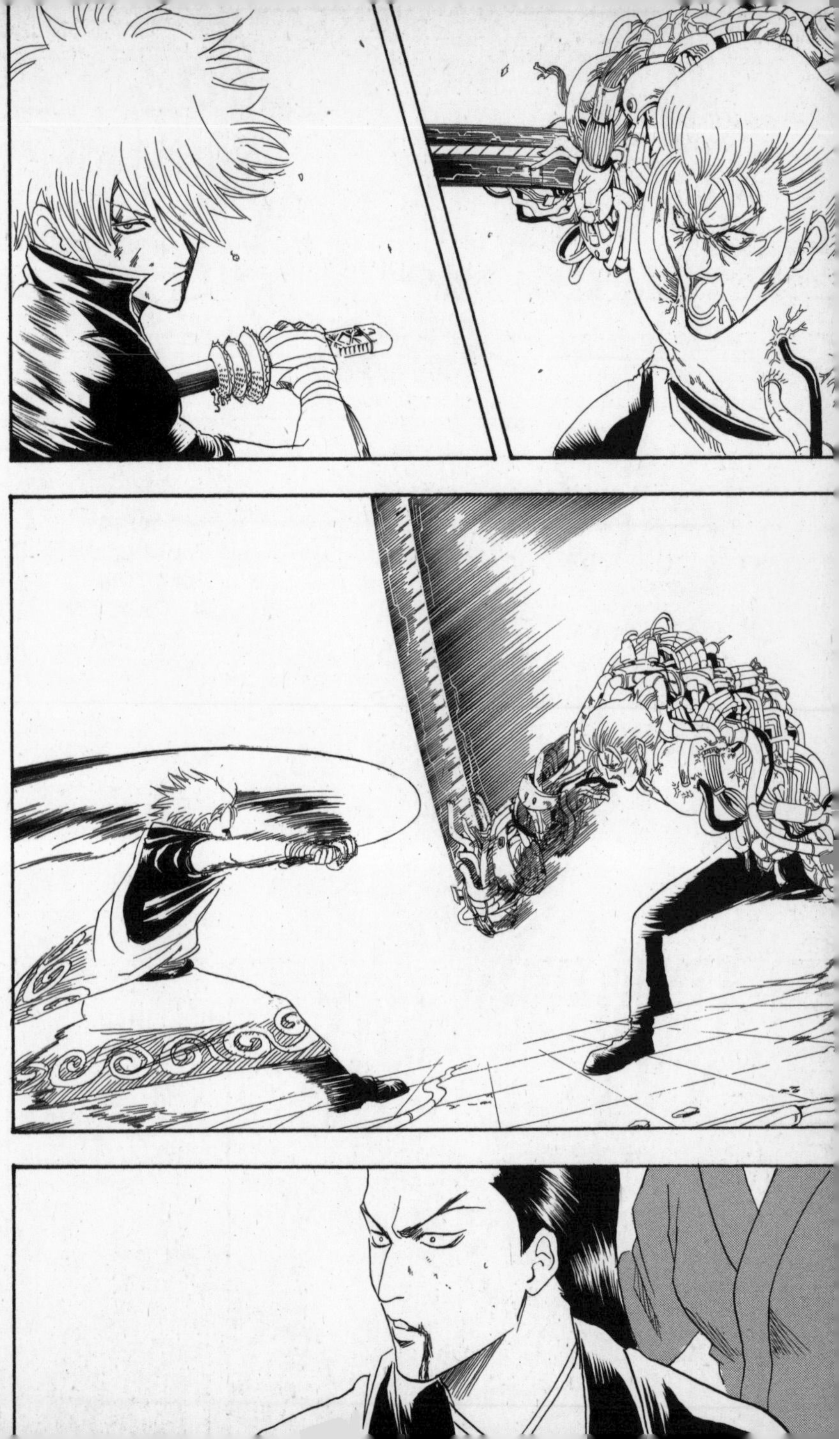

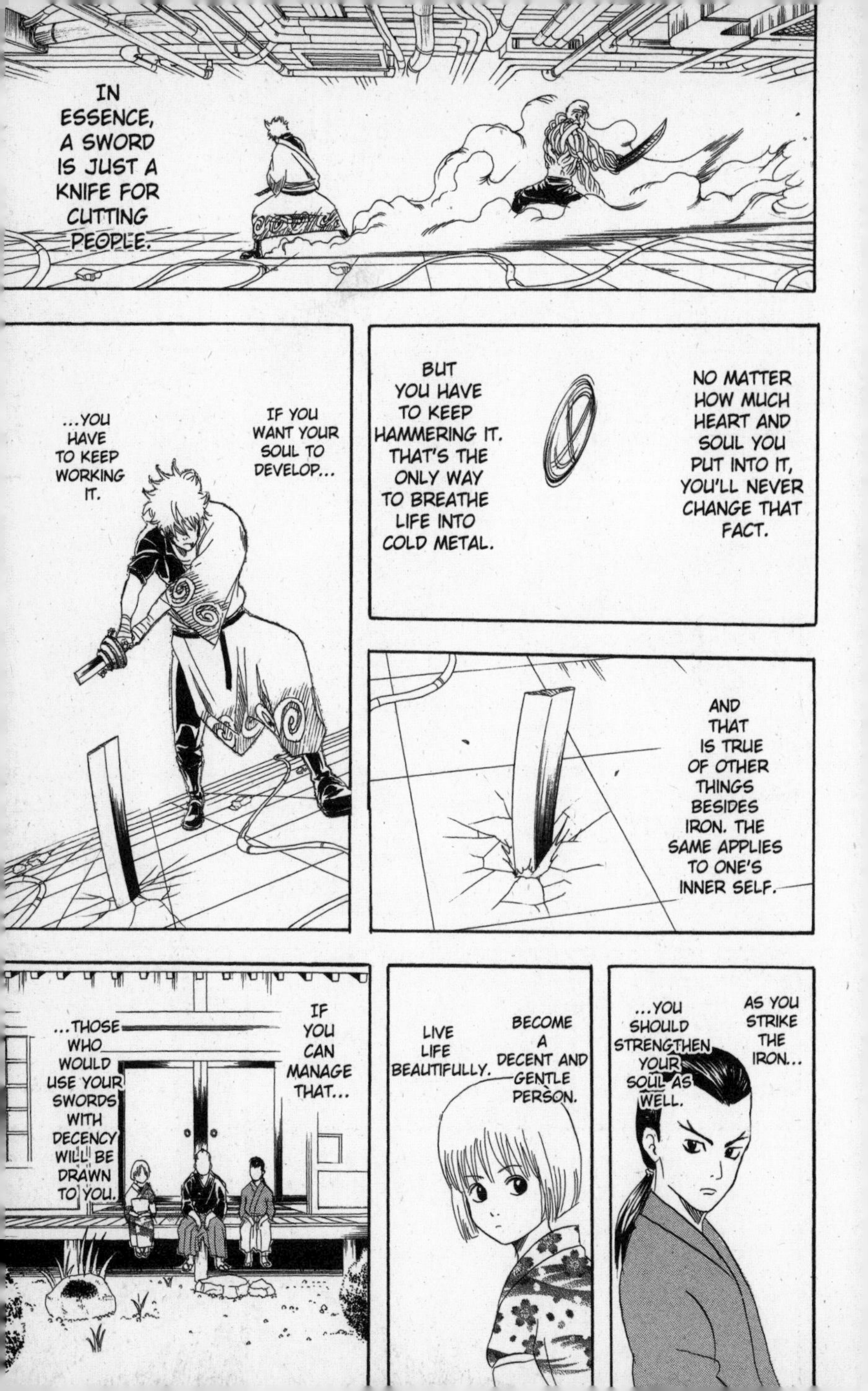
IN ESSENCE, A SWORD IS JUST A KNIFE FOR CUTTING PEOPLE.
NO MATTER HOW MUCH HEART AND SOUL YOU PUT INTO IT, YOU'LL NEVER CHANGE THAT FACT.
BUT YOU HAVE TO KEEP HAMMERING IT. THAT'S THE ONLY WAY TO BREATHE LIFE INTO COLD METAL.
AND THAT IS TRUE OF OTHER THINGS BESIDES IRON. THE SAME APPLIES TO ONE'S INNER SELF.
IF YOU WANT YOUR SOUL TO DEVELOP...
...YOU HAVE TO KEEP WORKING IT.
AS YOU STRIKE THE IRON...
...YOU SHOULD STRENGTHEN YOUR SOUL AS WELL.
BECOME A DECENT AND GENTLE PERSON.
LIVE LIFE BEAUTIFULLY.
IF YOU CAN MANAGE THAT...
...THOSE WHO WOULD USE YOUR SWORDS WITH DECENCY WILL BE DRAWN TO YOU.

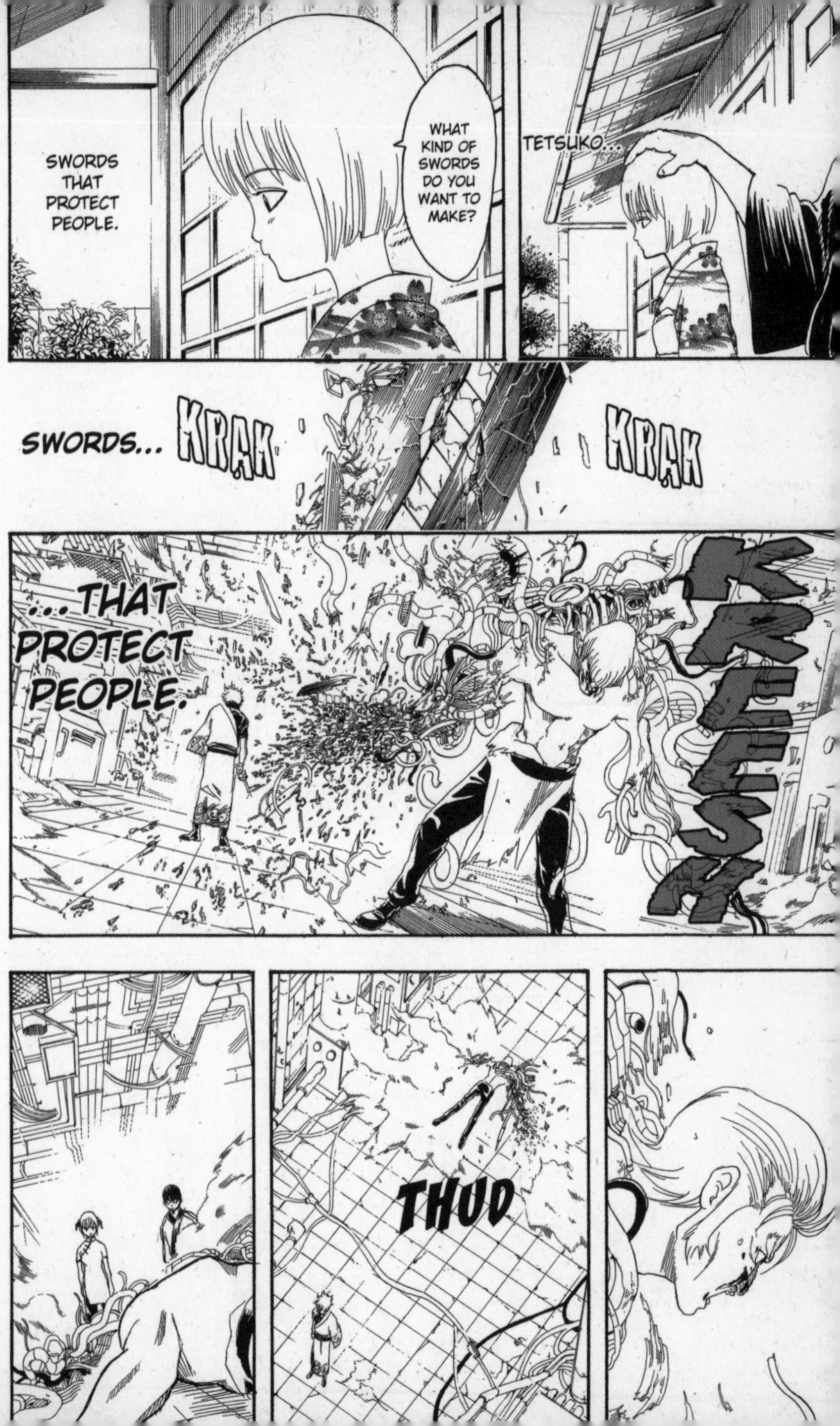
TETSUKO...
WHAT KIND OF SWORDS DO YOU WANT TO MAKE?
SWORDS THAT PROTECT PEOPLE.
KRAK
KRAK
SWORDS...
KRESSH
...THAT PROTECT PEOPLE.
THUD

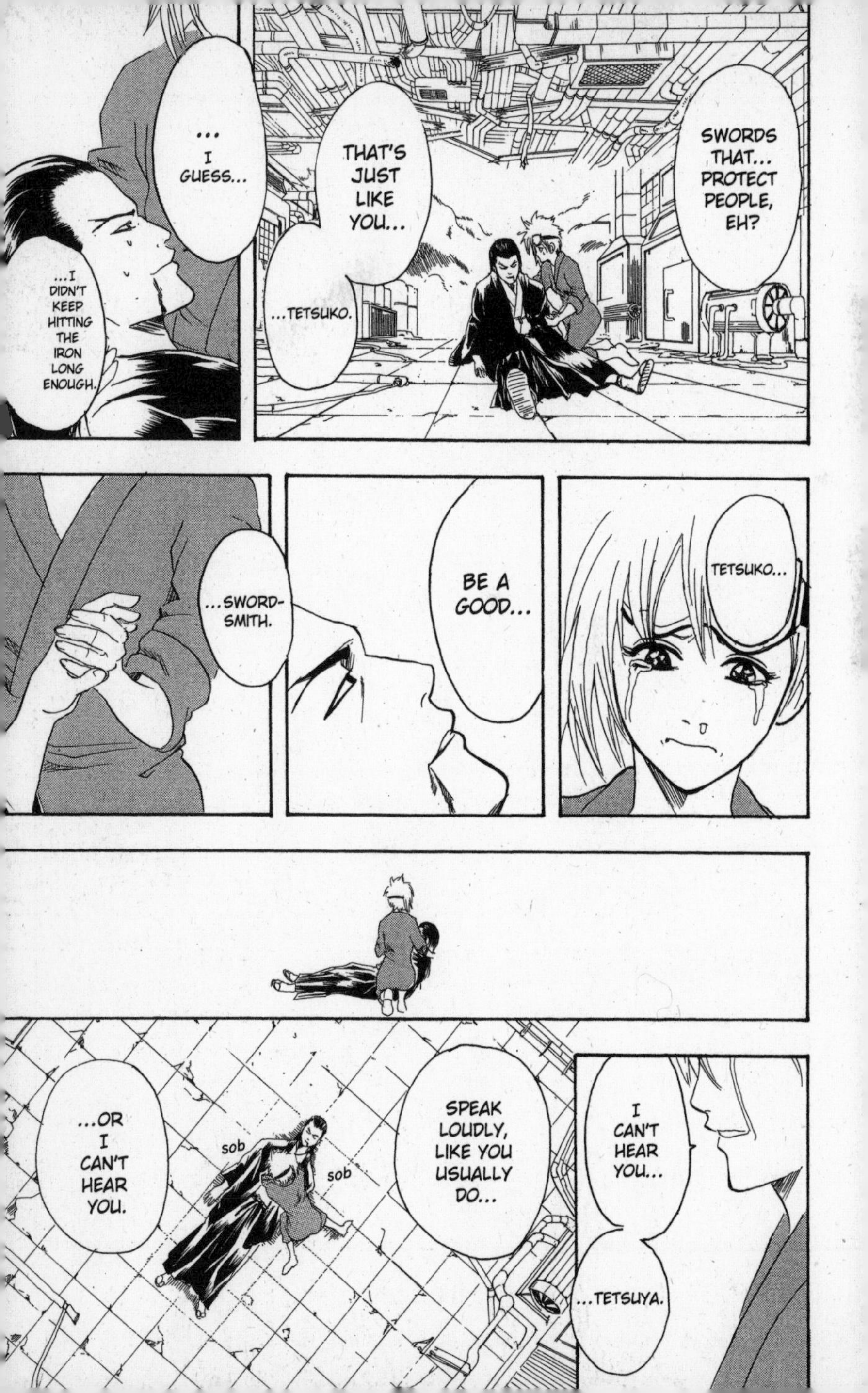
SWORDS THAT... PROTECT PEOPLE, EH?
THAT'S JUST LIKE YOU...
...TETSUKO.
... I GUESS...
...I DIDN'T KEEP HITTING THE IRON LONG ENOUGH.
TETSUKO...
BE A GOOD...
...SWORD-SMITH.
I CAN'T HEAR YOU...
...TETSUYA.
SPEAK LOUDLY, LIKE YOU USUALLY DO...
sob
sob
...OR I CAN'T HEAR YOU.

Gin Tama Fan Art!

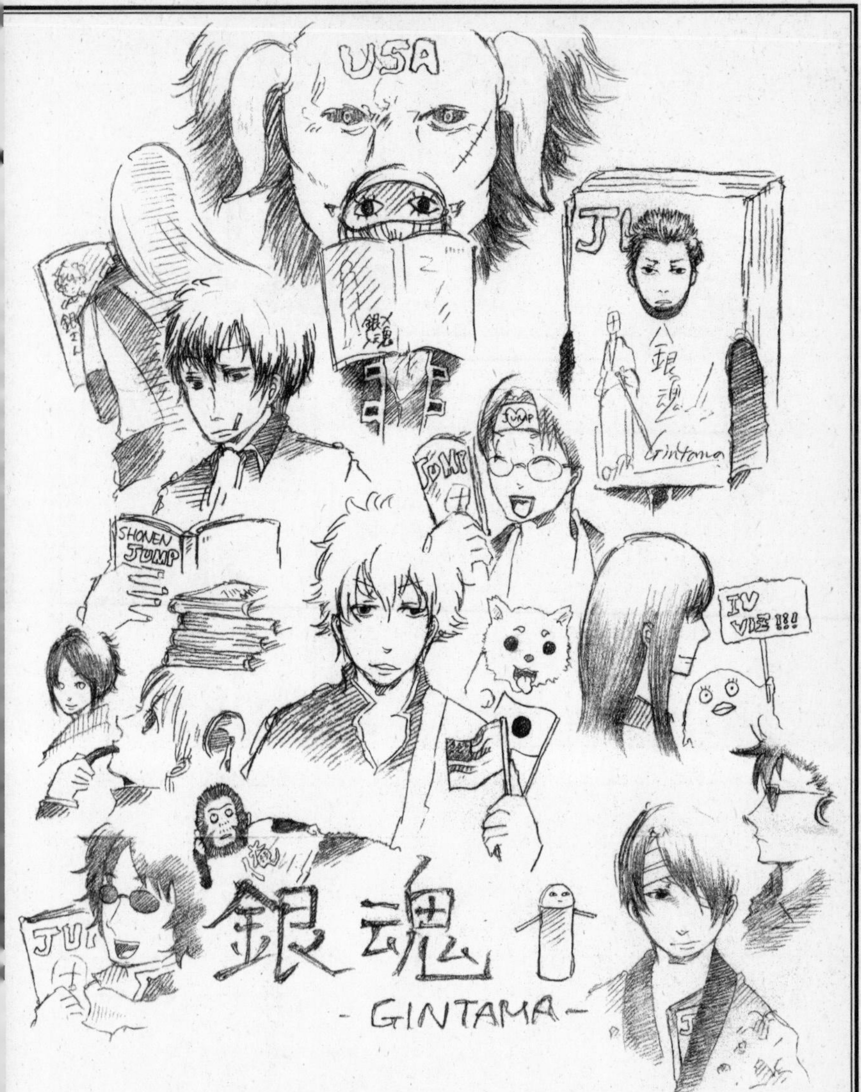
USA
SHONEN JUMP
Gintama
銀魂
-GINTAMA-

By S. Nishikawa

For details on how to submit your Gin Tama Fan Art, see page 166!

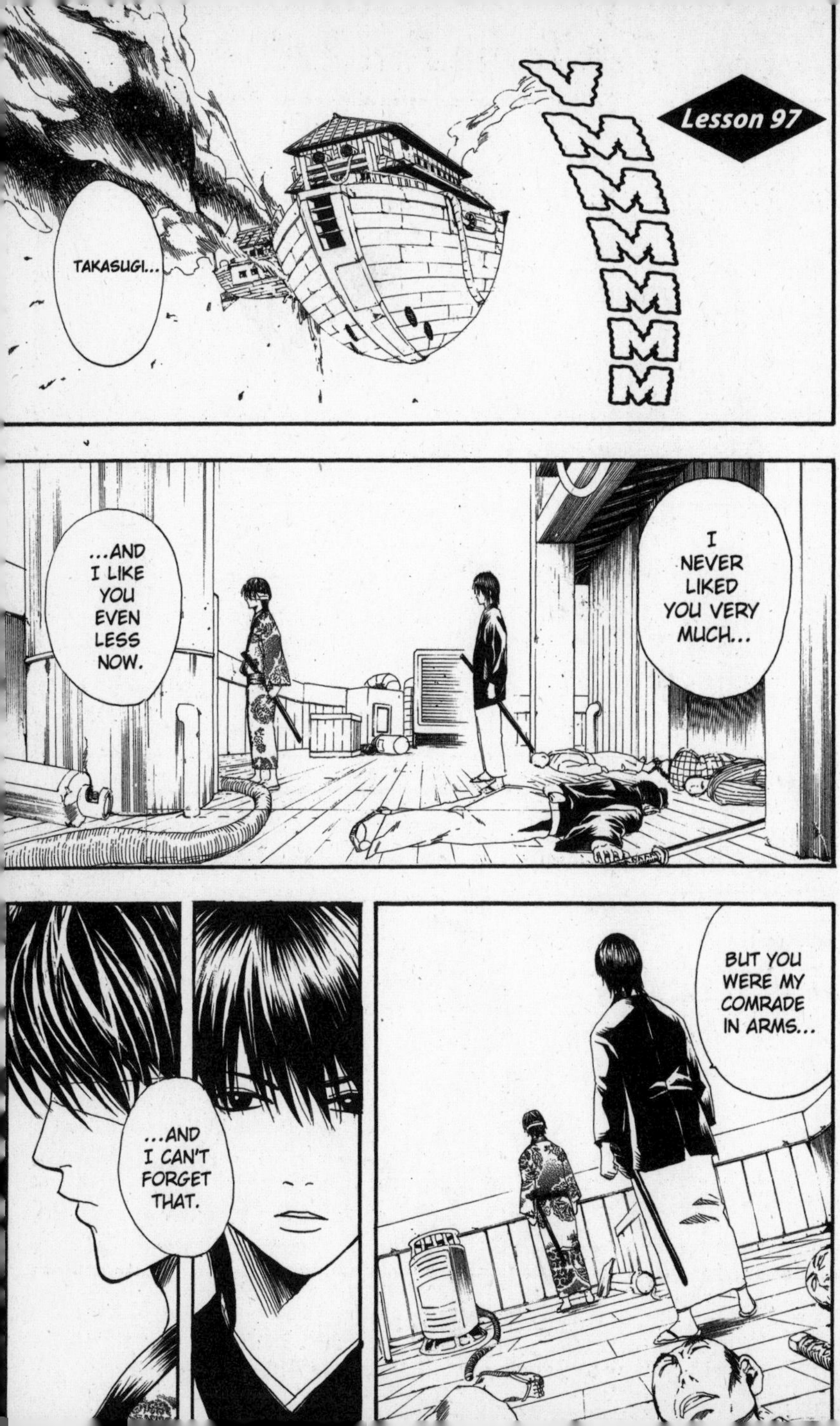
Lesson 97
VMMMMMM
TAKASUGI...
I NEVER LIKED YOU VERY MUCH...
...AND I LIKE YOU EVEN LESS NOW.
BUT YOU WERE MY COMRADE IN ARMS...
...AND I CAN'T FORGET THAT.

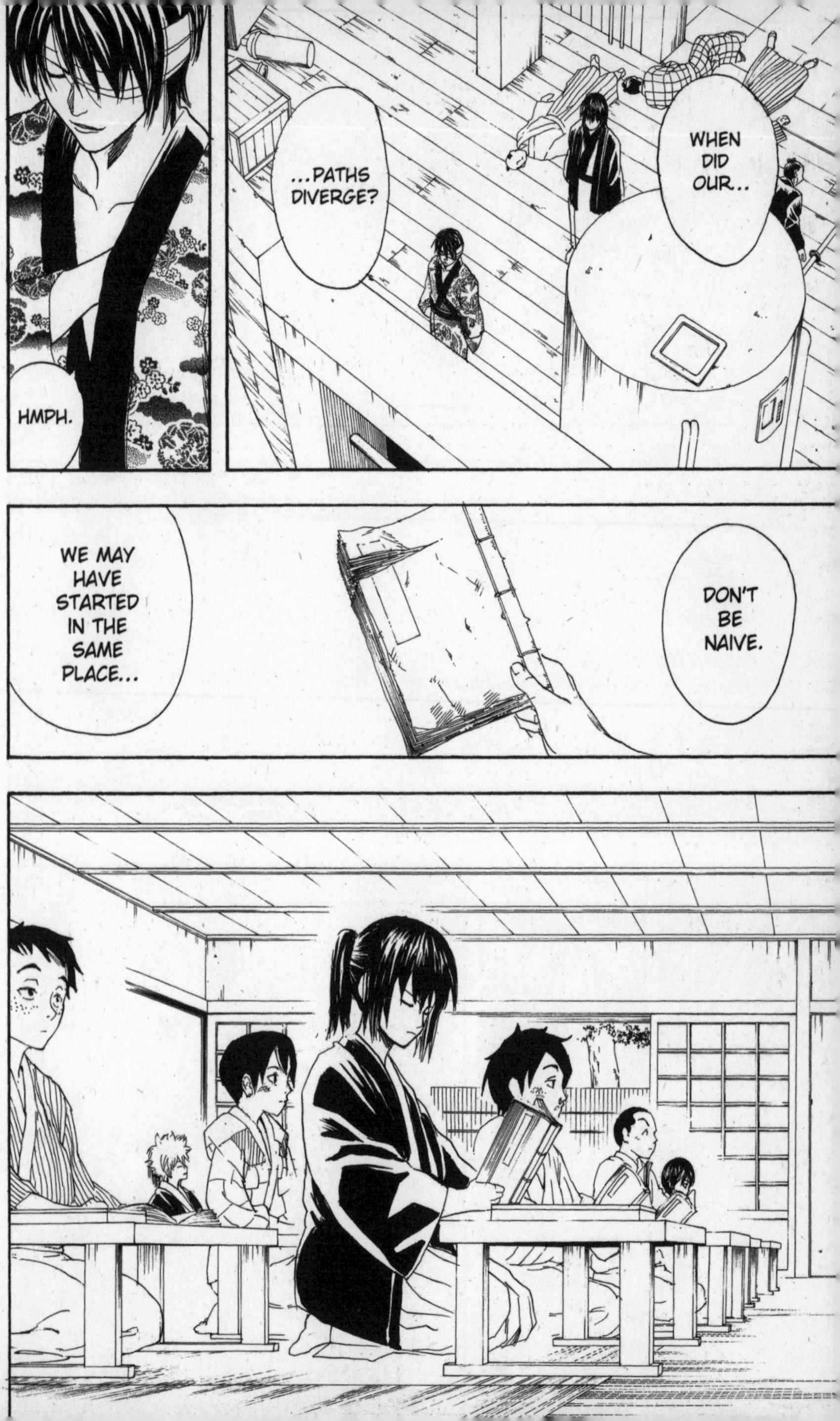
WHEN DID OUR...
...PATHS DIVERGE?
HMPH.
DON'T BE NAIVE.
WE MAY HAVE STARTED IN THE SAME PLACE...

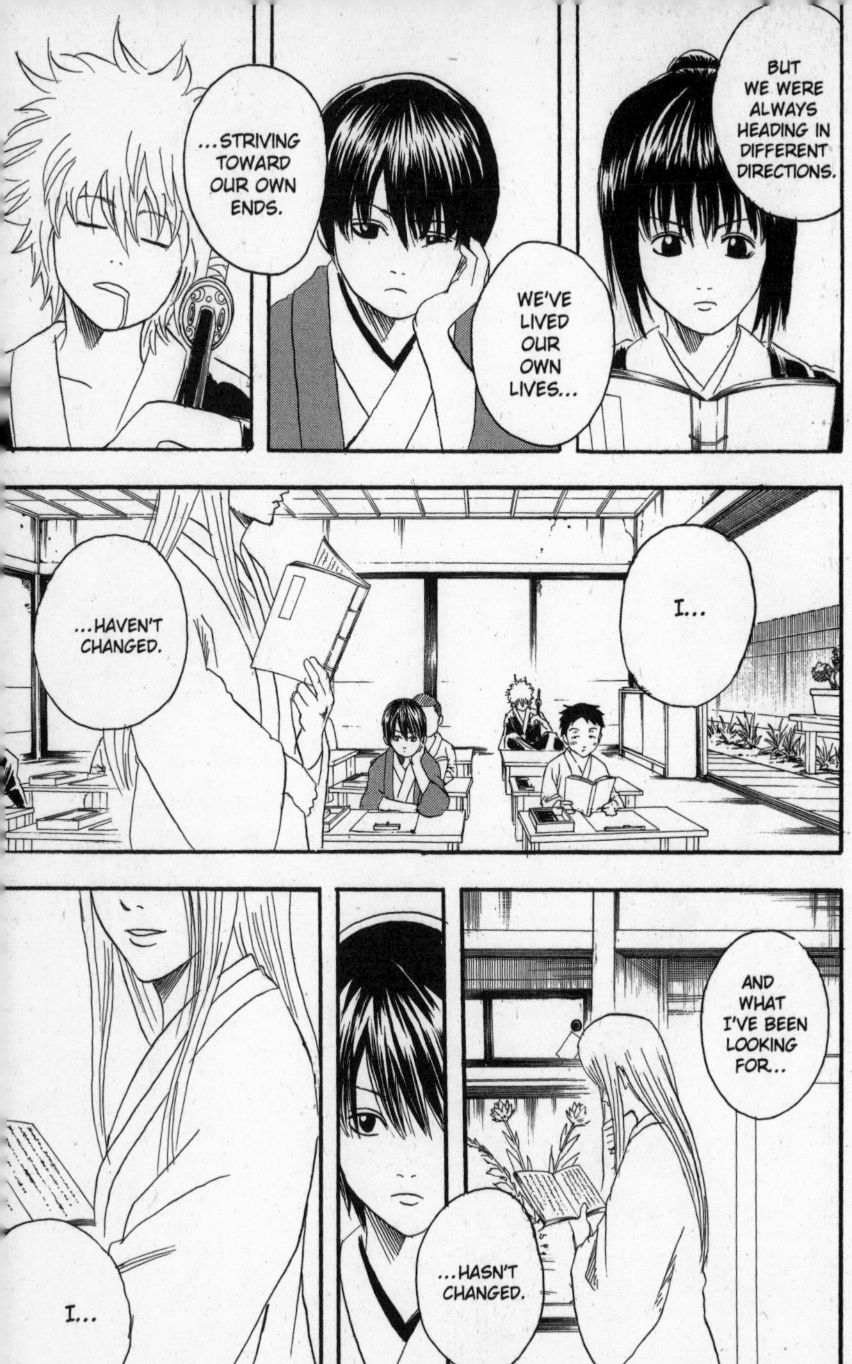
BUT WE WERE ALWAYS HEADING IN DIFFERENT DIRECTIONS.
WE'VE LIVED OUR OWN LIVES...
...STRIVING TOWARD OUR OWN ENDS.
I...
...HAVEN'T CHANGED.
AND WHAT I'VE BEEN LOOKING FOR...
...HASN'T CHANGED.
I...

Lesson 97
If You're Prepared, You Don't Need to Worry

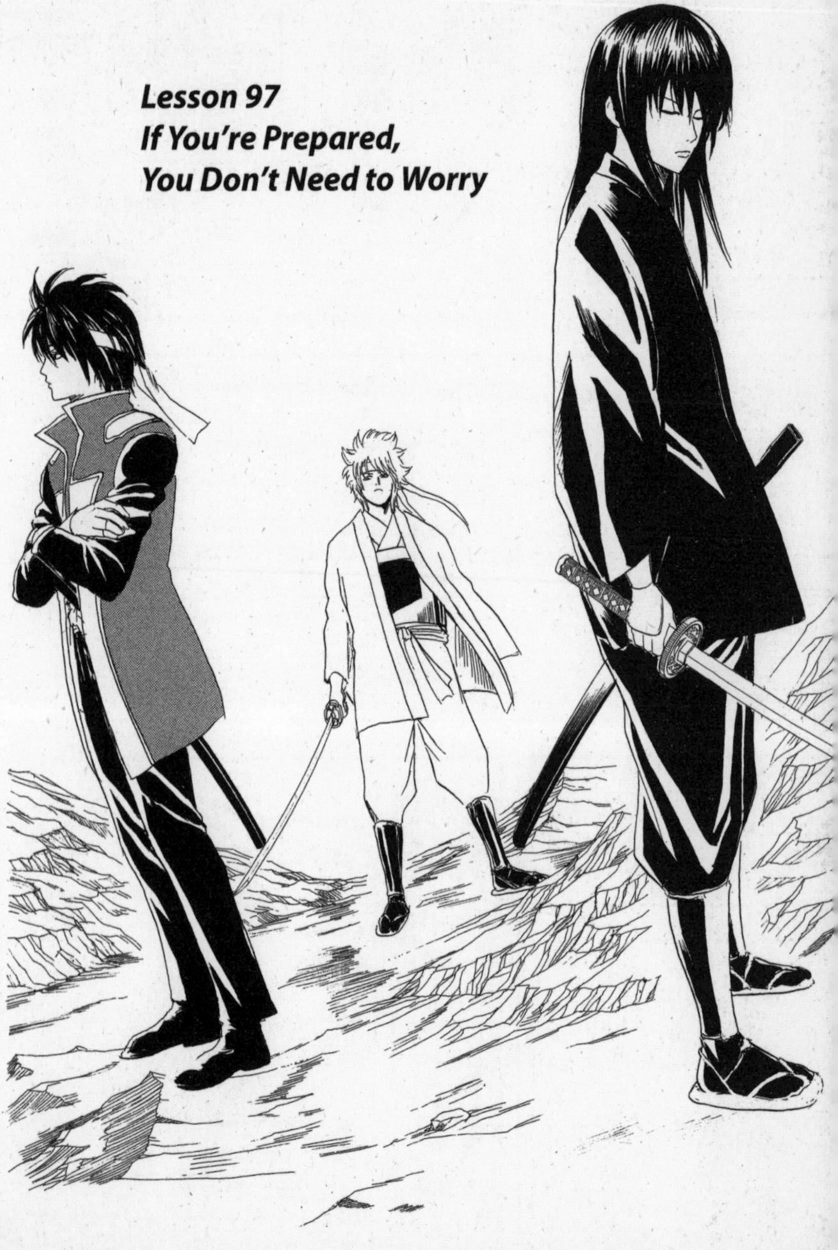

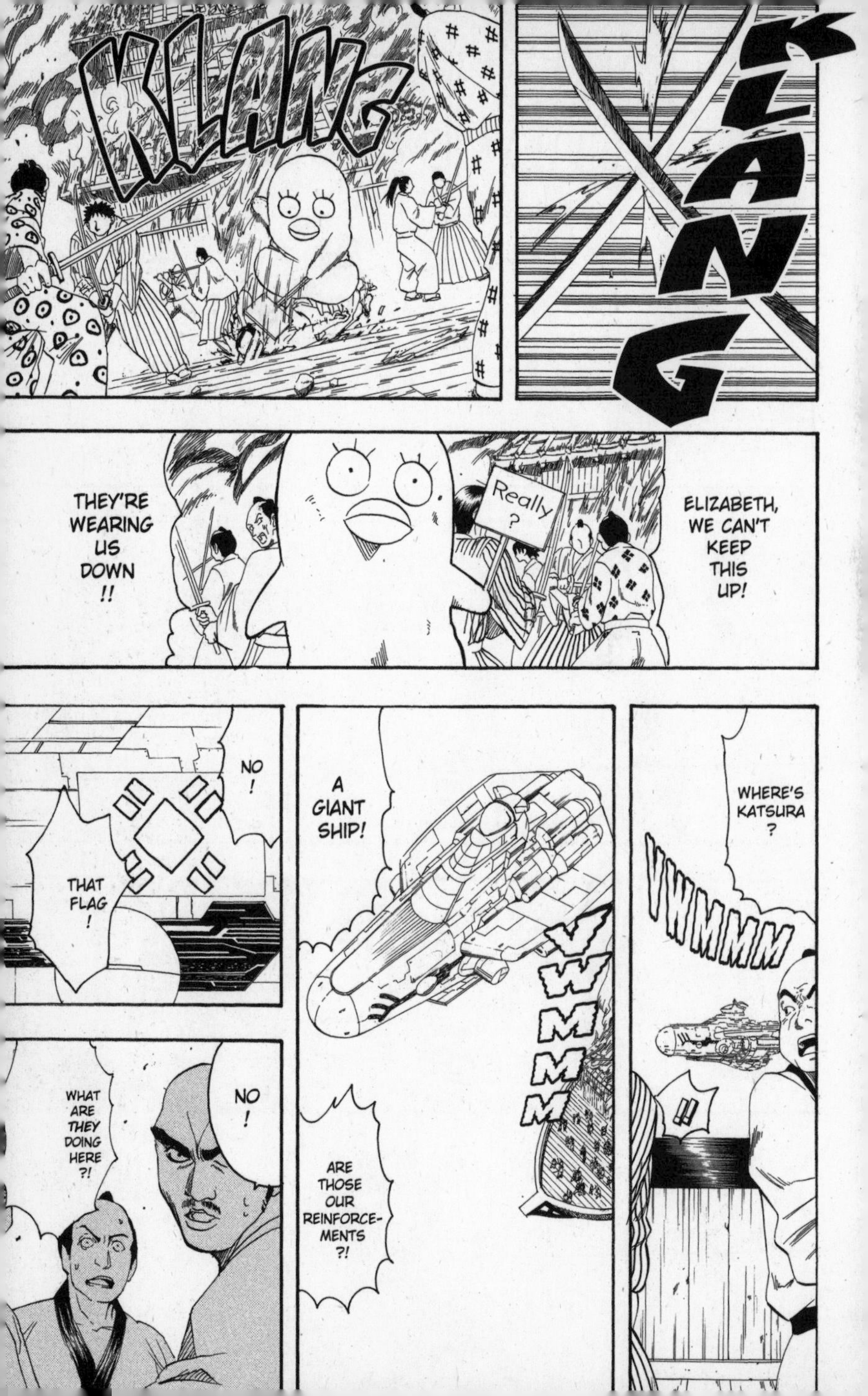
KLANG
KLANG
ELIZABETH, WE CAN'T KEEP THIS UP!
Really?
THEY'RE WEARING US DOWN!!
WHERE'S KATSURA?
VWMMMM
!!
A GIANT SHIP!
VWMMMM
ARE THOSE OUR REINFORCEMENTS?!
NO! THAT FLAG!
NO!
WHAT ARE THEY DOING HERE?!

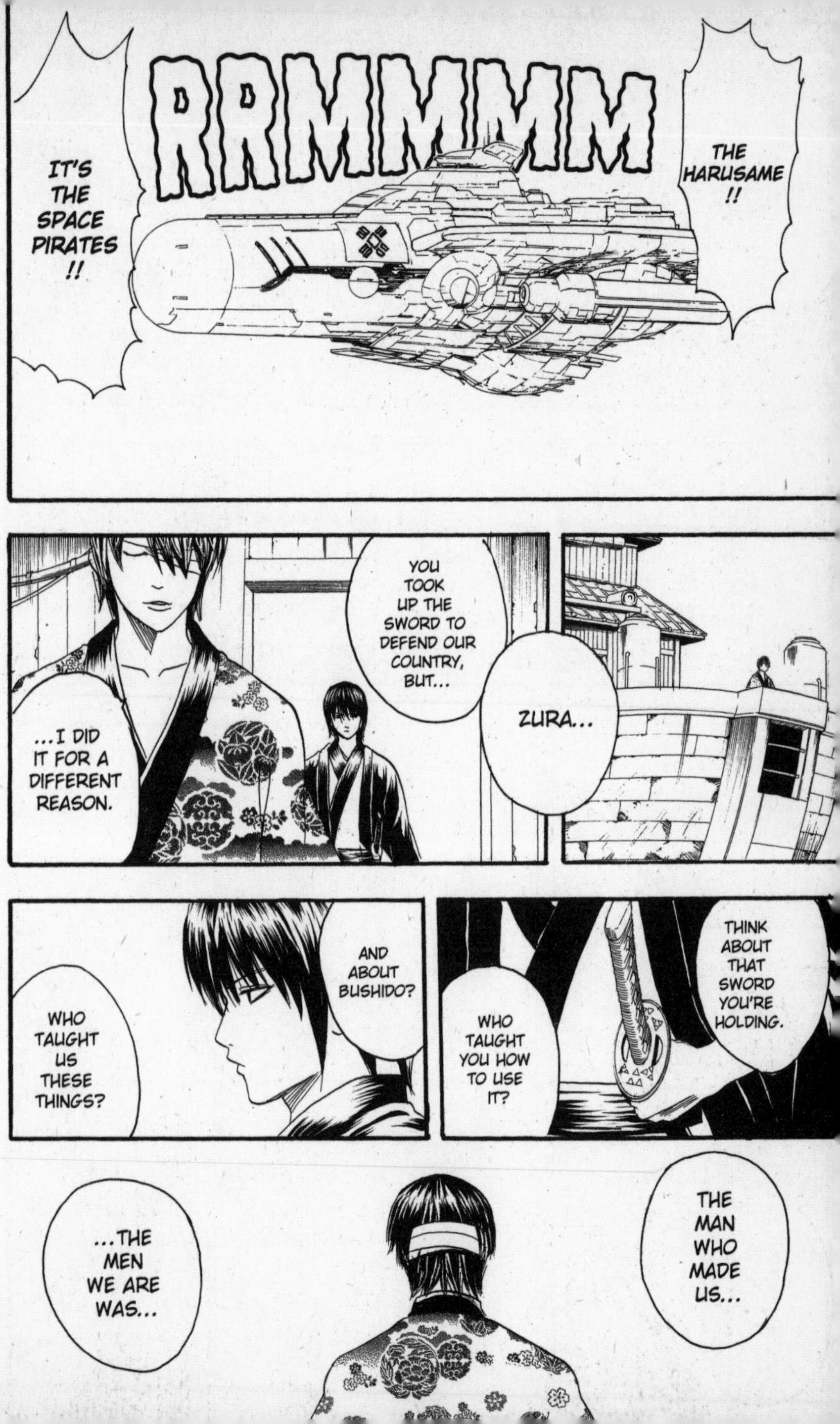
RRMMMM
THE HARUSAME !!
IT'S THE SPACE PIRATES !!
ZURA...
YOU TOOK UP THE SWORD TO DEFEND OUR COUNTRY, BUT...
...I DID IT FOR A DIFFERENT REASON.
THINK ABOUT THAT SWORD YOU'RE HOLDING.
WHO TAUGHT YOU HOW TO USE IT?
AND ABOUT BUSHIDO?
WHO TAUGHT US THESE THINGS?
THE MAN WHO MADE US...
...THE MEN WE ARE WAS...

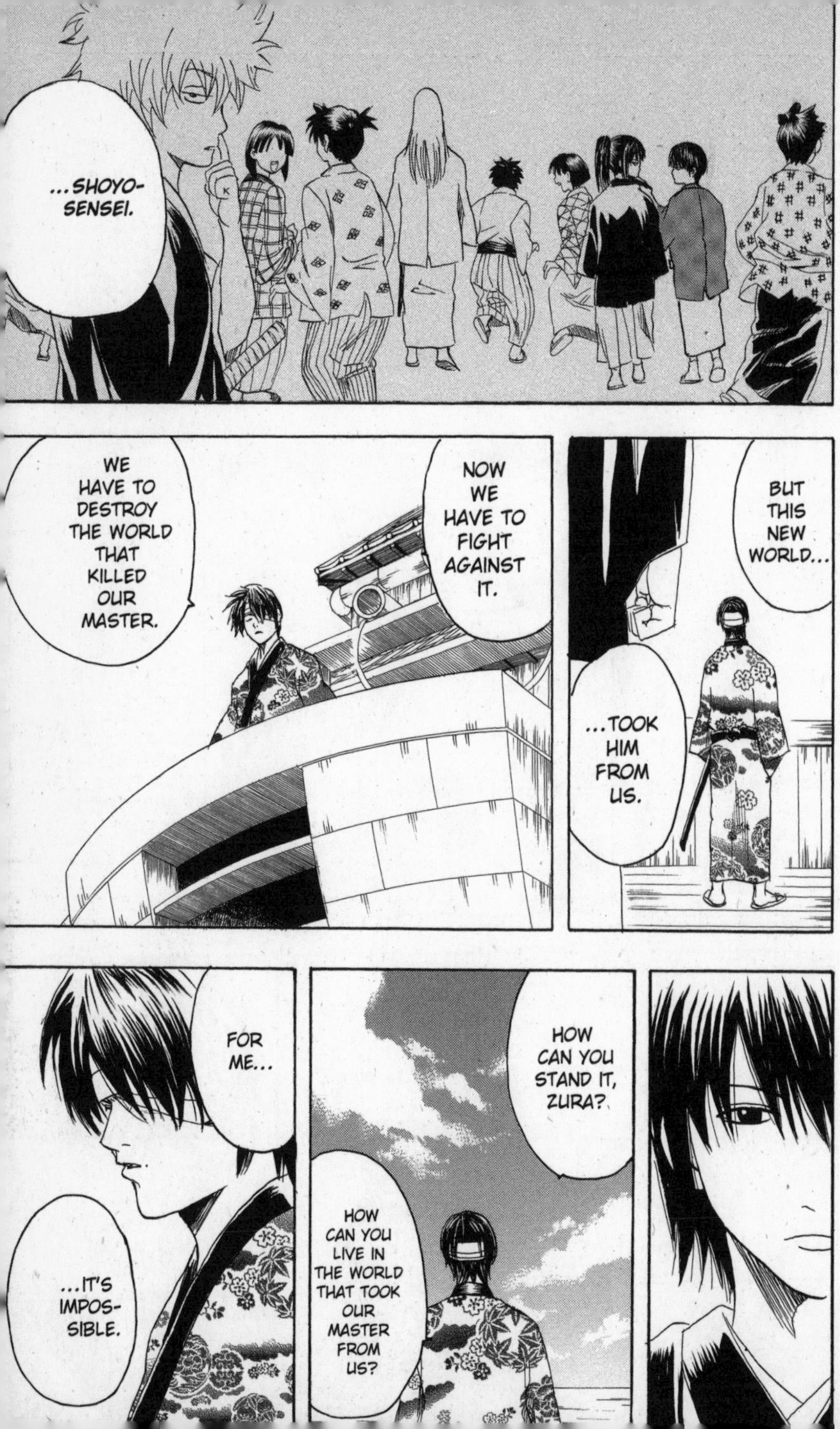
...SHOYO-SENSEI.
BUT THIS NEW WORLD...
...TOOK HIM FROM US.
NOW WE HAVE TO FIGHT AGAINST IT.
WE HAVE TO DESTROY THE WORLD THAT KILLED OUR MASTER.
HOW CAN YOU STAND IT, ZURA?
HOW CAN YOU LIVE IN THE WORLD THAT TOOK OUR MASTER FROM US?
FOR ME...
...IT'S IMPOSSIBLE.

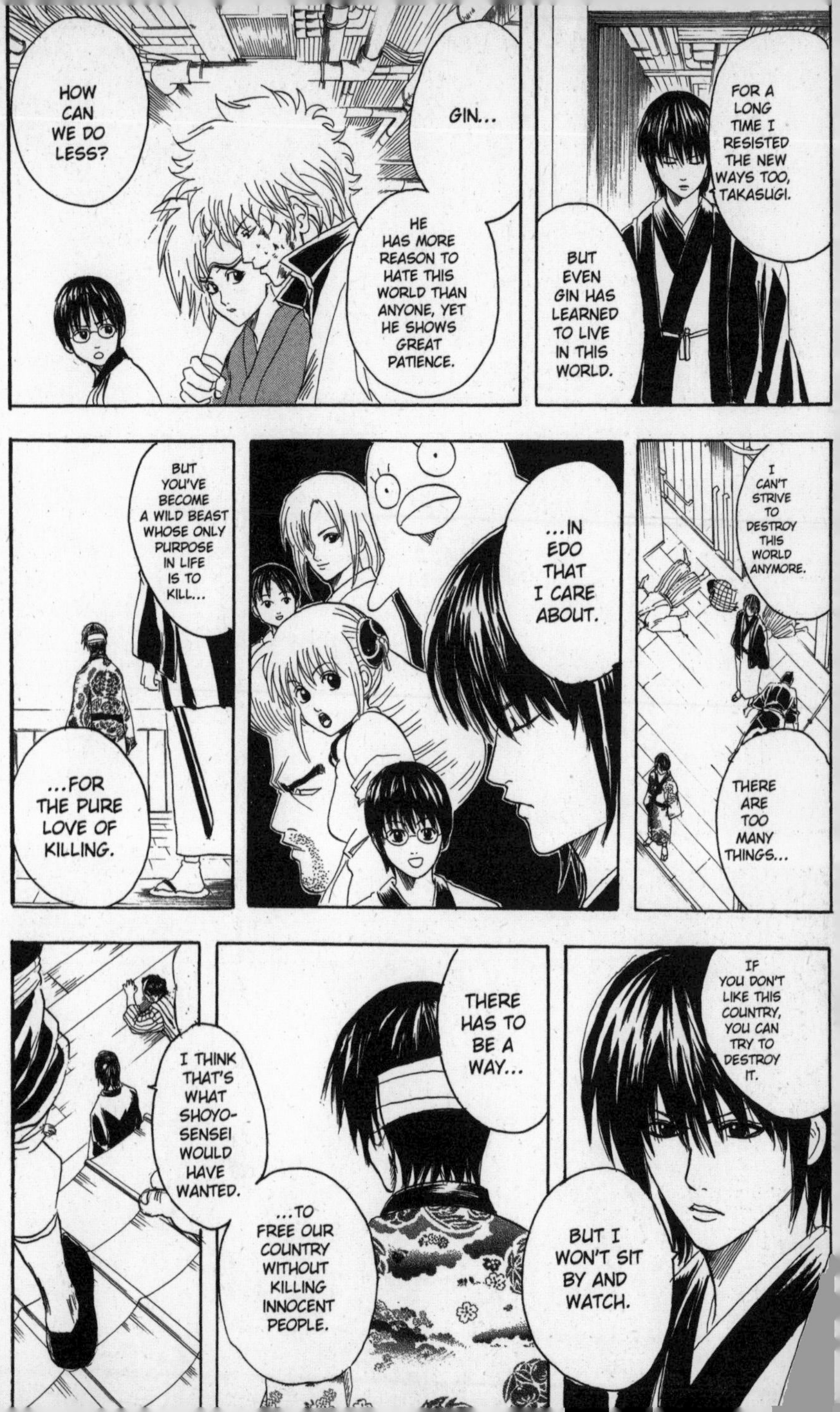
FOR A LONG TIME I RESISTED THE NEW WAYS TOO, TAKASUGI.
BUT EVEN GIN HAS LEARNED TO LIVE IN THIS WORLD.
GIN...
HE HAS MORE REASON TO HATE THIS WORLD THAN ANYONE, YET HE SHOWS GREAT PATIENCE.
HOW CAN WE DO LESS?
I CAN'T STRIVE TO DESTROY THIS WORLD ANYMORE.
THERE ARE TOO MANY THINGS...
...IN EDO THAT I CARE ABOUT.
BUT YOU'VE BECOME A WILD BEAST WHOSE ONLY PURPOSE IN LIFE IS TO KILL...
...FOR THE PURE LOVE OF KILLING.
IF YOU DON'T LIKE THIS COUNTRY, YOU CAN TRY TO DESTROY IT.
BUT I WON'T SIT BY AND WATCH.
THERE HAS TO BE A WAY...
...TO FREE OUR COUNTRY WITHOUT KILLING INNOCENT PEOPLE.
I THINK THAT'S WHAT SHOYO-SENSEI WOULD HAVE WANTED.

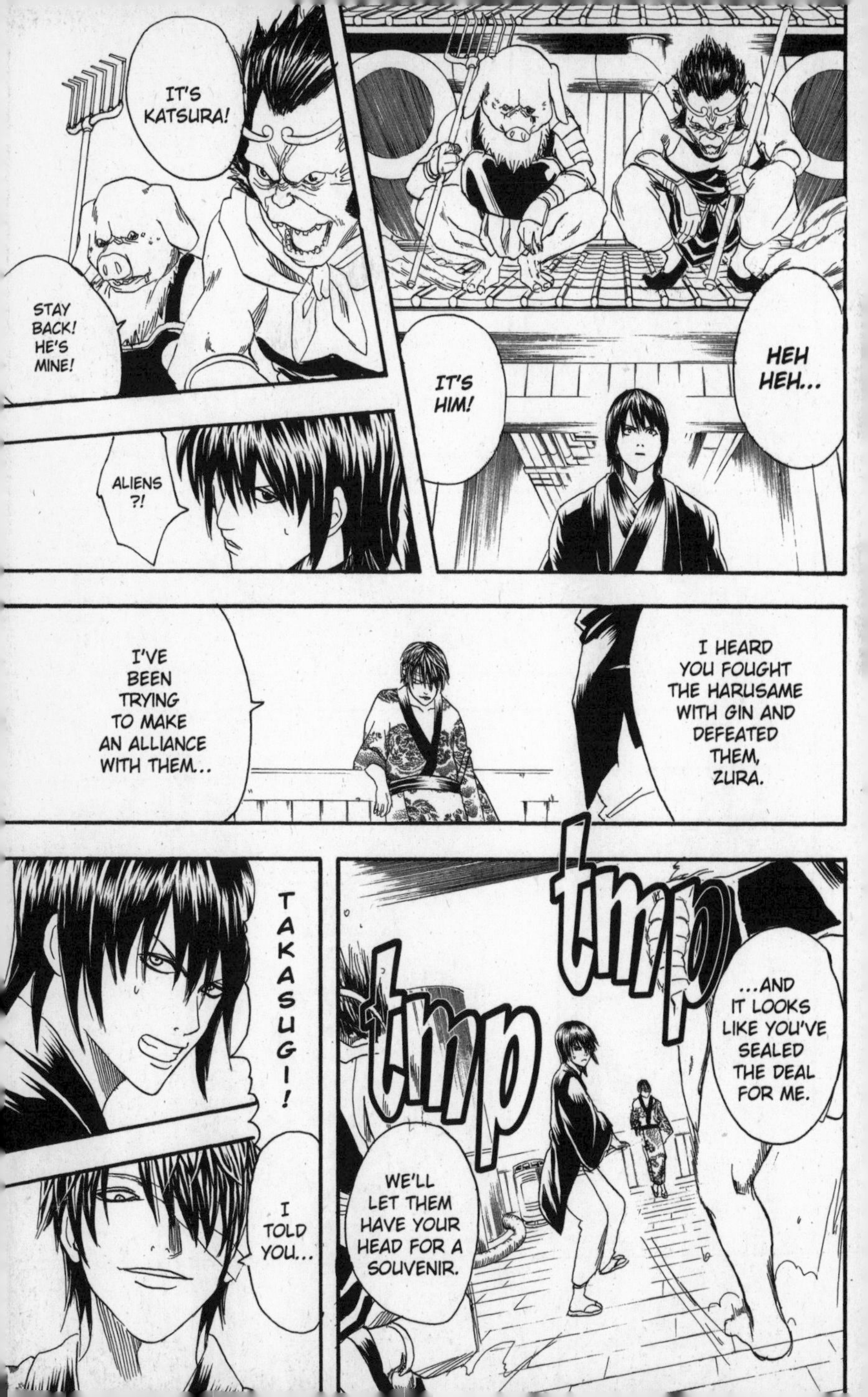
HEH HEH...
IT'S HIM!
IT'S KATSURA!
STAY BACK! HE'S MINE!
ALIENS ?!
I HEARD YOU FOUGHT THE HARUSAME WITH GIN AND DEFEATED THEM, ZURA.
I'VE BEEN TRYING TO MAKE AN ALLIANCE WITH THEM...
tmp
tmp
...AND IT LOOKS LIKE YOU'VE SEALED THE DEAL FOR ME.
WE'LL LET THEM HAVE YOUR HEAD FOR A SOUVENIR.
TAKASUGI!
I TOLD YOU...

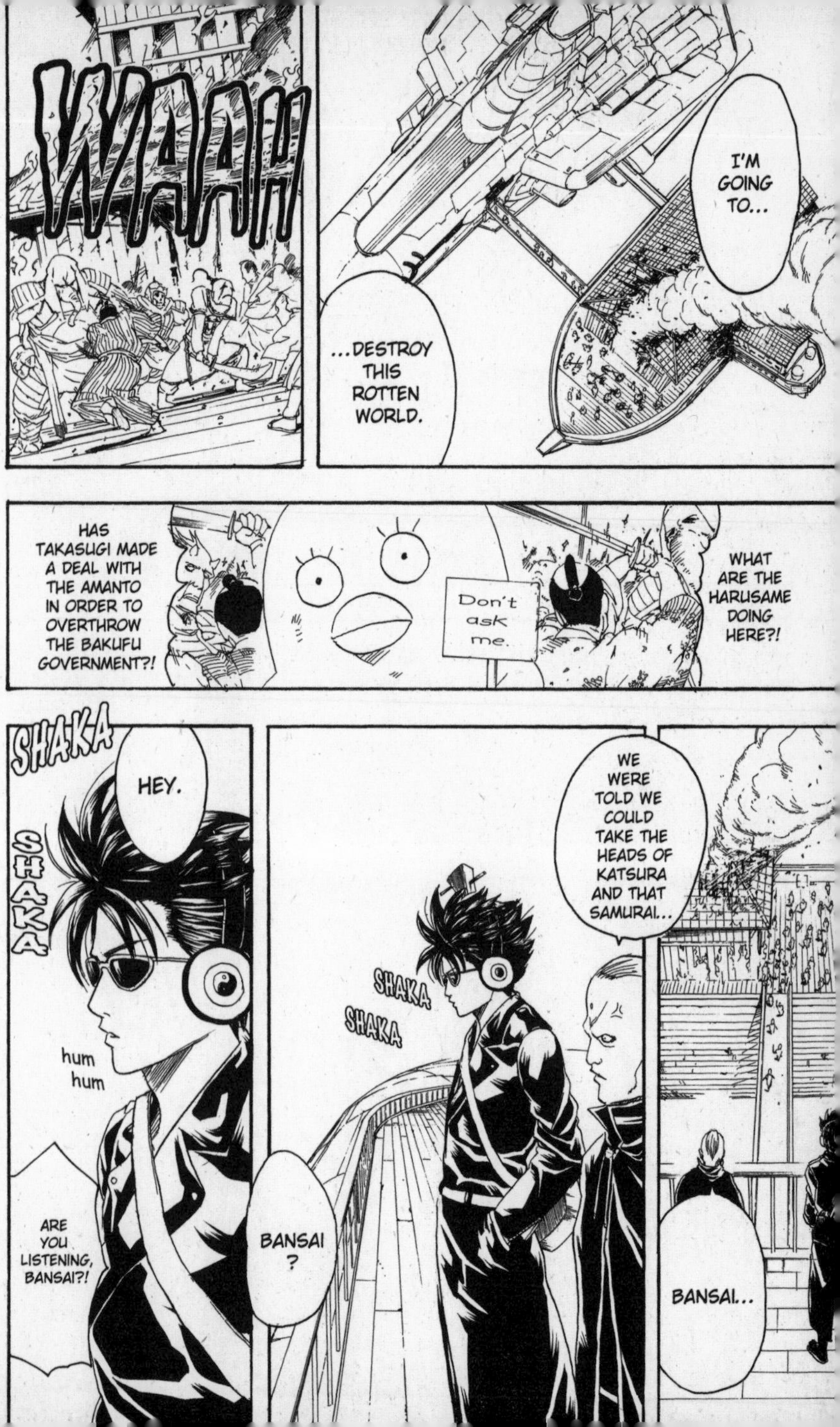
I'M GOING TO...
...DESTROY THIS ROTTEN WORLD.
WAAH
WHAT ARE THE HARUSAME DOING HERE?!
Don't ask me.
HAS TAKASUGI MADE A DEAL WITH THE AMANTO IN ORDER TO OVERTHROW THE BAKUFU GOVERNMENT?!
WE WERE TOLD WE COULD TAKE THE HEADS OF KATSURA AND THAT SAMURAI...
BANSAI...
SHAKA
SHAKA
BANSAI ?
SHAKA
HEY.
SHAKA SHAKA
hum hum
ARE YOU LISTENING, BANSAI?!

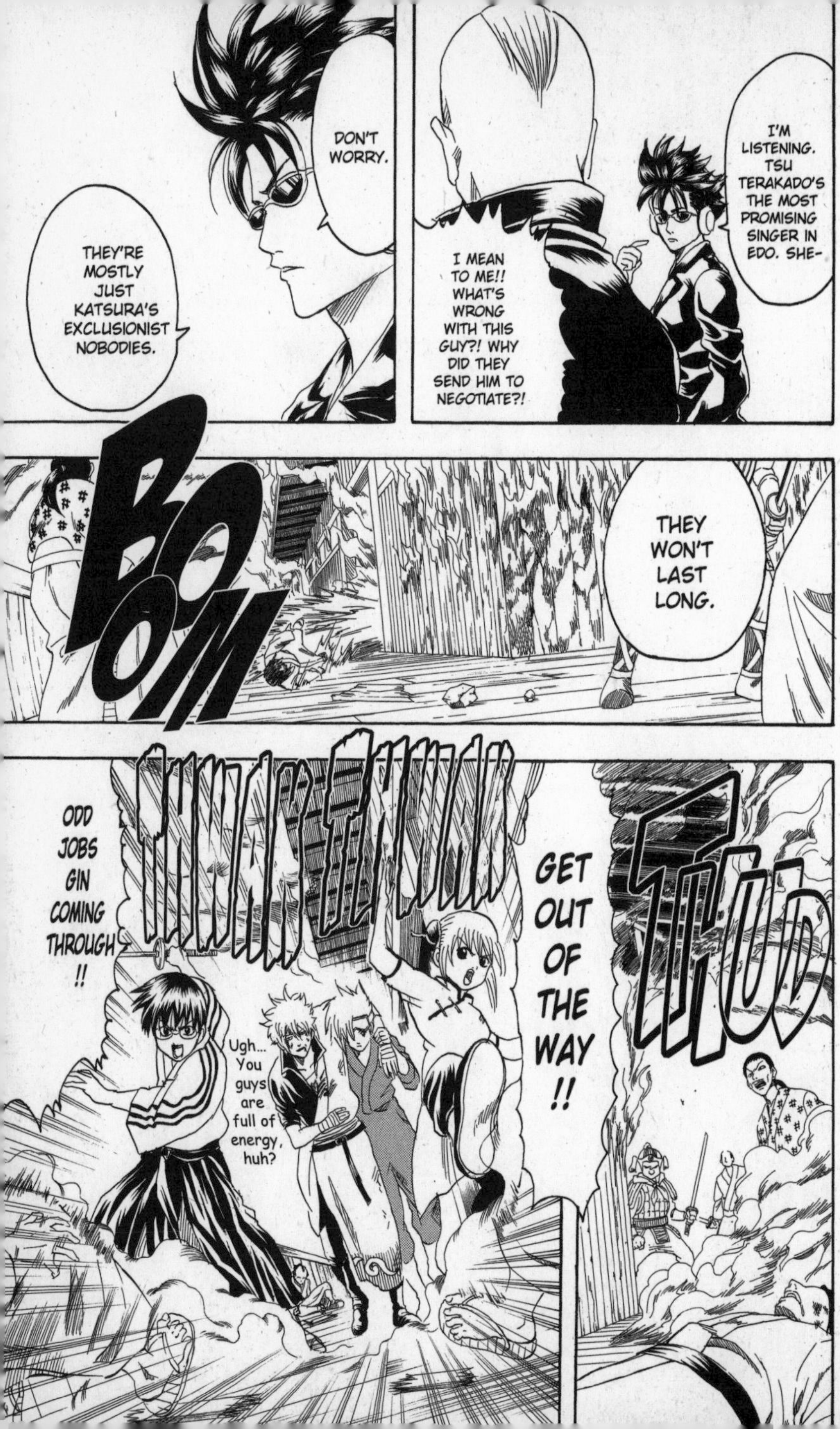
I'M LISTENING. TSU TERAKADO'S THE MOST PROMISING SINGER IN EDO. SHE-
I MEAN TO ME!! WHAT'S WRONG WITH THIS GUY?! WHY DID THEY SEND HIM TO NEGOTIATE?!
DON'T WORRY.
THEY'RE MOSTLY JUST KATSURA'S EXCLUSIONIST NOBODIES.
THEY WON'T LAST LONG.
BOOM
THUD
GET OUT OF THE WAY!!
ODD JOBS GIN COMING THROUGH!!
Ugh... You guys are full of energy, huh?

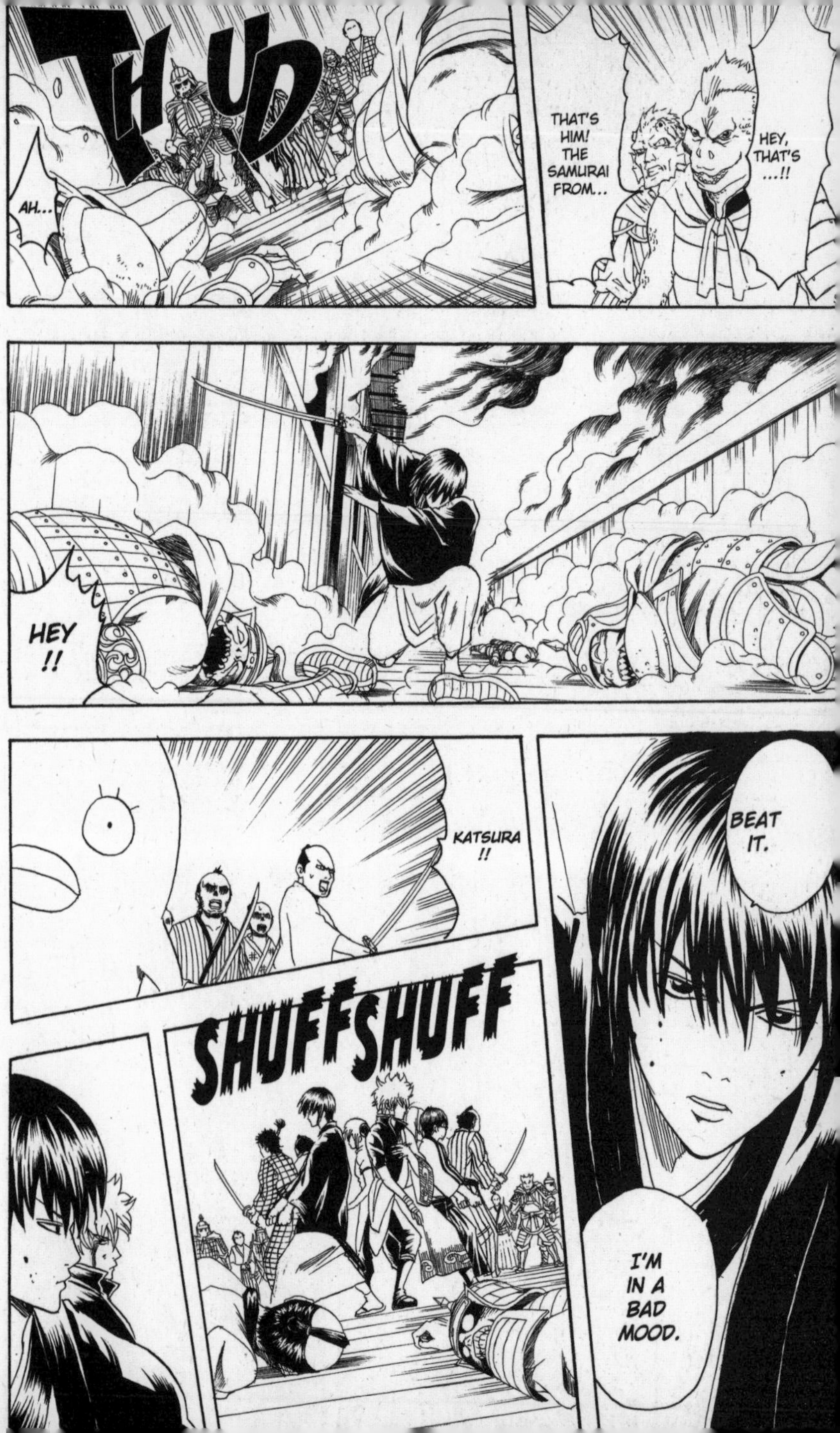
HEY, THAT'S ...!!
THAT'S HIM! THE SAMURAI FROM...
THUD
AH...
HEY !!
BEAT IT.
I'M IN A BAD MOOD.
KATSURA !!
SHUFFSHUFF

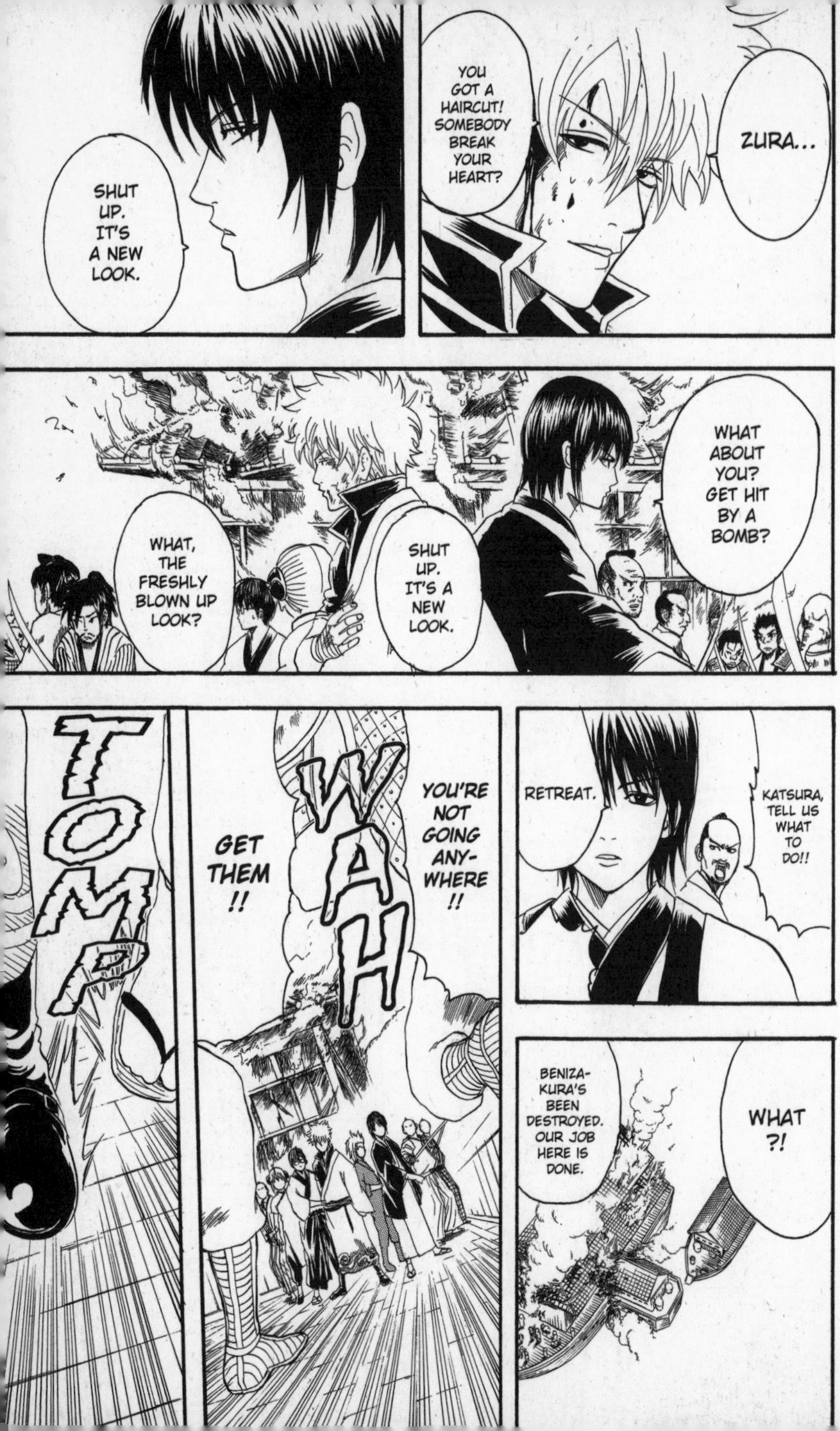
ZURA...
YOU GOT A HAIRCUT! SOMEBODY BREAK YOUR HEART?
SHUT UP. IT'S A NEW LOOK.
WHAT ABOUT YOU? GET HIT BY A BOMB?
SHUT UP. IT'S A NEW LOOK.
WHAT, THE FRESHLY BLOWN UP LOOK?
KATSURA, TELL US WHAT TO DO!!
RETREAT.
WHAT?!
BENIZA-KURA'S BEEN DESTROYED. OUR JOB HERE IS DONE.
YOU'RE NOT GOING ANY-WHERE!!
WAH
GET THEM!!
TOMP

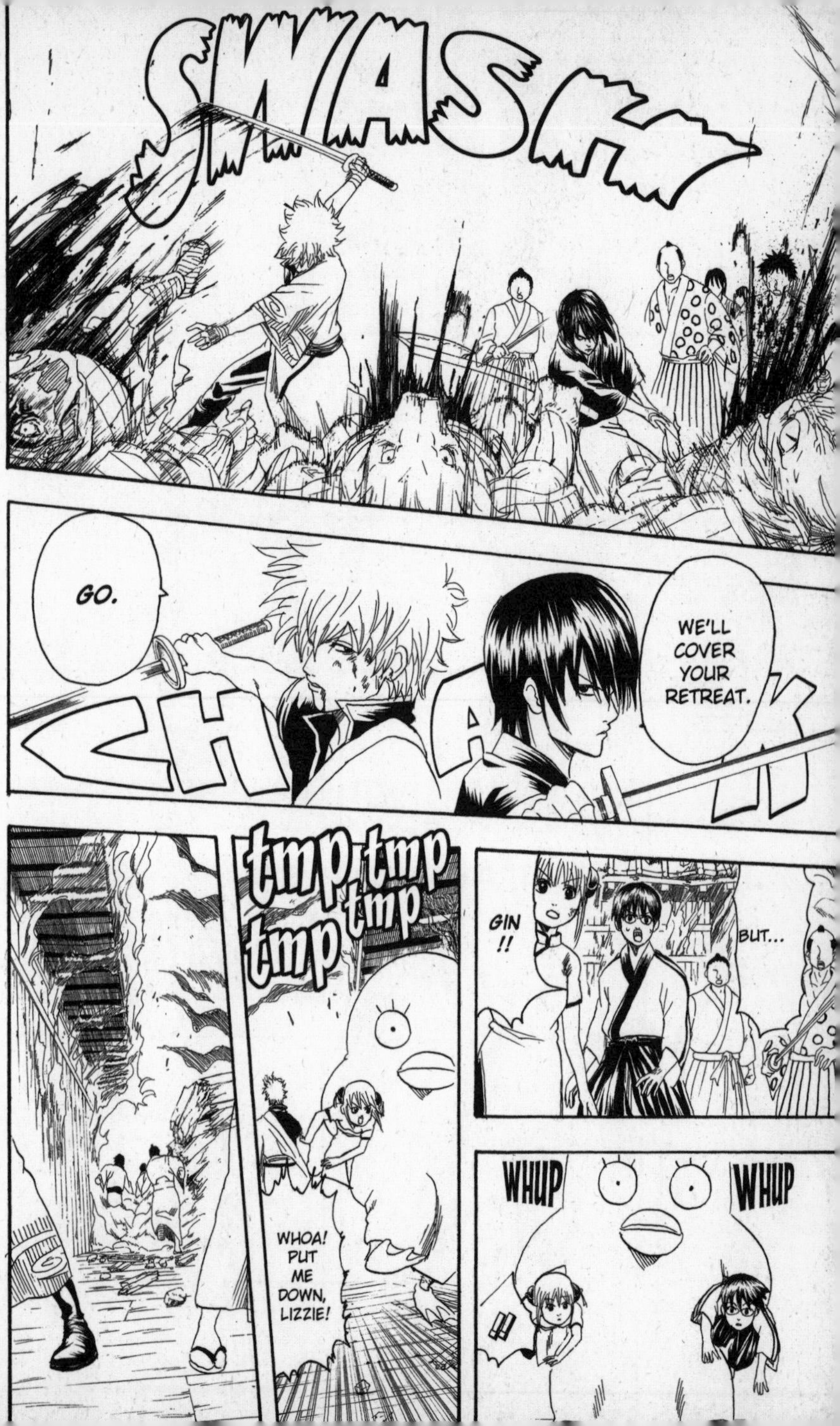
SWASH
WE'LL COVER YOUR RETREAT.
GO.
CHAK
BUT...
GIN !!
WHUP
WHUP
!!
tmp tmp tmp tmp
WHOA! PUT ME DOWN, LIZZIE!

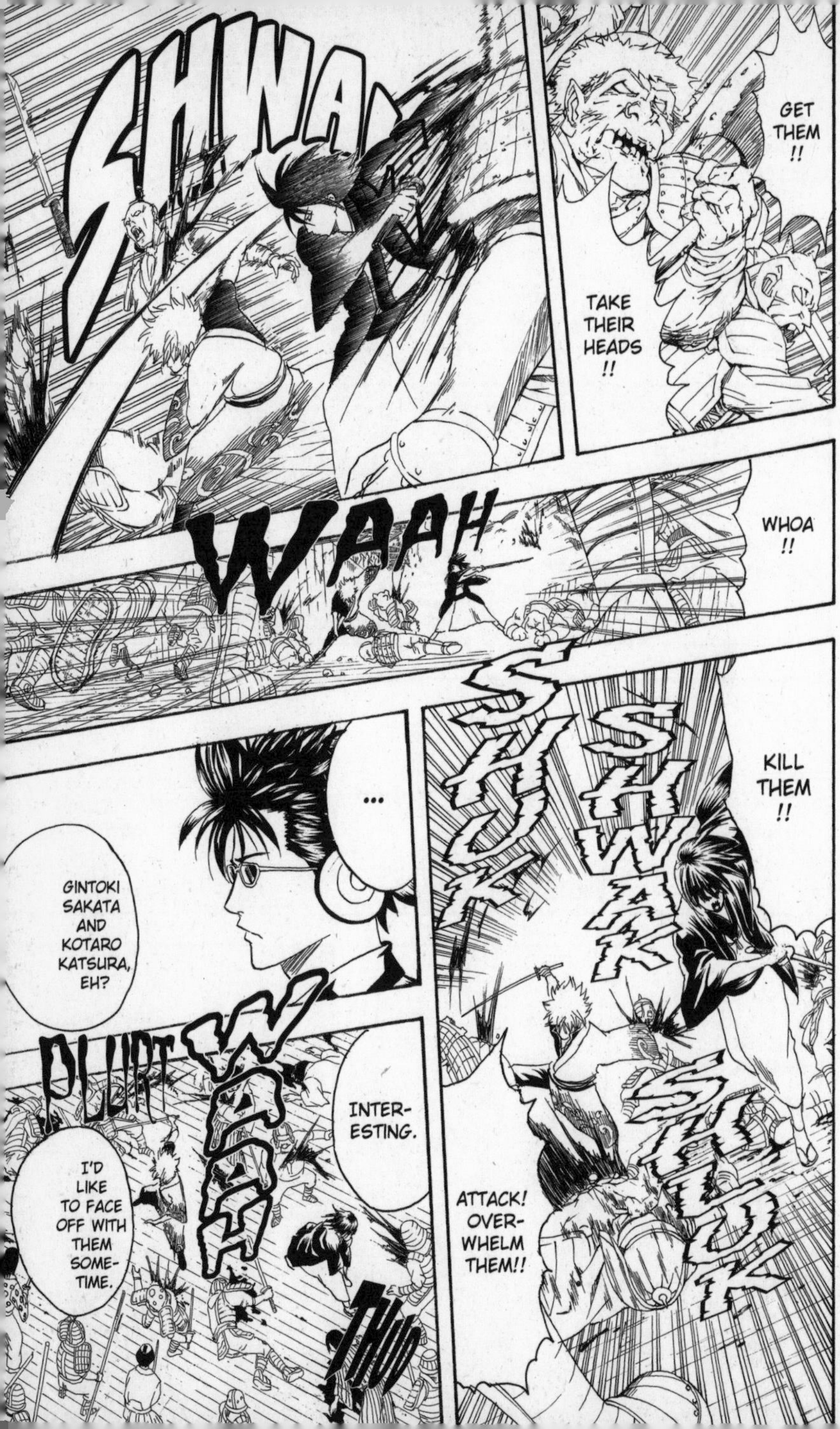
GET THEM !!
TAKE THEIR HEADS !!
SHWA
WHOA !!
WAAH
KILL THEM !!
SHUK
SHWAK
SHUK
ATTACK! OVER-WHELM THEM!!
...
GINTOKI SAKATA AND KOTARO KATSURA, EH?
INTER-ESTING.
I'D LIKE TO FACE OFF WITH THEM SOME-TIME.
PLURT
THUD

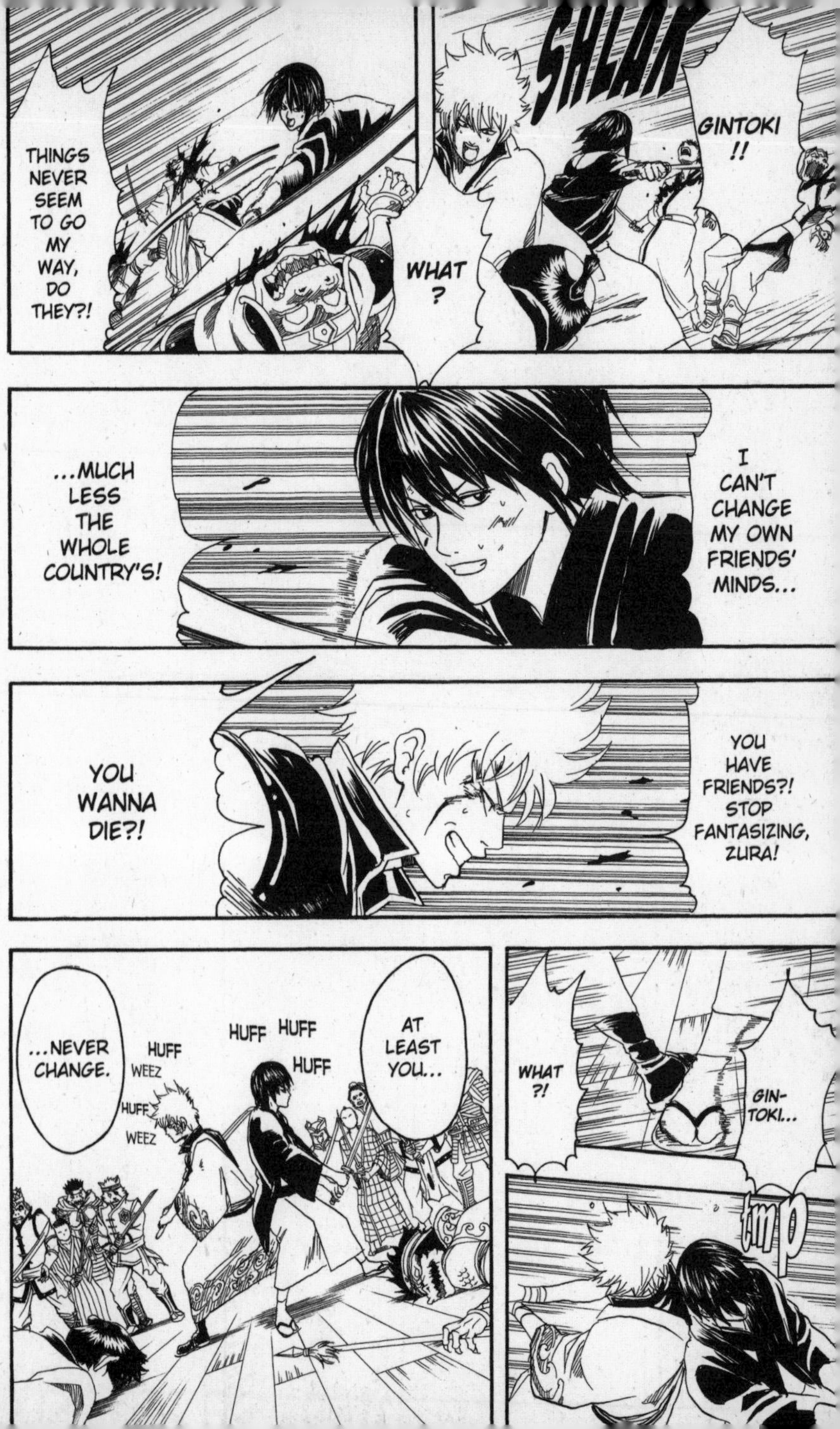
SHLAK
GINTOKI !!
WHAT ?
THINGS NEVER SEEM TO GO MY WAY, DO THEY?!
I CAN'T CHANGE MY OWN FRIENDS' MINDS...
...MUCH LESS THE WHOLE COUNTRY'S!
YOU HAVE FRIENDS?! STOP FANTASIZING, ZURA!
YOU WANNA DIE?!
GIN-TOKI...
WHAT ?!
tmp
AT LEAST YOU...
HUFF HUFF
HUFF
HUFF
WEEZ
HUFF
WEEZ
...NEVER CHANGE.

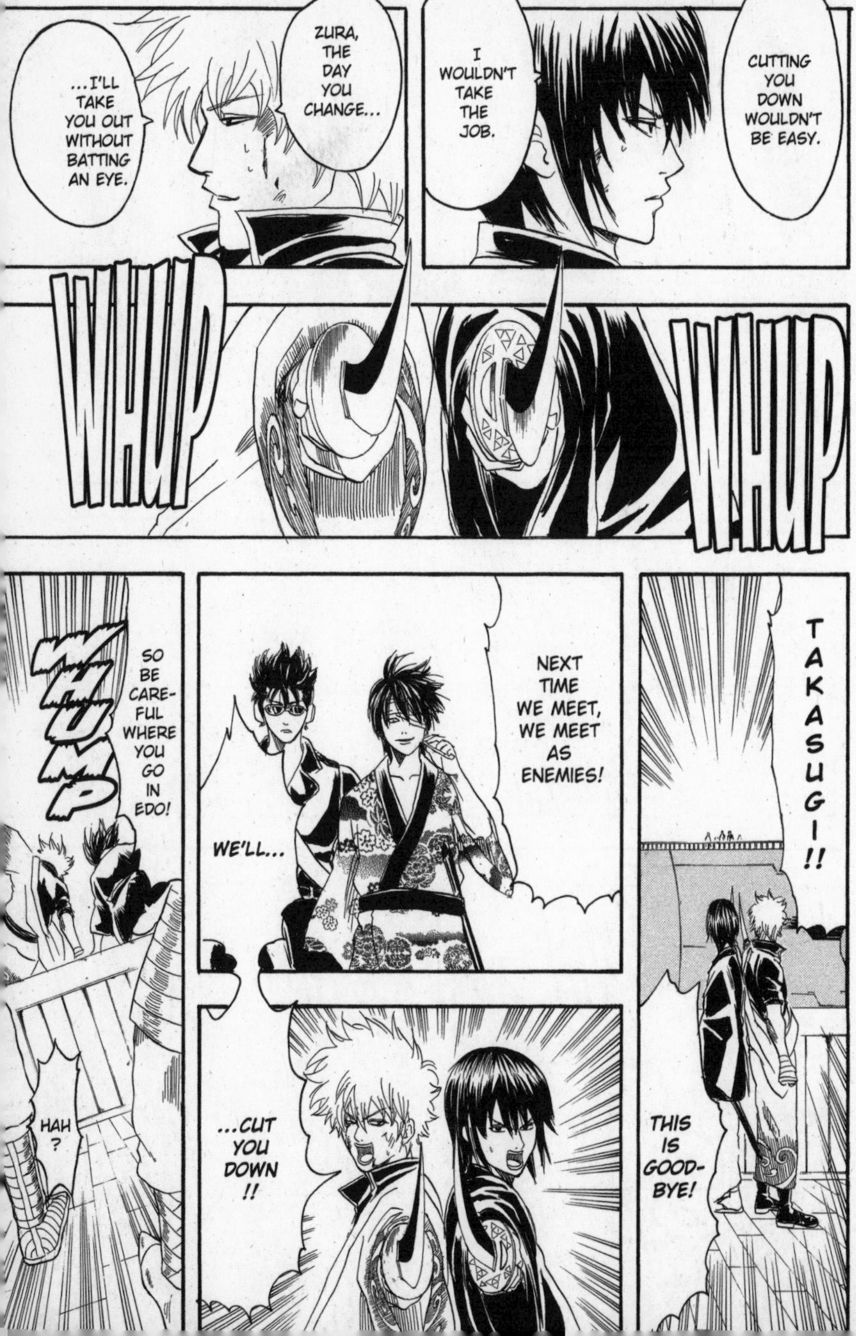
CUTTING YOU DOWN WOULDN'T BE EASY.
I WOULDN'T TAKE THE JOB.
ZURA, THE DAY YOU CHANGE...
...I'LL TAKE YOU OUT WITHOUT BATTING AN EYE.
WHUP
WHUP
TAKASUGI!!
THIS IS GOOD-BYE!
NEXT TIME WE MEET, WE MEET AS ENEMIES!
WE'LL...
...CUT YOU DOWN!!
WHUMP
SO BE CARE-FUL WHERE YOU GO IN EDO!
HAH?

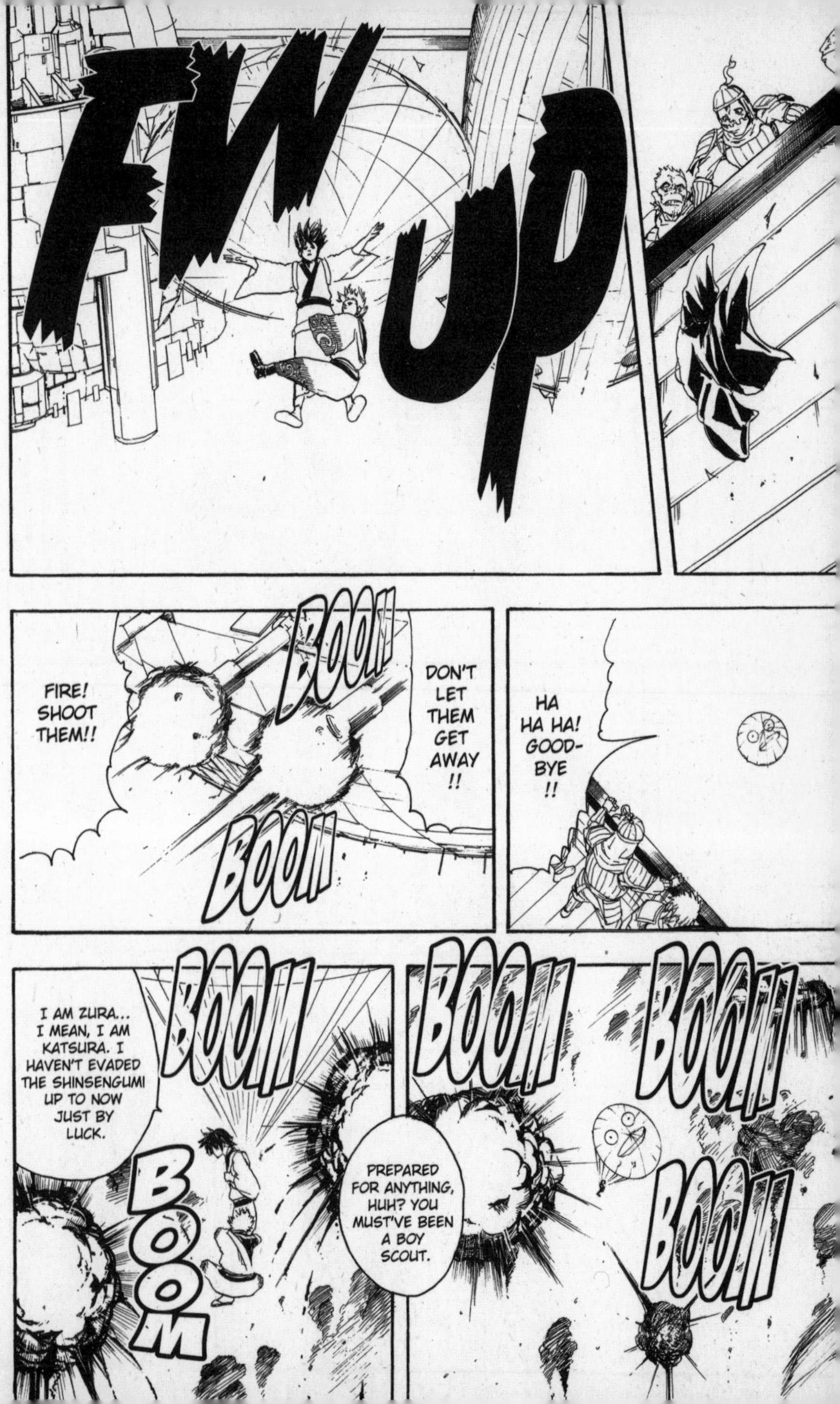
FWUP
HA HA HA! GOODBYE!!
DON'T LET THEM GET AWAY!!
BOOM
FIRE! SHOOT THEM!!
BOOM
BOOM
BOOM
BOOM
PREPARED FOR ANYTHING, HUH? YOU MUST'VE BEEN A BOY SCOUT.
BOOM
I AM ZURA... I MEAN, I AM KATSURA. I HAVEN'T EVADED THE SHINSENGUMI UP TO NOW JUST BY LUCK.
BOOM

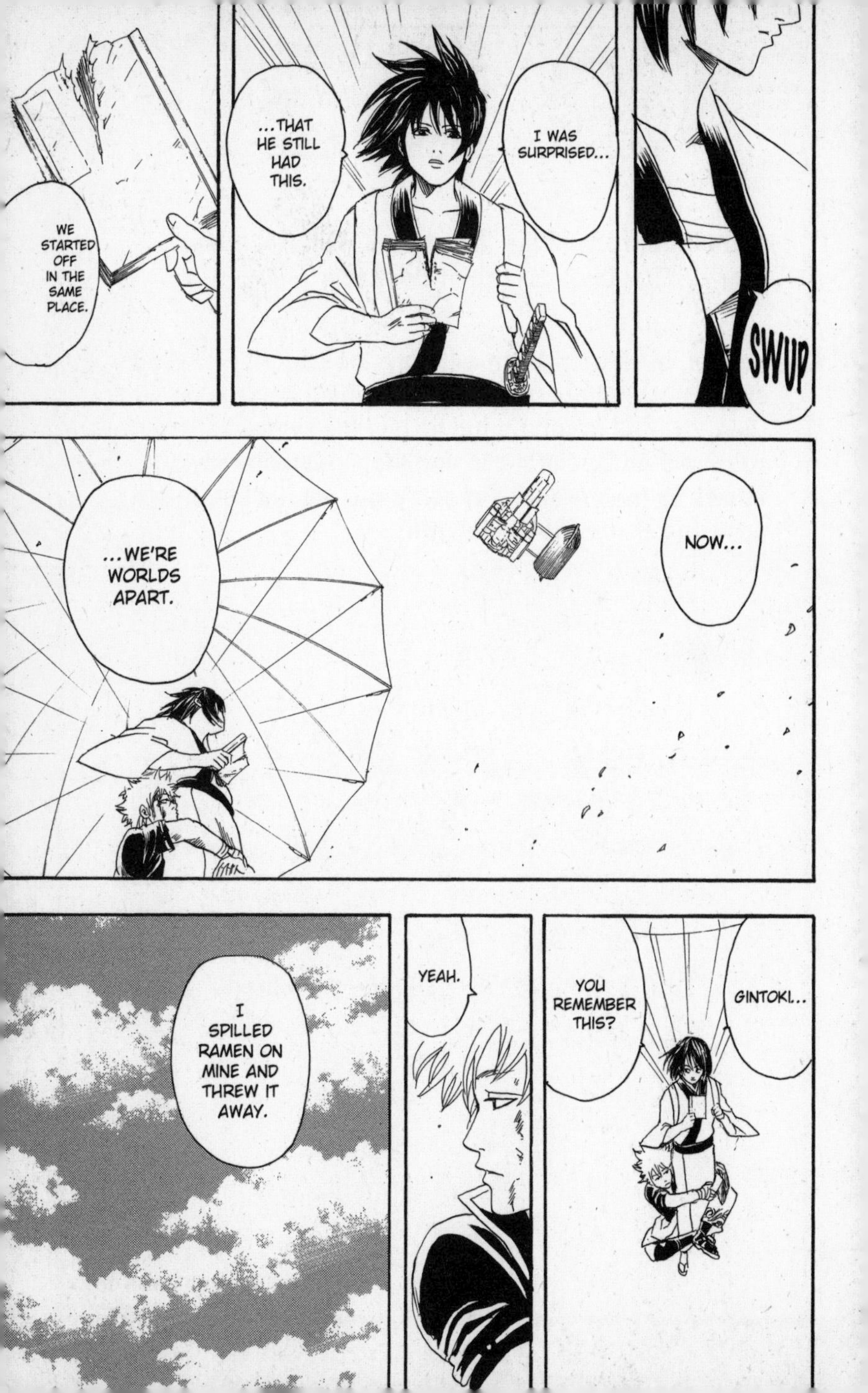
SWUP
I WAS SURPRISED...
...THAT HE STILL HAD THIS.
WE STARTED OFF IN THE SAME PLACE.
NOW...
...WE'RE WORLDS APART.
GINTOKI...
YOU REMEMBER THIS?
YEAH.
I SPILLED RAMEN ON MINE AND THREW IT AWAY.

Sorachi's Q&A
Hanging with the Readers #33

\<Question from I Like Jastaways Just Because
They're Jastaways-san of Osakao\>

Sensei, in volume 1 Gin-san says he bought his wooden sword on a school trip, but in volume 5 he says he buys them by mail order. So did he buy the sword he had in volume 1 on a school trip and then subsequently buy others by mail order? I'm sorry, but details like these drive me crazy! Please tell me.

\<Answer\>

No, it doesn't mean that. He buys all his swords by mail order. Statements like, "I bought it on a school trip" and "I got it from a hermit at Lake Toya," are Gin's own embellishments. I guess Lake Toya is a special place for him.

(Q&A #33 is on page 86)

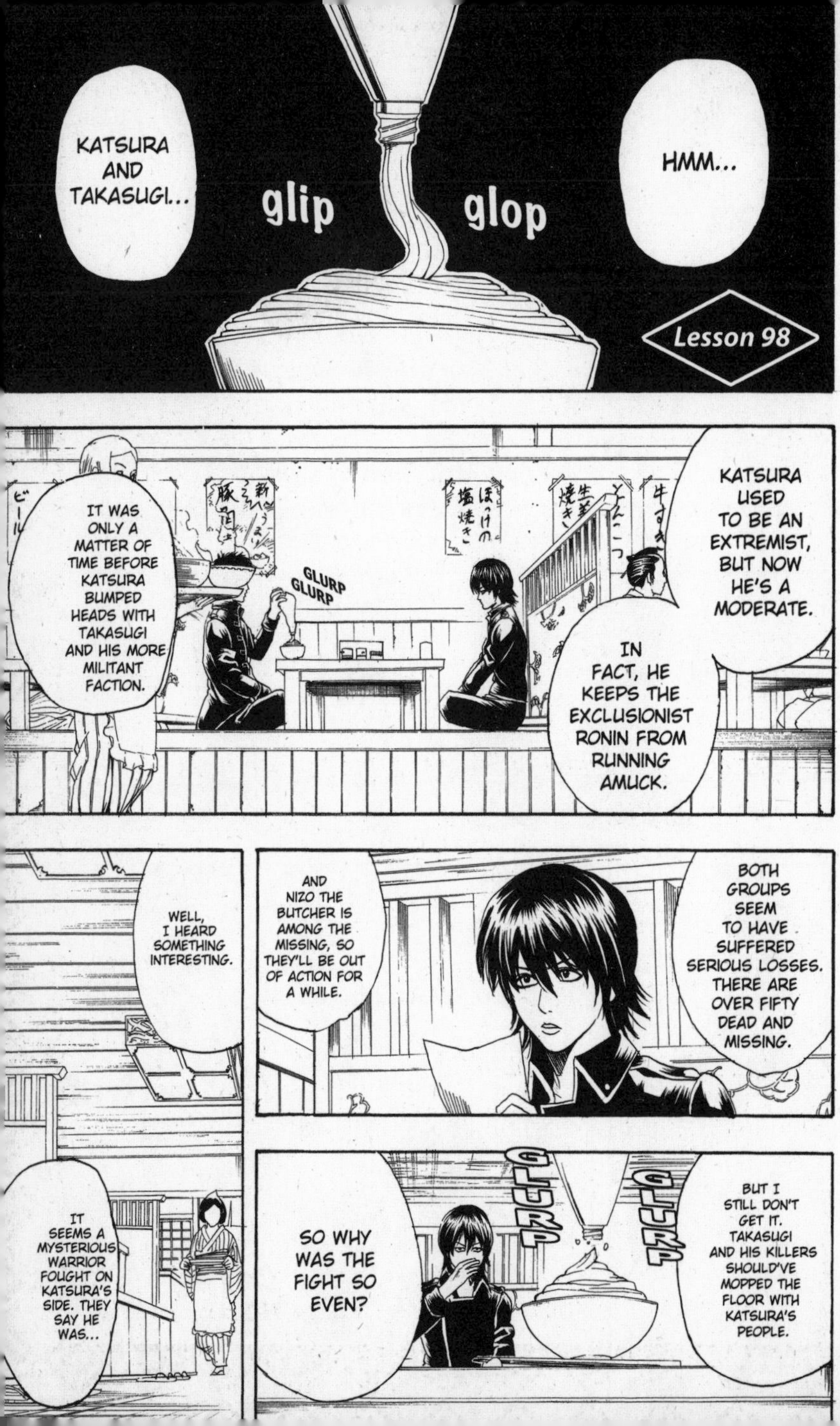
HMM...
glop
glip
KATSURA AND TAKASUGI...
Lesson 98
KATSURA USED TO BE AN EXTREMIST, BUT NOW HE'S A MODERATE.
IN FACT, HE KEEPS THE EXCLUSIONIST RONIN FROM RUNNING AMUCK.
ほっけの塩焼き
GLURP GLURP
IT WAS ONLY A MATTER OF TIME BEFORE KATSURA BUMPED HEADS WITH TAKASUGI AND HIS MORE MILITANT FACTION.
BOTH GROUPS SEEM TO HAVE SUFFERED SERIOUS LOSSES. THERE ARE OVER FIFTY DEAD AND MISSING.
AND NIZO THE BUTCHER IS AMONG THE MISSING, SO THEY'LL BE OUT OF ACTION FOR A WHILE.
WELL, I HEARD SOMETHING INTERESTING.
BUT I STILL DON'T GET IT. TAKASUGI AND HIS KILLERS SHOULD'VE MOPPED THE FLOOR WITH KATSURA'S PEOPLE.
GLURP
GLURP
SO WHY WAS THE FIGHT SO EVEN?
IT SEEMS A MYSTERIOUS WARRIOR FOUGHT ON KATSURA'S SIDE. THEY SAY HE WAS...

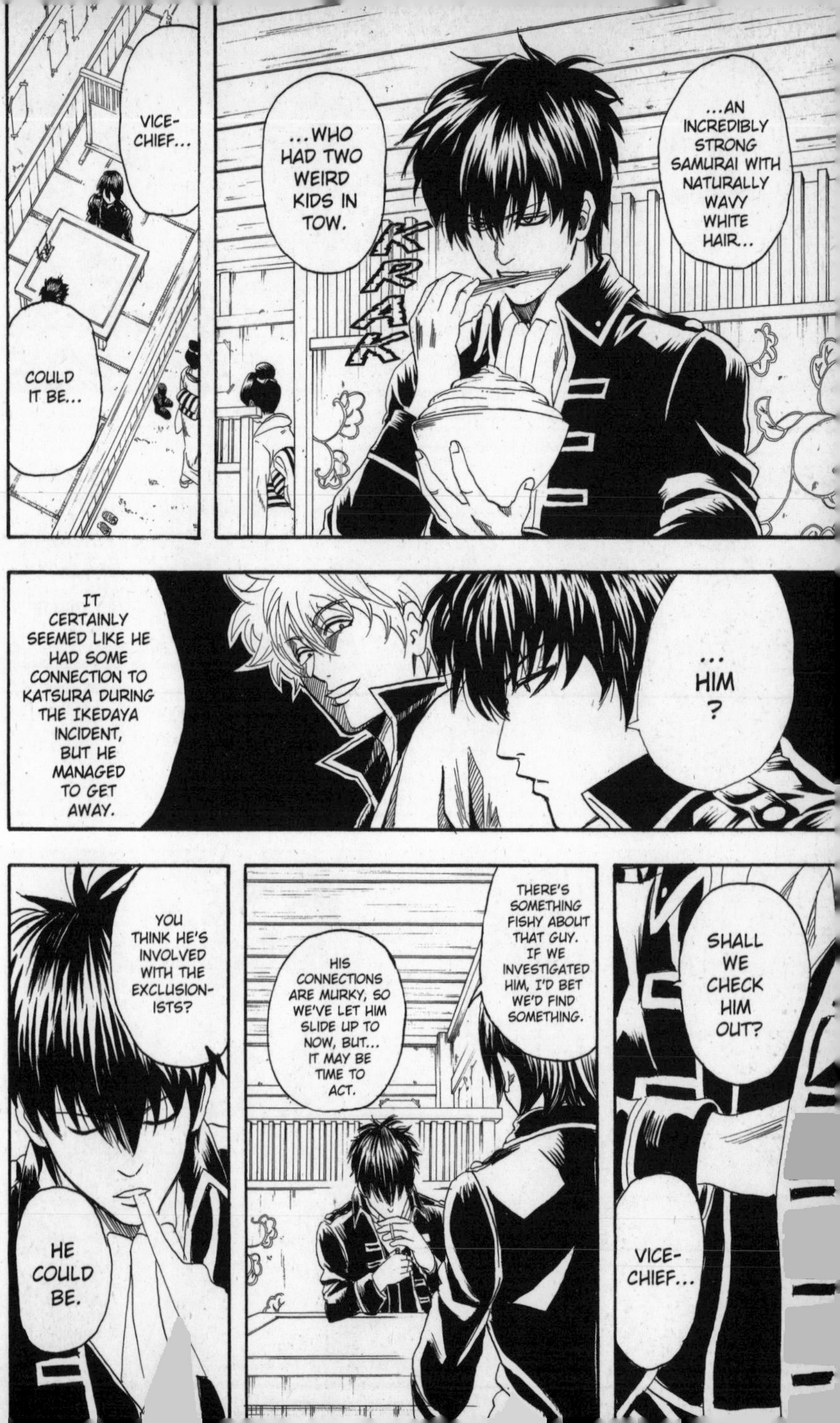
...AN INCREDIBLY STRONG SAMURAI WITH NATURALLY WAVY WHITE HAIR...
...WHO HAD TWO WEIRD KIDS IN TOW.
KRAK
VICE-CHIEF...
COULD IT BE...
...HIM?
IT CERTAINLY SEEMED LIKE HE HAD SOME CONNECTION TO KATSURA DURING THE IKEDAYA INCIDENT, BUT HE MANAGED TO GET AWAY.
SHALL WE CHECK HIM OUT?
VICE-CHIEF...
THERE'S SOMETHING FISHY ABOUT THAT GUY. IF WE INVESTIGATED HIM, I'D BET WE'D FIND SOMETHING.
HIS CONNECTIONS ARE MURKY, SO WE'VE LET HIM SLIDE UP TO NOW, BUT... IT MAY BE TIME TO ACT.
YOU THINK HE'S INVOLVED WITH THE EXCLUSION-ISTS?
HE COULD BE.

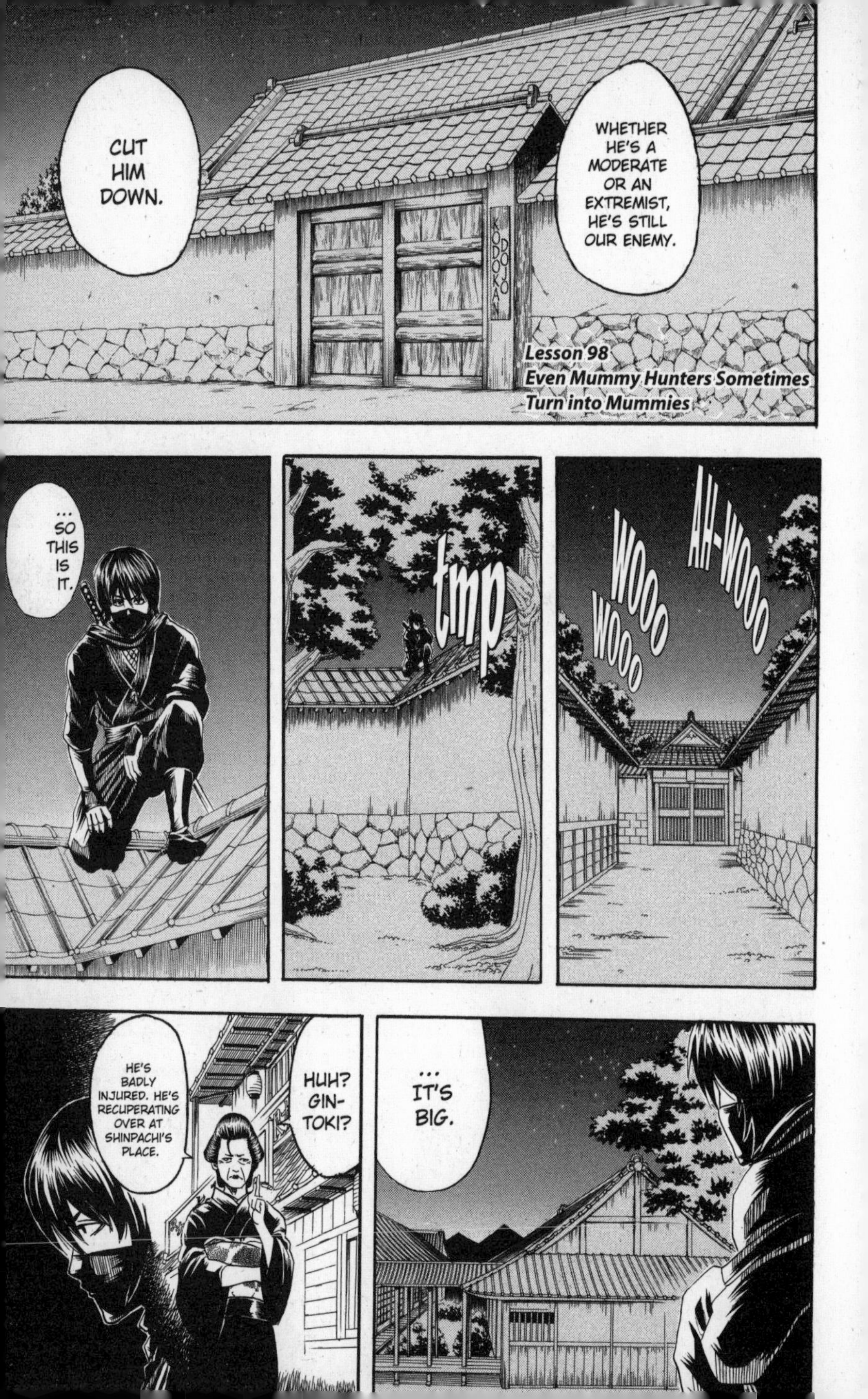
WHETHER HE'S A MODERATE OR AN EXTREMIST, HE'S STILL OUR ENEMY.
KODOKAN DOJO
CUT HIM DOWN.
Lesson 98
Even Mummy Hunters Sometimes Turn into Mummies
AH-WOOO
WOOO WOOO
WOOO
tmp
... SO THIS IS IT.
... IT'S BIG.
HUH? GIN-TOKI?
HE'S BADLY INJURED. HE'S RECUPERATING OVER AT SHINPACHI'S PLACE.

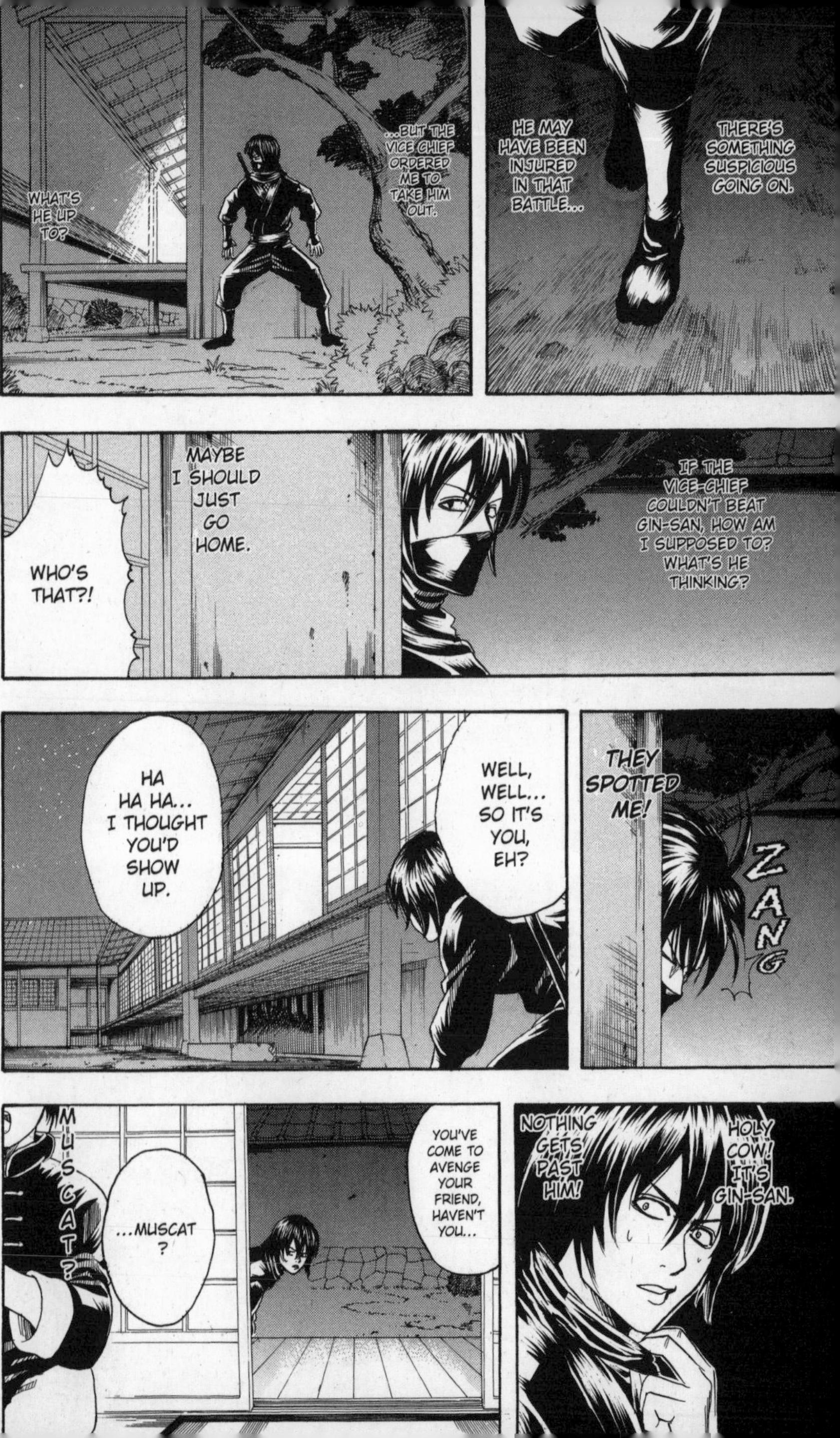
THERE'S SOMETHING SUSPICIOUS GOING ON.
HE MAY HAVE BEEN INJURED IN THAT BATTLE...
...BUT THE VICE CHIEF ORDERED ME TO TAKE HIM OUT.
WHAT'S HE UP TO?
IF THE VICE-CHIEF COULDN'T BEAT GIN-SAN, HOW AM I SUPPOSED TO? WHAT'S HE THINKING?
MAYBE I SHOULD JUST GO HOME.
WHO'S THAT?!
THEY SPOTTED ME!
ZANG
WELL, WELL... SO IT'S YOU, EH?
HA HA HA... I THOUGHT YOU'D SHOW UP.
HOLY COW! IT'S GIN-SAN.
NOTHING GETS PAST HIM!
YOU'VE COME TO AVENGE YOUR FRIEND, HAVEN'T YOU...
...MUSCAT?
MUSCAT?

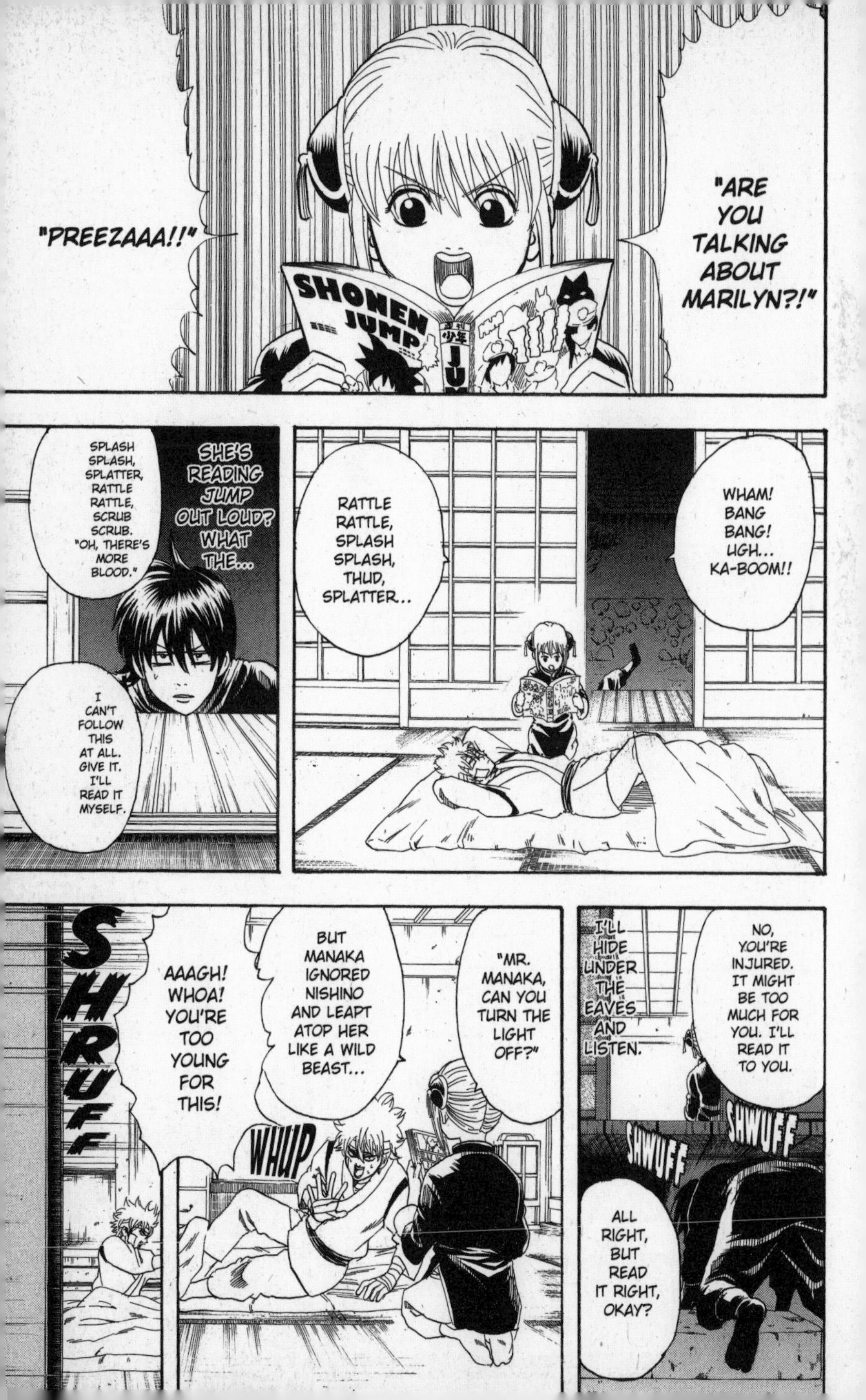
"ARE YOU TALKING ABOUT MARILYN?!"
"PREEZAAA!!"
SHONEN JUMP
WHAM! BANG BANG! UGH... KA-BOOM!!
RATTLE RATTLE, SPLASH SPLASH, THUD, SPLATTER...
SPLASH SPLASH, SPLATTER, RATTLE RATTLE, SCRUB SCRUB. "OH, THERE'S MORE BLOOD."
SHE'S READING JUMP OUT LOUD? WHAT THE...
I CAN'T FOLLOW THIS AT ALL. GIVE IT. I'LL READ IT MYSELF.
NO, YOU'RE INJURED. IT MIGHT BE TOO MUCH FOR YOU. I'LL READ IT TO YOU.
I'LL HIDE UNDER THE EAVES AND LISTEN.
SHWUFF
SHWUFF
ALL RIGHT, BUT READ IT RIGHT, OKAY?
"MR. MANAKA, CAN YOU TURN THE LIGHT OFF?"
BUT MANAKA IGNORED NISHINO AND LEAPT ATOP HER LIKE A WILD BEAST...
AAAGH! WHOA! YOU'RE TOO YOUNG FOR THIS!
WHUP
SHRUFF

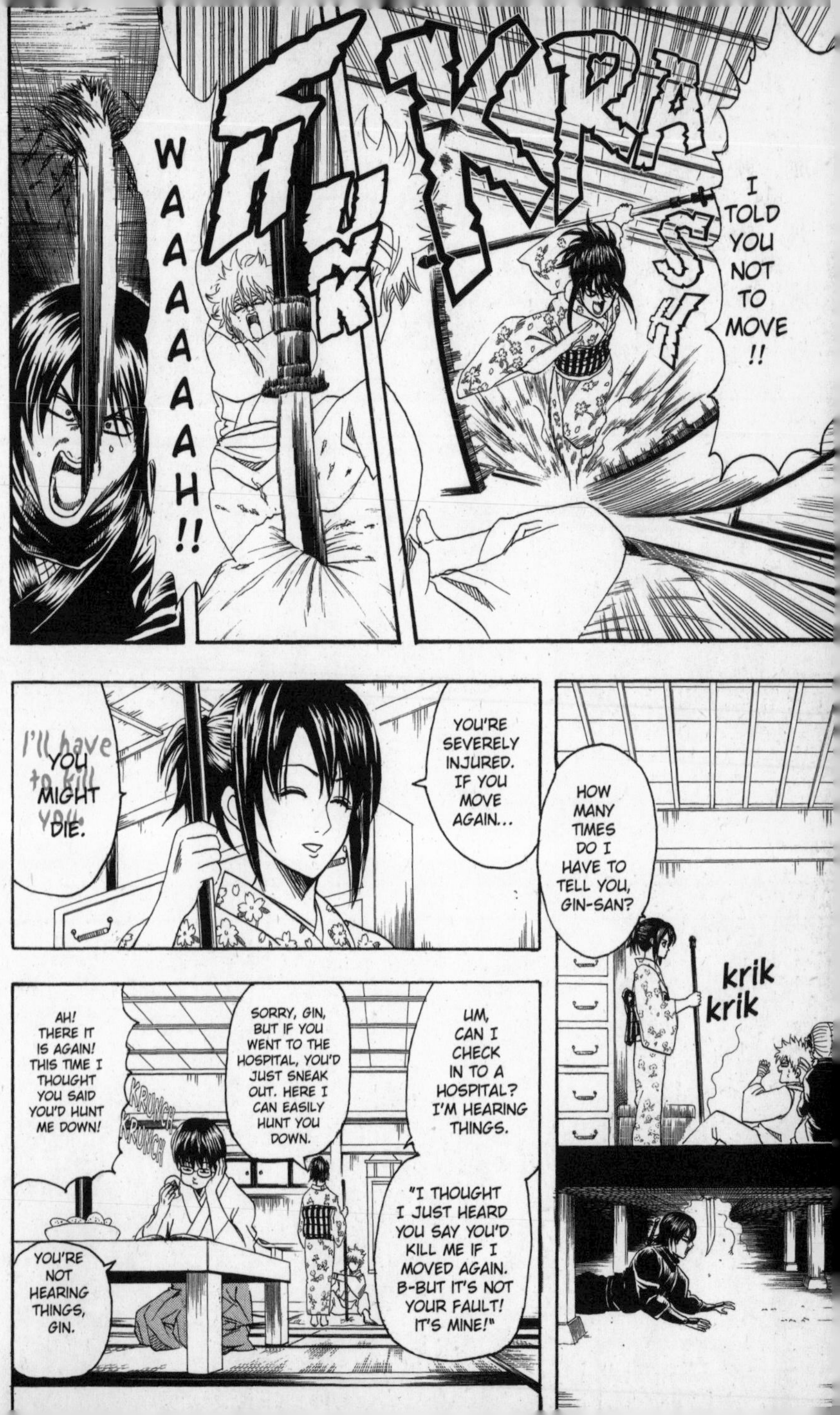
I TOLD YOU NOT TO MOVE !!
KRASH
THUNK
WAAAAAAAAH!!
HOW MANY TIMES DO I HAVE TO TELL YOU, GIN-SAN?
krik krik
YOU'RE SEVERELY INJURED. IF YOU MOVE AGAIN...
YOU MIGHT DIE.
I'll have to kill you.
UM, CAN I CHECK IN TO A HOSPITAL? I'M HEARING THINGS.
"I THOUGHT I JUST HEARD YOU SAY YOU'D KILL ME IF I MOVED AGAIN. B-BUT IT'S NOT YOUR FAULT! IT'S MINE!"
SORRY, GIN, BUT IF YOU WENT TO THE HOSPITAL, YOU'D JUST SNEAK OUT. HERE I CAN EASILY HUNT YOU DOWN.
KRUNCH KRUNCH
AH! THERE IT IS AGAIN! THIS TIME I THOUGHT YOU SAID YOU'D HUNT ME DOWN!
YOU'RE NOT HEARING THINGS, GIN.

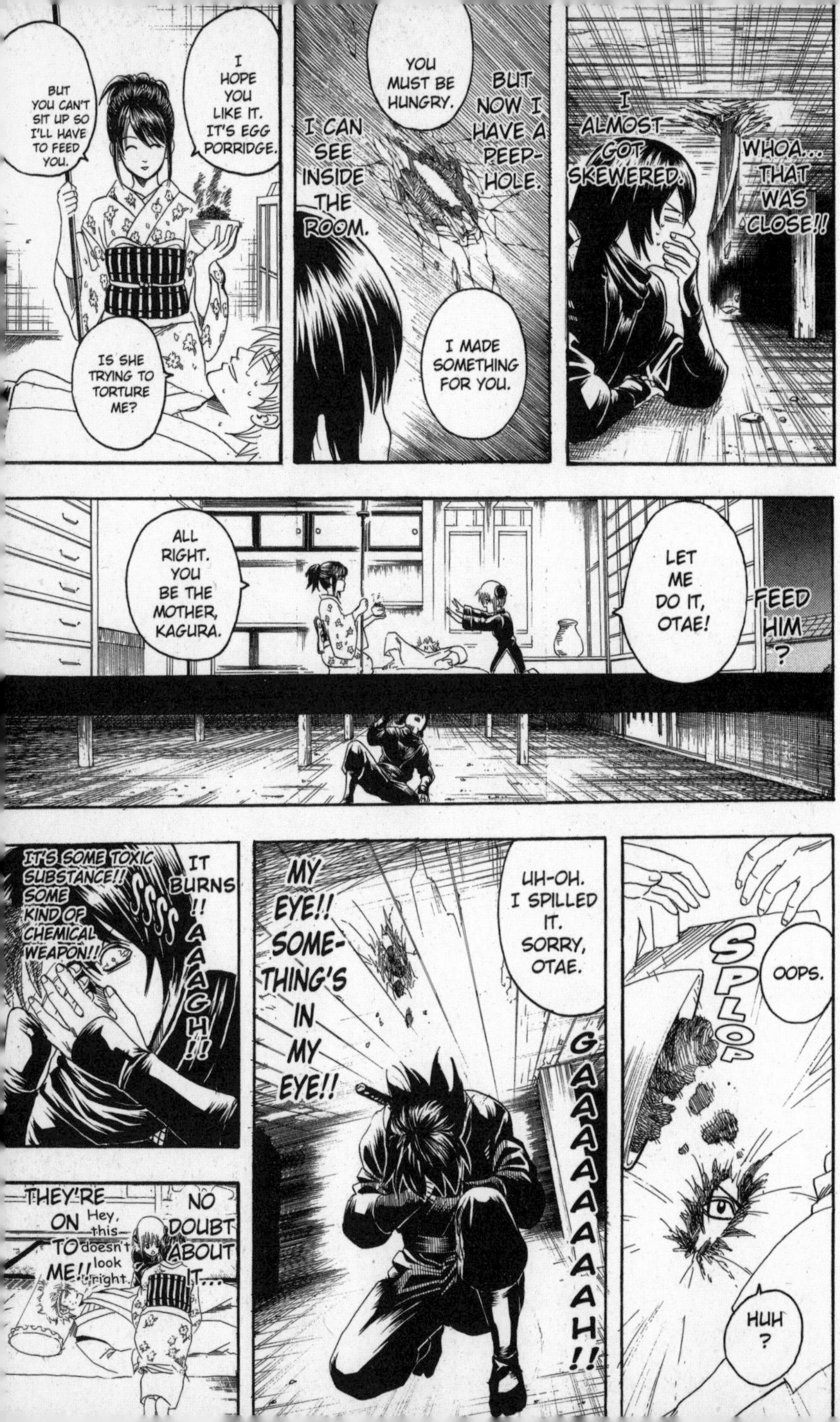
WHOA... THAT WAS CLOSE!!
I ALMOST GOT SKEWERED.
BUT NOW I HAVE A PEEP-HOLE.
YOU MUST BE HUNGRY.
I CAN SEE INSIDE THE ROOM.
I MADE SOMETHING FOR YOU.
I HOPE YOU LIKE IT. IT'S EGG PORRIDGE.
BUT YOU CAN'T SIT UP SO I'LL HAVE TO FEED YOU.
IS SHE TRYING TO TORTURE ME?
FEED HIM?
LET ME DO IT, OTAE!
ALL RIGHT. YOU BE THE MOTHER, KAGURA.
OOPS.
SPLOP
HUH?
UH-OH. I SPILLED IT. SORRY, OTAE.
GAAAAAAAAAAAAH!!
MY EYE!! SOMETHING'S IN MY EYE!!
IT BURNS!!
AAAAGH!!
SSSS
IT'S SOME TOXIC SUBSTANCE!! SOME KIND OF CHEMICAL WEAPON!!
NO DOUBT ABOUT IT...
THEY'RE ON TO ME!!
Hey, this doesn't look right.

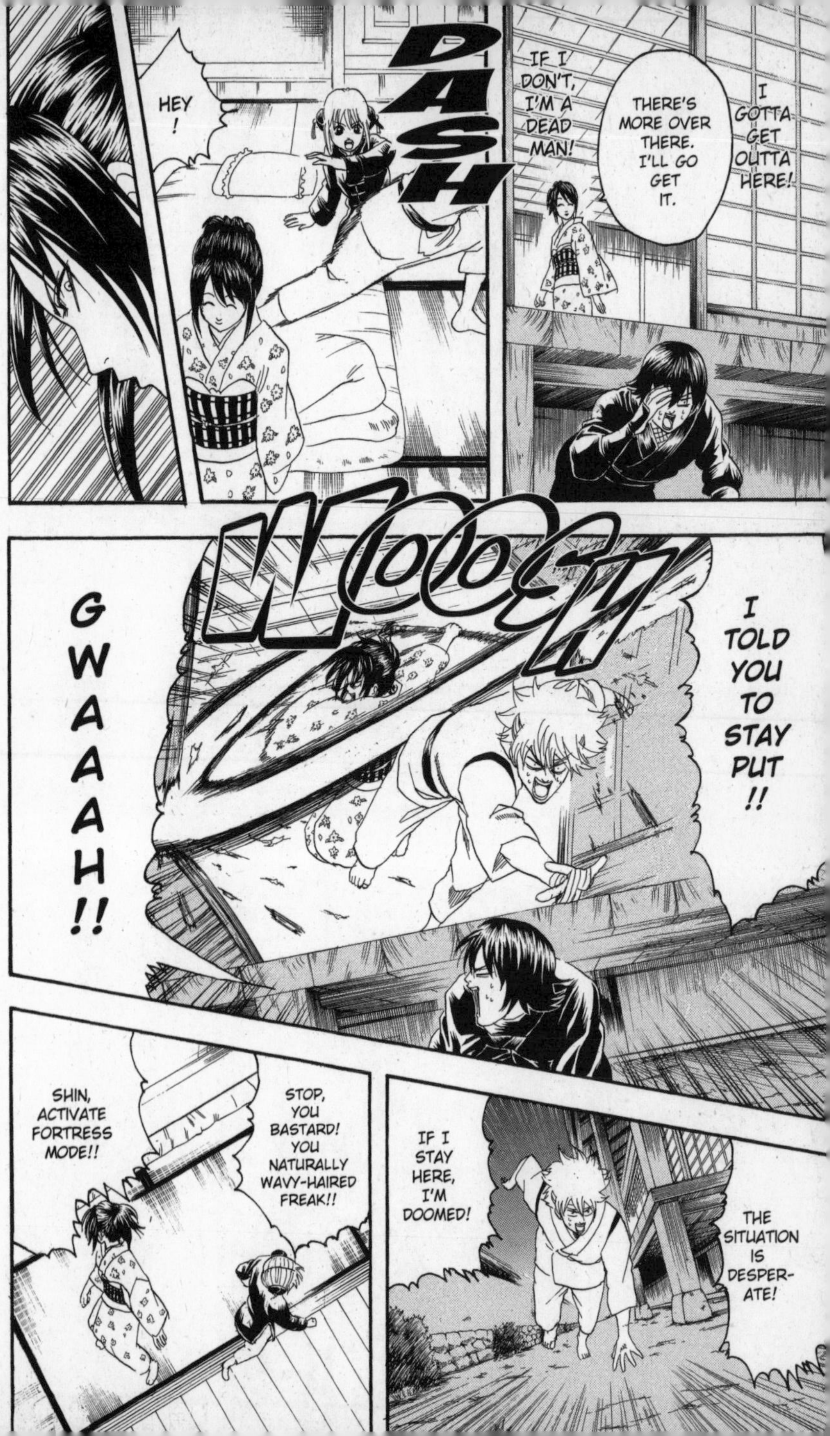
I GOTTA GET OUTTA HERE!
THERE'S MORE OVER THERE. I'LL GO GET IT.
IF I DON'T, I'M A DEAD MAN!
DASH
HEY!
WOOOSH
I TOLD YOU TO STAY PUT!!
GWAAAAH!!
THE SITUATION IS DESPER-ATE!
IF I STAY HERE, I'M DOOMED!
STOP, YOU BASTARD! YOU NATURALLY WAVY-HAIRED FREAK!!
SHIN, ACTIVATE FORTRESS MODE!!

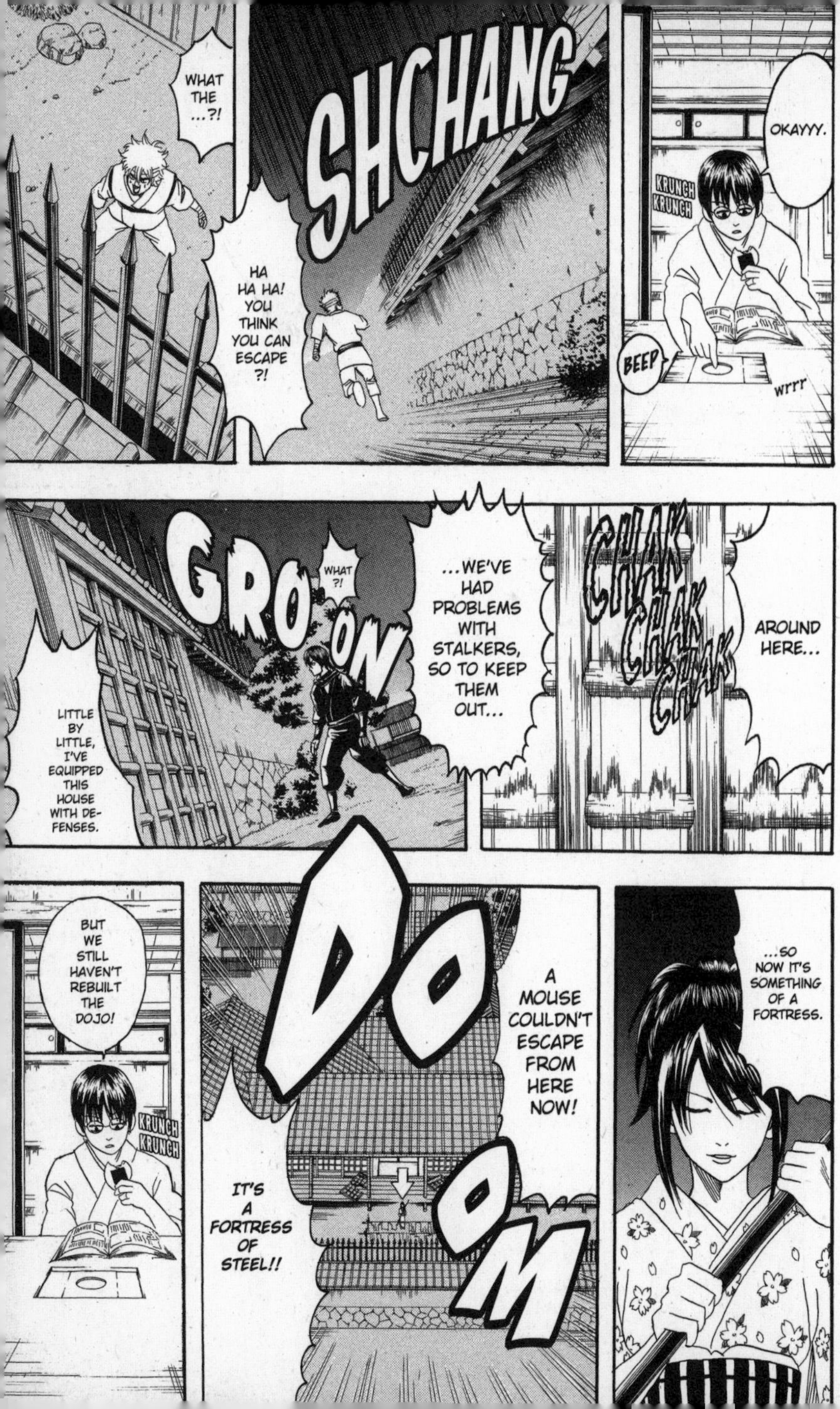
OKAYYY.
KRUNCH KRUNCH
BEEP
wrrr
SHCHANG
HA HA HA! YOU THINK YOU CAN ESCAPE?!
WHAT THE ...?!
AROUND HERE...
CHAK CHAK CHAK
...WE'VE HAD PROBLEMS WITH STALKERS, SO TO KEEP THEM OUT...
GRO ON
WHAT?!
LITTLE BY LITTLE, I'VE EQUIPPED THIS HOUSE WITH DE-FENSES.
...SO NOW IT'S SOMETHING OF A FORTRESS.
A MOUSE COULDN'T ESCAPE FROM HERE NOW!
DOOOM
IT'S A FORTRESS OF STEEL!!
BUT WE STILL HAVEN'T REBUILT THE DOJO!
KRUNCH KRUNCH

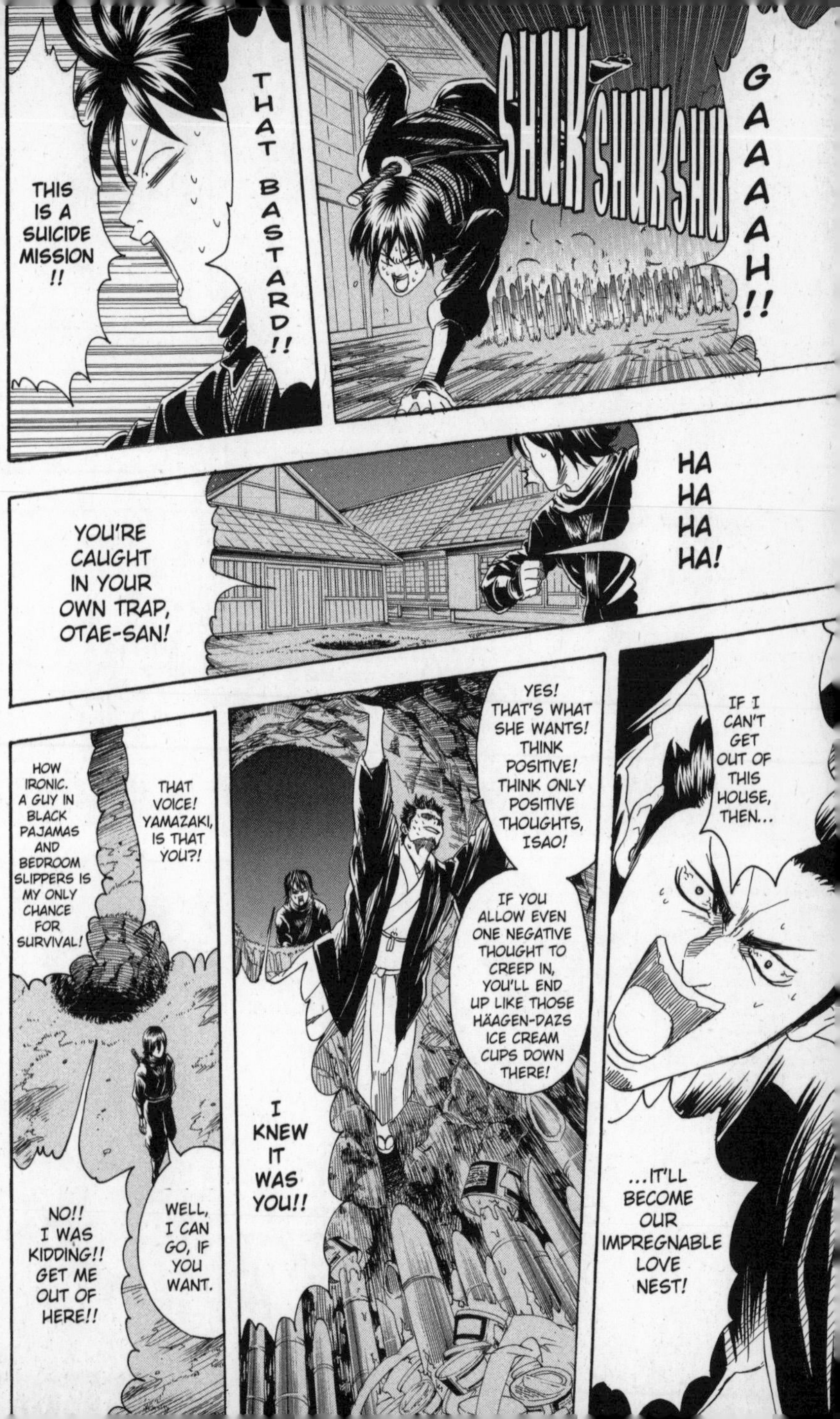
SHUK SHUKSHU
GAAAAAH!!
THAT BASTARD!!
THIS IS A SUICIDE MISSION!!
HA HA HA HA!
YOU'RE CAUGHT IN YOUR OWN TRAP, OTAE-SAN!
IF I CAN'T GET OUT OF THIS HOUSE, THEN...
...IT'LL BECOME OUR IMPREGNABLE LOVE NEST!
YES! THAT'S WHAT SHE WANTS! THINK POSITIVE! THINK ONLY POSITIVE THOUGHTS, ISAO!
IF YOU ALLOW EVEN ONE NEGATIVE THOUGHT TO CREEP IN, YOU'LL END UP LIKE THOSE HÄAGEN-DAZS ICE CREAM CUPS DOWN THERE!
I KNEW IT WAS YOU!!
THAT VOICE! YAMAZAKI, IS THAT YOU?!
HOW IRONIC. A GUY IN BLACK PAJAMAS AND BEDROOM SLIPPERS IS MY ONLY CHANCE FOR SURVIVAL!
WELL, I CAN GO, IF YOU WANT.
NO!! I WAS KIDDING!! GET ME OUT OF HERE!!

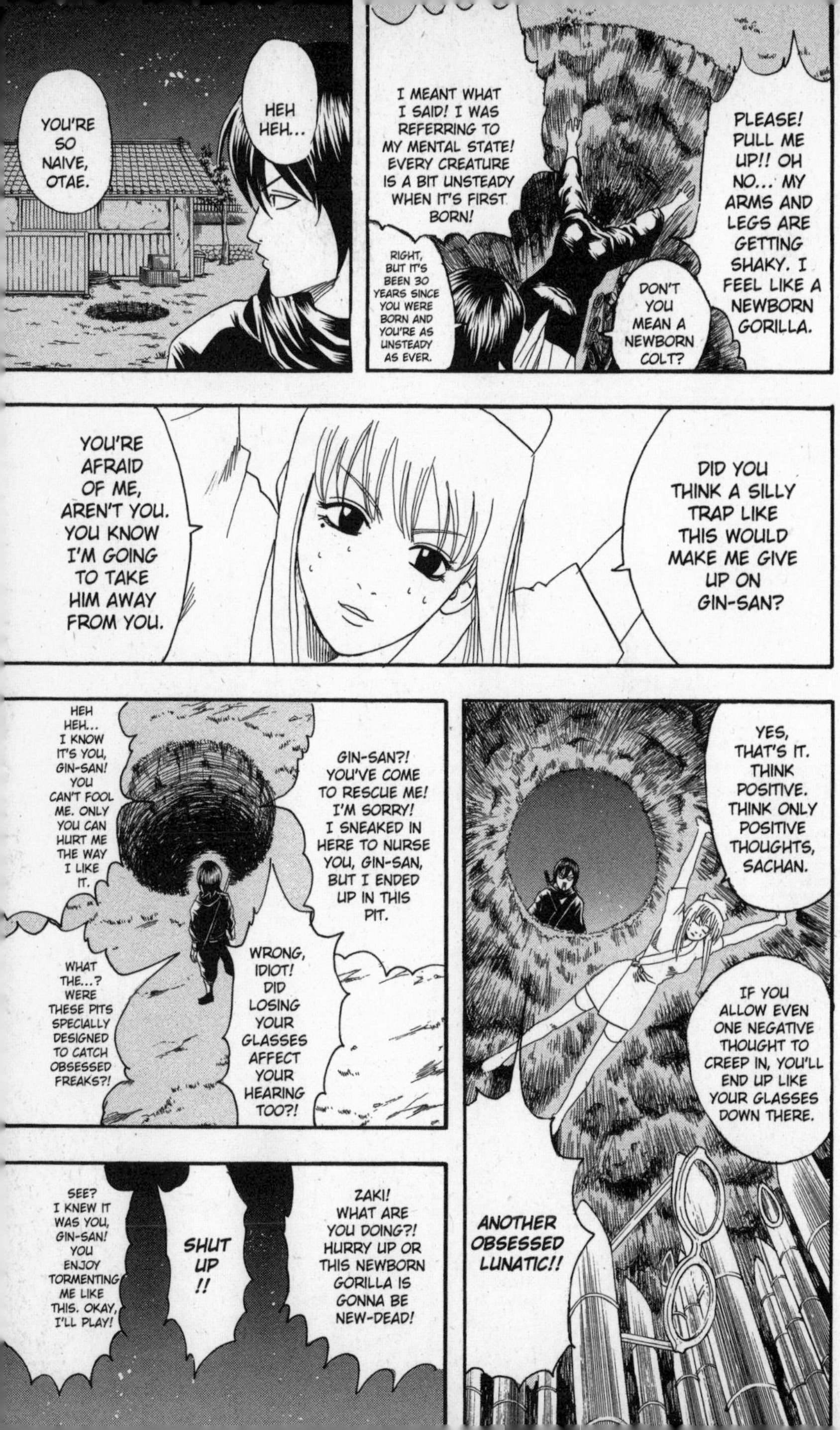
PLEASE! PULL ME UP!! OH NO... MY ARMS AND LEGS ARE GETTING SHAKY. I FEEL LIKE A NEWBORN GORILLA.
DON'T YOU MEAN A NEWBORN COLT?
I MEANT WHAT I SAID! I WAS REFERRING TO MY MENTAL STATE! EVERY CREATURE IS A BIT UNSTEADY WHEN IT'S FIRST BORN!
RIGHT, BUT IT'S BEEN 30 YEARS SINCE YOU WERE BORN AND YOU'RE AS UNSTEADY AS EVER.
HEH HEH...
YOU'RE SO NAIVE, OTAE.
DID YOU THINK A SILLY TRAP LIKE THIS WOULD MAKE ME GIVE UP ON GIN-SAN?
YOU'RE AFRAID OF ME, AREN'T YOU. YOU KNOW I'M GOING TO TAKE HIM AWAY FROM YOU.
YES, THAT'S IT. THINK POSITIVE. THINK ONLY POSITIVE THOUGHTS, SACHAN.
IF YOU ALLOW EVEN ONE NEGATIVE THOUGHT TO CREEP IN, YOU'LL END UP LIKE YOUR GLASSES DOWN THERE.
ANOTHER OBSESSED LUNATIC!!
GIN-SAN?! YOU'VE COME TO RESCUE ME! I'M SORRY! I SNEAKED IN HERE TO NURSE YOU, GIN-SAN, BUT I ENDED UP IN THIS PIT.
HEH HEH... I KNOW IT'S YOU, GIN-SAN! YOU CAN'T FOOL ME. ONLY YOU CAN HURT ME THE WAY I LIKE IT.
WRONG, IDIOT! DID LOSING YOUR GLASSES AFFECT YOUR HEARING TOO?!
WHAT THE...? WERE THESE PITS SPECIALLY DESIGNED TO CATCH OBSESSED FREAKS?!
ZAKI! WHAT ARE YOU DOING?! HURRY UP OR THIS NEWBORN GORILLA IS GONNA BE NEW-DEAD!
SHUT UP!!
SEE? I KNEW IT WAS YOU, GIN-SAN! YOU ENJOY TORMENTING ME LIKE THIS. OKAY, I'LL PLAY!

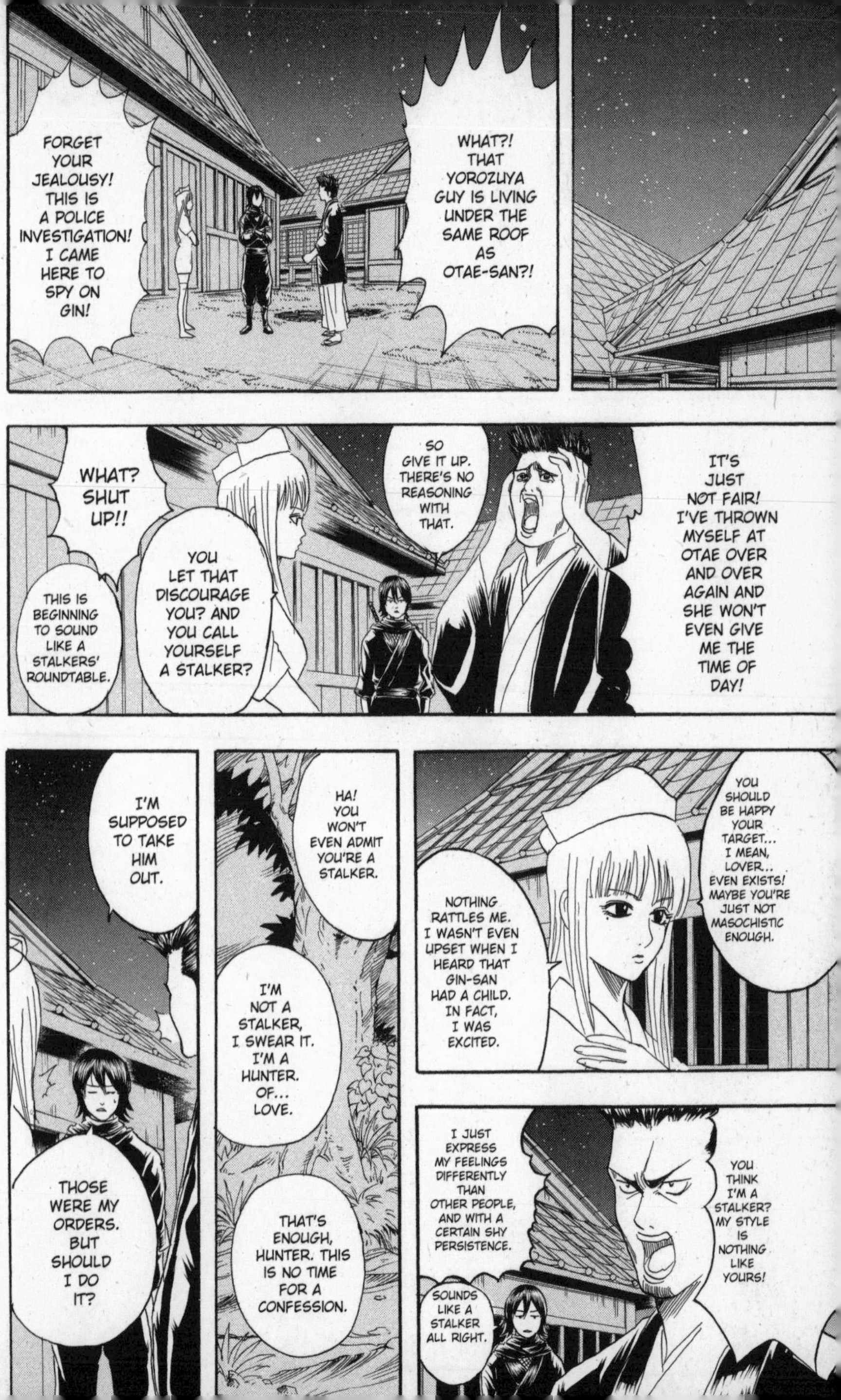
WHAT?! THAT YOROZUYA GUY IS LIVING UNDER THE SAME ROOF AS OTAE-SAN?!
FORGET YOUR JEALOUSY! THIS IS A POLICE INVESTIGATION! I CAME HERE TO SPY ON GIN!
IT'S JUST NOT FAIR! I'VE THROWN MYSELF AT OTAE OVER AND OVER AGAIN AND SHE WON'T EVEN GIVE ME THE TIME OF DAY!
SO GIVE IT UP. THERE'S NO REASONING WITH THAT.
WHAT? SHUT UP!!
YOU LET THAT DISCOURAGE YOU? AND YOU CALL YOURSELF A STALKER?
THIS IS BEGINNING TO SOUND LIKE A STALKERS' ROUNDTABLE.
YOU SHOULD BE HAPPY YOUR TARGET... I MEAN, LOVER... EVEN EXISTS! MAYBE YOU'RE JUST NOT MASOCHISTIC ENOUGH.
NOTHING RATTLES ME. I WASN'T EVEN UPSET WHEN I HEARD THAT GIN-SAN HAD A CHILD. IN FACT, I WAS EXCITED.
YOU THINK I'M A STALKER? MY STYLE IS NOTHING LIKE YOURS!
I JUST EXPRESS MY FEELINGS DIFFERENTLY THAN OTHER PEOPLE, AND WITH A CERTAIN SHY PERSISTENCE.
SOUNDS LIKE A STALKER ALL RIGHT.
HA! YOU WON'T EVEN ADMIT YOU'RE A STALKER.
I'M NOT A STALKER, I SWEAR IT. I'M A HUNTER. OF... LOVE.
THAT'S ENOUGH, HUNTER. THIS IS NO TIME FOR A CONFESSION.
I'M SUPPOSED TO TAKE HIM OUT.
THOSE WERE MY ORDERS. BUT SHOULD I DO IT?

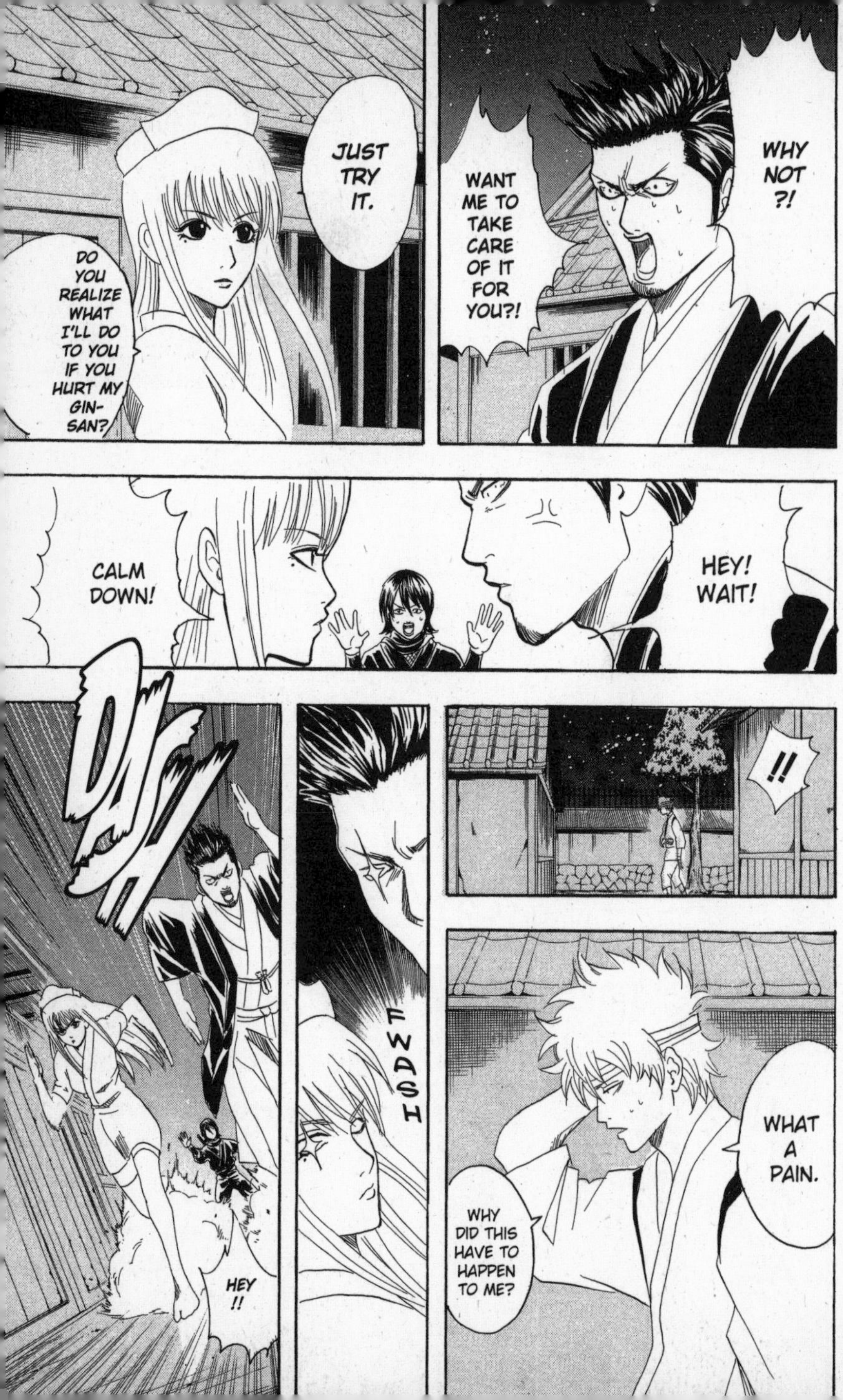
WHY NOT ?!
WANT ME TO TAKE CARE OF IT FOR YOU?!
JUST TRY IT.
DO YOU REALIZE WHAT I'LL DO TO YOU IF YOU HURT MY GIN-SAN?
HEY! WAIT!
CALM DOWN!
!!
WHAT A PAIN.
WHY DID THIS HAVE TO HAPPEN TO ME?
FWASH
HEY !!

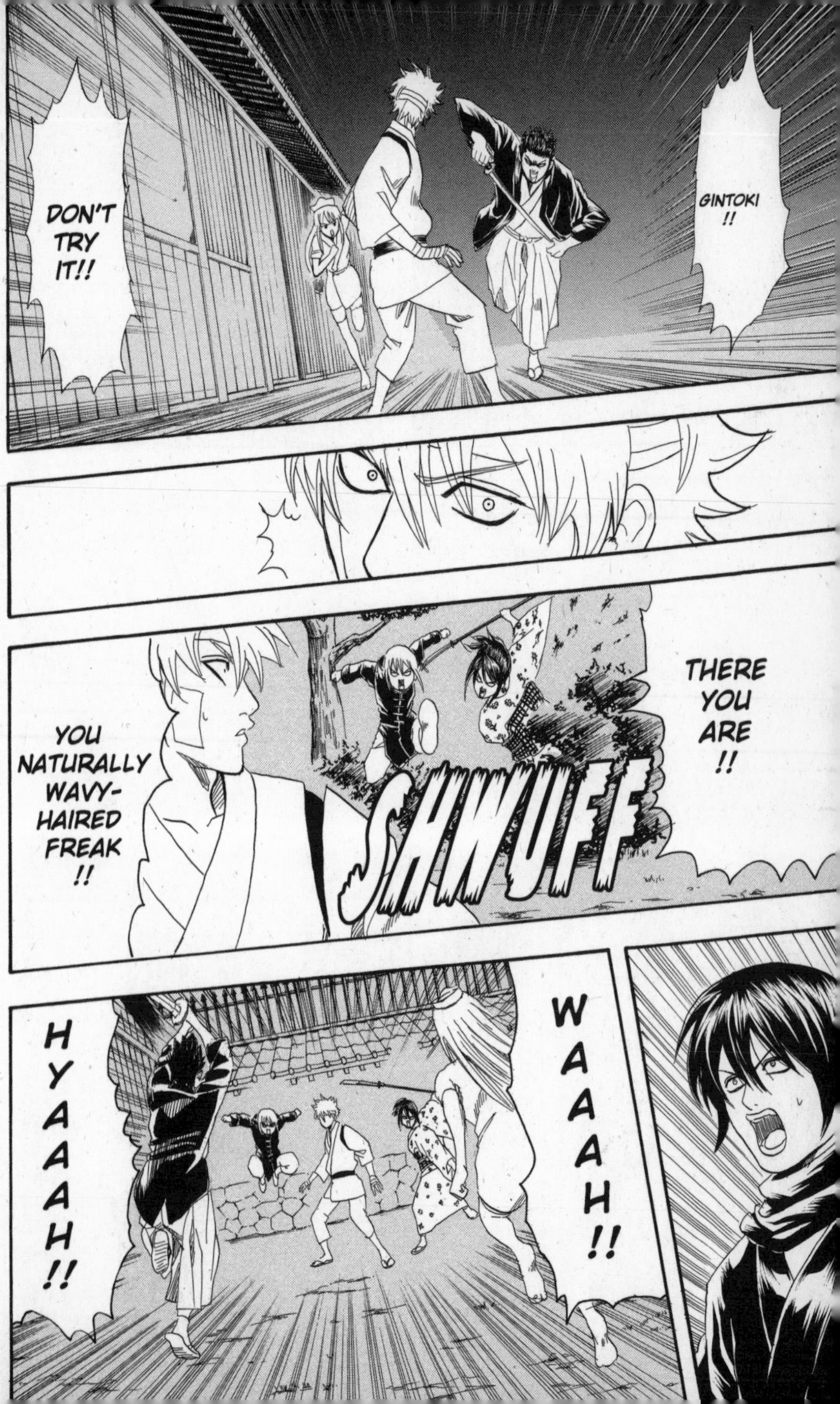
GINTOKI !!
DON'T TRY IT!!
THERE YOU ARE !!
SHWUFF
YOU NATURALLY WAVY-HAIRED FREAK !!
WAAAAH!!
HYAAAAH!!

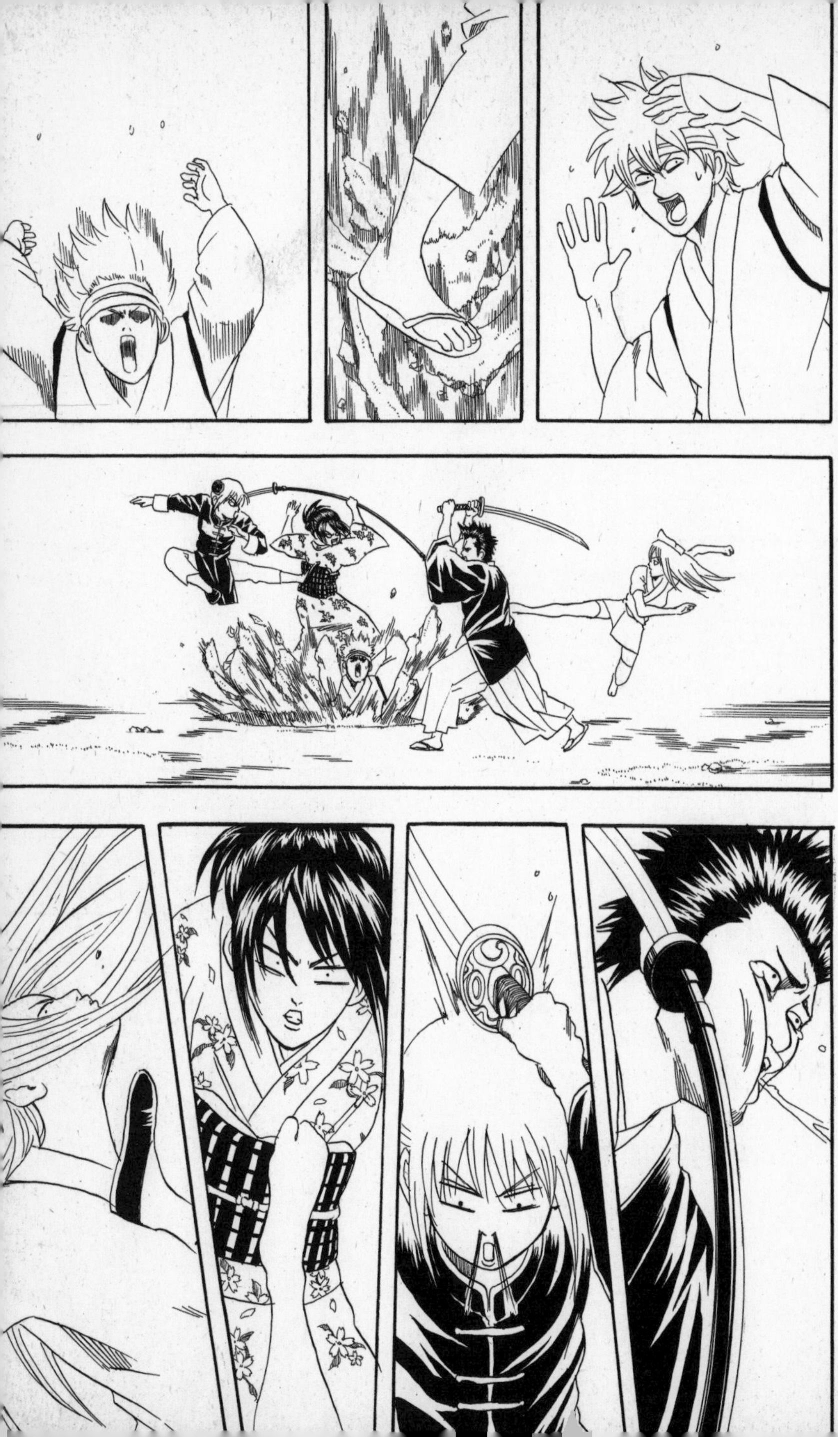

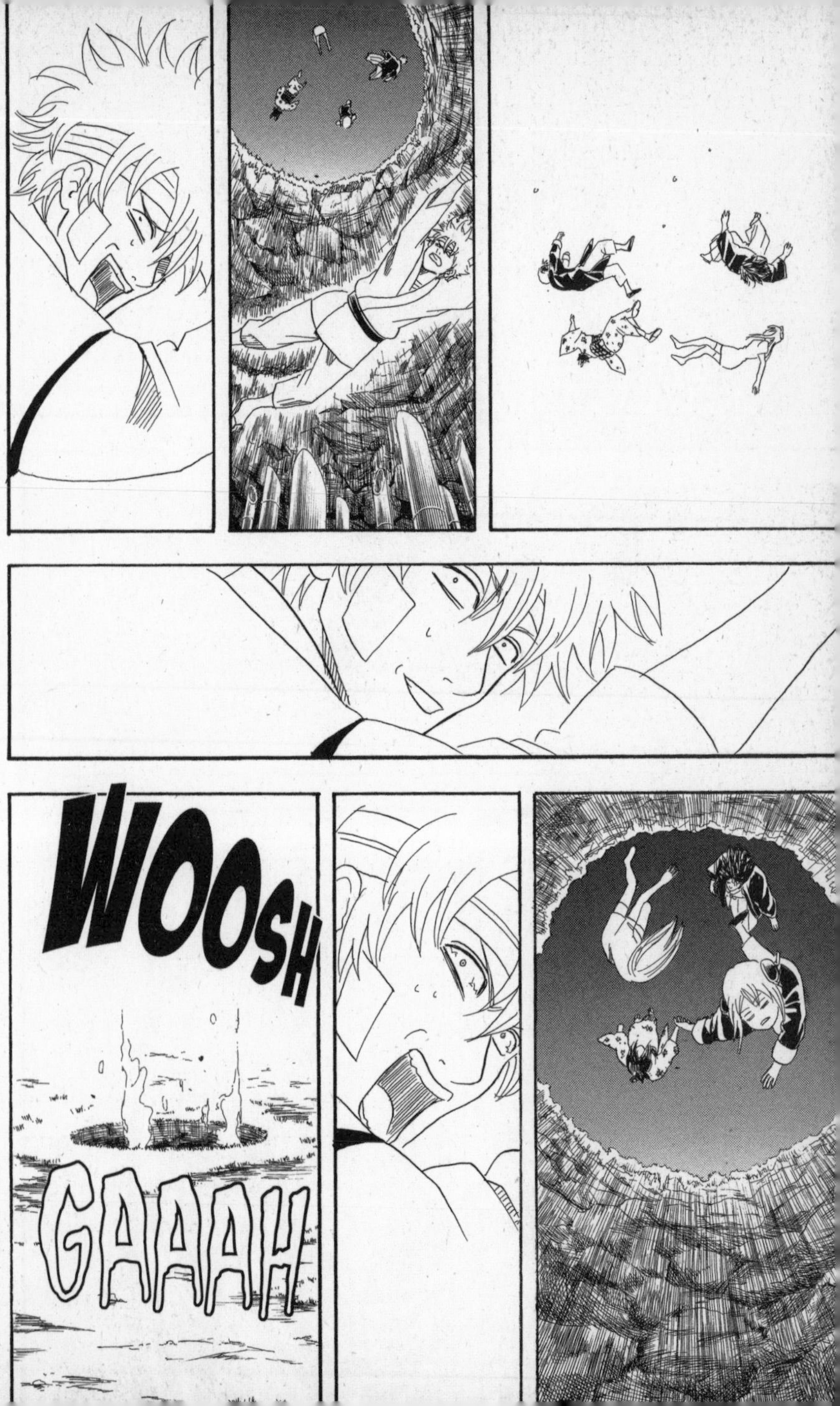
WOOSH
GAAAH

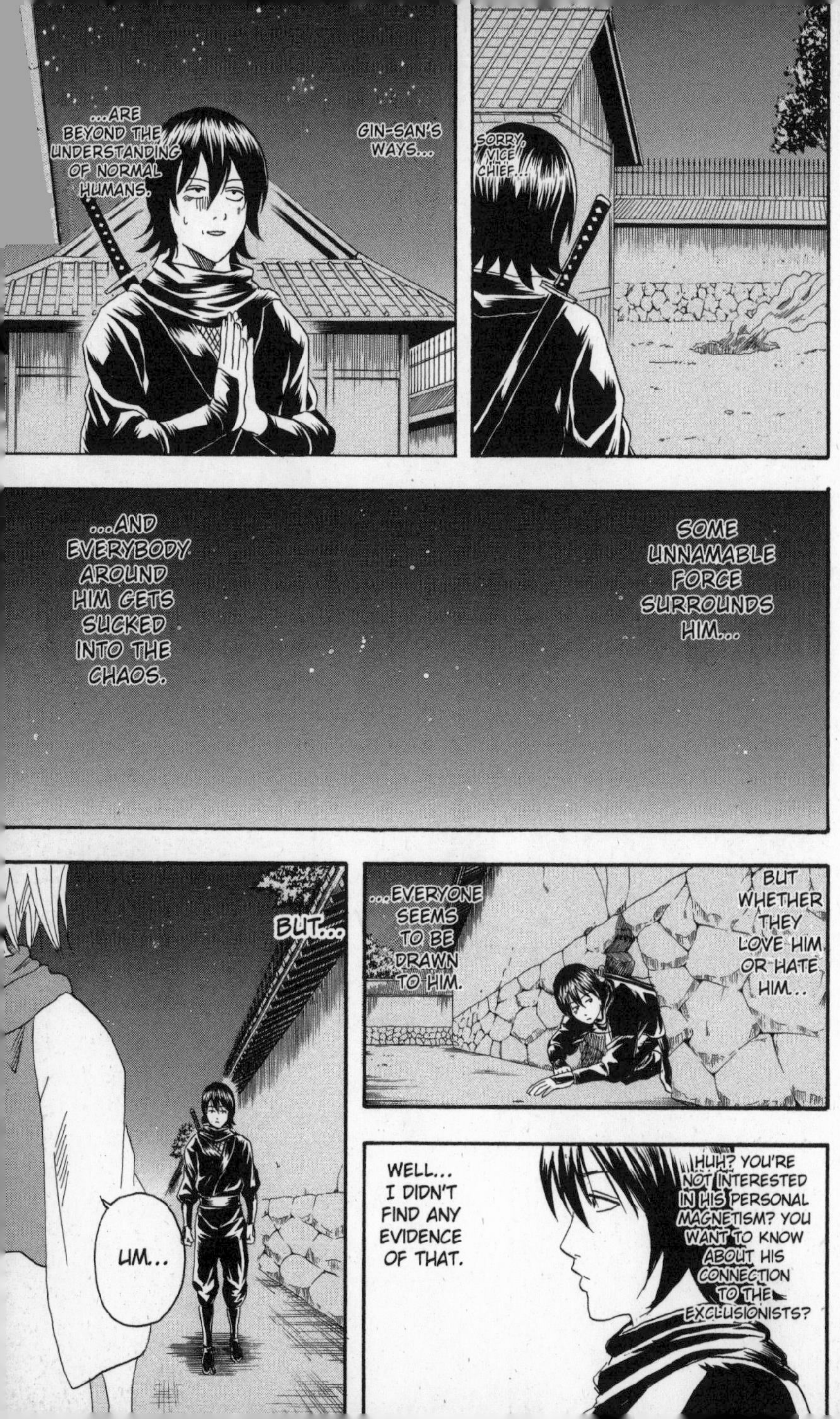
SORRY, VICE CHIEF...
GIN-SAN'S WAYS...
...ARE BEYOND THE UNDERSTANDING OF NORMAL HUMANS.
SOME UNNAMABLE FORCE SURROUNDS HIM...
...AND EVERYBODY AROUND HIM GETS SUCKED INTO THE CHAOS.
BUT WHETHER THEY LOVE HIM OR HATE HIM...
...EVERYONE SEEMS TO BE DRAWN TO HIM.
HUH? YOU'RE NOT INTERESTED IN HIS PERSONAL MAGNETISM? YOU WANT TO KNOW ABOUT HIS CONNECTION TO THE EXCLUSIONISTS?
WELL... I DIDN'T FIND ANY EVIDENCE OF THAT.
BUT...
UM...

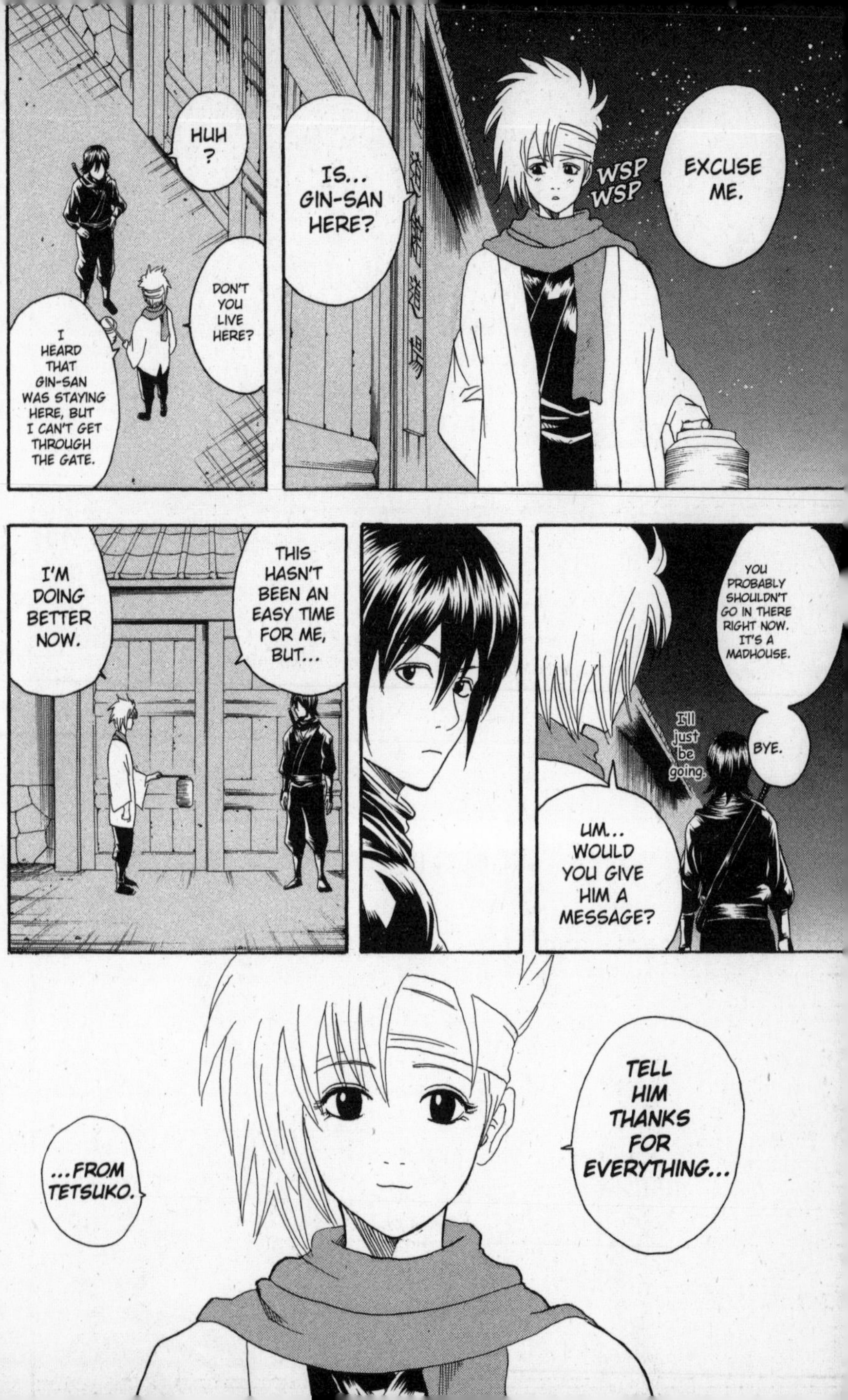
EXCUSE ME.
WSP WSP
IS... GIN-SAN HERE?
HUH ?
DON'T YOU LIVE HERE?
I HEARD THAT GIN-SAN WAS STAYING HERE, BUT I CAN'T GET THROUGH THE GATE.
YOU PROBABLY SHOULDN'T GO IN THERE RIGHT NOW. IT'S A MADHOUSE.
BYE.
I'll just be going.
UM... WOULD YOU GIVE HIM A MESSAGE?
THIS HASN'T BEEN AN EASY TIME FOR ME, BUT...
I'M DOING BETTER NOW.
TELL HIM THANKS FOR EVERYTHING...
...FROM TETSUKO.

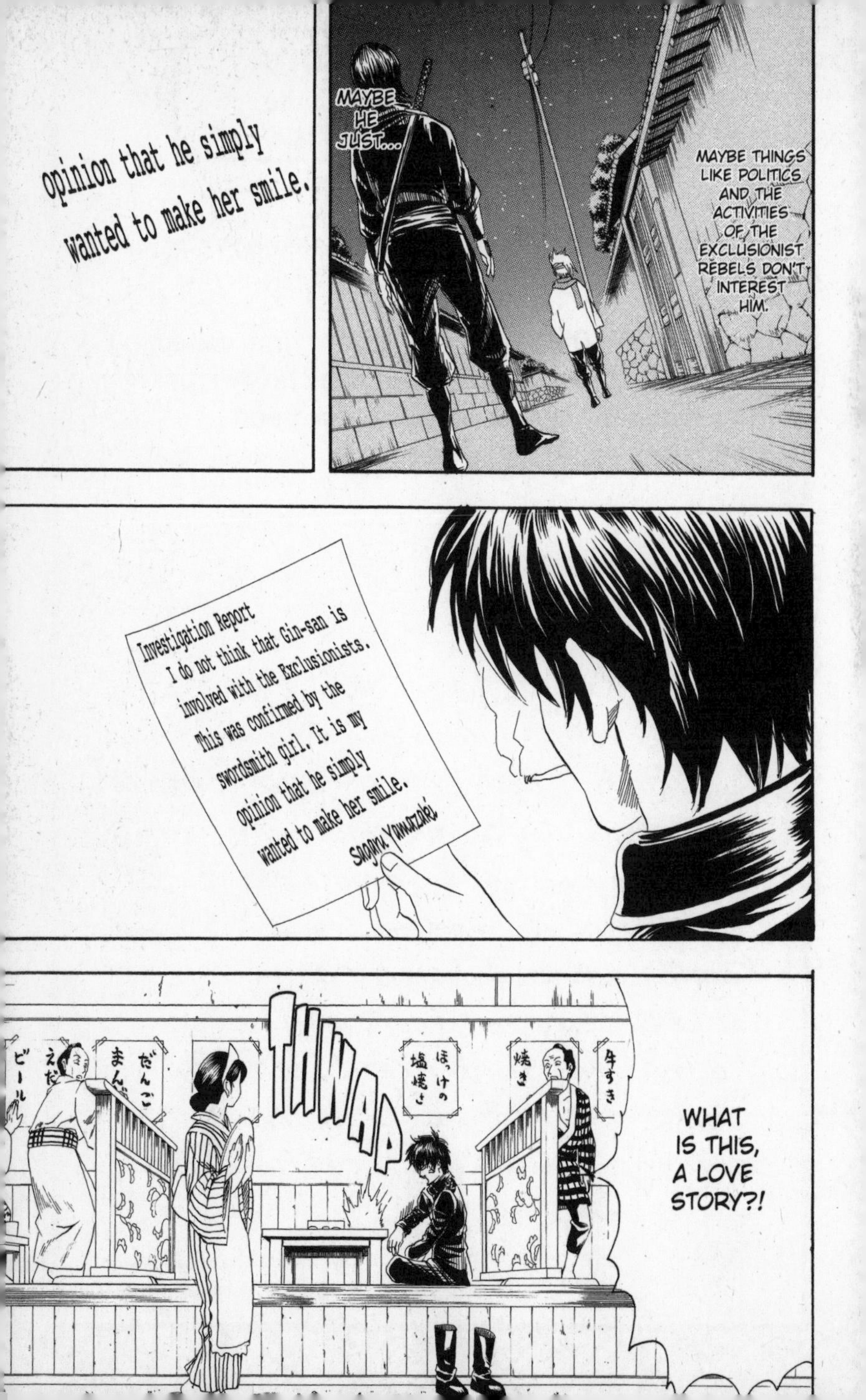
MAYBE THINGS LIKE POLITICS AND THE ACTIVITIES OF THE EXCLUSIONIST REBELS DON'T INTEREST HIM.
MAYBE HE JUST...
opinion that he simply wanted to make her smile.
Investigation Report
I do not think that Gin-san is involved with the Exclusionists. This was confirmed by the swordsmith girl. It is my opinion that he simply wanted to make her smile.
Sagaru Yamazaki
WHAT IS THIS, A LOVE STORY?!
THWAP
牛すき
ほっけの塩焼き

Sorachi's Q&A
Hanging with the Readers #34

<Question from Johnny-san of Fukushima Prefecture>

It seems like Otose-san has a hard time collecting rent from Gin-san. How much does he owe her? How much is his rent, anyway? I've been wondering about these things.

<Answer>

The rent is 60,000 yen ($600). That's very reasonable for Kabukicho. But the Yorozuya work freelance, so sometimes Gin has a lot of money and sometimes he's broke. And it's never cheap to feed Kagura and Sadaharu, so he's always strapped for cash.

He may not look like it, but Gin works pretty hard. Still, he's usually about two months behind in his rent.

(Q&A #35 is on page 106)

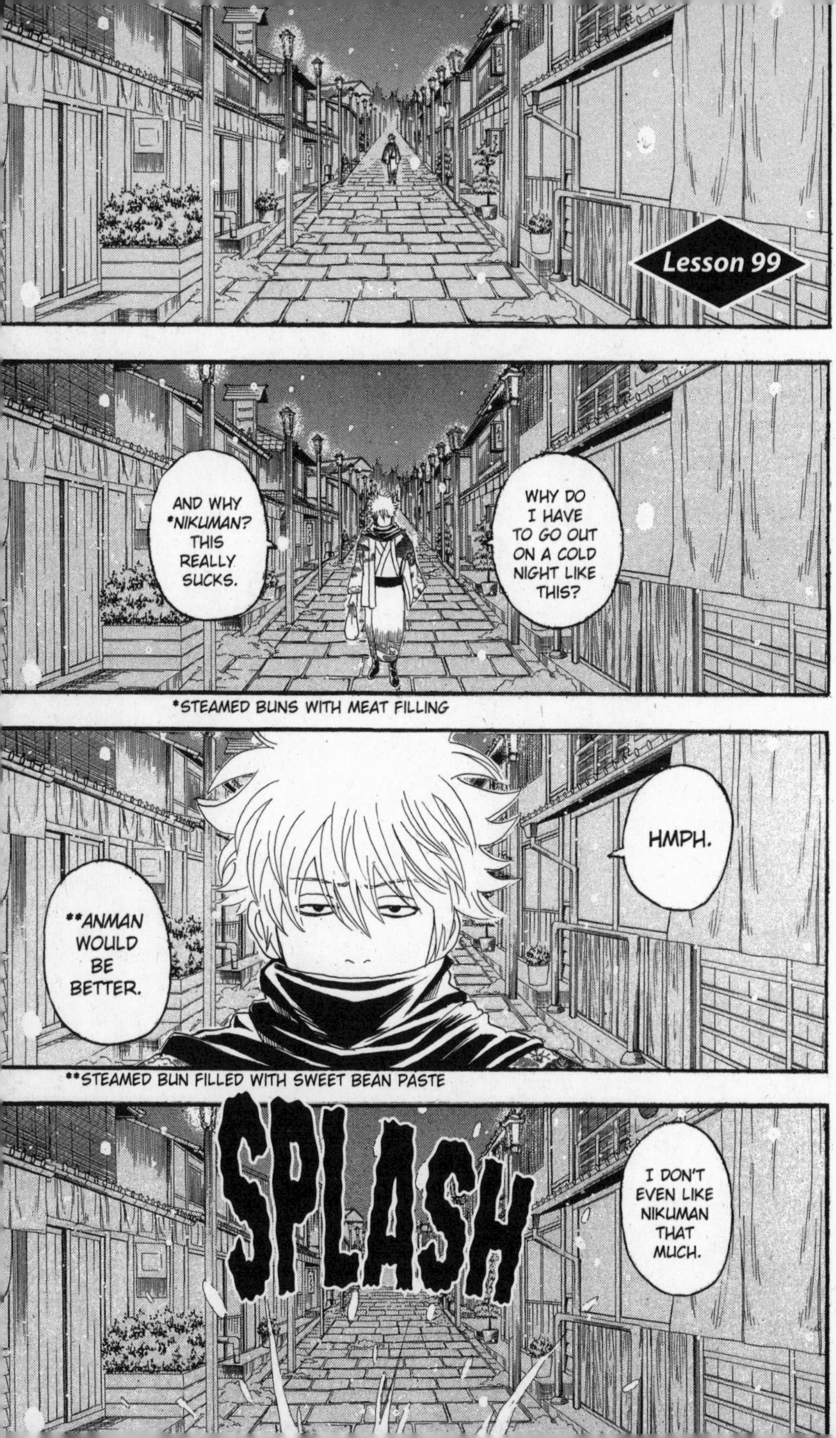
Lesson 99
WHY DO I HAVE TO GO OUT ON A COLD NIGHT LIKE THIS?
AND WHY *NIKUMAN? THIS REALLY SUCKS.
HMPH.
**ANMAN WOULD BE BETTER.
I DON'T EVEN LIKE NIKUMAN THAT MUCH.
SPLASH

*STEAMED BUNS WITH MEAT FILLING

**STEAMED BUN FILLED WITH SWEET BEAN PASTE

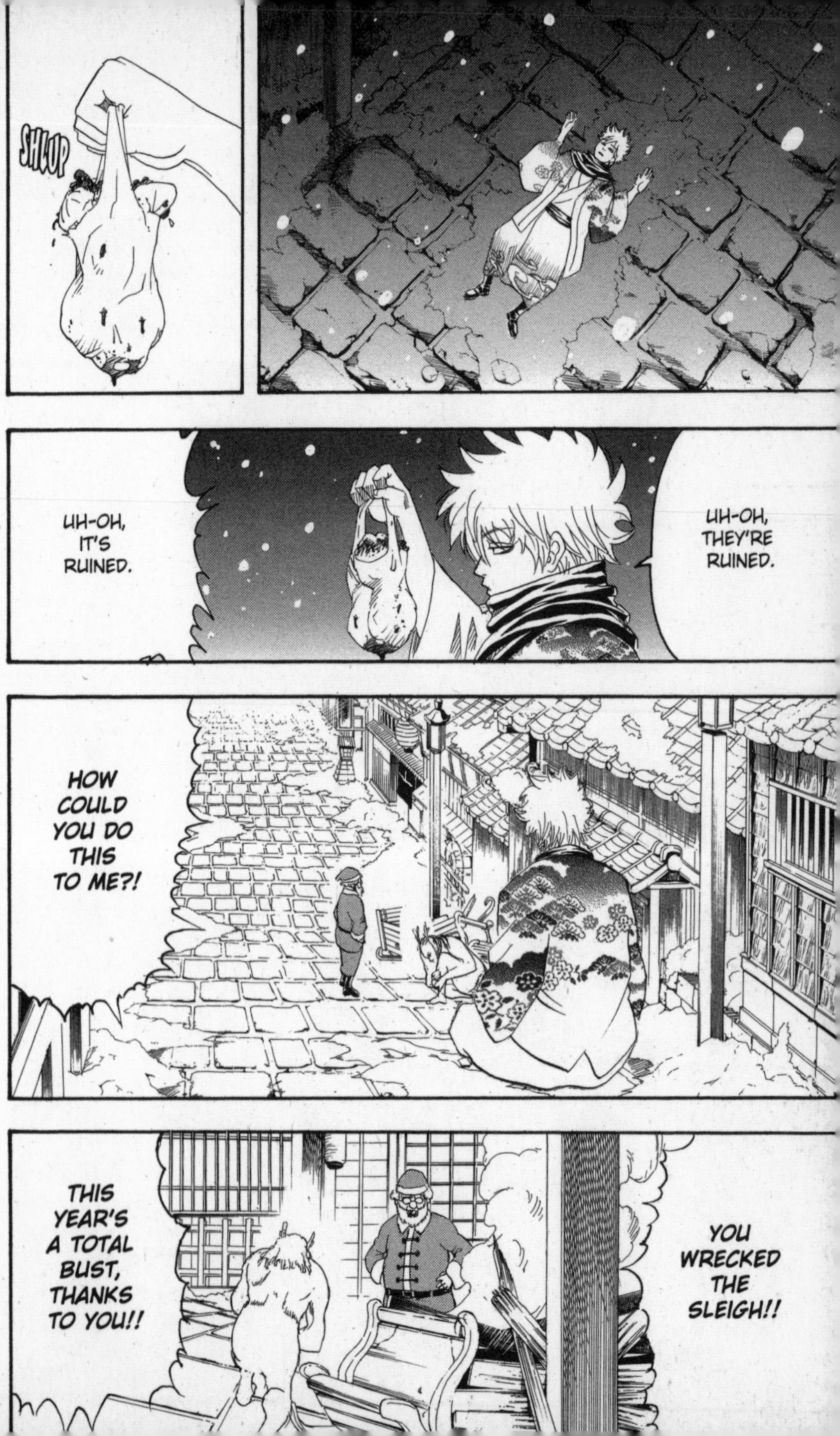
SHLUP
UH-OH, THEY'RE RUINED.
UH-OH, IT'S RUINED.
HOW COULD YOU DO THIS TO ME?!
YOU WRECKED THE SLEIGH!!
THIS YEAR'S A TOTAL BUST, THANKS TO YOU!!

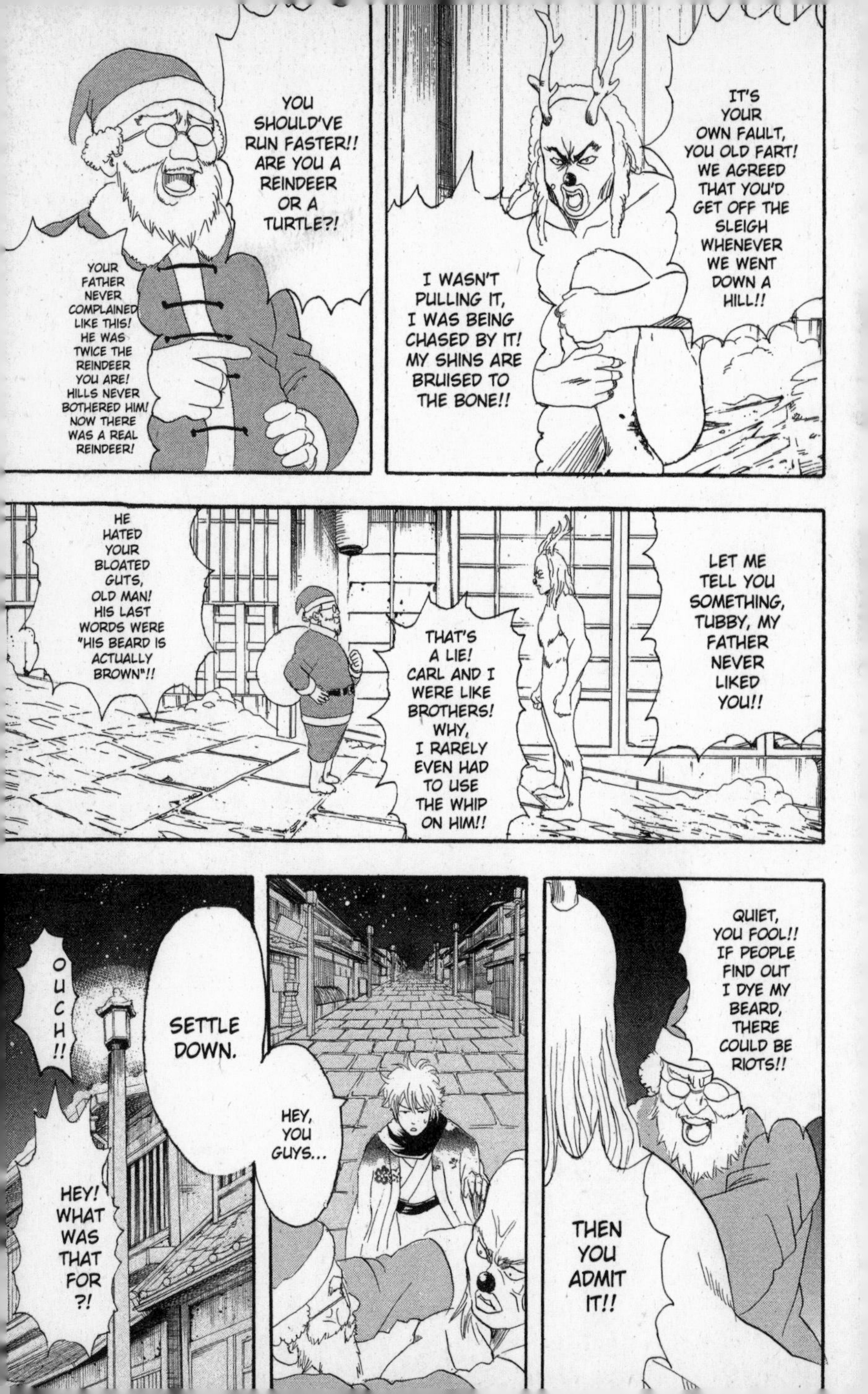
IT'S YOUR OWN FAULT, YOU OLD FART! WE AGREED THAT YOU'D GET OFF THE SLEIGH WHENEVER WE WENT DOWN A HILL!!
I WASN'T PULLING IT, I WAS BEING CHASED BY IT! MY SHINS ARE BRUISED TO THE BONE!!
YOU SHOULD'VE RUN FASTER!! ARE YOU A REINDEER OR A TURTLE?!
YOUR FATHER NEVER COMPLAINED LIKE THIS! HE WAS TWICE THE REINDEER YOU ARE! HILLS NEVER BOTHERED HIM! NOW THERE WAS A REAL REINDEER!
LET ME TELL YOU SOMETHING, TUBBY, MY FATHER NEVER LIKED YOU!!
THAT'S A LIE! CARL AND I WERE LIKE BROTHERS! WHY, I RARELY EVEN HAD TO USE THE WHIP ON HIM!!
HE HATED YOUR BLOATED GUTS, OLD MAN! HIS LAST WORDS WERE "HIS BEARD IS ACTUALLY BROWN"!!
QUIET, YOU FOOL!! IF PEOPLE FIND OUT I DYE MY BEARD, THERE COULD BE RIOTS!!
THEN YOU ADMIT IT!!
HEY, YOU GUYS...
SETTLE DOWN.
OUCH!!
HEY! WHAT WAS THAT FOR?!

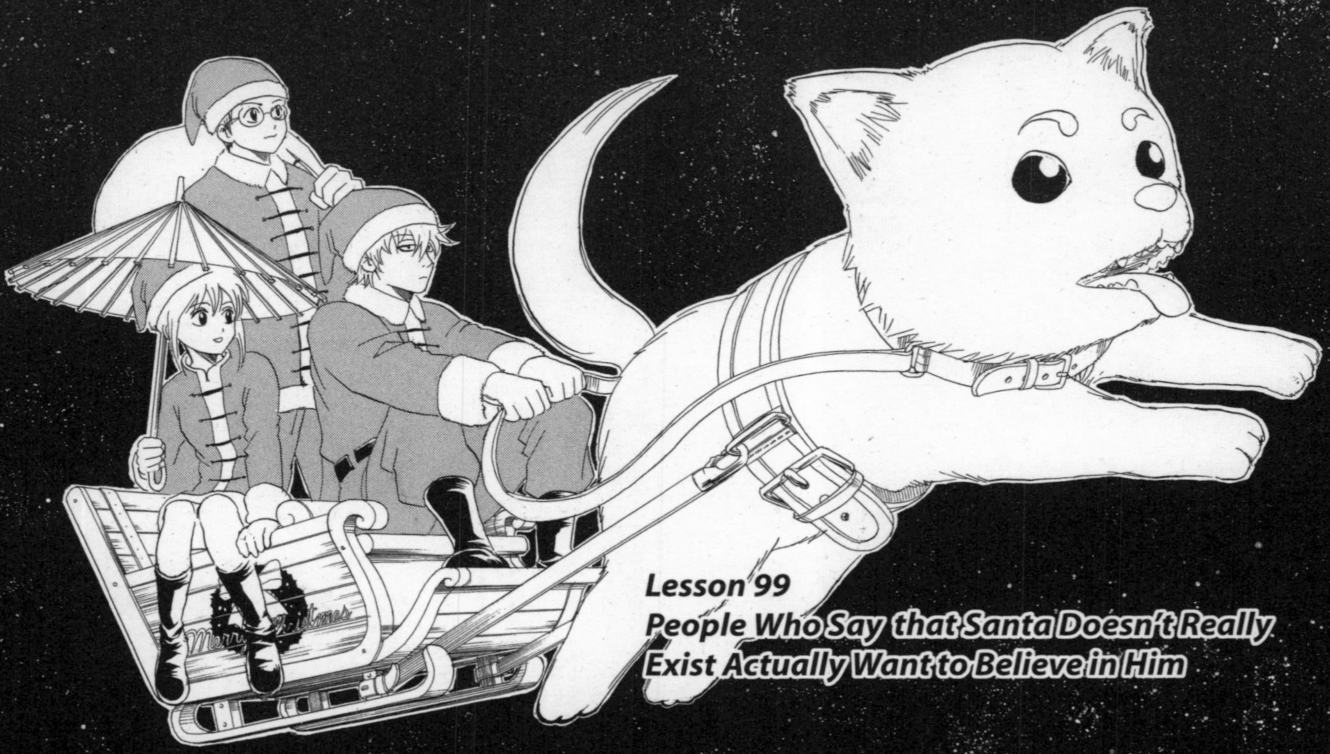

Lesson 99
People Who Say that Santa Doesn't Really Exist Actually Want to Believe in Him

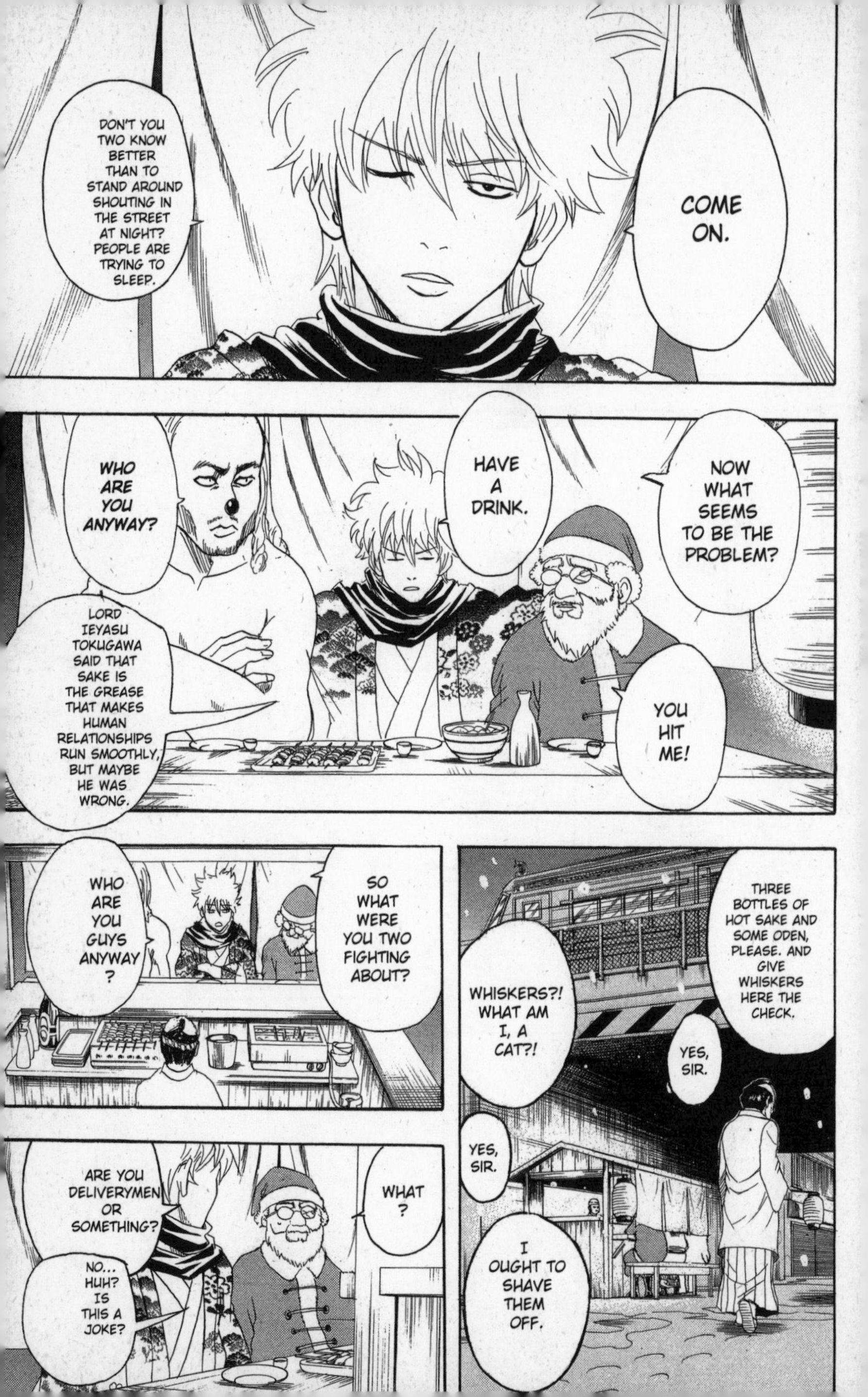
COME ON.
DON'T YOU TWO KNOW BETTER THAN TO STAND AROUND SHOUTING IN THE STREET AT NIGHT? PEOPLE ARE TRYING TO SLEEP.
NOW WHAT SEEMS TO BE THE PROBLEM?
HAVE A DRINK.
WHO ARE YOU ANYWAY?
YOU HIT ME!
LORD IEYASU TOKUGAWA SAID THAT SAKE IS THE GREASE THAT MAKES HUMAN RELATIONSHIPS RUN SMOOTHLY, BUT MAYBE HE WAS WRONG.
THREE BOTTLES OF HOT SAKE AND SOME ODEN, PLEASE. AND GIVE WHISKERS HERE THE CHECK.
YES, SIR.
WHISKERS?! WHAT AM I, A CAT?!
YES, SIR.
I OUGHT TO SHAVE THEM OFF.
SO WHAT WERE YOU TWO FIGHTING ABOUT?
WHO ARE YOU GUYS ANYWAY?
WHAT?
ARE YOU DELIVERYMEN OR SOMETHING?
NO... HUH? IS THIS A JOKE?

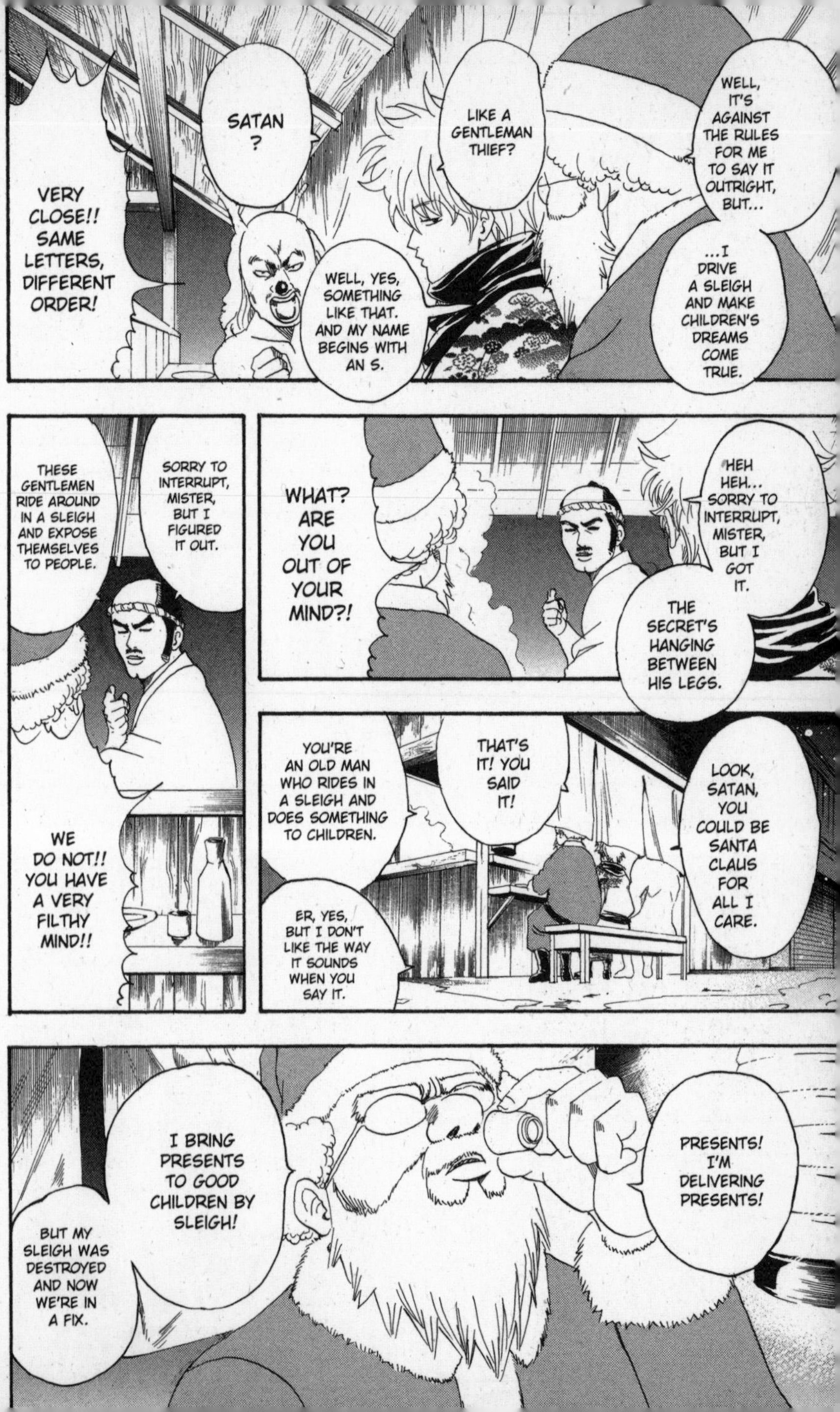
WELL, IT'S AGAINST THE RULES FOR ME TO SAY IT OUTRIGHT, BUT...
...I DRIVE A SLEIGH AND MAKE CHILDREN'S DREAMS COME TRUE.
LIKE A GENTLEMAN THIEF?
WELL, YES, SOMETHING LIKE THAT. AND MY NAME BEGINS WITH AN S.
SATAN?
VERY CLOSE!! SAME LETTERS, DIFFERENT ORDER!
HEH HEH... SORRY TO INTERRUPT, MISTER, BUT I GOT IT.
THE SECRET'S HANGING BETWEEN HIS LEGS.
WHAT? ARE YOU OUT OF YOUR MIND?!
LOOK, SATAN, YOU COULD BE SANTA CLAUS FOR ALL I CARE.
THAT'S IT! YOU SAID IT!
YOU'RE AN OLD MAN WHO RIDES IN A SLEIGH AND DOES SOMETHING TO CHILDREN.
ER, YES, BUT I DON'T LIKE THE WAY IT SOUNDS WHEN YOU SAY IT.
SORRY TO INTERRUPT, MISTER, BUT I FIGURED IT OUT.
THESE GENTLEMEN RIDE AROUND IN A SLEIGH AND EXPOSE THEMSELVES TO PEOPLE.
WE DO NOT!! YOU HAVE A VERY FILTHY MIND!!
PRESENTS! I'M DELIVERING PRESENTS!
I BRING PRESENTS TO GOOD CHILDREN BY SLEIGH!
BUT MY SLEIGH WAS DESTROYED AND NOW WE'RE IN A FIX.

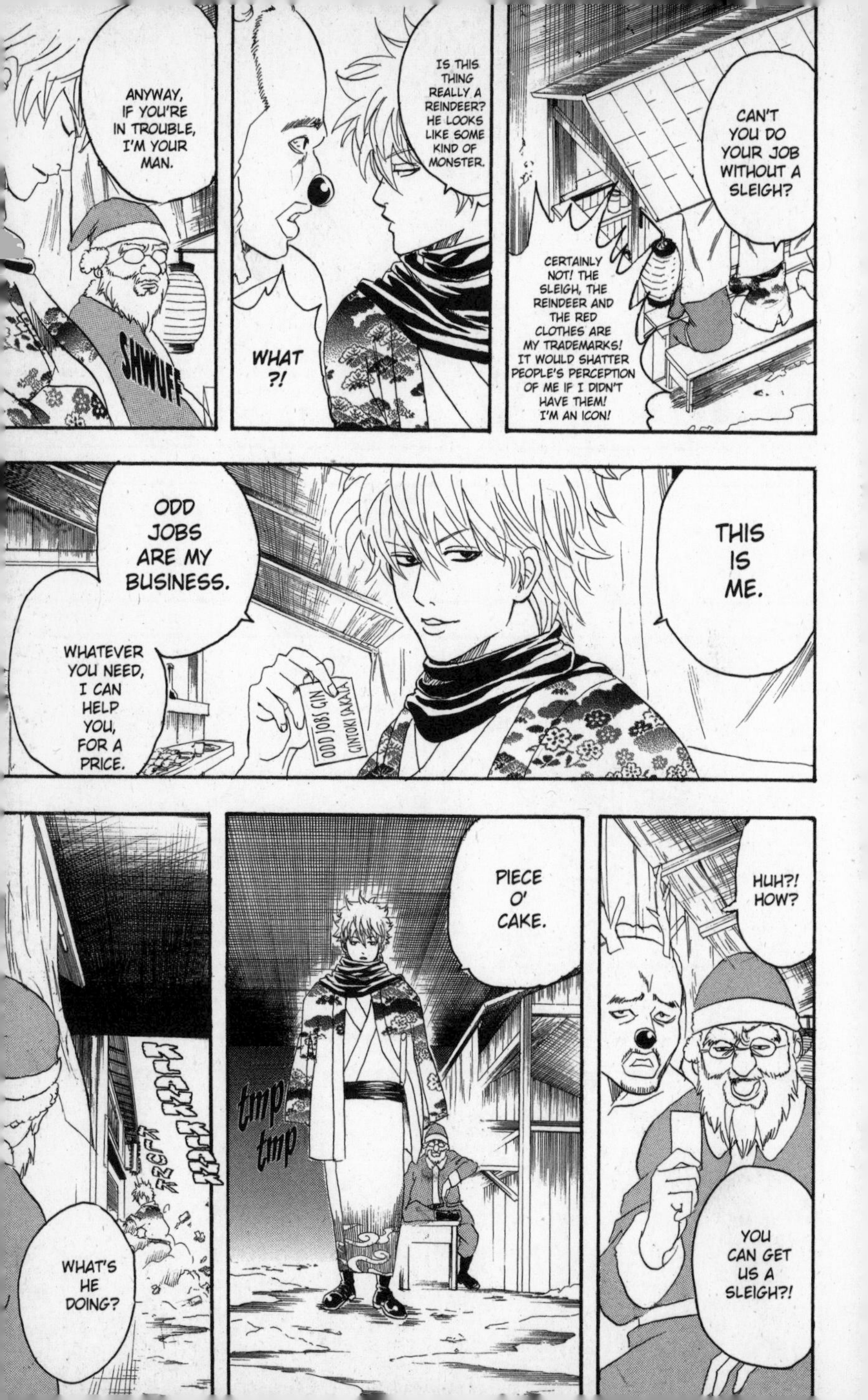

CAN'T YOU DO YOUR JOB WITHOUT A SLEIGH?
CERTAINLY NOT! THE SLEIGH, THE REINDEER AND THE RED CLOTHES ARE MY TRADEMARKS! IT WOULD SHATTER PEOPLE'S PERCEPTION OF ME IF I DIDN'T HAVE THEM! I'M AN ICON!
IS THIS THING REALLY A REINDEER? HE LOOKS LIKE SOME KIND OF MONSTER.
WHAT ?!
ANYWAY, IF YOU'RE IN TROUBLE, I'M YOUR MAN.
SHWUFF
THIS IS ME.
ODD JOBS ARE MY BUSINESS.
WHATEVER YOU NEED, I CAN HELP YOU, FOR A PRICE.
ODD JOBS GIN
GINTOKI SAKATA
HUH?! HOW?
YOU CAN GET US A SLEIGH?!
PIECE O' CAKE.
tmp tmp
KLANK KLANK
KLONK
WHAT'S HE DOING?

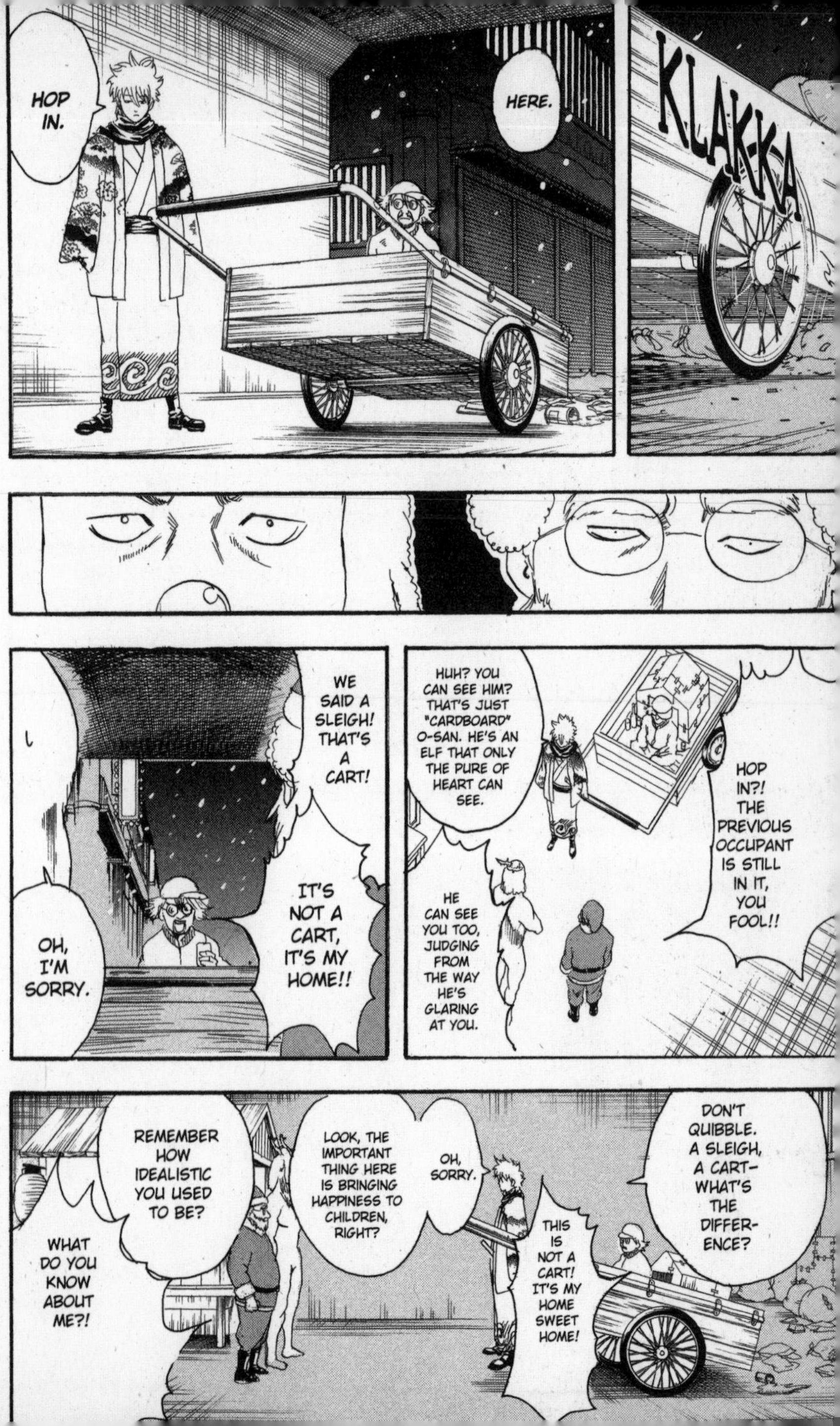
KLAKKA
HERE.
HOP IN.
HOP IN?! THE PREVIOUS OCCUPANT IS STILL IN IT, YOU FOOL!!
HUH? YOU CAN SEE HIM? THAT'S JUST "CARDBOARD" O-SAN. HE'S AN ELF THAT ONLY THE PURE OF HEART CAN SEE.
HE CAN SEE YOU TOO, JUDGING FROM THE WAY HE'S GLARING AT YOU.
WE SAID A SLEIGH! THAT'S A CART!
IT'S NOT A CART, IT'S MY HOME!!
OH, I'M SORRY.
DON'T QUIBBLE. A SLEIGH, A CART—WHAT'S THE DIFFERENCE?
THIS IS NOT A CART! IT'S MY HOME SWEET HOME!
OH, SORRY.
LOOK, THE IMPORTANT THING HERE IS BRINGING HAPPINESS TO CHILDREN, RIGHT?
REMEMBER HOW IDEALISTIC YOU USED TO BE?
WHAT DO YOU KNOW ABOUT ME?!

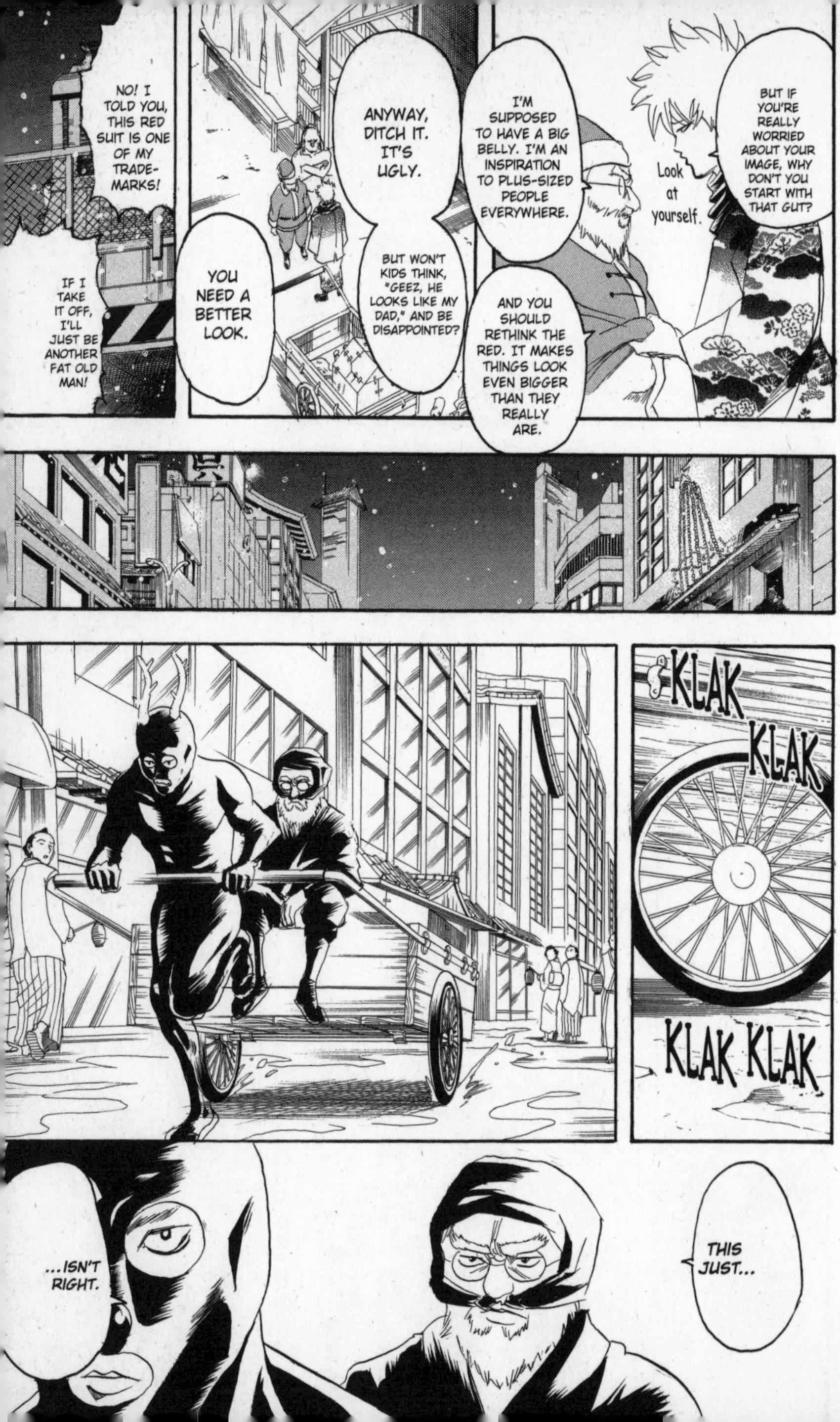
BUT IF YOU'RE REALLY WORRIED ABOUT YOUR IMAGE, WHY DON'T YOU START WITH THAT GUT?
Look at yourself.
I'M SUPPOSED TO HAVE A BIG BELLY. I'M AN INSPIRATION TO PLUS-SIZED PEOPLE EVERYWHERE.
AND YOU SHOULD RETHINK THE RED. IT MAKES THINGS LOOK EVEN BIGGER THAN THEY REALLY ARE.
ANYWAY, DITCH IT. IT'S UGLY.
BUT WON'T KIDS THINK, "GEEZ, HE LOOKS LIKE MY DAD," AND BE DISAPPOINTED?
YOU NEED A BETTER LOOK.
NO! I TOLD YOU, THIS RED SUIT IS ONE OF MY TRADE-MARKS!
IF I TAKE IT OFF, I'LL JUST BE ANOTHER FAT OLD MAN!
KLAK KLAK
KLAK KLAK
THIS JUST...
...ISN'T RIGHT.

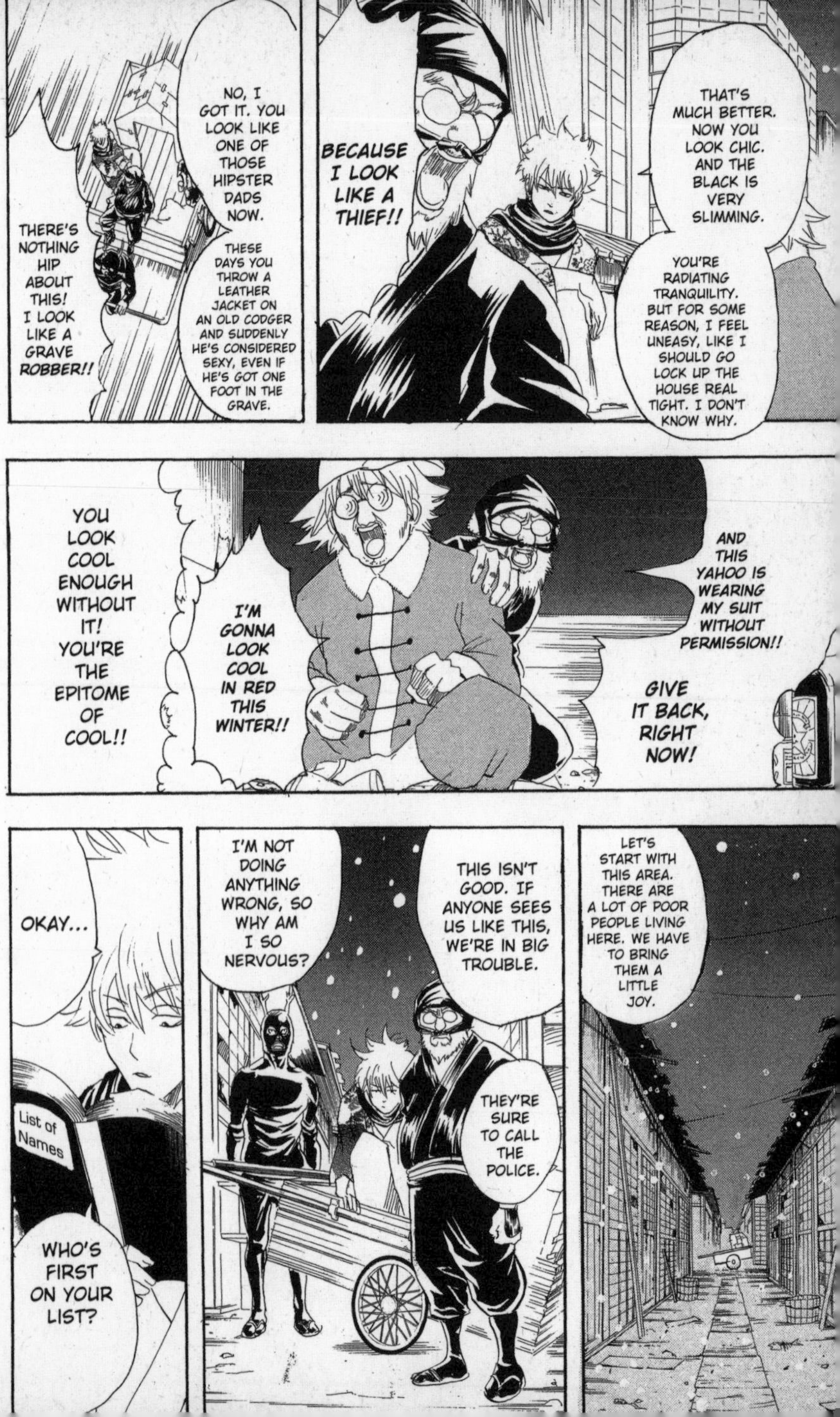

THAT'S MUCH BETTER. NOW YOU LOOK CHIC. AND THE BLACK IS VERY SLIMMING.
YOU'RE RADIATING TRANQUILITY. BUT FOR SOME REASON, I FEEL UNEASY, LIKE I SHOULD GO LOCK UP THE HOUSE REAL TIGHT. I DON'T KNOW WHY.
BECAUSE I LOOK LIKE A THIEF!!
NO, I GOT IT. YOU LOOK LIKE ONE OF THOSE HIPSTER DADS NOW.
THESE DAYS YOU THROW A LEATHER JACKET ON AN OLD CODGER AND SUDDENLY HE'S CONSIDERED SEXY, EVEN IF HE'S GOT ONE FOOT IN THE GRAVE.
THERE'S NOTHING HIP ABOUT THIS! I LOOK LIKE A GRAVE ROBBER!!
AND THIS YAHOO IS WEARING MY SUIT WITHOUT PERMISSION!!
GIVE IT BACK, RIGHT NOW!
I'M GONNA LOOK COOL IN RED THIS WINTER!!
YOU LOOK COOL ENOUGH WITHOUT IT! YOU'RE THE EPITOME OF COOL!!
LET'S START WITH THIS AREA. THERE ARE A LOT OF POOR PEOPLE LIVING HERE. WE HAVE TO BRING THEM A LITTLE JOY.
THIS ISN'T GOOD. IF ANYONE SEES US LIKE THIS, WE'RE IN BIG TROUBLE.
I'M NOT DOING ANYTHING WRONG, SO WHY AM I SO NERVOUS?
THEY'RE SURE TO CALL THE POLICE.
OKAY...
List of Names
WHO'S FIRST ON YOUR LIST?

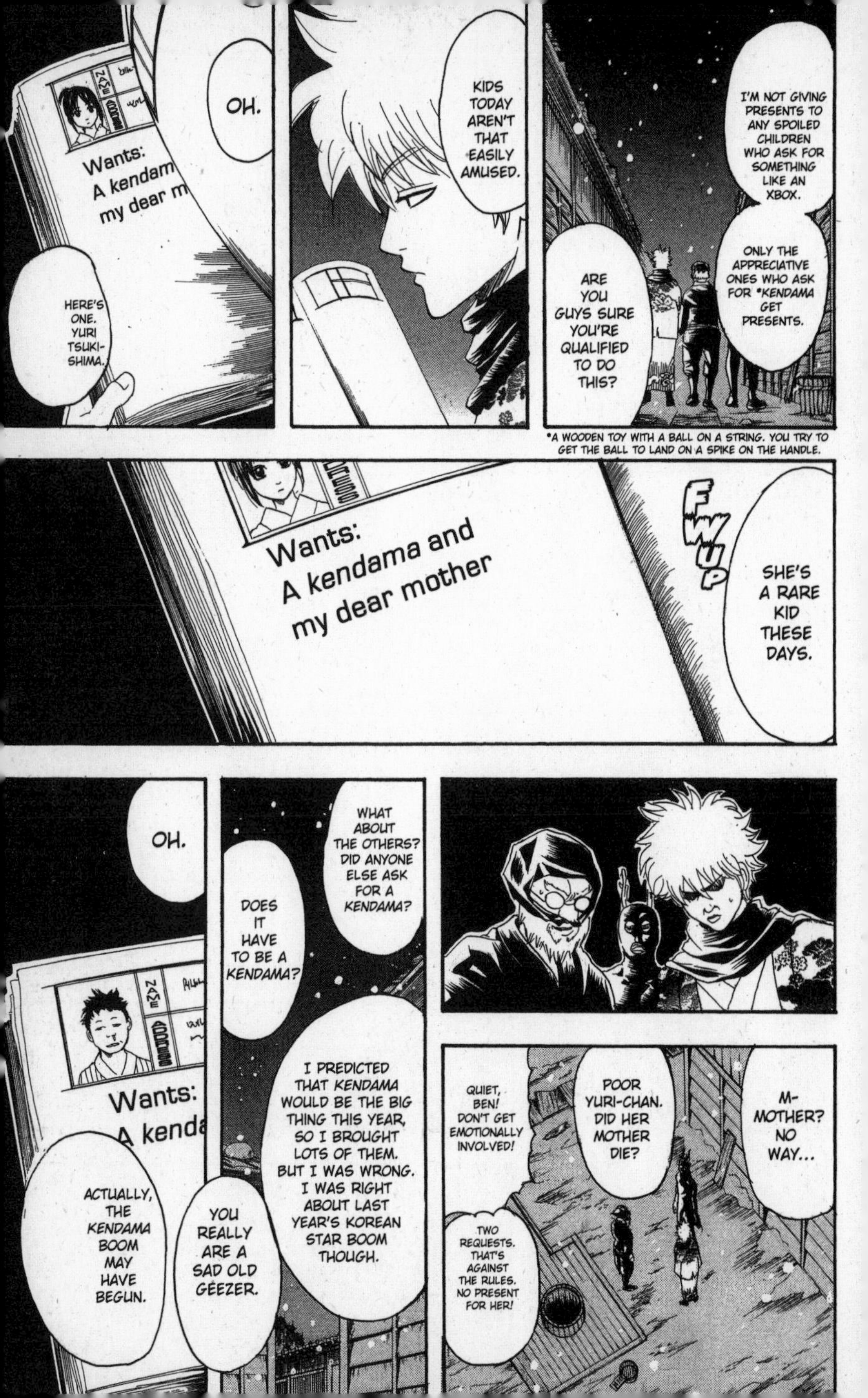
I'M NOT GIVING PRESENTS TO ANY SPOILED CHILDREN WHO ASK FOR SOMETHING LIKE AN XBOX.
ONLY THE APPRECIATIVE ONES WHO ASK FOR *KENDAMA GET PRESENTS.
ARE YOU GUYS SURE YOU'RE QUALIFIED TO DO THIS?
KIDS TODAY AREN'T THAT EASILY AMUSED.
OH.
Wants: A kendam my dear m
HERE'S ONE. YURI TSUKISHIMA.
FWUP
SHE'S A RARE KID THESE DAYS.
Wants: A kendama and my dear mother
M-MOTHER? NO WAY...
POOR YURI-CHAN. DID HER MOTHER DIE?
QUIET, BEN! DON'T GET EMOTIONALLY INVOLVED!
TWO REQUESTS. THAT'S AGAINST THE RULES. NO PRESENT FOR HER!
WHAT ABOUT THE OTHERS? DID ANYONE ELSE ASK FOR A KENDAMA?
DOES IT HAVE TO BE A KENDAMA?
I PREDICTED THAT KENDAMA WOULD BE THE BIG THING THIS YEAR, SO I BROUGHT LOTS OF THEM. BUT I WAS WRONG. I WAS RIGHT ABOUT LAST YEAR'S KOREAN STAR BOOM THOUGH.
YOU REALLY ARE A SAD OLD GEEZER.
OH.
Wants: A kenda
ACTUALLY, THE KENDAMA BOOM MAY HAVE BEGUN.
*A WOODEN TOY WITH A BALL ON A STRING. YOU TRY TO GET THE BALL TO LAND ON A SPIKE ON THE HANDLE.

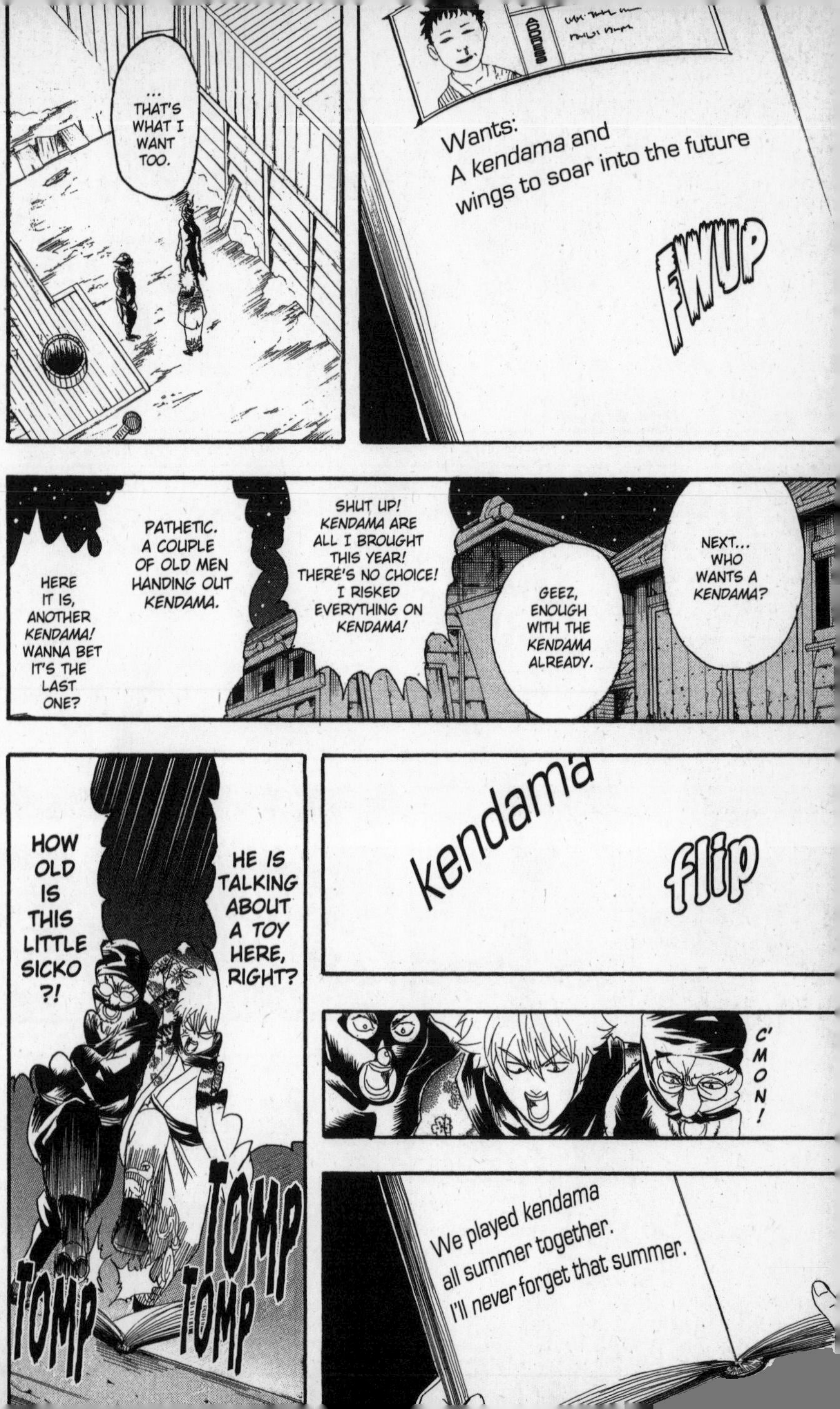
Wants:
A kendama and
wings to soar into the future
FWUP
... THAT'S WHAT I WANT TOO.
NEXT... WHO WANTS A KENDAMA?
GEEZ, ENOUGH WITH THE KENDAMA ALREADY.
SHUT UP! KENDAMA ARE ALL I BROUGHT THIS YEAR! THERE'S NO CHOICE! I RISKED EVERYTHING ON KENDAMA!
PATHETIC. A COUPLE OF OLD MEN HANDING OUT KENDAMA.
HERE IT IS, ANOTHER KENDAMA! WANNA BET IT'S THE LAST ONE?
kendama
flip
C'MON!
We played kendama
all summer together.
I'll never forget that summer.
HE IS TALKING ABOUT A TOY HERE, RIGHT?
HOW OLD IS THIS LITTLE SICKO?!
TOMP TOMP
TOMP TOMP

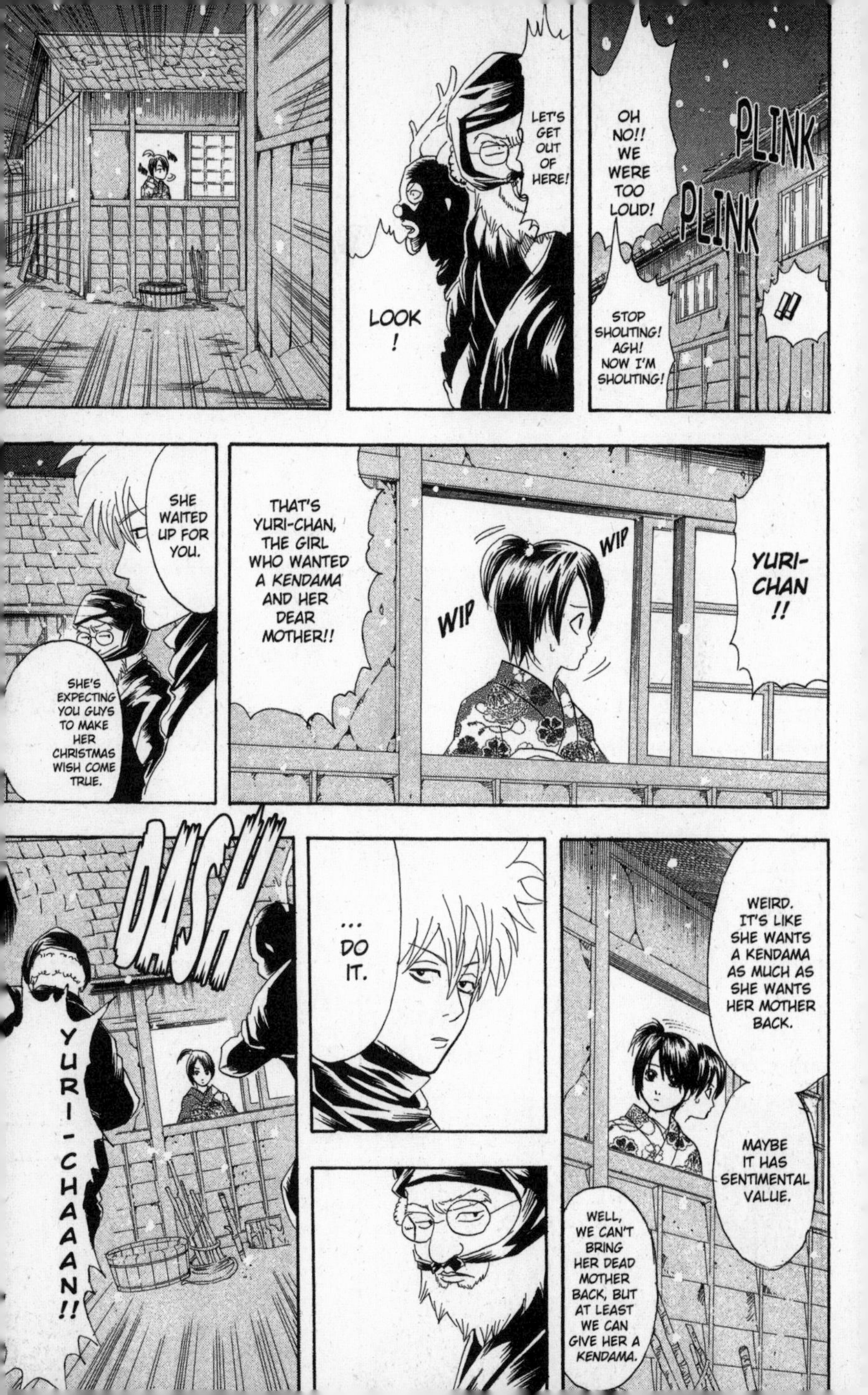

OH NO!! WE WERE TOO LOUD!
PLINK
PLINK
!!
STOP SHOUTING! AGH! NOW I'M SHOUTING!
LET'S GET OUT OF HERE!
LOOK!
YURI-CHAN!!
WIP
WIP
THAT'S YURI-CHAN, THE GIRL WHO WANTED A KENDAMA AND HER DEAR MOTHER!!
SHE WAITED UP FOR YOU.
SHE'S EXPECTING YOU GUYS TO MAKE HER CHRISTMAS WISH COME TRUE.
WEIRD. IT'S LIKE SHE WANTS A KENDAMA AS MUCH AS SHE WANTS HER MOTHER BACK.
MAYBE IT HAS SENTIMENTAL VALUE.
WELL, WE CAN'T BRING HER DEAD MOTHER BACK, BUT AT LEAST WE CAN GIVE HER A KENDAMA.
... DO IT.
DASH
YURI-CHAAAAN!!

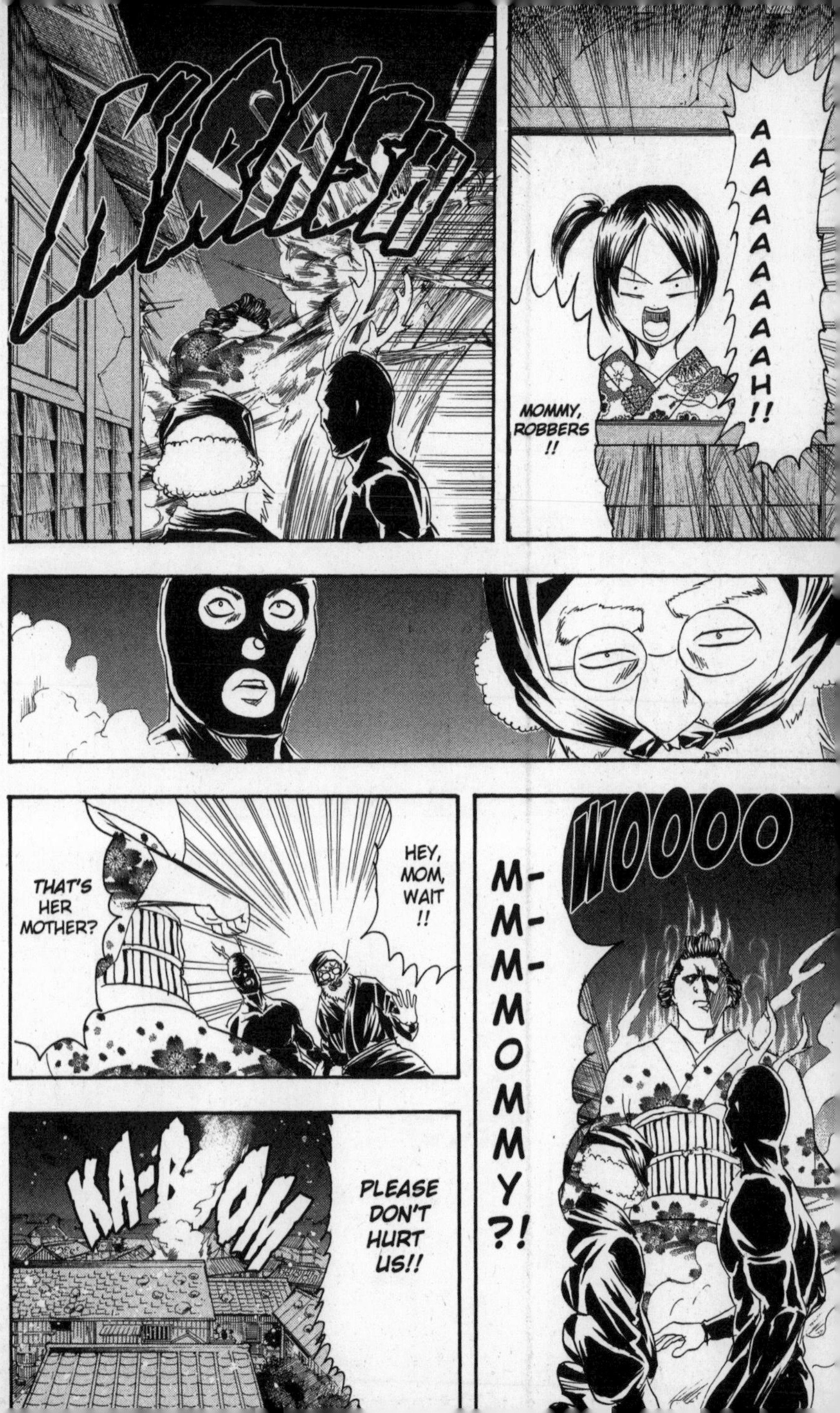
AAAAAAAAAAAAH!!
MOMMY, ROBBERS!!
WOOOO
M-M-M-MOMMOMMY?!
HEY, MOM, WAIT!!
THAT'S HER MOTHER?
PLEASE DON'T HURT US!!
KA-BOOM

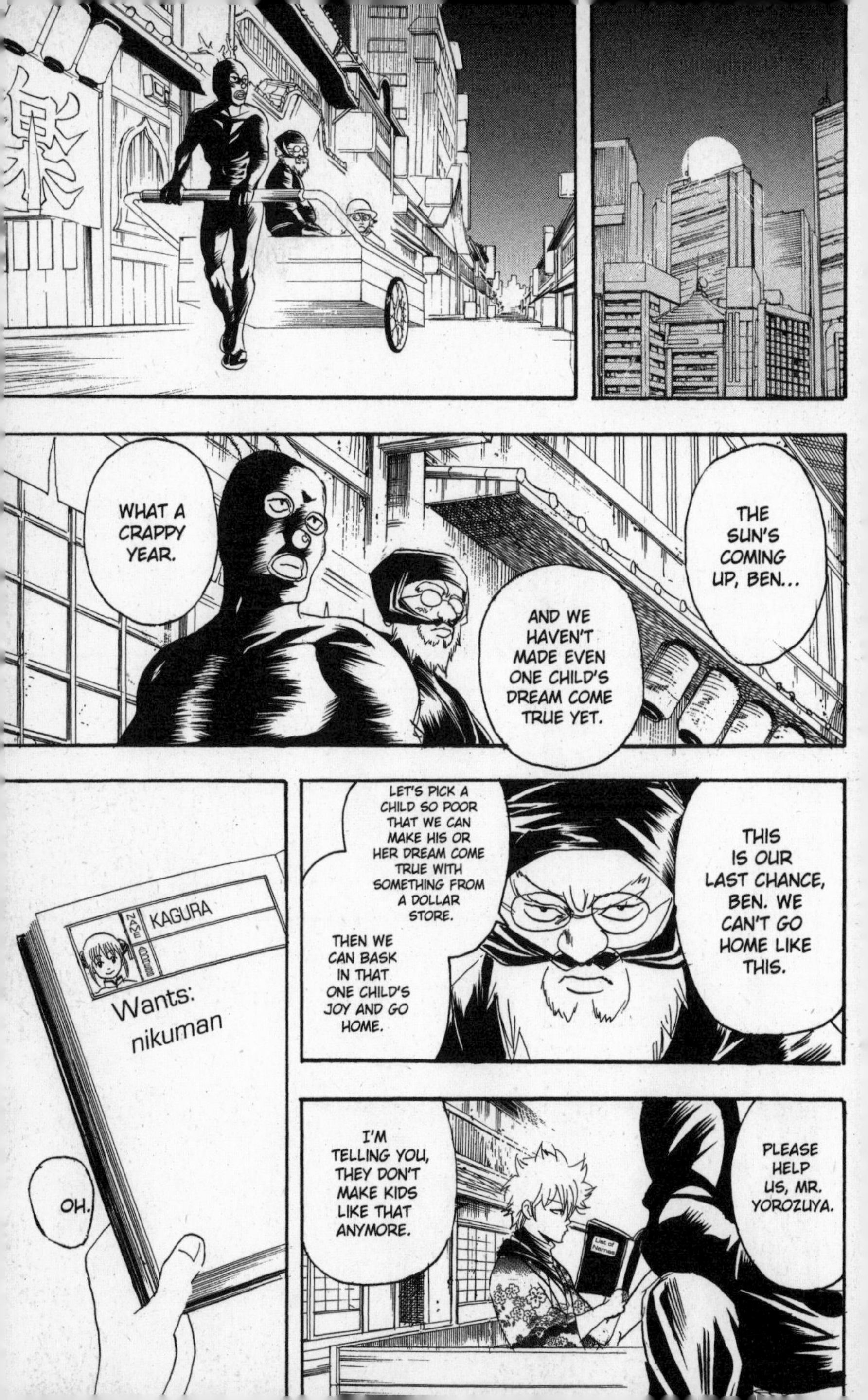
THE SUN'S COMING UP, BEN...
AND WE HAVEN'T MADE EVEN ONE CHILD'S DREAM COME TRUE YET.
WHAT A CRAPPY YEAR.
THIS IS OUR LAST CHANCE, BEN. WE CAN'T GO HOME LIKE THIS.
LET'S PICK A CHILD SO POOR THAT WE CAN MAKE HIS OR HER DREAM COME TRUE WITH SOMETHING FROM A DOLLAR STORE.
THEN WE CAN BASK IN THAT ONE CHILD'S JOY AND GO HOME.
PLEASE HELP US, MR. YOROZUYA.
I'M TELLING YOU, THEY DON'T MAKE KIDS LIKE THAT ANYMORE.
List of Names
NAME
KAGURA
Wants: nikuman
OH.

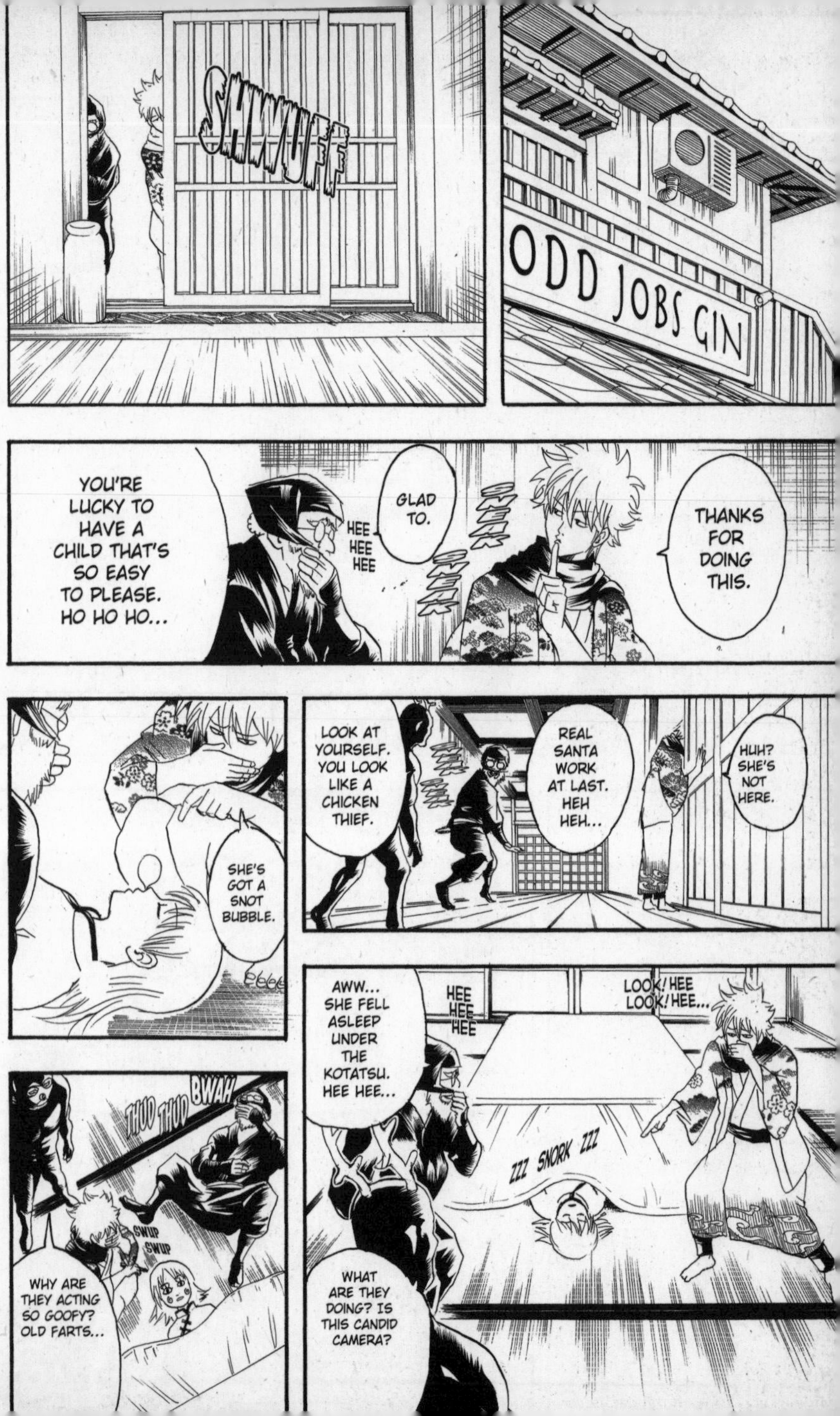
ODD JOBS GIN
SHWUFF
THANKS FOR DOING THIS.
SNEAK SNEAK
GLAD TO.
HEE HEE HEE
YOU'RE LUCKY TO HAVE A CHILD THAT'S SO EASY TO PLEASE. HO HO HO...
HUH? SHE'S NOT HERE.
REAL SANTA WORK AT LAST. HEH HEH...
LOOK AT YOURSELF. YOU LOOK LIKE A CHICKEN THIEF.
SHE'S GOT A SNOT BUBBLE.
LOOK! LOOK! HEE HEE...
HEE HEE HEE
AWW... SHE FELL ASLEEP UNDER THE KOTATSU. HEE HEE...
ZZZ SNORK ZZZ
WHAT ARE THEY DOING? IS THIS CANDID CAMERA?
BWAH
THUD THUD
SWUP SWUP
WHY ARE THEY ACTING SO GOOFY? OLD FARTS...

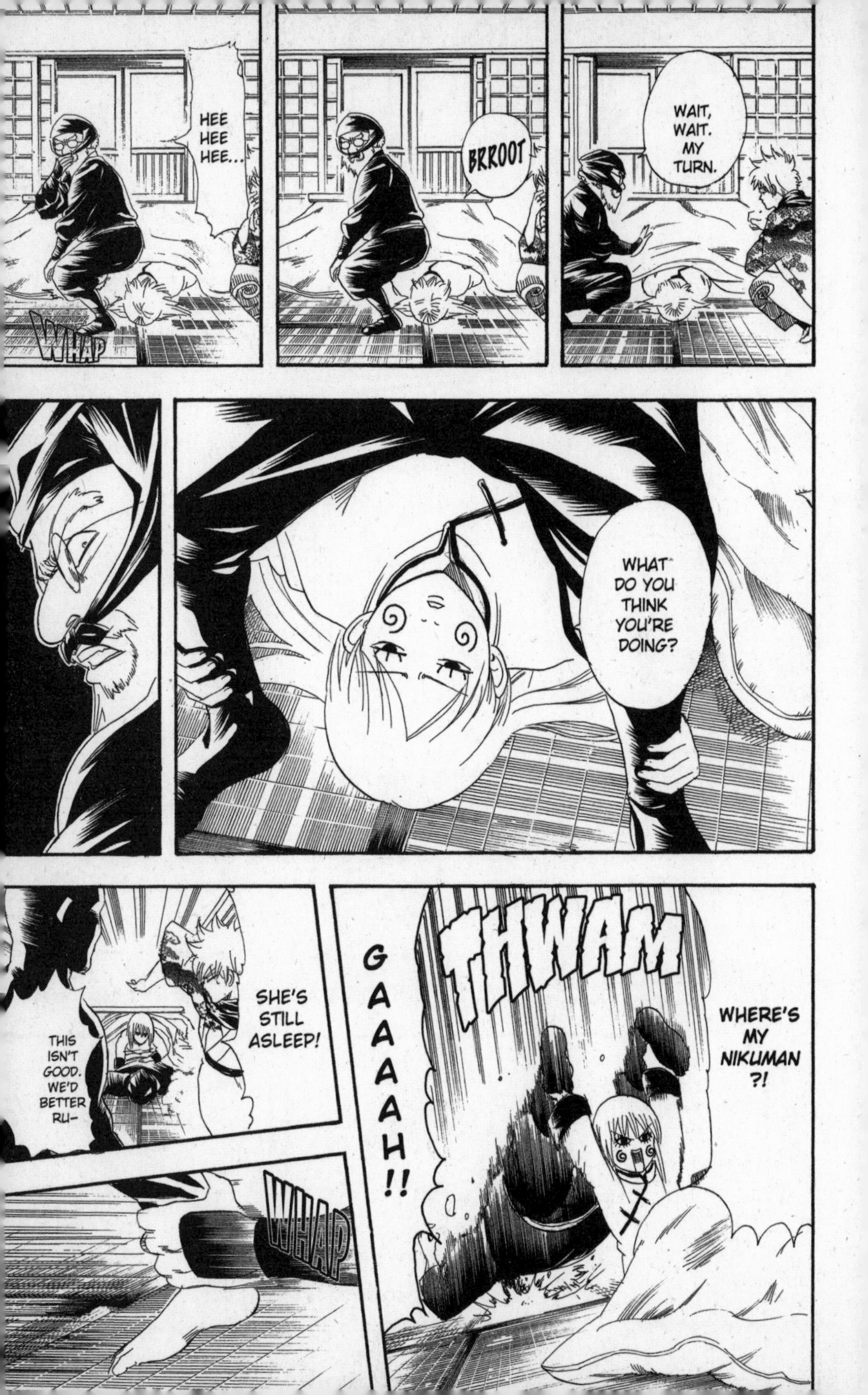
WAIT, WAIT. MY TURN.
BRROOT
HEE HEE HEE...
WHAP
WHAT DO YOU THINK YOU'RE DOING?
WHERE'S MY NIKUMAN ?!
THWAM
GAAAAAH!!
SHE'S STILL ASLEEP!
THIS ISN'T GOOD. WE'D BETTER RU-
WHAP

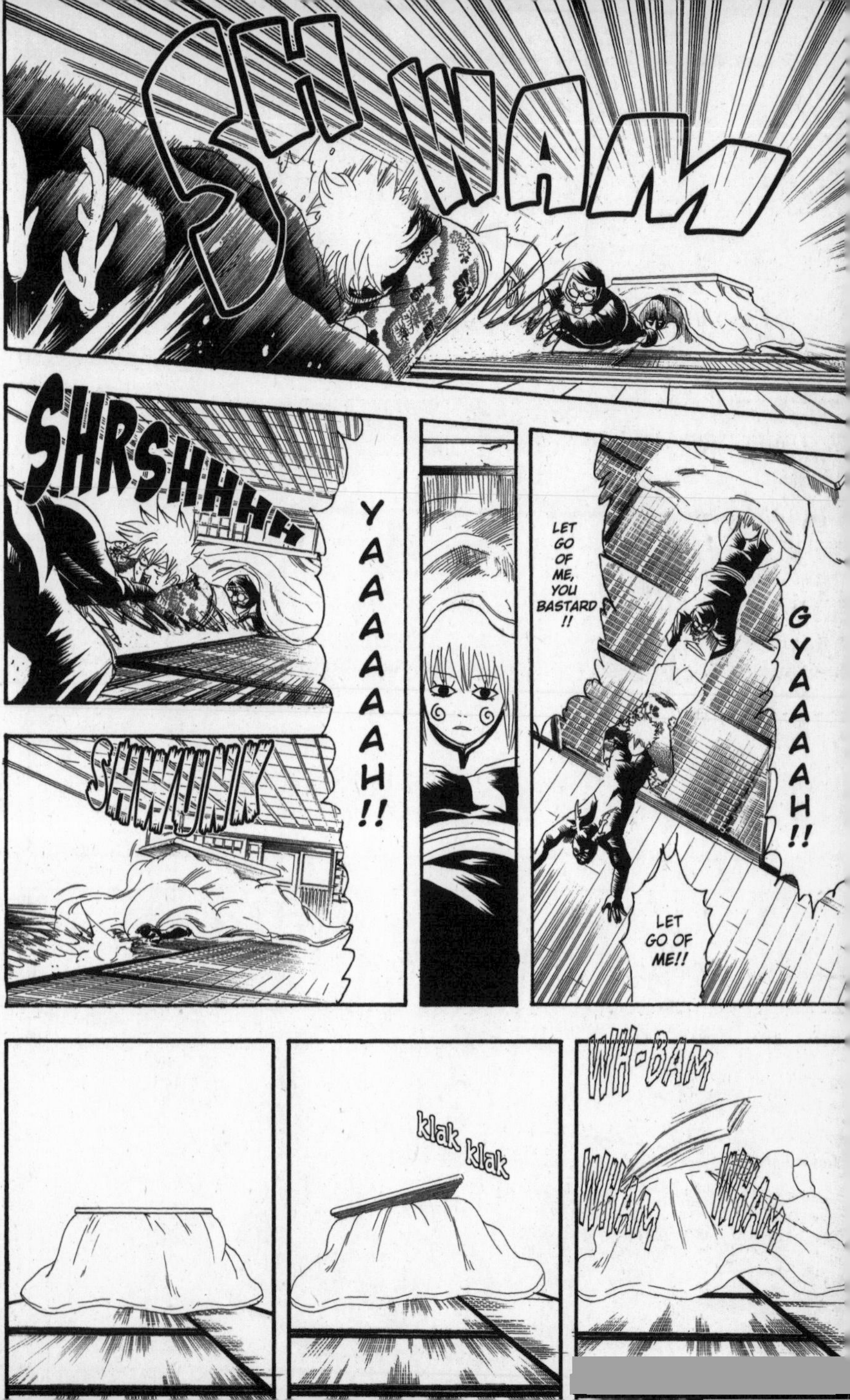
SH WAM
LET GO OF ME, YOU BASTARD!!
GYAAAAH!!
LET GO OF ME!!
SHRSHHHHH
YAAAAAAH!!
SHWUNK
WH-BAM
WHAM
WHAM
klak klak

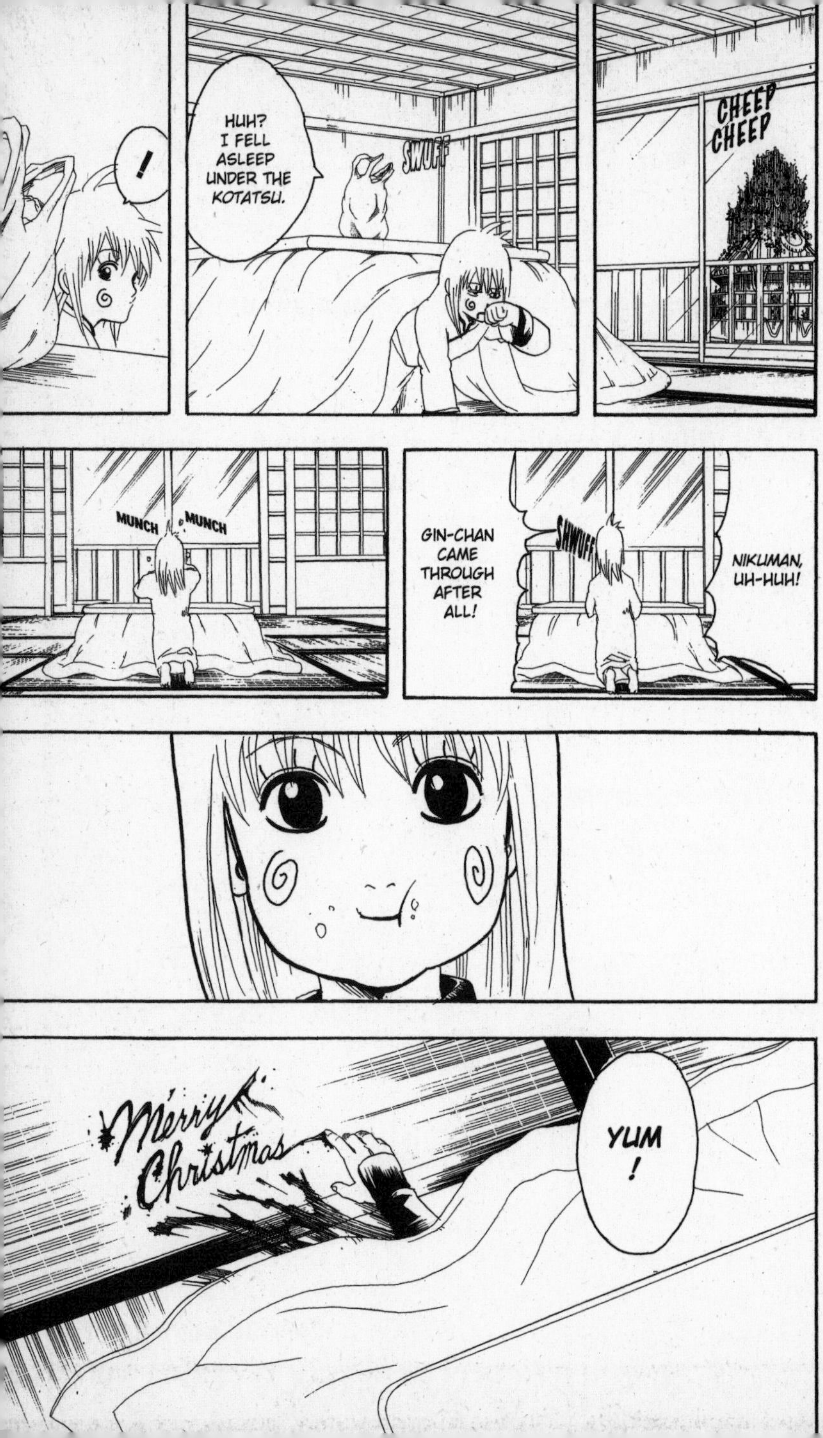
CHEEP CHEEP
HUH? I FELL ASLEEP UNDER THE KOTATSU.
SWUFF
!
NIKUMAN, UH-HUH!
SHWUFF
GIN-CHAN CAME THROUGH AFTER ALL!
MUNCH MUNCH
YUM!
Merry Christmas

<Question from I May Be An Inhabitant of the Sadistic Planet-san from Tokyo>

Don't you sometimes feel regret while writing *Gin Tama*, Sorachi Sensei?

<Answer>

I feel regret when I receive a letter like this.

(Q&A #36 is on page 126)

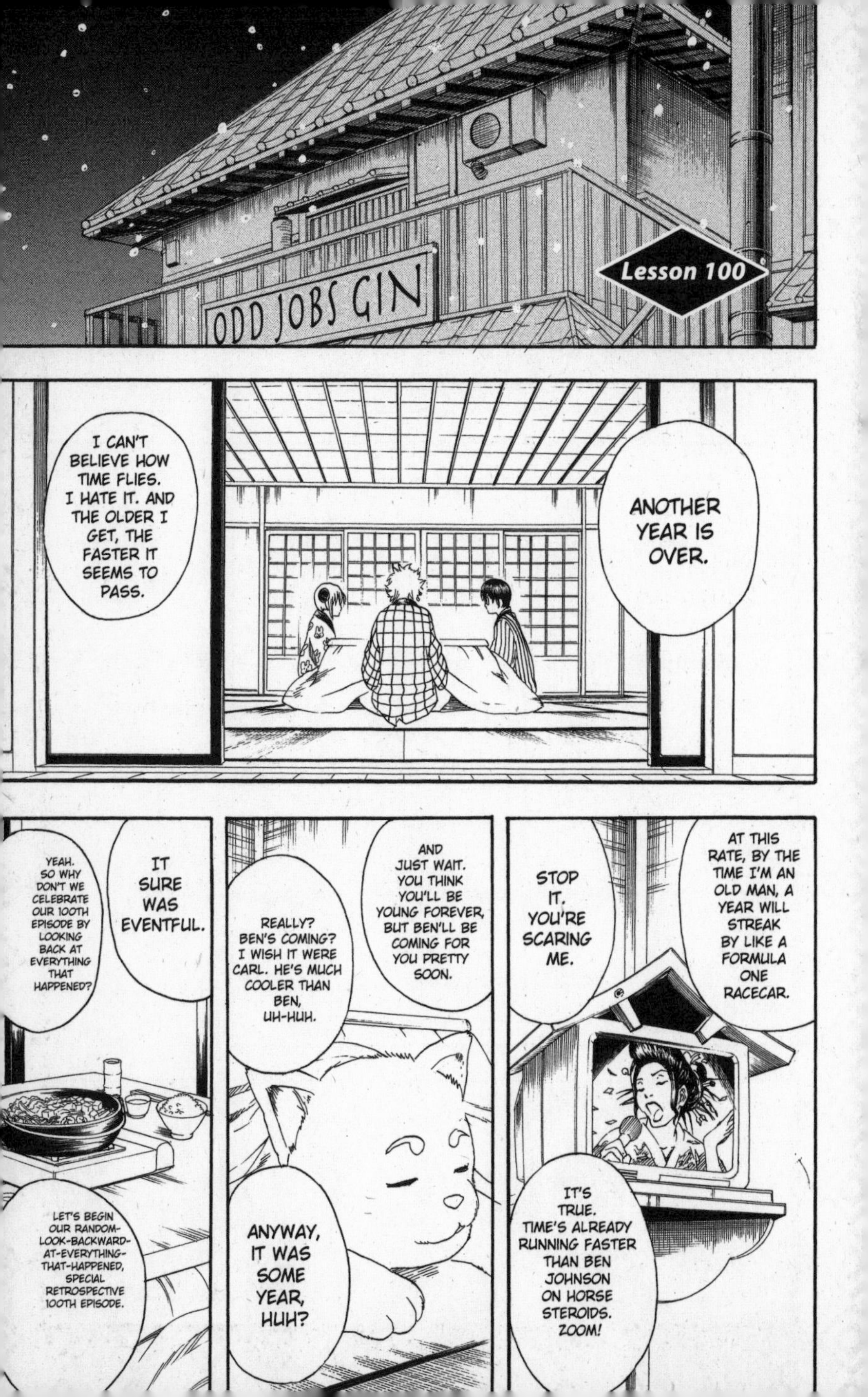
Lesson 100
ODD JOBS GIN
ANOTHER YEAR IS OVER.
I CAN'T BELIEVE HOW TIME FLIES. I HATE IT. AND THE OLDER I GET, THE FASTER IT SEEMS TO PASS.
AT THIS RATE, BY THE TIME I'M AN OLD MAN, A YEAR WILL STREAK BY LIKE A FORMULA ONE RACECAR.
STOP IT. YOU'RE SCARING ME.
IT'S TRUE. TIME'S ALREADY RUNNING FASTER THAN BEN JOHNSON ON HORSE STEROIDS. ZOOM!
AND JUST WAIT. YOU THINK YOU'LL BE YOUNG FOREVER, BUT BEN'LL BE COMING FOR YOU PRETTY SOON.
REALLY? BEN'S COMING? I WISH IT WERE CARL. HE'S MUCH COOLER THAN BEN, UH-HUH.
ANYWAY, IT WAS SOME YEAR, HUH?
IT SURE WAS EVENTFUL.
YEAH. SO WHY DON'T WE CELEBRATE OUR 100TH EPISODE BY LOOKING BACK AT EVERYTHING THAT HAPPENED?
LET'S BEGIN OUR RANDOM-LOOK-BACKWARD-AT-EVERYTHING-THAT-HAPPENED, SPECIAL RETROSPECTIVE 100TH EPISODE.

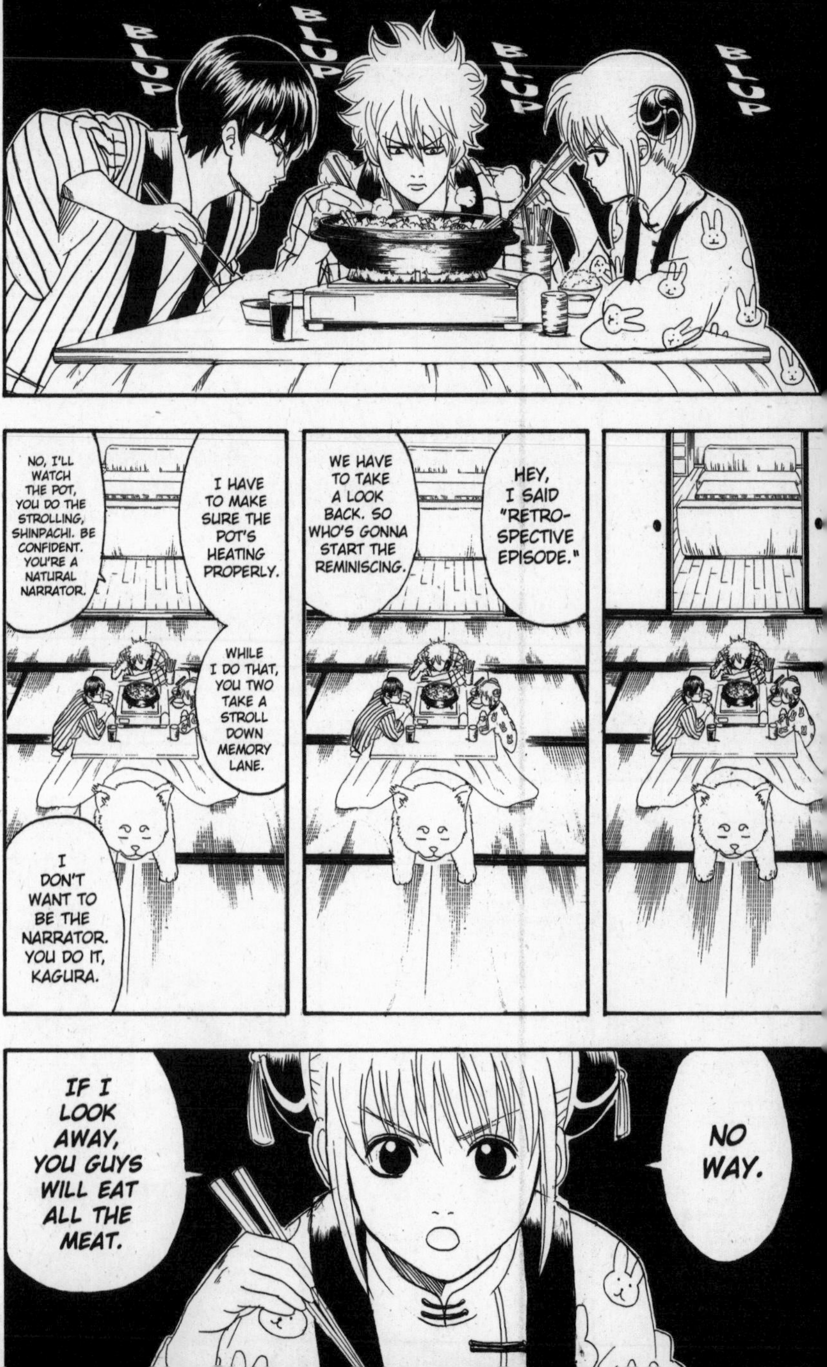
BLUP
BLUP
BLUP
BLUP
HEY, I SAID "RETRO-SPECTIVE EPISODE."
WE HAVE TO TAKE A LOOK BACK. SO WHO'S GONNA START THE REMINISCING.
I HAVE TO MAKE SURE THE POT'S HEATING PROPERLY.
WHILE I DO THAT, YOU TWO TAKE A STROLL DOWN MEMORY LANE.
NO, I'LL WATCH THE POT, YOU DO THE STROLLING, SHINPACHI. BE CONFIDENT. YOU'RE A NATURAL NARRATOR.
I DON'T WANT TO BE THE NARRATOR. YOU DO IT, KAGURA.
NO WAY.
IF I LOOK AWAY, YOU GUYS WILL EAT ALL THE MEAT.

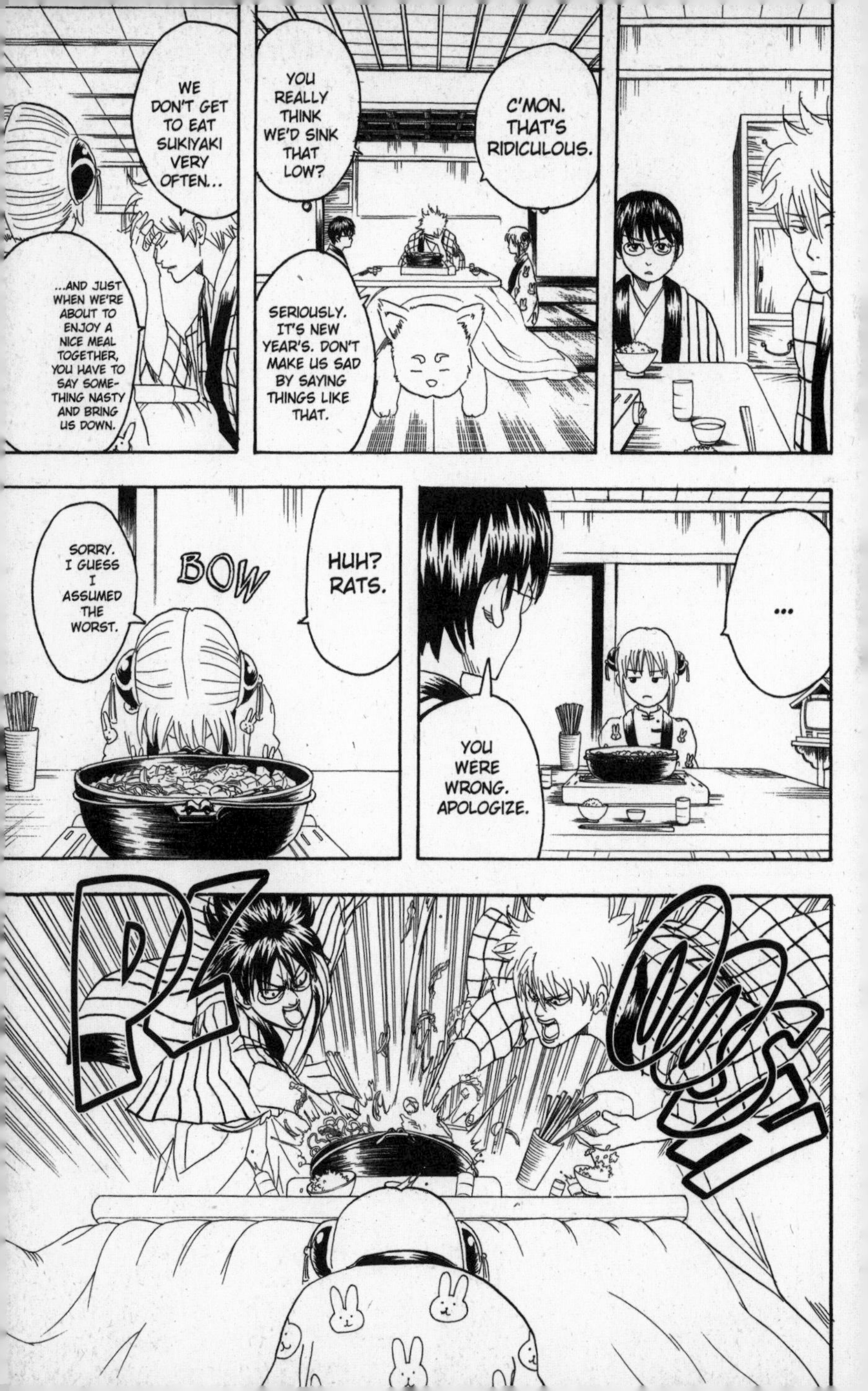
C'MON. THAT'S RIDICULOUS.
YOU REALLY THINK WE'D SINK THAT LOW?
SERIOUSLY. IT'S NEW YEAR'S. DON'T MAKE US SAD BY SAYING THINGS LIKE THAT.
WE DON'T GET TO EAT SUKIYAKI VERY OFTEN...
...AND JUST WHEN WE'RE ABOUT TO ENJOY A NICE MEAL TOGETHER, YOU HAVE TO SAY SOME-THING NASTY AND BRING US DOWN.
...
YOU WERE WRONG. APOLOGIZE.
HUH? RATS.
BOW
SORRY. I GUESS I ASSUMED THE WORST.

Lesson 100
A Shared Soup Pot Is a Microcosm of Life

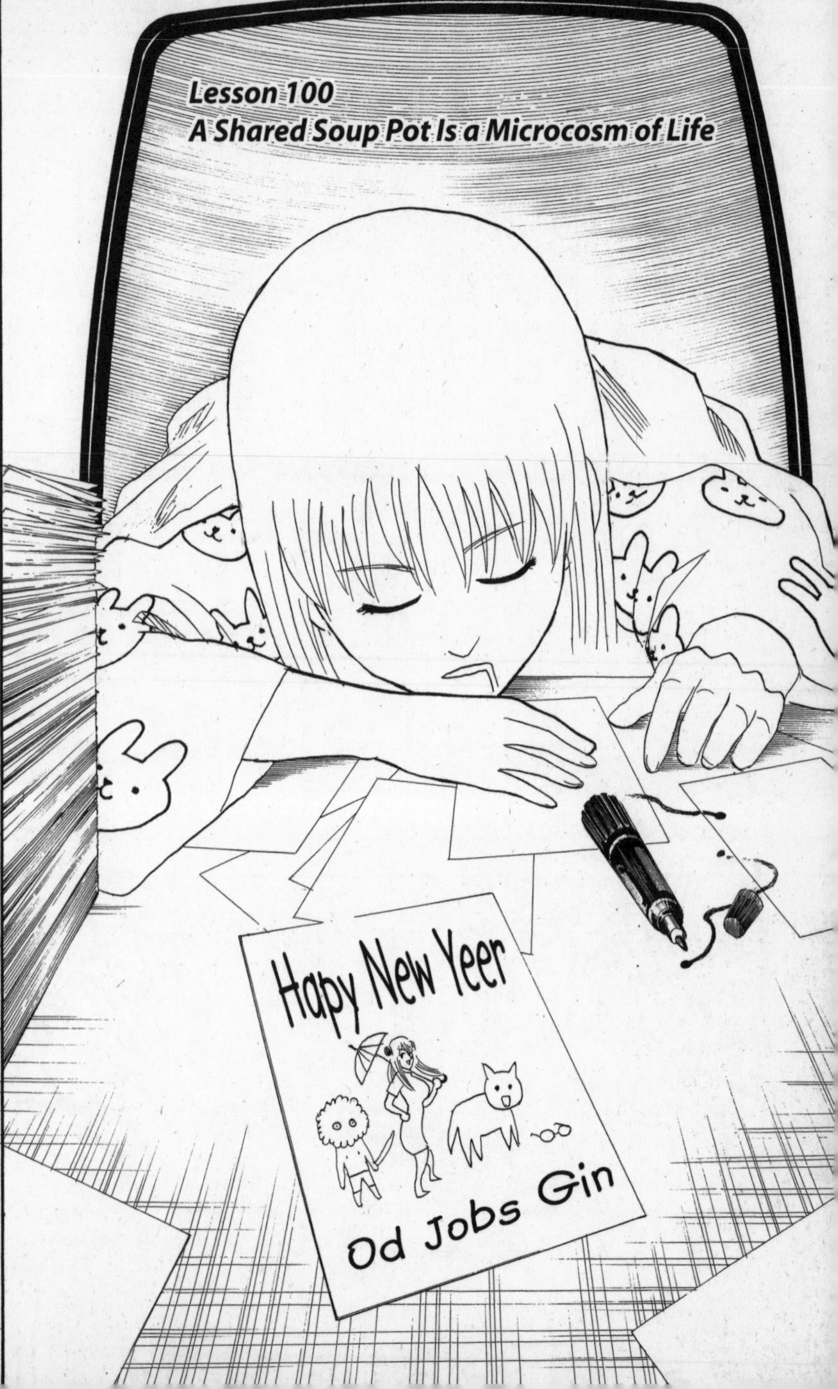
Hapy New Yeer
Od Jobs Gin

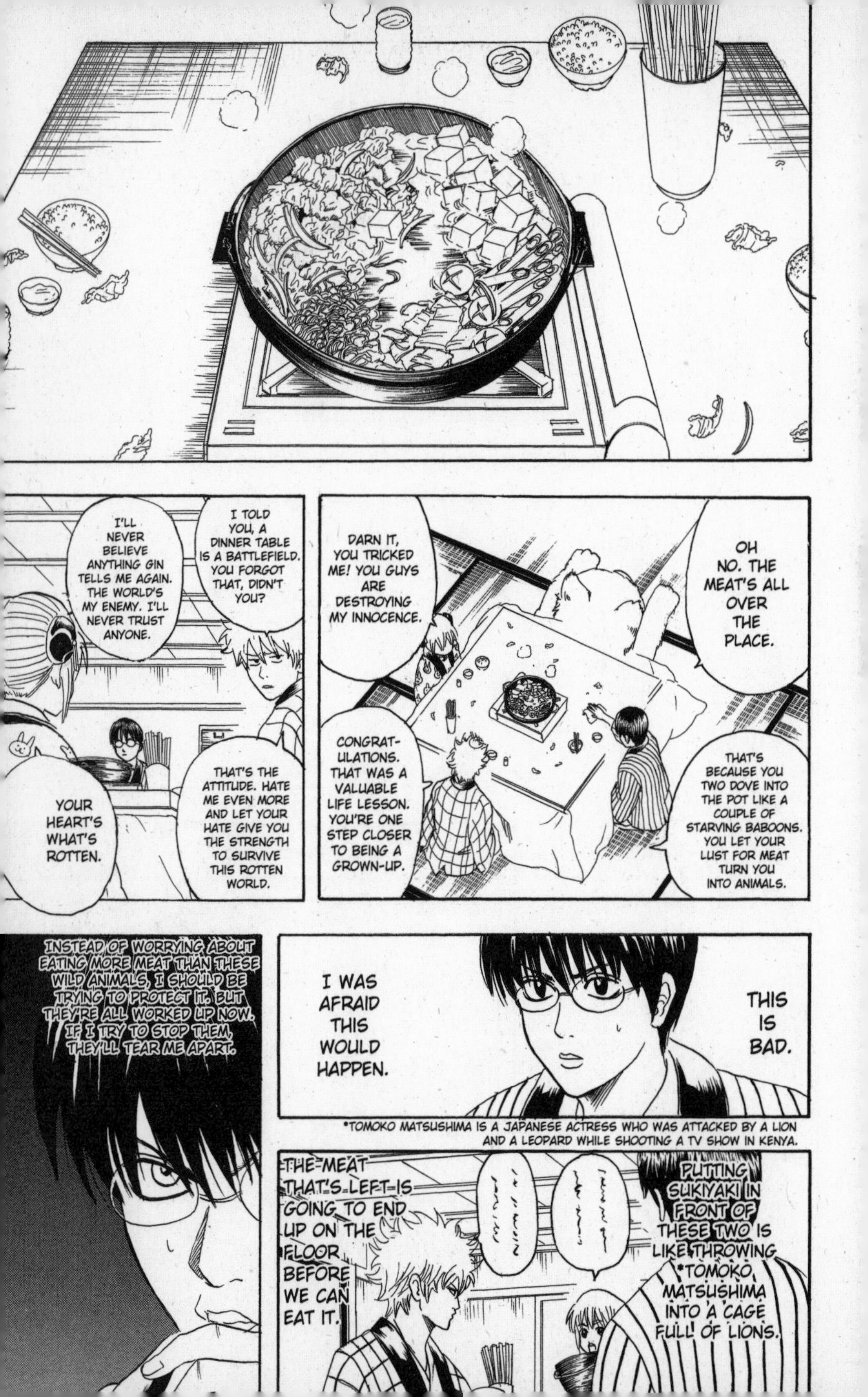
OH NO. THE MEAT'S ALL OVER THE PLACE.
DARN IT, YOU TRICKED ME! YOU GUYS ARE DESTROYING MY INNOCENCE.
THAT'S BECAUSE YOU TWO DOVE INTO THE POT LIKE A COUPLE OF STARVING BABOONS. YOU LET YOUR LUST FOR MEAT TURN YOU INTO ANIMALS.
CONGRATULATIONS. THAT WAS A VALUABLE LIFE LESSON. YOU'RE ONE STEP CLOSER TO BEING A GROWN-UP.
I TOLD YOU, A DINNER TABLE IS A BATTLEFIELD. YOU FORGOT THAT, DIDN'T YOU?
I'LL NEVER BELIEVE ANYTHING GIN TELLS ME AGAIN. THE WORLD'S MY ENEMY. I'LL NEVER TRUST ANYONE.
THAT'S THE ATTITUDE. HATE ME EVEN MORE AND LET YOUR HATE GIVE YOU THE STRENGTH TO SURVIVE THIS ROTTEN WORLD.
YOUR HEART'S WHAT'S ROTTEN.
THIS IS BAD.
I WAS AFRAID THIS WOULD HAPPEN.
*TOMOKO MATSUSHIMA IS A JAPANESE ACTRESS WHO WAS ATTACKED BY A LION AND A LEOPARD WHILE SHOOTING A TV SHOW IN KENYA.
PUTTING SUKIYAKI IN FRONT OF THESE TWO IS LIKE THROWING *TOMOKO MATSUSHIMA INTO A CAGE FULL OF LIONS.
THE MEAT THAT'S LEFT IS GOING TO END UP ON THE FLOOR BEFORE WE CAN EAT IT.
INSTEAD OF WORRYING ABOUT EATING MORE MEAT THAN THESE WILD ANIMALS, I SHOULD BE TRYING TO PROTECT IT. BUT THEY'RE ALL WORKED UP NOW. IF I TRY TO STOP THEM, THEY'LL TEAR ME APART.

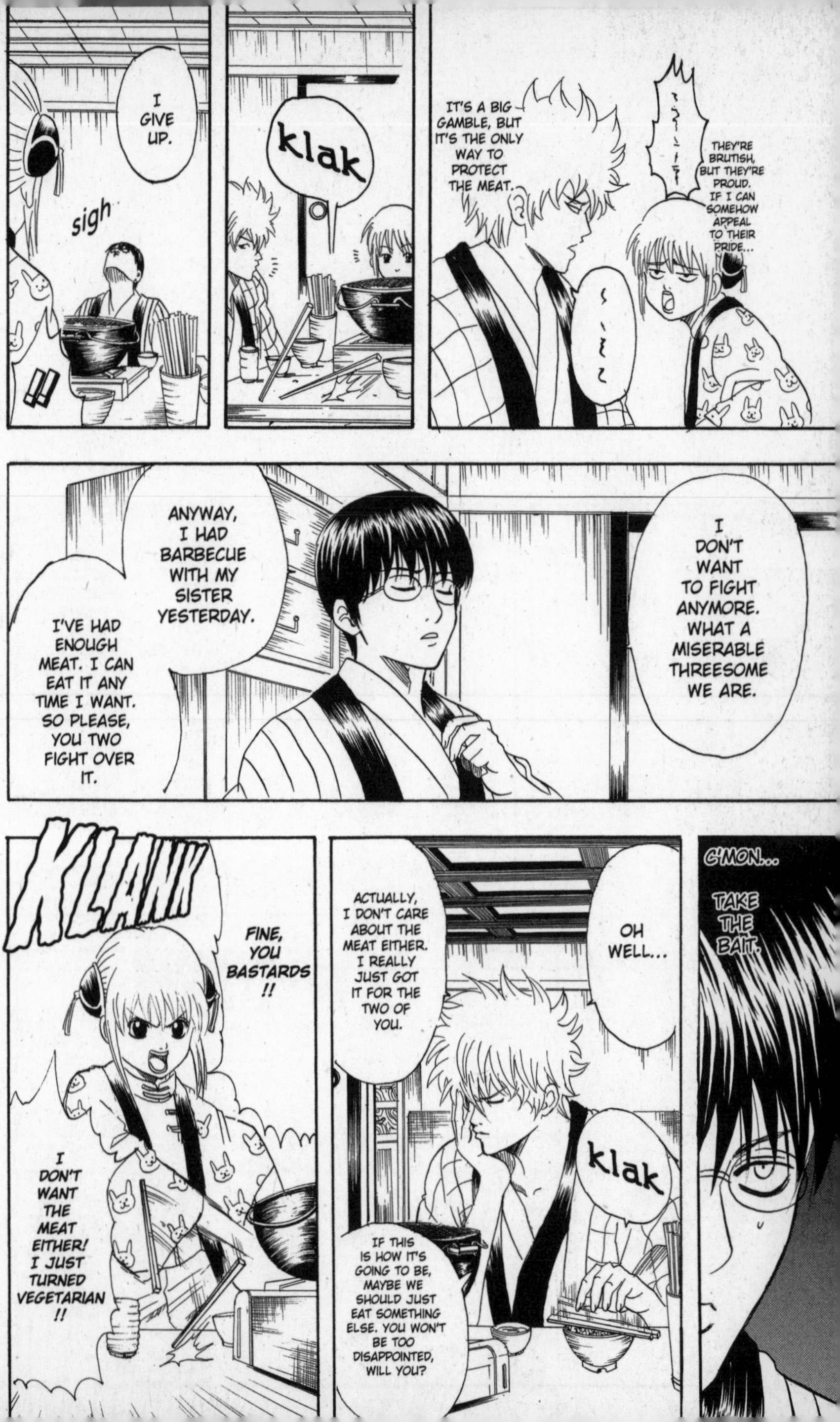
THEY'RE BRUTISH, BUT THEY'RE PROUD. IF I CAN SOMEHOW APPEAL TO THEIR PRIDE...
IT'S A BIG GAMBLE, BUT IT'S THE ONLY WAY TO PROTECT THE MEAT.
klak
I GIVE UP.
sigh
I DON'T WANT TO FIGHT ANYMORE. WHAT A MISERABLE THREESOME WE ARE.
ANYWAY, I HAD BARBECUE WITH MY SISTER YESTERDAY.
I'VE HAD ENOUGH MEAT. I CAN EAT IT ANY TIME I WANT. SO PLEASE, YOU TWO FIGHT OVER IT.
C'MON...
TAKE THE BAIT.
OH WELL...
ACTUALLY, I DON'T CARE ABOUT THE MEAT EITHER. I REALLY JUST GOT IT FOR THE TWO OF YOU.
klak
IF THIS IS HOW IT'S GOING TO BE, MAYBE WE SHOULD JUST EAT SOMETHING ELSE. YOU WON'T BE TOO DISAPPOINTED, WILL YOU?
KLANK
FINE, YOU BASTARDS !!
I DON'T WANT THE MEAT EITHER! I JUST TURNED VEGETARIAN !!

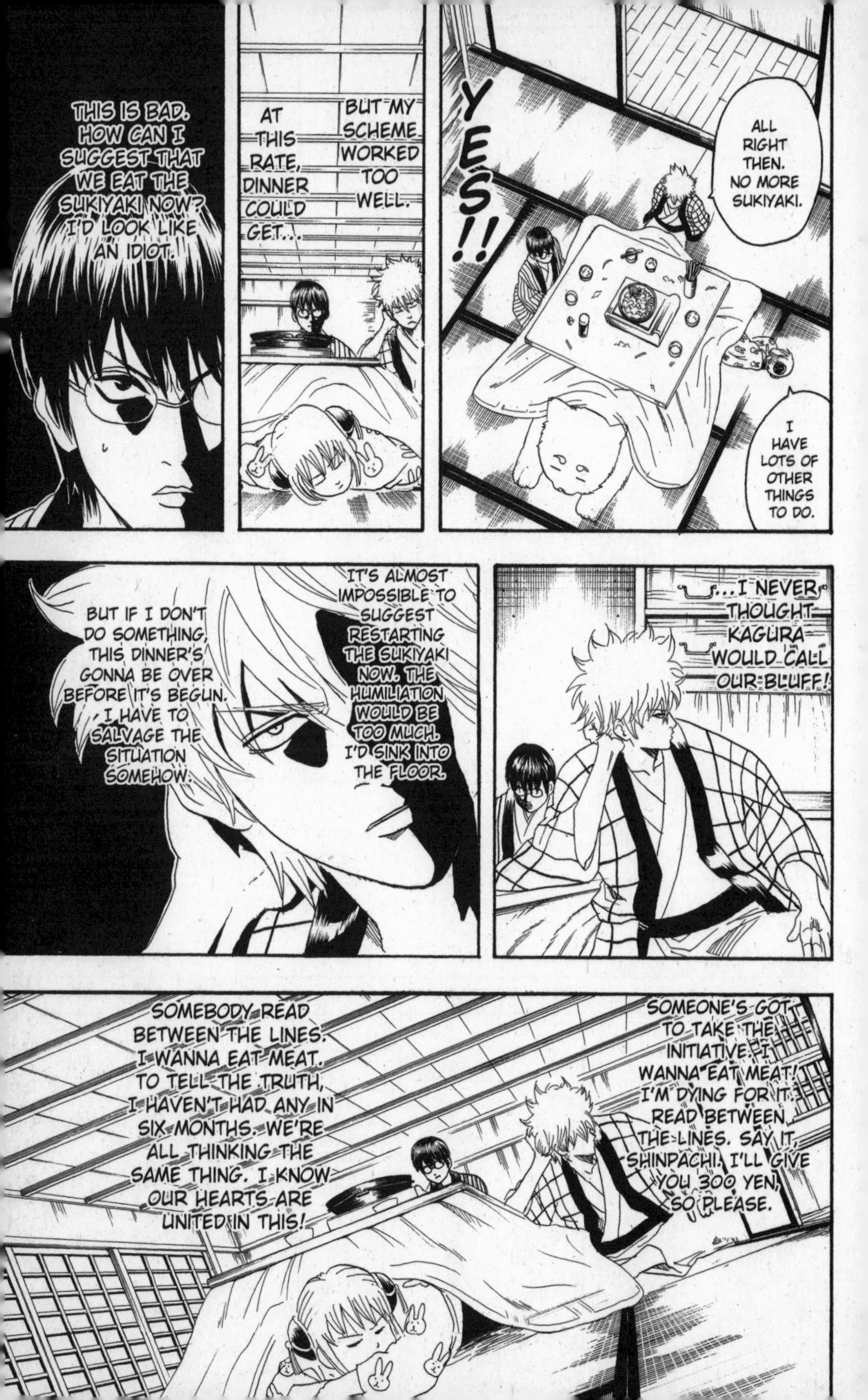
ALL RIGHT THEN. NO MORE SUKIYAKI.
I HAVE LOTS OF OTHER THINGS TO DO.
YES!!
BUT MY SCHEME WORKED TOO WELL.
AT THIS RATE, DINNER COULD GET...
THIS IS BAD. HOW CAN I SUGGEST THAT WE EAT THE SUKIYAKI NOW? I'D LOOK LIKE AN IDIOT.
...I NEVER THOUGHT KAGURA WOULD CALL OUR BLUFF!
IT'S ALMOST IMPOSSIBLE TO SUGGEST RESTARTING THE SUKIYAKI NOW. THE HUMILIATION WOULD BE TOO MUCH. I'D SINK INTO THE FLOOR.
BUT IF I DON'T DO SOMETHING, THIS DINNER'S GONNA BE OVER BEFORE IT'S BEGUN. I HAVE TO SALVAGE THE SITUATION SOMEHOW.
SOMEONE'S GOT TO TAKE THE INITIATIVE. I WANNA EAT MEAT! I'M DYING FOR IT. READ BETWEEN THE LINES. SAY IT, SHINPACHI. I'LL GIVE YOU 300 YEN, SO PLEASE.
SOMEBODY READ BETWEEN THE LINES. I WANNA EAT MEAT. TO TELL THE TRUTH, I HAVEN'T HAD ANY IN SIX MONTHS. WE'RE ALL THINKING THE SAME THING. I KNOW OUR HEARTS ARE UNITED IN THIS!

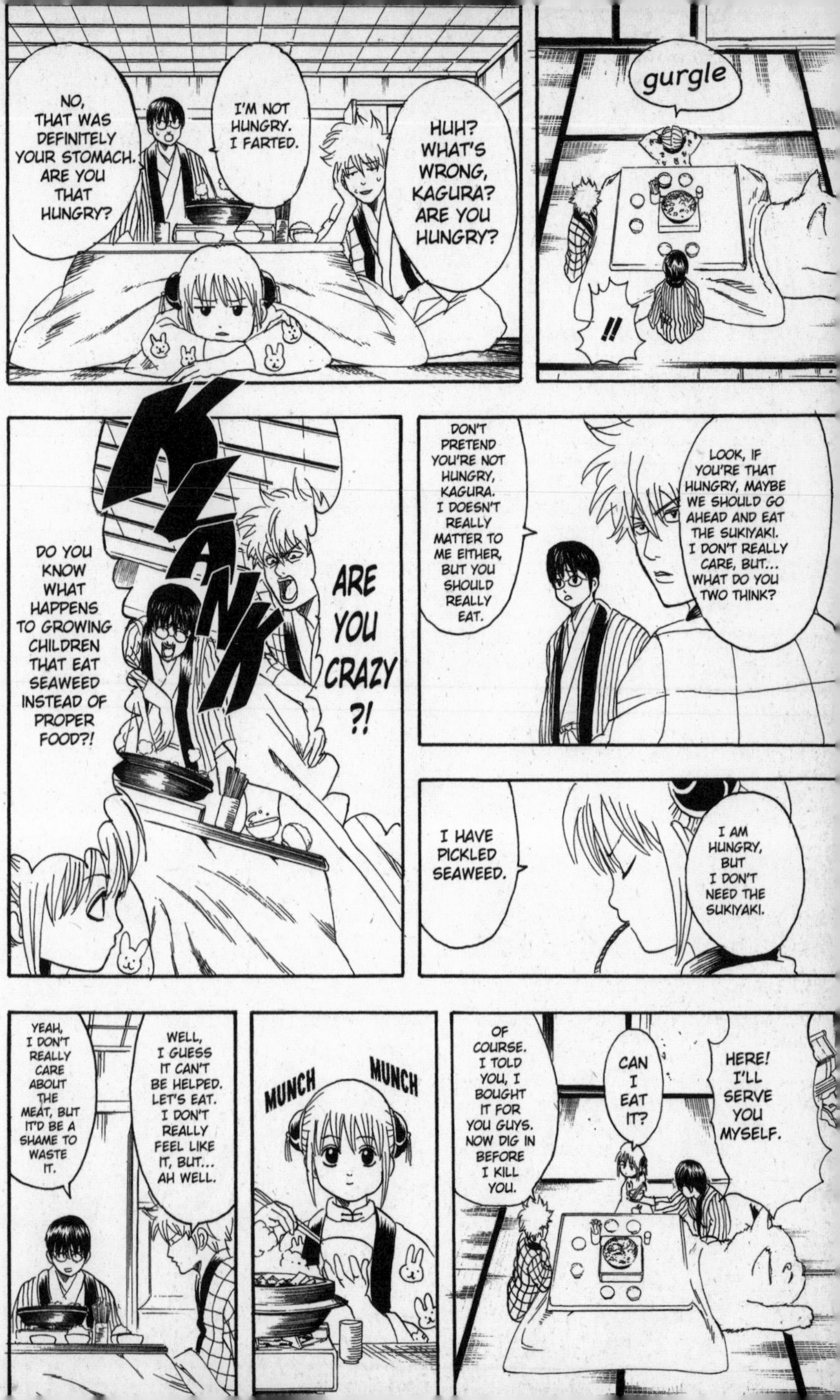
gurgle
!!
HUH? WHAT'S WRONG, KAGURA? ARE YOU HUNGRY?
I'M NOT HUNGRY. I FARTED.
NO, THAT WAS DEFINITELY YOUR STOMACH. ARE YOU THAT HUNGRY?
LOOK, IF YOU'RE THAT HUNGRY, MAYBE WE SHOULD GO AHEAD AND EAT THE SUKIYAKI. I DON'T REALLY CARE, BUT... WHAT DO YOU TWO THINK?
DON'T PRETEND YOU'RE NOT HUNGRY, KAGURA. I DOESN'T REALLY MATTER TO ME EITHER, BUT YOU SHOULD REALLY EAT.
I AM HUNGRY, BUT I DON'T NEED THE SUKIYAKI.
I HAVE PICKLED SEAWEED.
KLANK
ARE YOU CRAZY?!
DO YOU KNOW WHAT HAPPENS TO GROWING CHILDREN THAT EAT SEAWEED INSTEAD OF PROPER FOOD?!
HERE! I'LL SERVE YOU MYSELF.
CAN I EAT IT?
OF COURSE. I TOLD YOU, I BOUGHT IT FOR YOU GUYS. NOW DIG IN BEFORE I KILL YOU.
MUNCH
MUNCH
WELL, I GUESS IT CAN'T BE HELPED. LET'S EAT. I DON'T REALLY FEEL LIKE IT, BUT... AH WELL.
YEAH, I DON'T REALLY CARE ABOUT THE MEAT, BUT IT'D BE A SHAME TO WASTE IT.

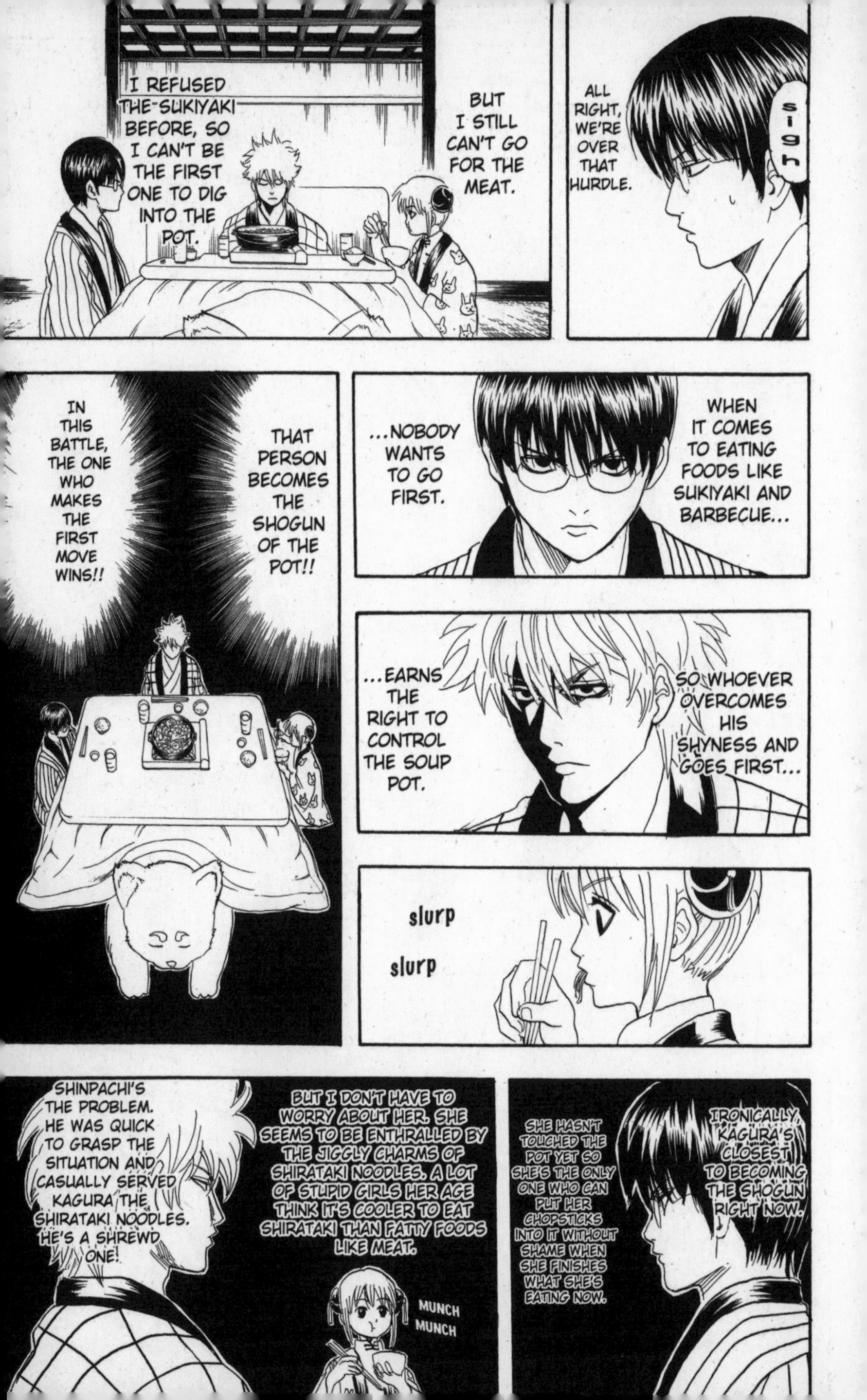

sigh
ALL RIGHT, WE'RE OVER THAT HURDLE.
BUT I STILL CAN'T GO FOR THE MEAT.
I REFUSED THE SUKIYAKI BEFORE, SO I CAN'T BE THE FIRST ONE TO DIG INTO THE POT.
WHEN IT COMES TO EATING FOODS LIKE SUKIYAKI AND BARBECUE...
...NOBODY WANTS TO GO FIRST.
SO WHOEVER OVERCOMES HIS SHYNESS AND GOES FIRST...
...EARNS THE RIGHT TO CONTROL THE SOUP POT.
slurp
slurp
THAT PERSON BECOMES THE SHOGUN OF THE POT!!
IN THIS BATTLE, THE ONE WHO MAKES THE FIRST MOVE WINS!!
IRONICALLY, KAGURA'S CLOSEST TO BECOMING THE SHOGUN RIGHT NOW.
SHE HASN'T TOUCHED THE POT YET SO SHE'S THE ONLY ONE WHO CAN PUT HER CHOPSTICKS INTO IT WITHOUT SHAME WHEN SHE FINISHES WHAT SHE'S EATING NOW.
BUT I DON'T HAVE TO WORRY ABOUT HER. SHE SEEMS TO BE ENTHRALLED BY THE JIGGLY CHARMS OF SHIRATAKI NOODLES. A LOT OF STUPID GIRLS HER AGE THINK IT'S COOLER TO EAT SHIRATAKI THAN FATTY FOODS LIKE MEAT.
SHINPACHI'S THE PROBLEM. HE WAS QUICK TO GRASP THE SITUATION AND CASUALLY SERVED KAGURA THE SHIRATAKI NOODLES. HE'S A SHREWD ONE!
MUNCH
MUNCH

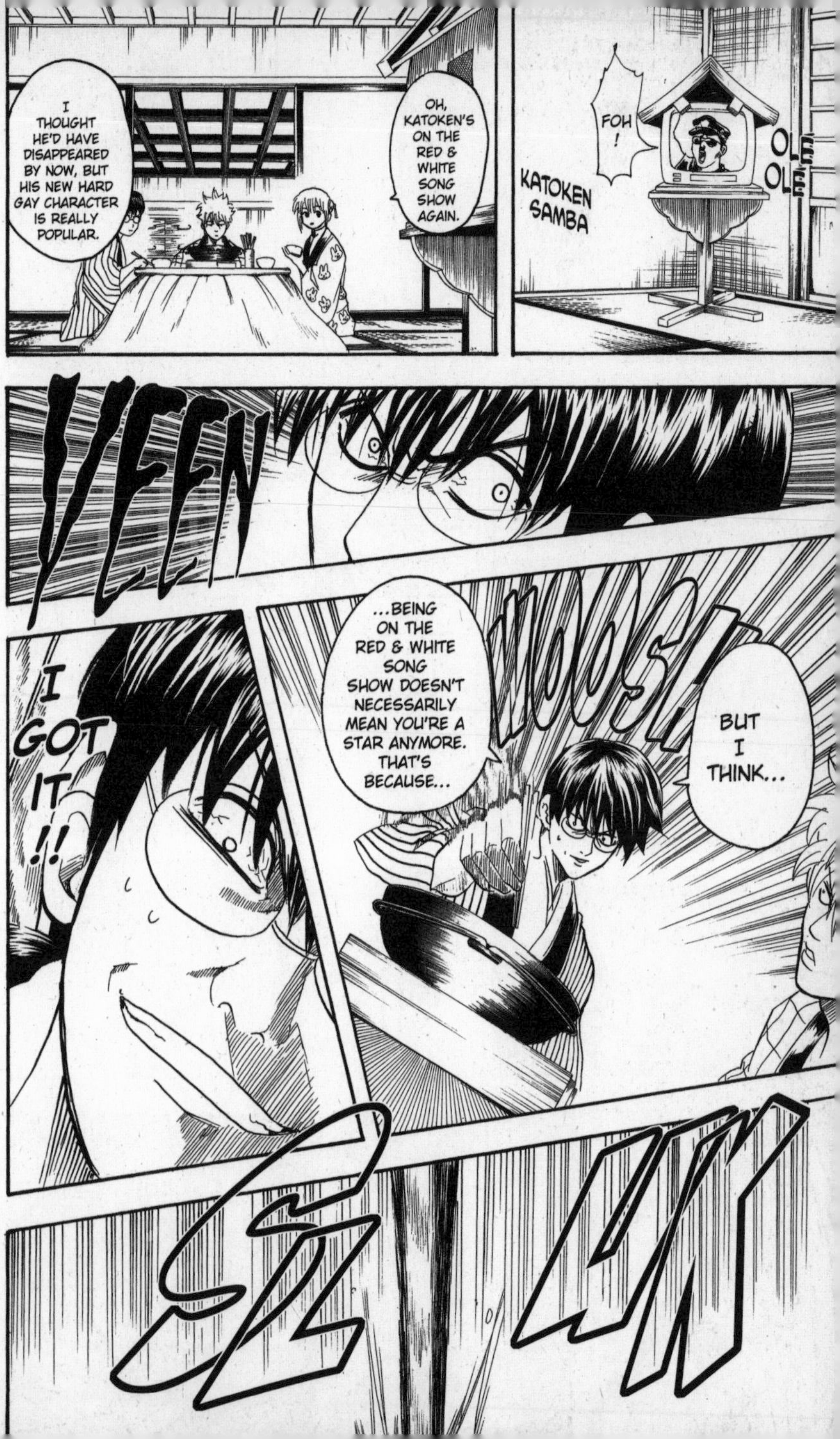
FOH!
OLE OLE
KATOKEN SAMBA
OH, KATOKEN'S ON THE RED & WHITE SONG SHOW AGAIN.
I THOUGHT HE'D HAVE DISAPPEARED BY NOW, BUT HIS NEW HARD GAY CHARACTER IS REALLY POPULAR.
YEEN
BUT I THINK...
...BEING ON THE RED & WHITE SONG SHOW DOESN'T NECESSARILY MEAN YOU'RE A STAR ANYMORE. THAT'S BECAUSE...
I GOT IT!!

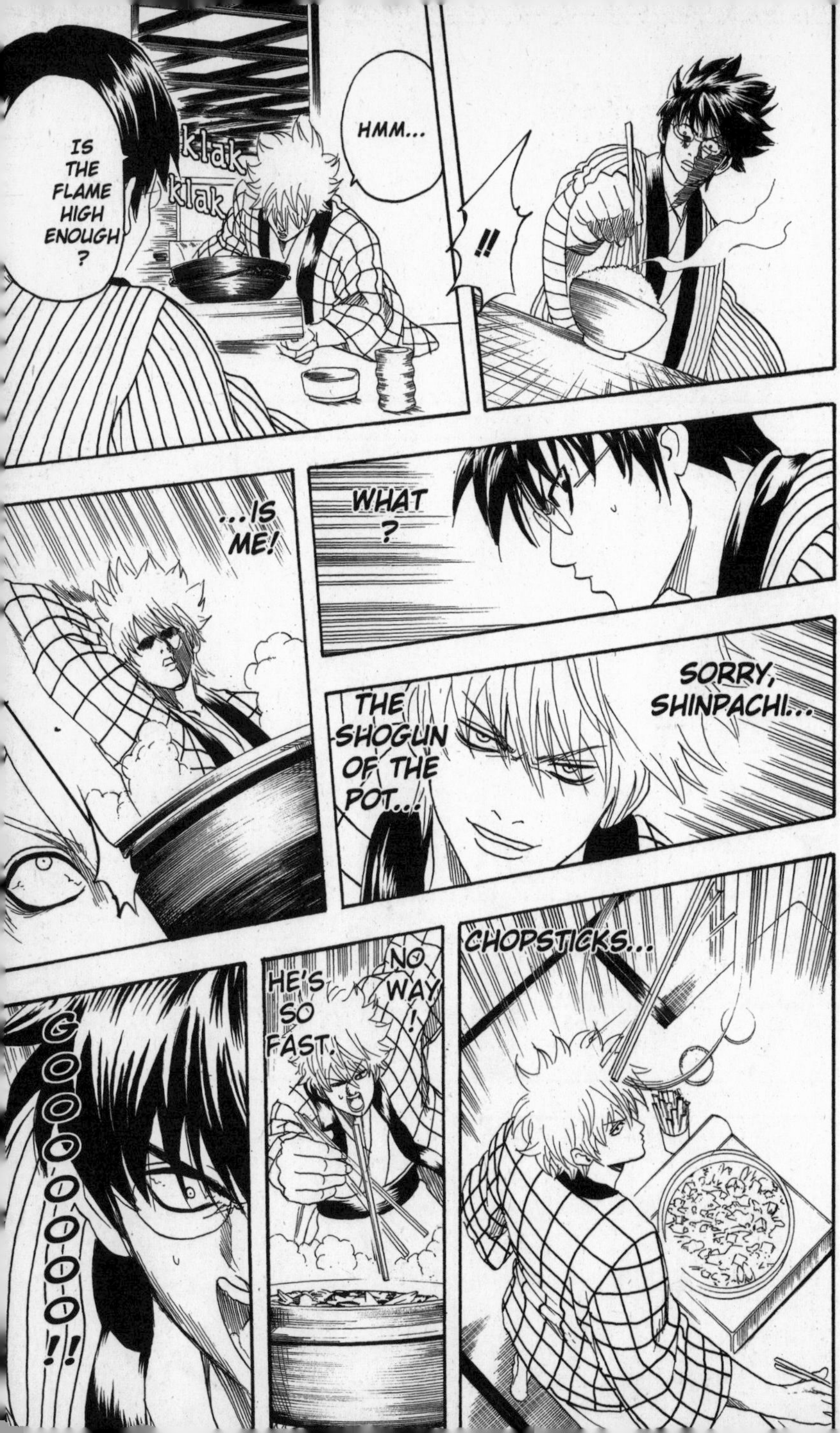
!!
HMM...
klak
klak
IS THE FLAME HIGH ENOUGH?
WHAT?
SORRY, SHINPACHI...
THE SHOGUN OF THE POT...
...IS ME!
CHOPSTICKS...
NO WAY!
HE'S SO FAST.
GOOOOOOOOOO!!

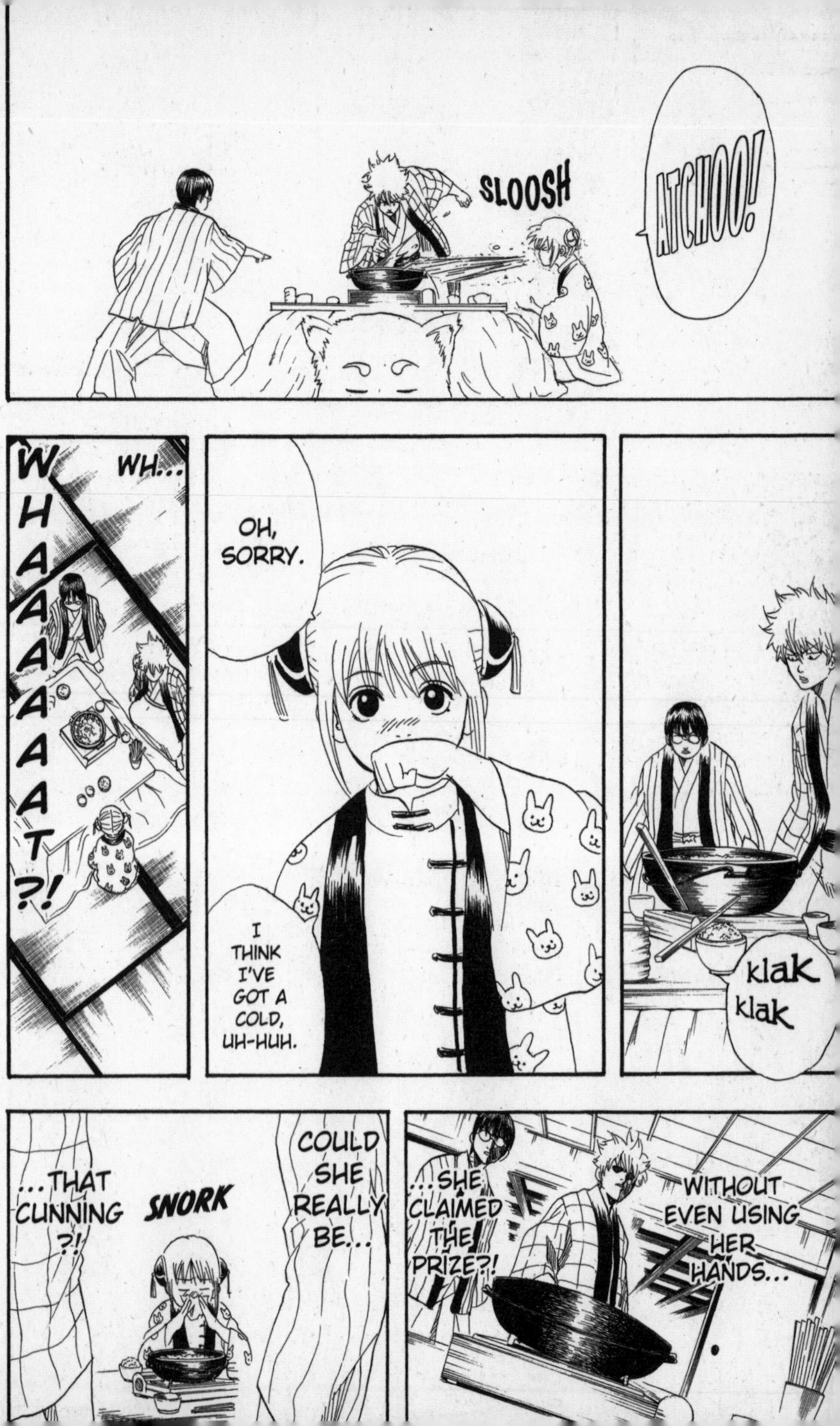
ATCHOO!
SLOOSH
klak klak
OH, SORRY.
I THINK I'VE GOT A COLD, UH-HUH.
WH...
WHAAAAAAAAAT?!
WITHOUT EVEN USING HER HANDS...
...SHE CLAIMED THE PRIZE?!
COULD SHE REALLY BE...
SNORK
...THAT CUNNING?!

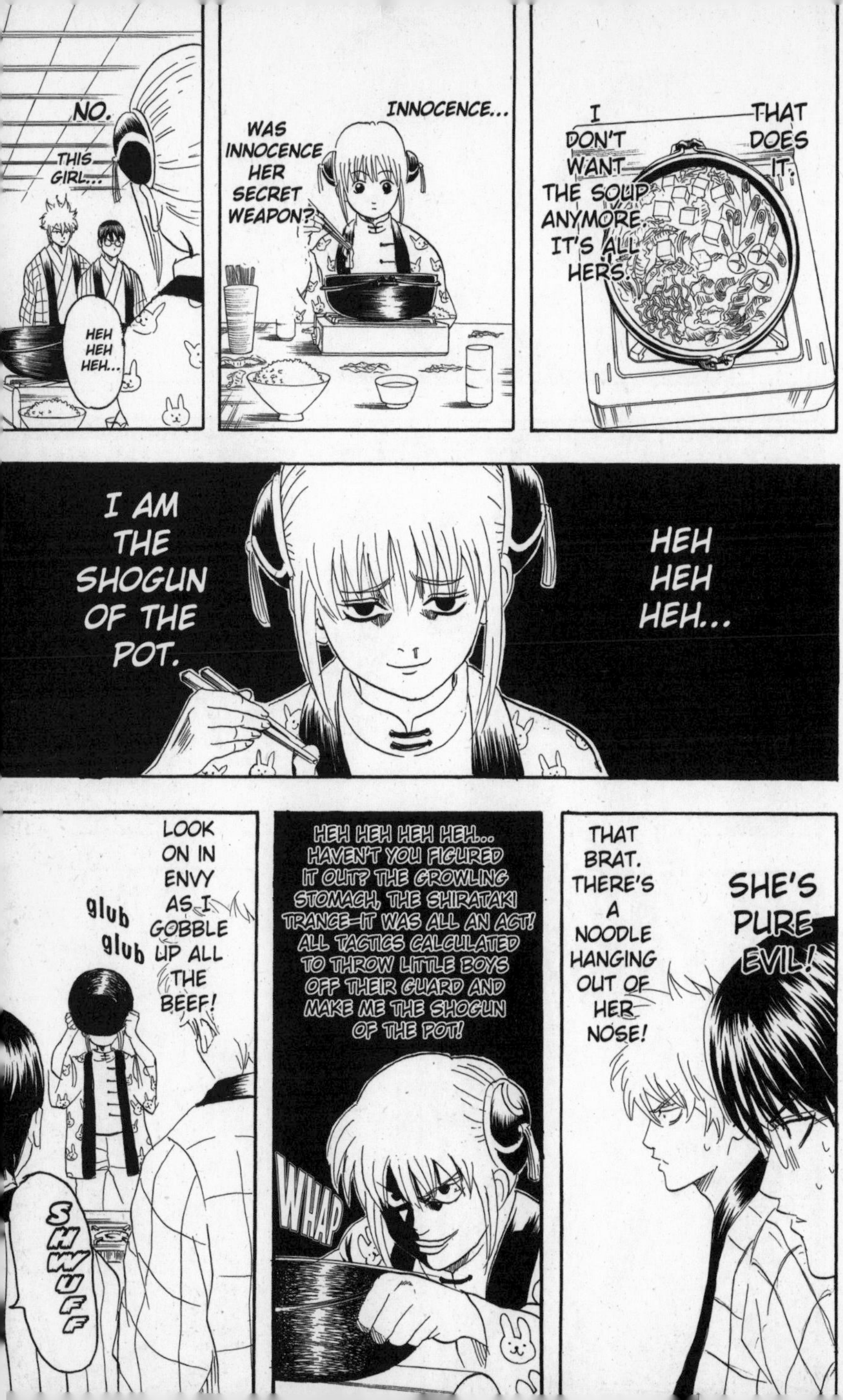
THAT DOES IT.
I DON'T WANT THE SOUP ANYMORE. IT'S ALL HERS.
INNOCENCE...
WAS INNOCENCE HER SECRET WEAPON?
NO.
THIS GIRL...
HEH HEH HEH...
HEH HEH HEH...
I AM THE SHOGUN OF THE POT.
SHE'S PURE EVIL!
THAT BRAT. THERE'S A NOODLE HANGING OUT OF HER NOSE!
HEH HEH HEH HEH... HAVEN'T YOU FIGURED IT OUT? THE GROWLING STOMACH, THE SHIRATAKI TRANCE—IT WAS ALL AN ACT! ALL TACTICS CALCULATED TO THROW LITTLE BOYS OFF THEIR GUARD AND MAKE ME THE SHOGUN OF THE POT!
WHAP
LOOK ON IN ENVY AS I GOBBLE UP ALL THE BEEF!
glub glub
SHWUFF

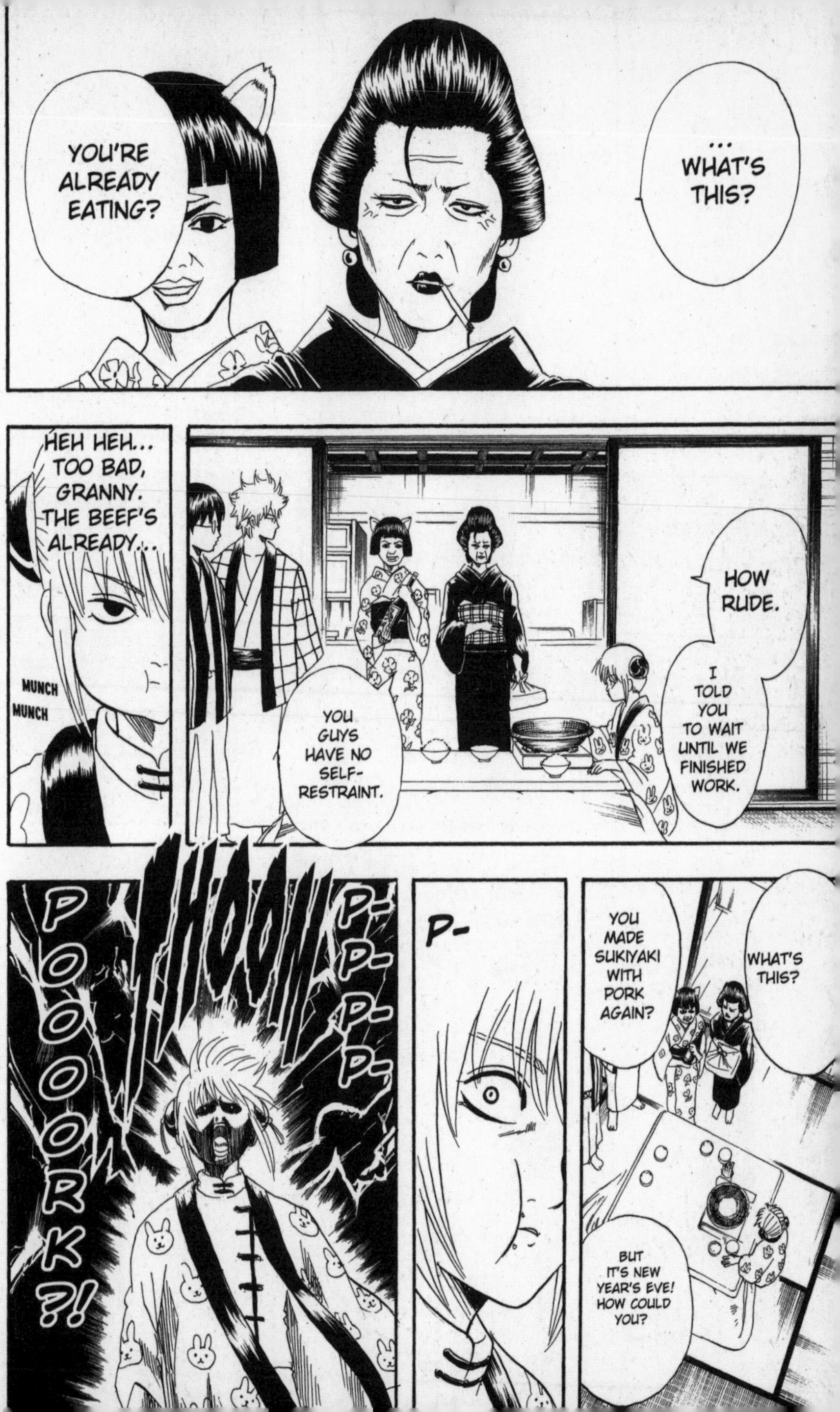
... WHAT'S THIS?
YOU'RE ALREADY EATING?
HOW RUDE.
I TOLD YOU TO WAIT UNTIL WE FINISHED WORK.
YOU GUYS HAVE NO SELF-RESTRAINT.
HEH HEH... TOO BAD, GRANNY. THE BEEF'S ALREADY...
MUNCH MUNCH
WHAT'S THIS?
YOU MADE SUKIYAKI WITH PORK AGAIN?
BUT IT'S NEW YEAR'S EVE! HOW COULD YOU?
P-
P-P-P-P-
POOOORK?!
WHOOM!

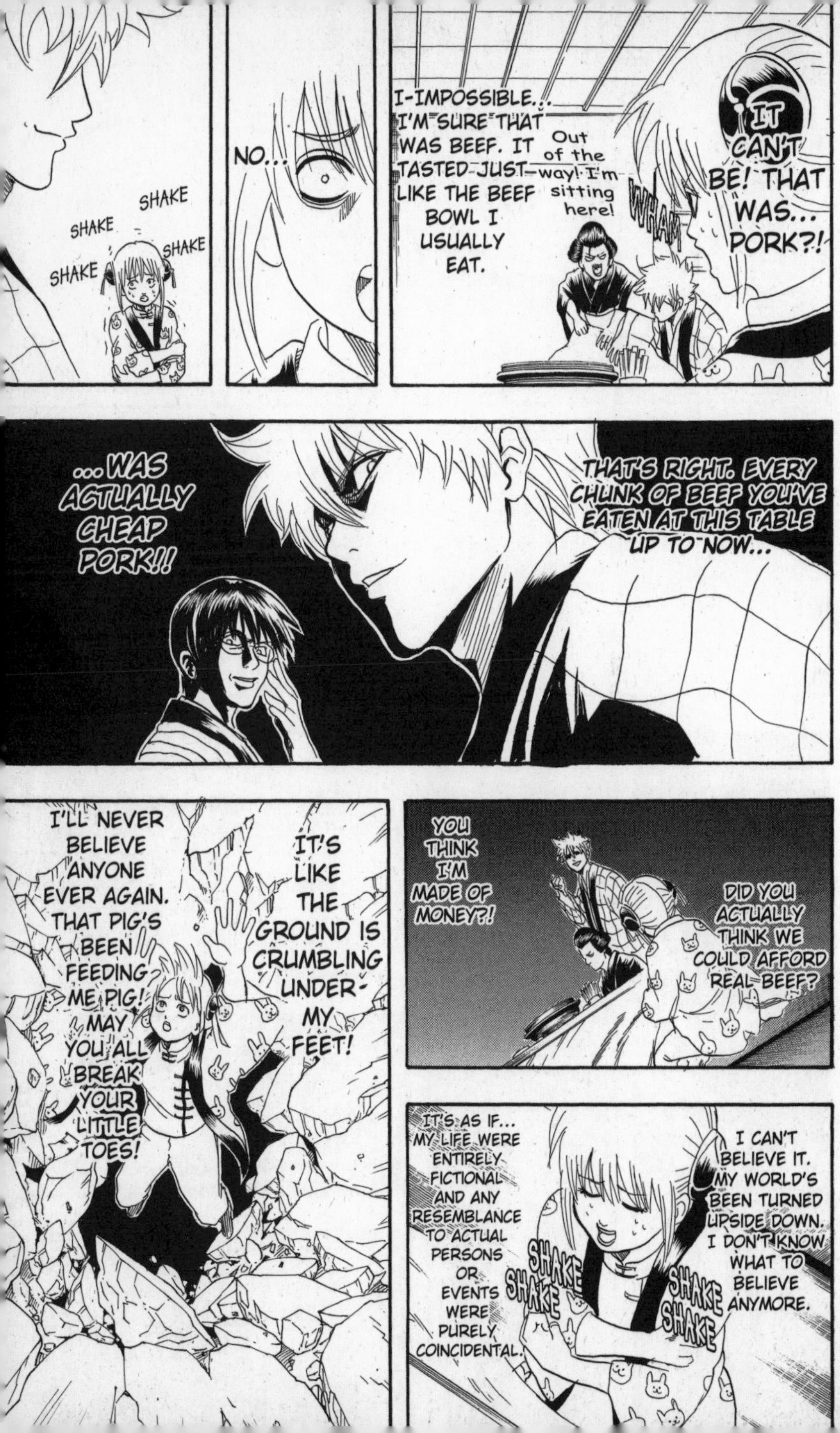
IT CAN'T BE! THAT WAS... PORK?!
I-IMPOSSIBLE... I'M SURE THAT WAS BEEF. IT TASTED JUST LIKE THE BEEF BOWL I USUALLY EAT.
Out of the way! I'm sitting here!
WHAM
NO...
SHAKE
SHAKE
SHAKE
SHAKE
THAT'S RIGHT. EVERY CHUNK OF BEEF YOU'VE EATEN AT THIS TABLE UP TO NOW...
...WAS ACTUALLY CHEAP PORK!!
DID YOU ACTUALLY THINK WE COULD AFFORD REAL BEEF?
YOU THINK I'M MADE OF MONEY?!
I CAN'T BELIEVE IT. MY WORLD'S BEEN TURNED UPSIDE DOWN. I DON'T KNOW WHAT TO BELIEVE ANYMORE.
SHAKE SHAKE
SHAKE SHAKE
IT'S AS IF... MY LIFE WERE ENTIRELY FICTIONAL AND ANY RESEMBLANCE TO ACTUAL PERSONS OR EVENTS WERE PURELY COINCIDENTAL.
IT'S LIKE THE GROUND IS CRUMBLING UNDER MY FEET!
I'LL NEVER BELIEVE ANYONE EVER AGAIN. THAT PIG'S BEEN FEEDING ME PIG! MAY YOU ALL BREAK YOUR LITTLE TOES!

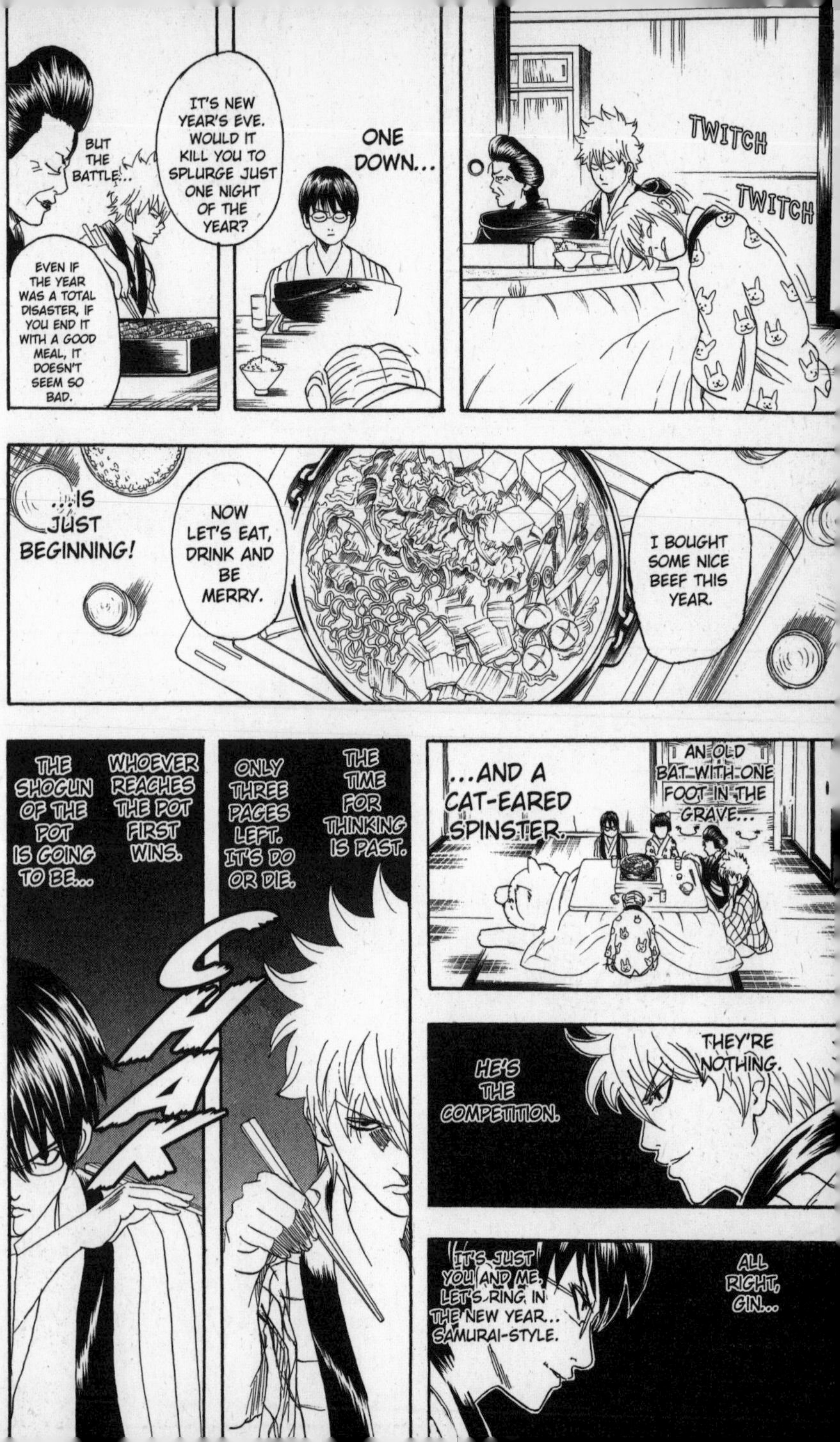
TWITCH
TWITCH
ONE DOWN...
IT'S NEW YEAR'S EVE. WOULD IT KILL YOU TO SPLURGE JUST ONE NIGHT OF THE YEAR?
BUT THE BATTLE...
EVEN IF THE YEAR WAS A TOTAL DISASTER, IF YOU END IT WITH A GOOD MEAL, IT DOESN'T SEEM SO BAD.
I BOUGHT SOME NICE BEEF THIS YEAR.
NOW LET'S EAT, DRINK AND BE MERRY.
...IS JUST BEGINNING!
AN OLD BAT WITH ONE FOOT IN THE GRAVE...
...AND A CAT-EARED SPINSTER.
THEY'RE NOTHING.
HE'S THE COMPETITION.
ALL RIGHT, GIN...
IT'S JUST YOU AND ME. LET'S RING IN THE NEW YEAR... SAMURAI-STYLE.
THE TIME FOR THINKING IS PAST.
ONLY THREE PAGES LEFT. IT'S DO OR DIE.
WHOEVER REACHES THE POT FIRST WINS.
THE SHOGUN OF THE POT IS GOING TO BE...

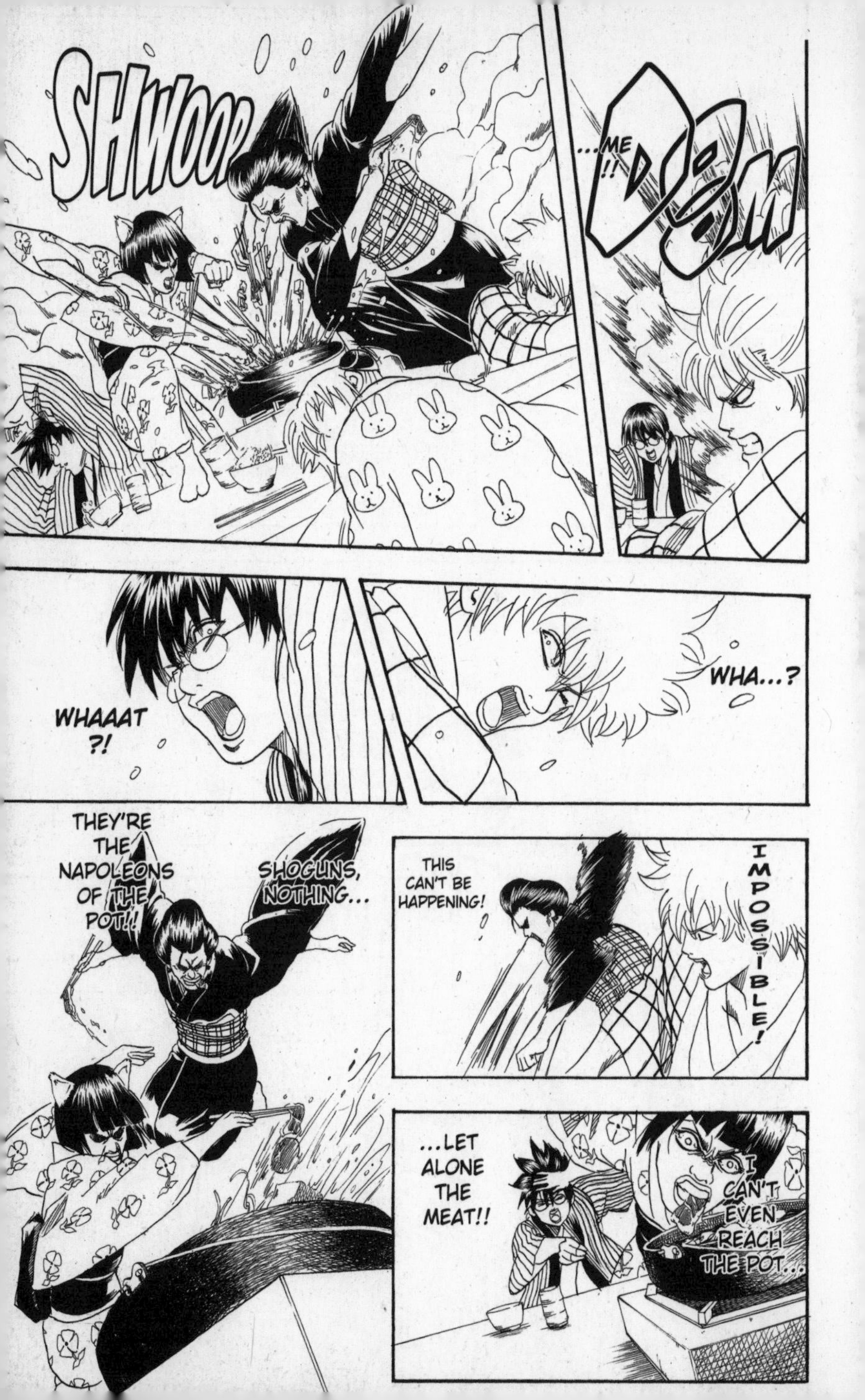
DOOM
...ME !!
SHWOOP
WHA...?
WHAAAT ?!
IMPOSSIBLE!
THIS CAN'T BE HAPPENING!
I CAN'T EVEN REACH THE POT...
...LET ALONE THE MEAT!!
SHOGUNS, NOTHING...
THEY'RE THE NAPOLEONS OF THE POT!!

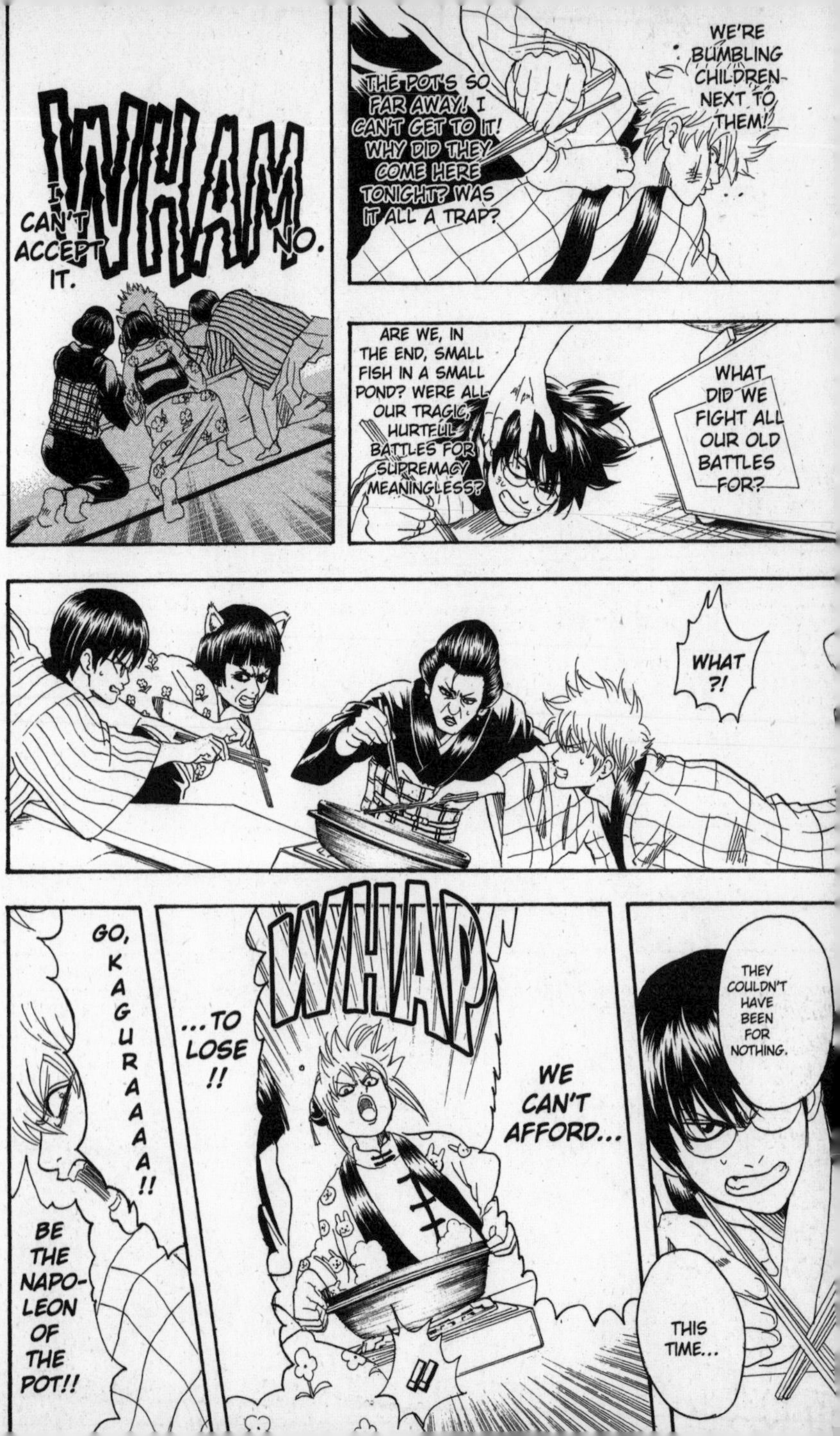
WE'RE BUMBLING CHILDREN NEXT TO THEM!
THE POT'S SO FAR AWAY! I CAN'T GET TO IT! WHY DID THEY COME HERE TONIGHT? WAS IT ALL A TRAP?
WHAT DID WE FIGHT ALL OUR OLD BATTLES FOR?
ARE WE, IN THE END, SMALL FISH IN A SMALL POND? WERE ALL OUR TRAGIC, HURTFUL BATTLES FOR SUPREMACY MEANINGLESS?
WHAM
NO.
I CAN'T ACCEPT IT.
WHAT ?!
THEY COULDN'T HAVE BEEN FOR NOTHING.
THIS TIME...
WHAP
WE CAN'T AFFORD...
...TO LOSE !!
!!
GO, KAGURAAAAAA!!
BE THE NAPOLEON OF THE POT!!

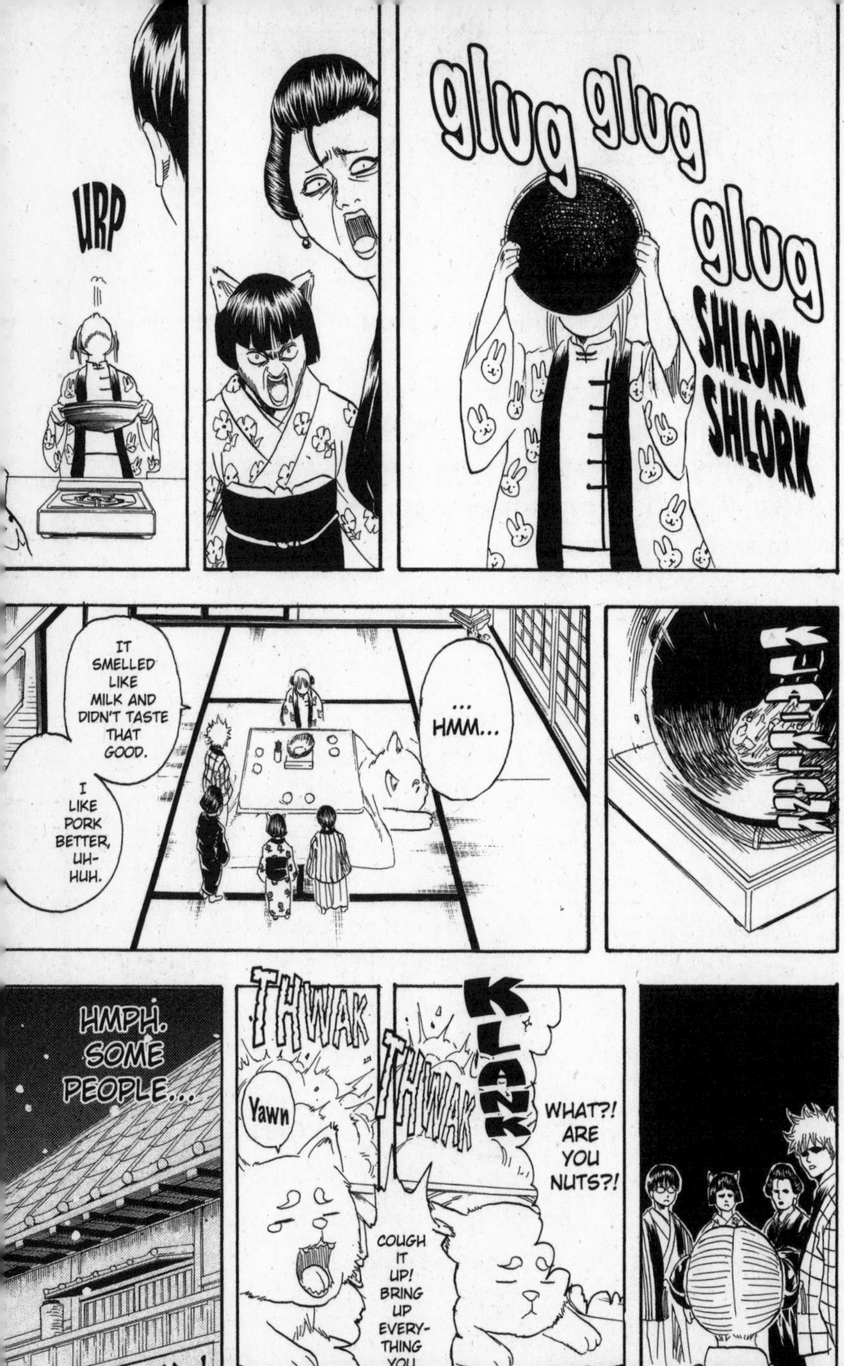

glug glug
glug
SHLORK
SHLORK
URP
... HMM...
IT SMELLED LIKE MILK AND DIDN'T TASTE THAT GOOD.
I LIKE PORK BETTER, UH-HUH.
KLANK
WHAT?! ARE YOU NUTS?!
THWAK
COUGH IT UP! BRING UP EVERY-THING YOU JUST ATE!!
THWAK
Yawn
HMPH. SOME PEOPLE...
D JOBS GIN

Sorachi's Q&A
Hanging with the Readers #36

<Question from Kudo-san of Aomori prefecture>

In *"The 58th Night,"* Lavi shouts, "These things happen in war!!" [see *D. Gray-man*, vol. 7, p.37] Is it my imagination or are there tears in his eyes? No, it can't be my imagination. Be a man and answer my question.

<Answer>

I think he was crying too. Well, Lavi's seen some hard times. He wants to believe that it couldn't be helped, but he can't help what he feels. That's how I see it. But then, I'm not Lavi so I can't really be sure. No, I'm not Lavi and this manga is not D.Gray-man! This postcard was sent to the letters section of D.Gray-man, the Discussion Room, but somehow it ended up here. I will personally deliver it to its intended destination, so don't worry, Kudo-san. But since Kudo-san probably doesn't read Gin Tama, he'll never know.

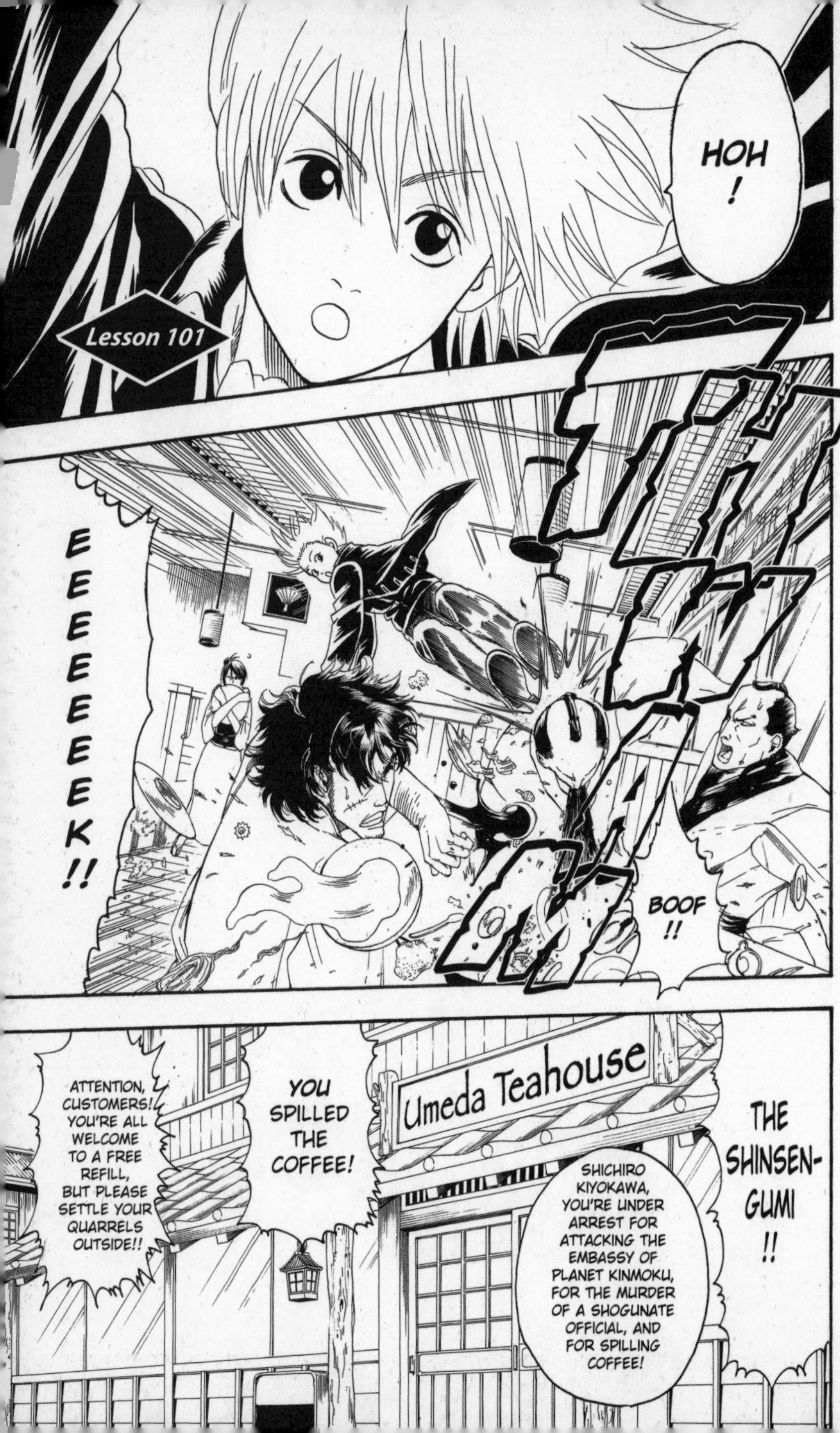
HOH!
Lesson 101
BOOF!!
EEEEEEEK!!
THE SHINSEN-GUMI!!
SHICHIRO KIYOKAWA, YOU'RE UNDER ARREST FOR ATTACKING THE EMBASSY OF PLANET KINMOKU, FOR THE MURDER OF A SHOGUNATE OFFICIAL, AND FOR SPILLING COFFEE!
Umeda Teahouse
YOU SPILLED THE COFFEE!
ATTENTION, CUSTOMERS! YOU'RE ALL WELCOME TO A FREE REFILL, BUT PLEASE SETTLE YOUR QUARRELS OUTSIDE!!

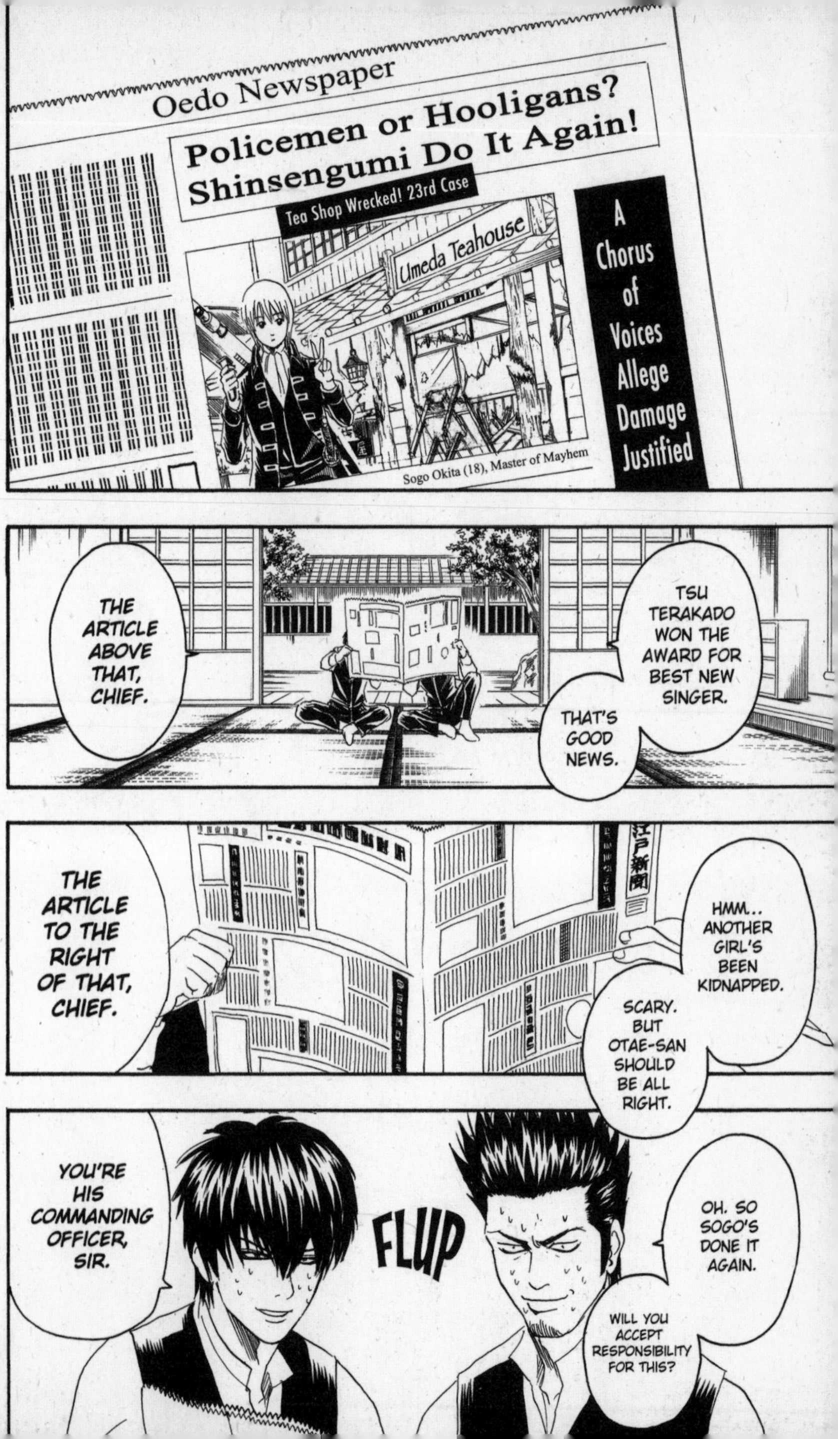
Oedo Newspaper
Policemen or Hooligans? Shinsengumi Do It Again!
Tea Shop Wrecked! 23rd Case
A Chorus of Voices Allege Damage Justified
Umeda Teahouse
Sogo Okita (18), Master of Mayhem
TSU TERAKADO WON THE AWARD FOR BEST NEW SINGER.
THAT'S GOOD NEWS.
THE ARTICLE ABOVE THAT, CHIEF.
江戸新聞
HMM... ANOTHER GIRL'S BEEN KIDNAPPED.
SCARY. BUT OTAE-SAN SHOULD BE ALL RIGHT.
THE ARTICLE TO THE RIGHT OF THAT, CHIEF.
OH. SO SOGO'S DONE IT AGAIN.
FLUP
WILL YOU ACCEPT RESPONSIBILITY FOR THIS?
YOU'RE HIS COMMANDING OFFICER, SIR.

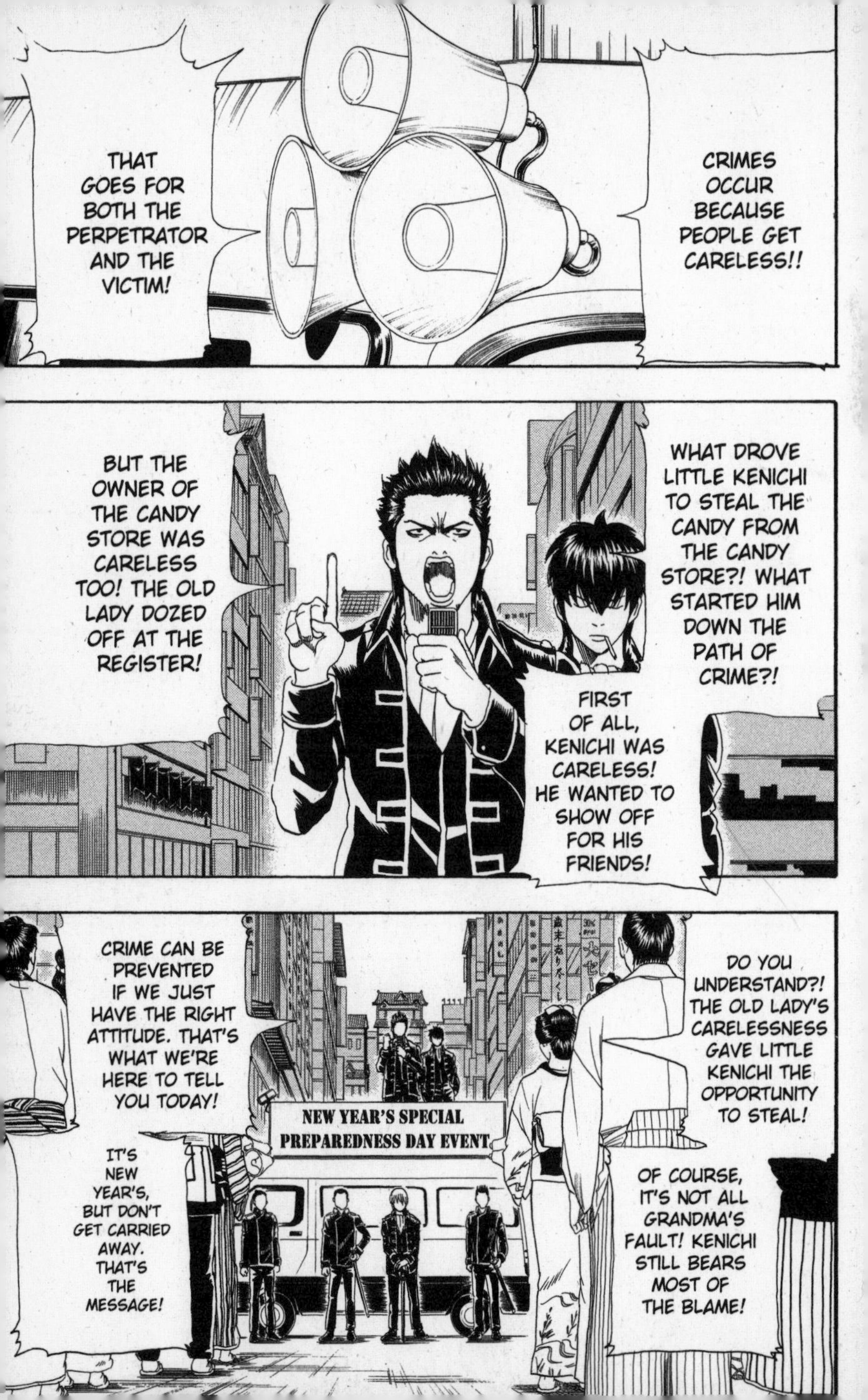
CRIMES OCCUR BECAUSE PEOPLE GET CARELESS!!
THAT GOES FOR BOTH THE PERPETRATOR AND THE VICTIM!
WHAT DROVE LITTLE KENICHI TO STEAL THE CANDY FROM THE CANDY STORE?! WHAT STARTED HIM DOWN THE PATH OF CRIME?!
FIRST OF ALL, KENICHI WAS CARELESS! HE WANTED TO SHOW OFF FOR HIS FRIENDS!
BUT THE OWNER OF THE CANDY STORE WAS CARELESS TOO! THE OLD LADY DOZED OFF AT THE REGISTER!
DO YOU UNDERSTAND?! THE OLD LADY'S CARELESSNESS GAVE LITTLE KENICHI THE OPPORTUNITY TO STEAL!
OF COURSE, IT'S NOT ALL GRANDMA'S FAULT! KENICHI STILL BEARS MOST OF THE BLAME!
CRIME CAN BE PREVENTED IF WE JUST HAVE THE RIGHT ATTITUDE. THAT'S WHAT WE'RE HERE TO TELL YOU TODAY!
NEW YEAR'S SPECIAL PREPAREDNESS DAY EVENT
IT'S NEW YEAR'S, BUT DON'T GET CARRIED AWAY. THAT'S THE MESSAGE!

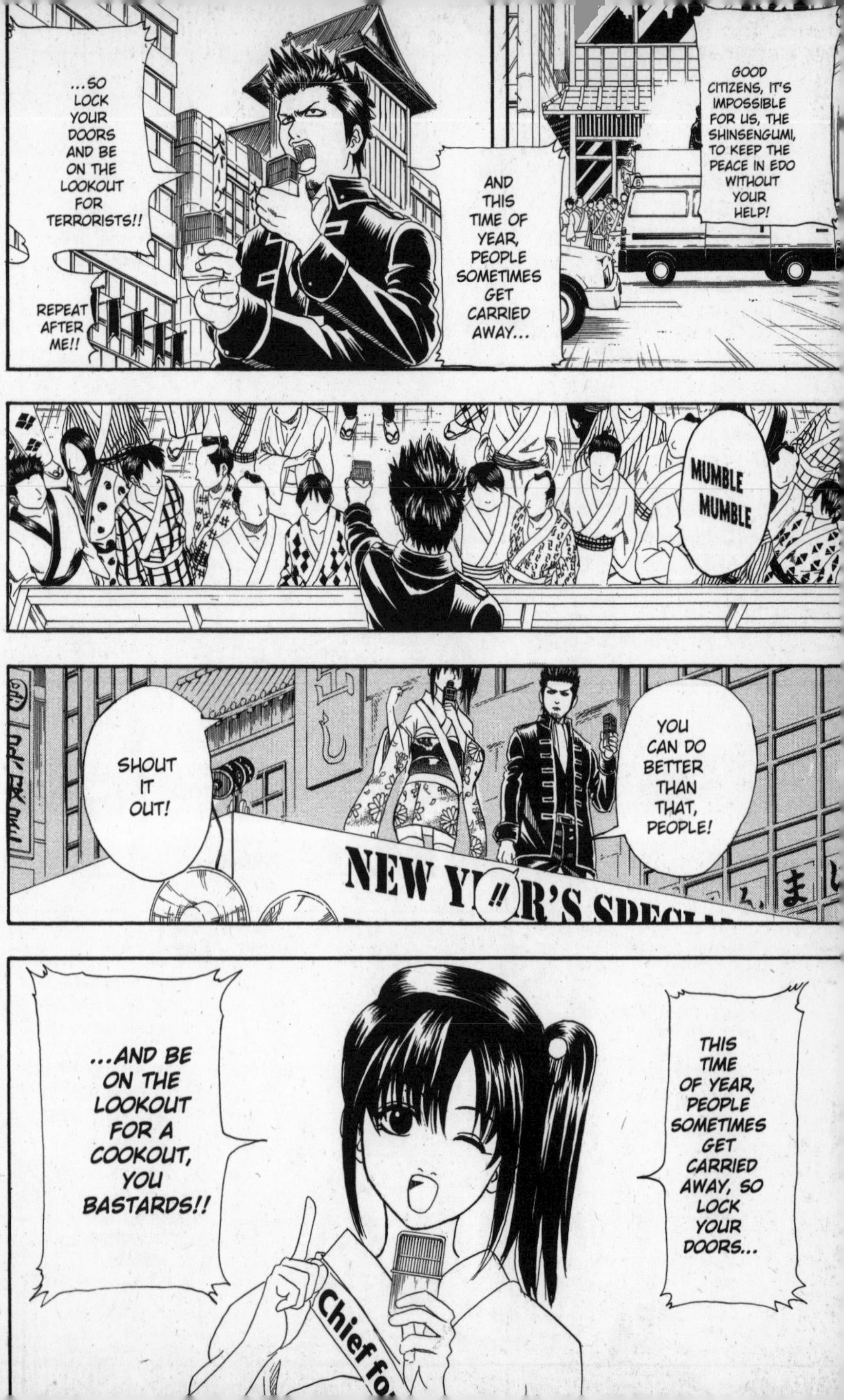
GOOD CITIZENS, IT'S IMPOSSIBLE FOR US, THE SHINSENGUMI, TO KEEP THE PEACE IN EDO WITHOUT YOUR HELP!
AND THIS TIME OF YEAR, PEOPLE SOMETIMES GET CARRIED AWAY...
...SO LOCK YOUR DOORS AND BE ON THE LOOKOUT FOR TERRORISTS!!
REPEAT AFTER ME!!
MUMBLE MUMBLE
YOU CAN DO BETTER THAN THAT, PEOPLE!
SHOUT IT OUT!
!!
THIS TIME OF YEAR, PEOPLE SOMETIMES GET CARRIED AWAY, SO LOCK YOUR DOORS...
...AND BE ON THE LOOKOUT FOR A COOKOUT, YOU BASTARDS!!

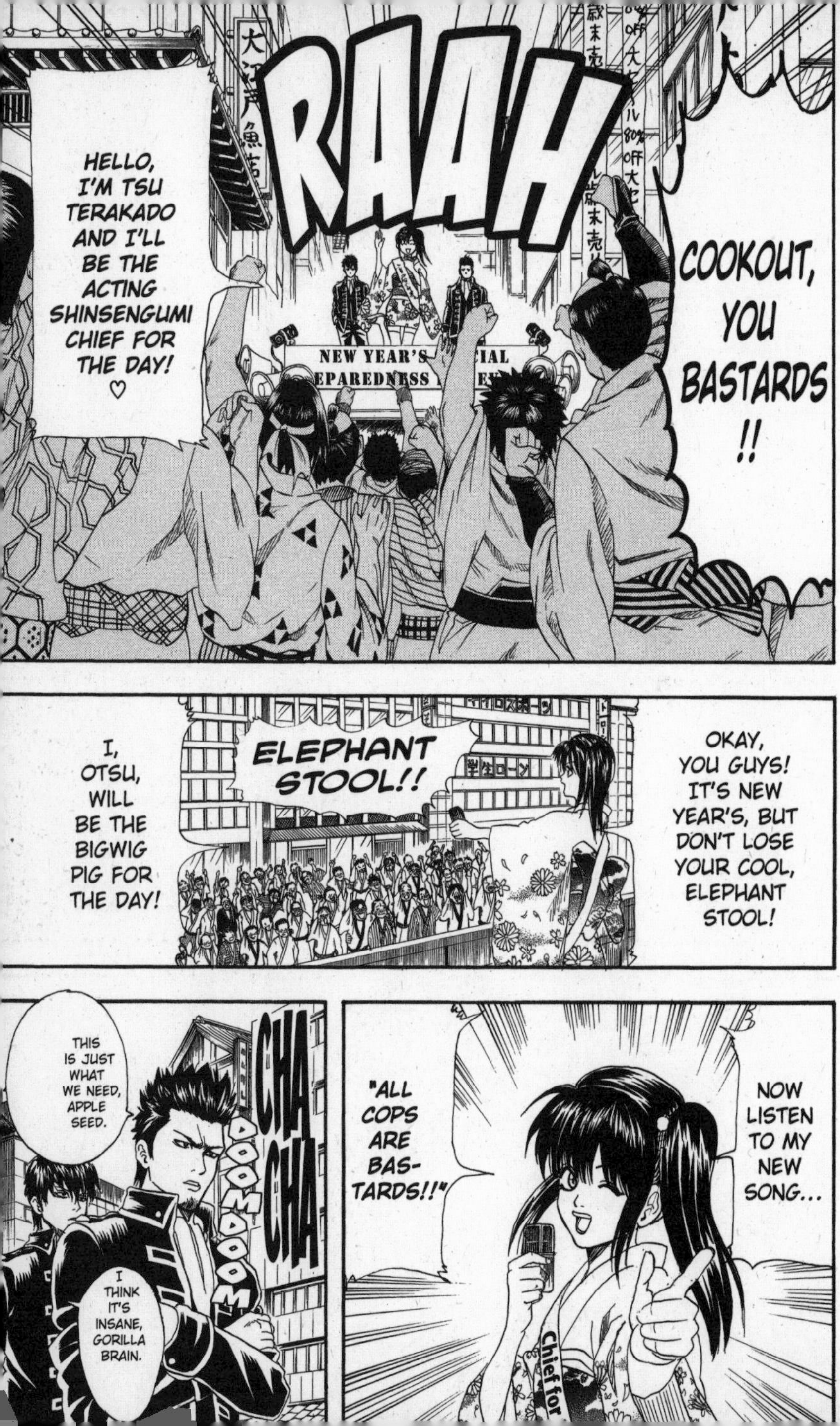
RAAH
COOKOUT, YOU BASTARDS!!
HELLO, I'M TSU TERAKADO AND I'LL BE THE ACTING SHINSENGUMI CHIEF FOR THE DAY! ♡
NEW YEAR'S
OKAY, YOU GUYS! IT'S NEW YEAR'S, BUT DON'T LOSE YOUR COOL, ELEPHANT STOOL!
ELEPHANT STOOL!!
I, OTSU, WILL BE THE BIGWIG PIG FOR THE DAY!
NOW LISTEN TO MY NEW SONG...
"ALL COPS ARE BAS-TARDS!!"
Chief for
CHA CHA
DOOM DOOM
THIS IS JUST WHAT WE NEED, APPLE SEED.
I THINK IT'S INSANE, GORILLA BRAIN.

Lesson 101 Keep an Eye on the Chief for the Day

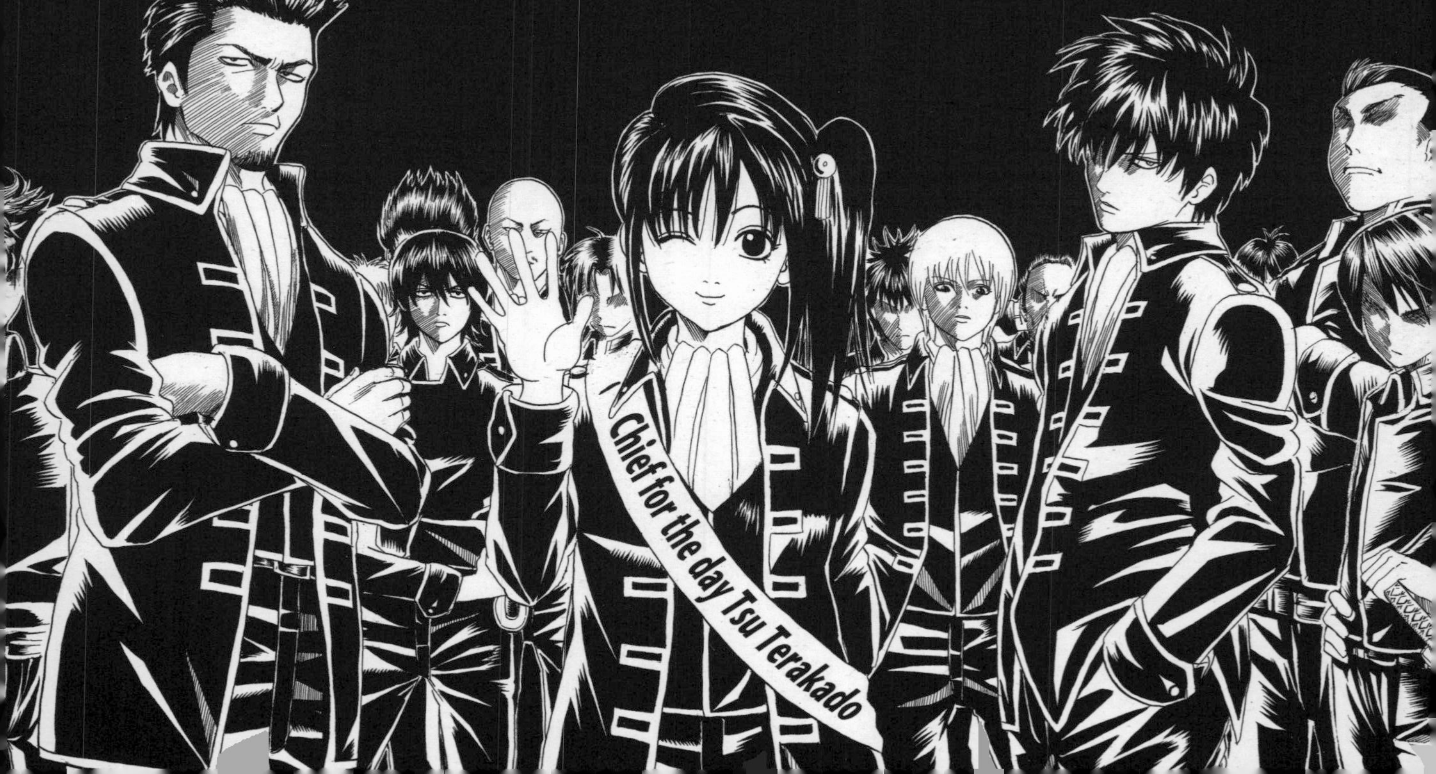
Chief for the day Tsu Terakado

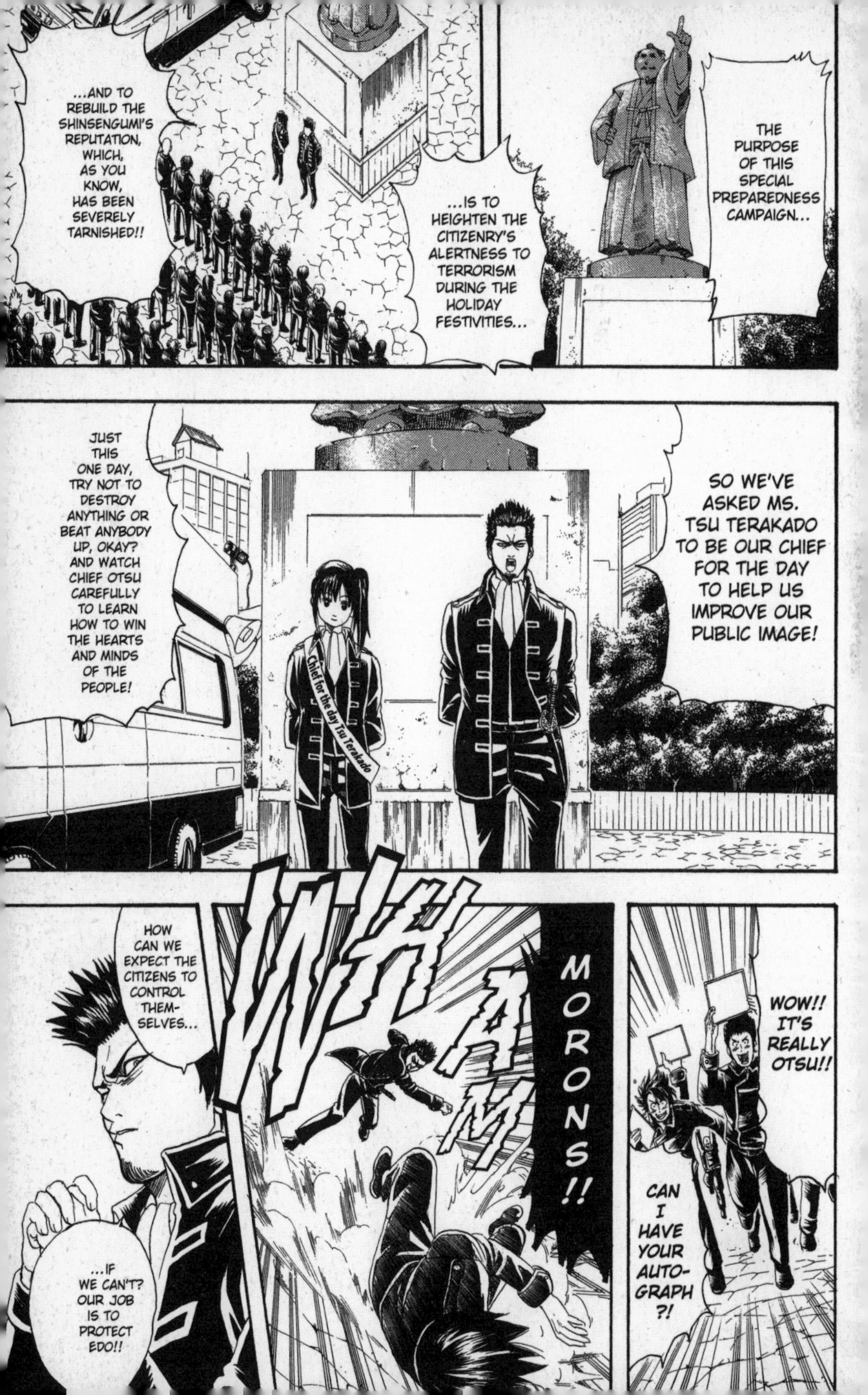
THE PURPOSE OF THIS SPECIAL PREPAREDNESS CAMPAIGN...
...IS TO HEIGHTEN THE CITIZENRY'S ALERTNESS TO TERRORISM DURING THE HOLIDAY FESTIVITIES...
...AND TO REBUILD THE SHINSENGUMI'S REPUTATION, WHICH, AS YOU KNOW, HAS BEEN SEVERELY TARNISHED!!
SO WE'VE ASKED MS. TSU TERAKADO TO BE OUR CHIEF FOR THE DAY TO HELP US IMPROVE OUR PUBLIC IMAGE!
Chief for the day Tsu Terakado
JUST THIS ONE DAY, TRY NOT TO DESTROY ANYTHING OR BEAT ANYBODY UP, OKAY? AND WATCH CHIEF OTSU CAREFULLY TO LEARN HOW TO WIN THE HEARTS AND MINDS OF THE PEOPLE!
WOW!! IT'S REALLY OTSU!!
CAN I HAVE YOUR AUTO-GRAPH?!
MORONS!!
WHAM
HOW CAN WE EXPECT THE CITIZENS TO CONTROL THEM-SELVES...
...IF WE CAN'T? OUR JOB IS TO PROTECT EDO!!

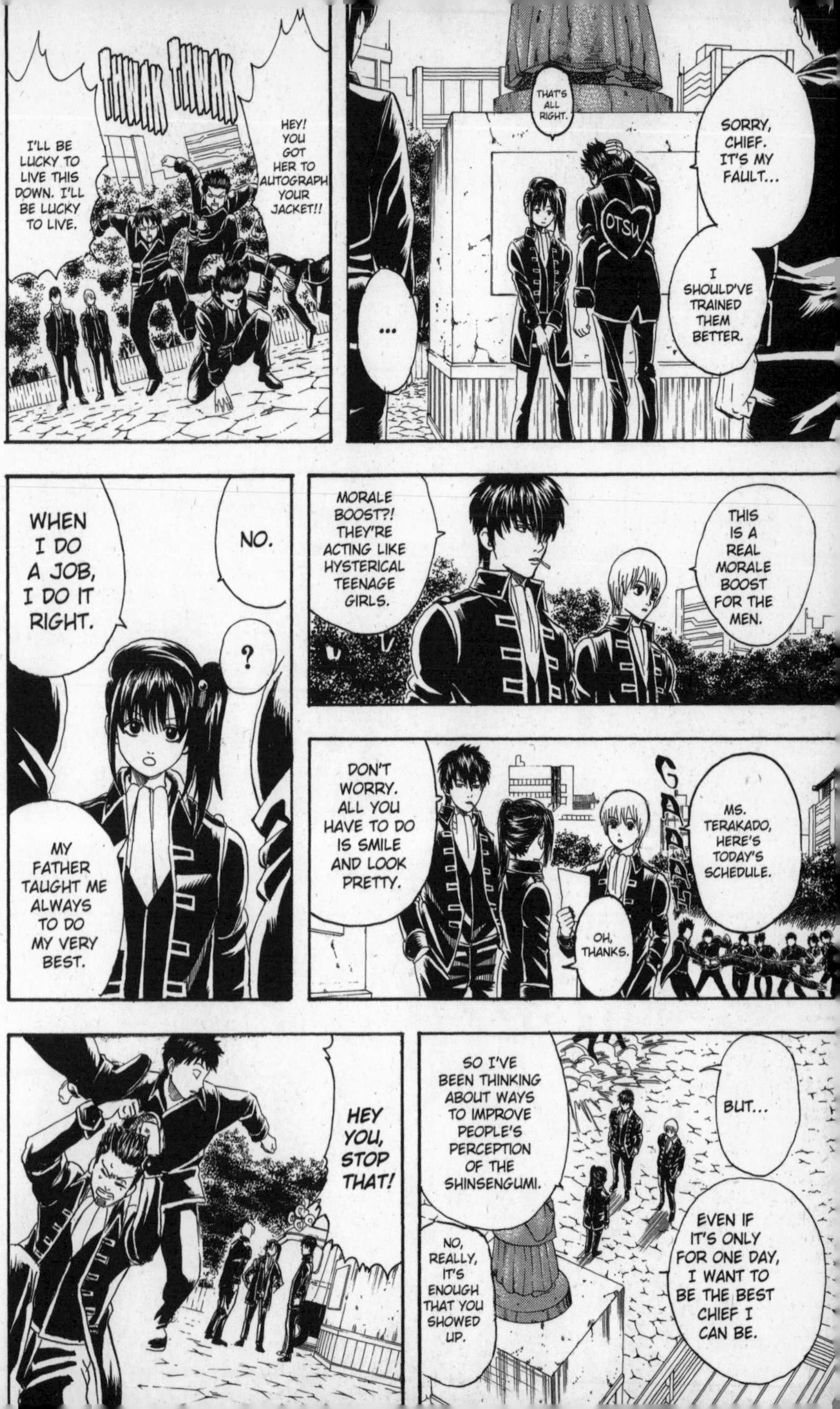
SORRY, CHIEF. IT'S MY FAULT...
I SHOULD'VE TRAINED THEM BETTER.
THAT'S ALL RIGHT.
...
THWAK THWAK
HEY! YOU GOT HER TO AUTOGRAPH YOUR JACKET!!
I'LL BE LUCKY TO LIVE THIS DOWN. I'LL BE LUCKY TO LIVE.
OTSU
THIS IS A REAL MORALE BOOST FOR THE MEN.
MORALE BOOST?! THEY'RE ACTING LIKE HYSTERICAL TEENAGE GIRLS.
MS. TERAKADO, HERE'S TODAY'S SCHEDULE.
OH, THANKS.
DON'T WORRY. ALL YOU HAVE TO DO IS SMILE AND LOOK PRETTY.
NO.
WHEN I DO A JOB, I DO IT RIGHT.
?
MY FATHER TAUGHT ME ALWAYS TO DO MY VERY BEST.
BUT...
EVEN IF IT'S ONLY FOR ONE DAY, I WANT TO BE THE BEST CHIEF I CAN BE.
SO I'VE BEEN THINKING ABOUT WAYS TO IMPROVE PEOPLE'S PERCEPTION OF THE SHINSENGUMI.
NO, REALLY, IT'S ENOUGH THAT YOU SHOWED UP.
HEY YOU, STOP THAT!

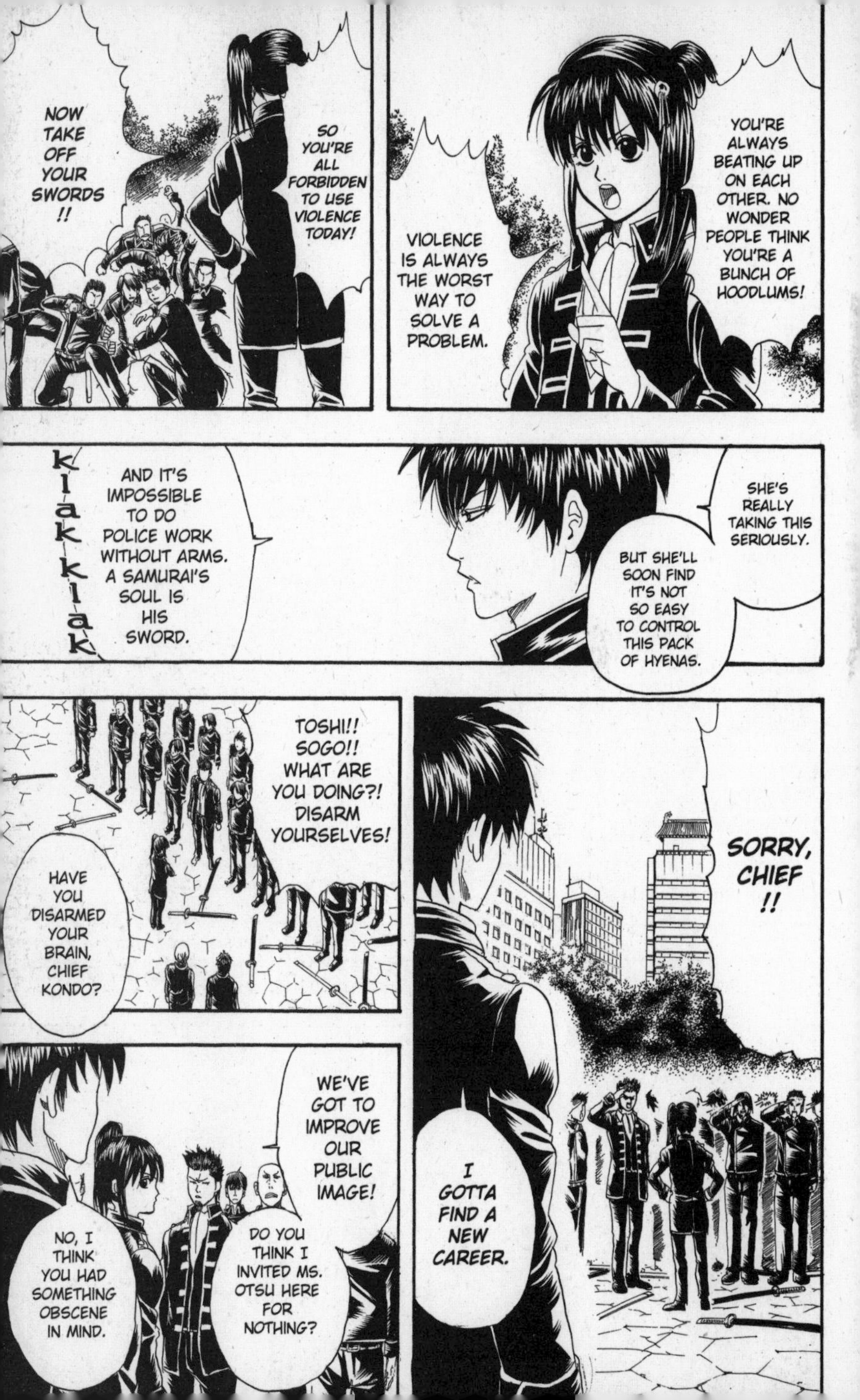
YOU'RE ALWAYS BEATING UP ON EACH OTHER. NO WONDER PEOPLE THINK YOU'RE A BUNCH OF HOODLUMS!
VIOLENCE IS ALWAYS THE WORST WAY TO SOLVE A PROBLEM.
SO YOU'RE ALL FORBIDDEN TO USE VIOLENCE TODAY!
NOW TAKE OFF YOUR SWORDS !!
SHE'S REALLY TAKING THIS SERIOUSLY.
BUT SHE'LL SOON FIND IT'S NOT SO EASY TO CONTROL THIS PACK OF HYENAS.
AND IT'S IMPOSSIBLE TO DO POLICE WORK WITHOUT ARMS. A SAMURAI'S SOUL IS HIS SWORD.
klak klak klak
SORRY, CHIEF !!
I GOTTA FIND A NEW CAREER.
TOSHI!! SOGO!! WHAT ARE YOU DOING?! DISARM YOURSELVES!
HAVE YOU DISARMED YOUR BRAIN, CHIEF KONDO?
WE'VE GOT TO IMPROVE OUR PUBLIC IMAGE!
DO YOU THINK I INVITED MS. OTSU HERE FOR NOTHING?
NO, I THINK YOU HAD SOMETHING OBSCENE IN MIND.

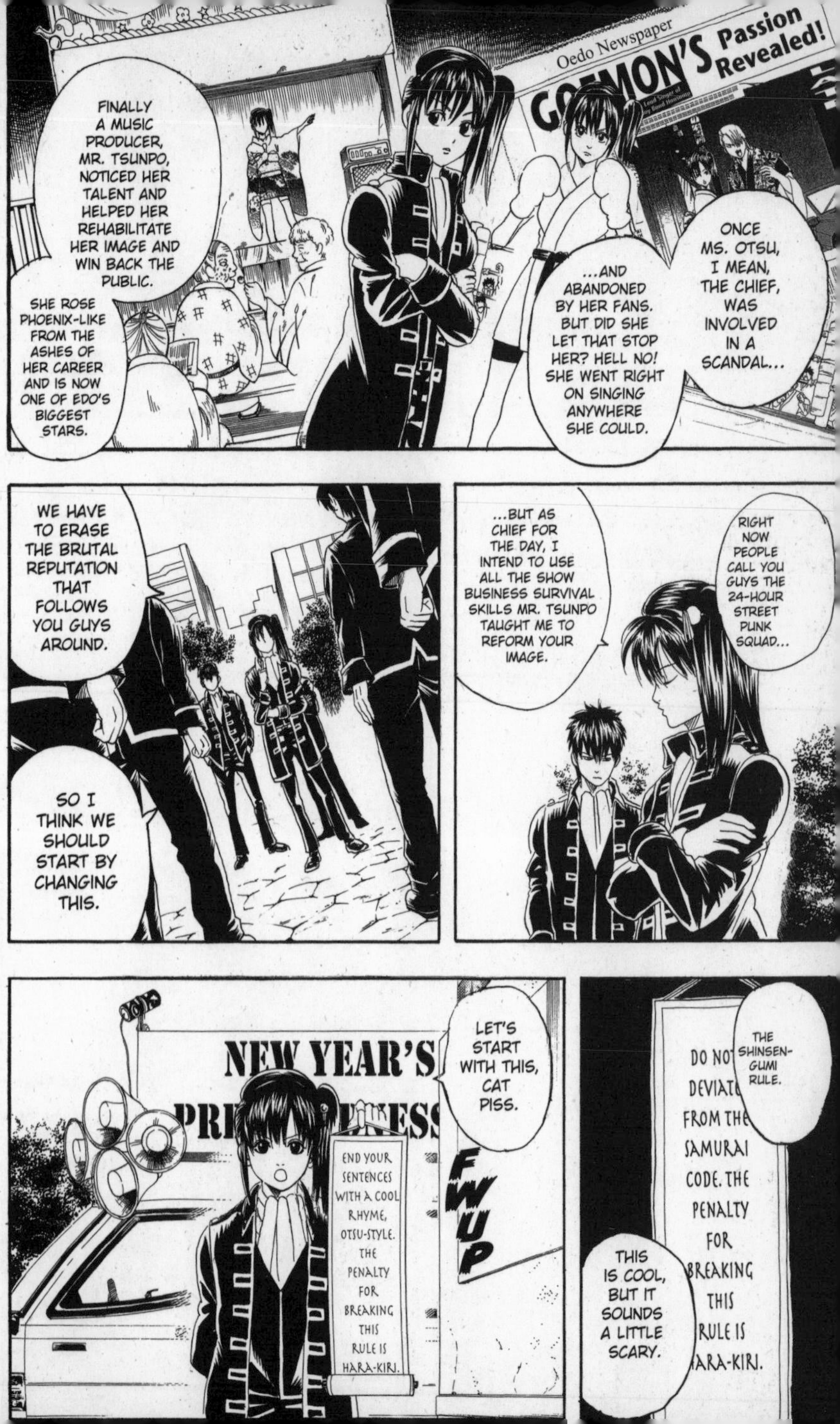
Oedo Newspaper
GOEMON'S Passion Revealed!
ONCE MS. OTSU, I MEAN, THE CHIEF, WAS INVOLVED IN A SCANDAL...
...AND ABANDONED BY HER FANS. BUT DID SHE LET THAT STOP HER? HELL NO! SHE WENT RIGHT ON SINGING ANYWHERE SHE COULD.
FINALLY A MUSIC PRODUCER, MR. TSUNPO, NOTICED HER TALENT AND HELPED HER REHABILITATE HER IMAGE AND WIN BACK THE PUBLIC.
SHE ROSE PHOENIX-LIKE FROM THE ASHES OF HER CAREER AND IS NOW ONE OF EDO'S BIGGEST STARS.
RIGHT NOW PEOPLE CALL YOU GUYS THE 24-HOUR STREET PUNK SQUAD...
...BUT AS CHIEF FOR THE DAY, I INTEND TO USE ALL THE SHOW BUSINESS SURVIVAL SKILLS MR. TSUNPO TAUGHT ME TO REFORM YOUR IMAGE.
WE HAVE TO ERASE THE BRUTAL REPUTATION THAT FOLLOWS YOU GUYS AROUND.
SO I THINK WE SHOULD START BY CHANGING THIS.
THE SHINSENGUMI RULE.
DO NO DEVIAT FROM THE SAMURAI CODE. THE PENALTY FOR BREAKING THIS RULE IS ARA-KIRI.
THIS IS COOL, BUT IT SOUNDS A LITTLE SCARY.
NEW YEAR'S
LET'S START WITH THIS, CAT PISS.
FWUP
END YOUR SENTENCES WITH A COOL RHYME, OTSU-STYLE. THE PENALTY FOR BREAKING THIS RULE IS HARA-KIRI.

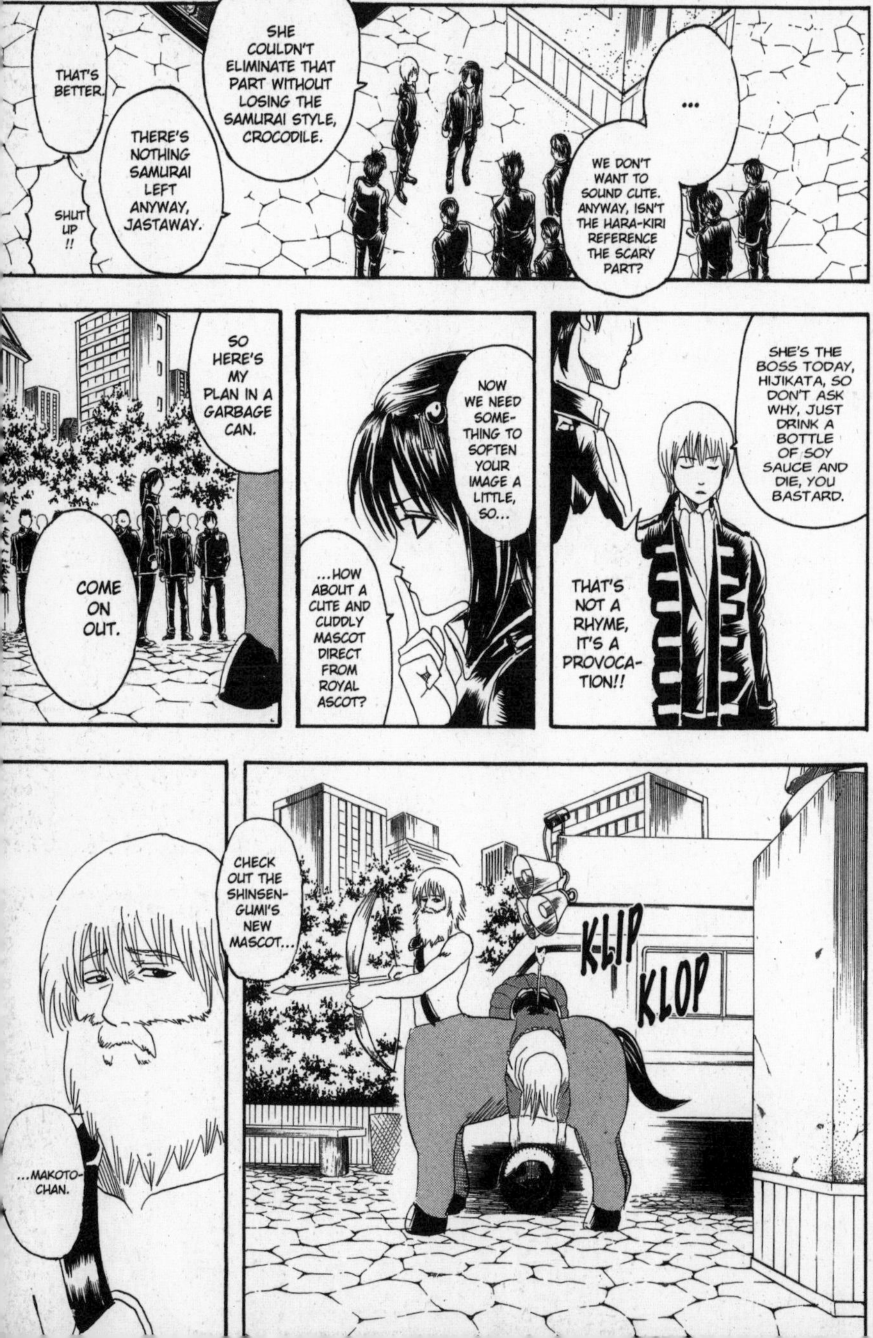
...
WE DON'T WANT TO SOUND CUTE. ANYWAY, ISN'T THE HARA-KIRI REFERENCE THE SCARY PART?
SHE COULDN'T ELIMINATE THAT PART WITHOUT LOSING THE SAMURAI STYLE, CROCODILE.
THERE'S NOTHING SAMURAI LEFT ANYWAY, JASTAWAY.
THAT'S BETTER.
SHUT UP!!
SHE'S THE BOSS TODAY, HIJIKATA, SO DON'T ASK WHY, JUST DRINK A BOTTLE OF SOY SAUCE AND DIE, YOU BASTARD.
THAT'S NOT A RHYME, IT'S A PROVOCATION!!
NOW WE NEED SOMETHING TO SOFTEN YOUR IMAGE A LITTLE, SO...
...HOW ABOUT A CUTE AND CUDDLY MASCOT DIRECT FROM ROYAL ASCOT?
SO HERE'S MY PLAN IN A GARBAGE CAN.
COME ON OUT.
CHECK OUT THE SHINSENGUMI'S NEW MASCOT...
KLIP
KLOP
...MAKOTO-CHAN.

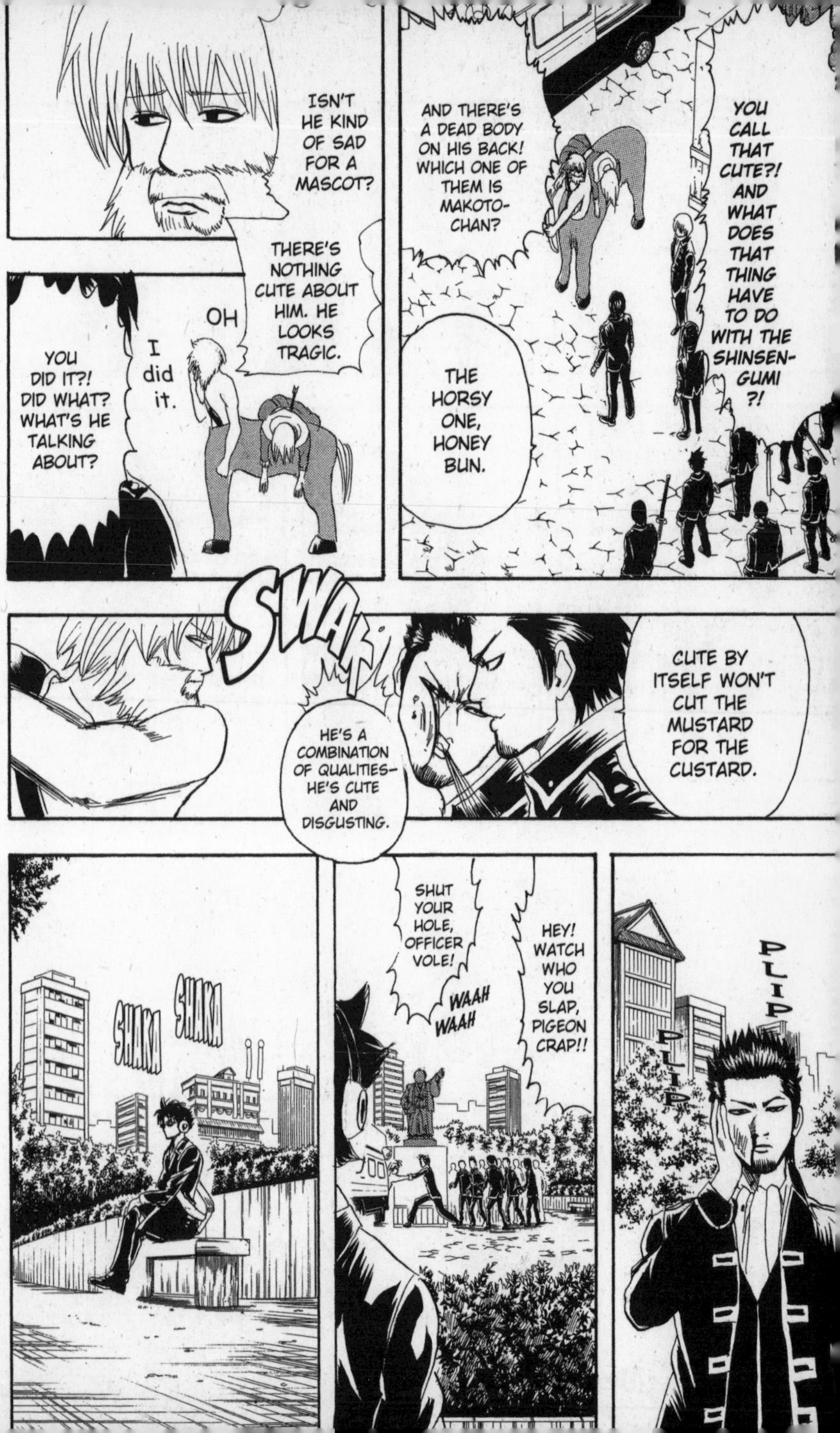

YOU CALL THAT CUTE?! AND WHAT DOES THAT THING HAVE TO DO WITH THE SHINSEN-GUMI ?!
AND THERE'S A DEAD BODY ON HIS BACK! WHICH ONE OF THEM IS MAKOTO-CHAN?
THE HORSY ONE, HONEY BUN.
ISN'T HE KIND OF SAD FOR A MASCOT?
THERE'S NOTHING CUTE ABOUT HIM. HE LOOKS TRAGIC.
OH
I did it.
YOU DID IT?! DID WHAT? WHAT'S HE TALKING ABOUT?
CUTE BY ITSELF WON'T CUT THE MUSTARD FOR THE CUSTARD.
SWAP
HE'S A COMBINATION OF QUALITIES-HE'S CUTE AND DISGUSTING.
PLIP
PLIP
PLIP
HEY! WATCH WHO YOU SLAP, PIGEON CRAP!!
SHUT YOUR HOLE, OFFICER VOLE!
WAAH WAAH
SHAKA
SHAKA

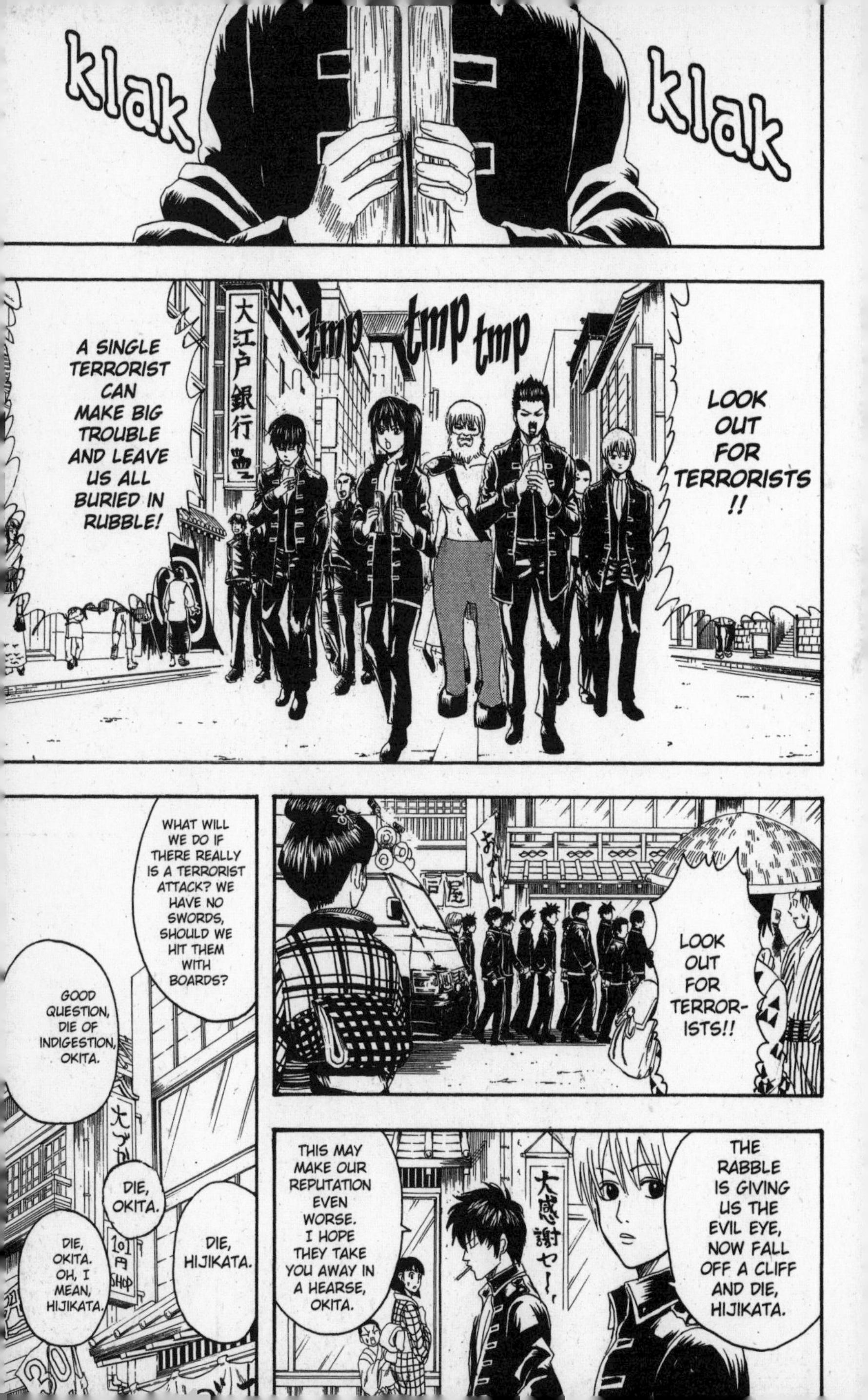
klak
klak
LOOK OUT FOR TERRORISTS!!
tmp tmp tmp
大江戸銀行
A SINGLE TERRORIST CAN MAKE BIG TROUBLE AND LEAVE US ALL BURIED IN RUBBLE!
LOOK OUT FOR TERROR-ISTS!!
THE RABBLE IS GIVING US THE EVIL EYE, NOW FALL OFF A CLIFF AND DIE, HIJIKATA.
THIS MAY MAKE OUR REPUTATION EVEN WORSE. I HOPE THEY TAKE YOU AWAY IN A HEARSE, OKITA.
WHAT WILL WE DO IF THERE REALLY IS A TERRORIST ATTACK? WE HAVE NO SWORDS, SHOULD WE HIT THEM WITH BOARDS?
GOOD QUESTION, DIE OF INDIGESTION, OKITA.
DIE, OKITA.
DIE, HIJIKATA.
DIE, OKITA. OH, I MEAN, HIJIKATA.

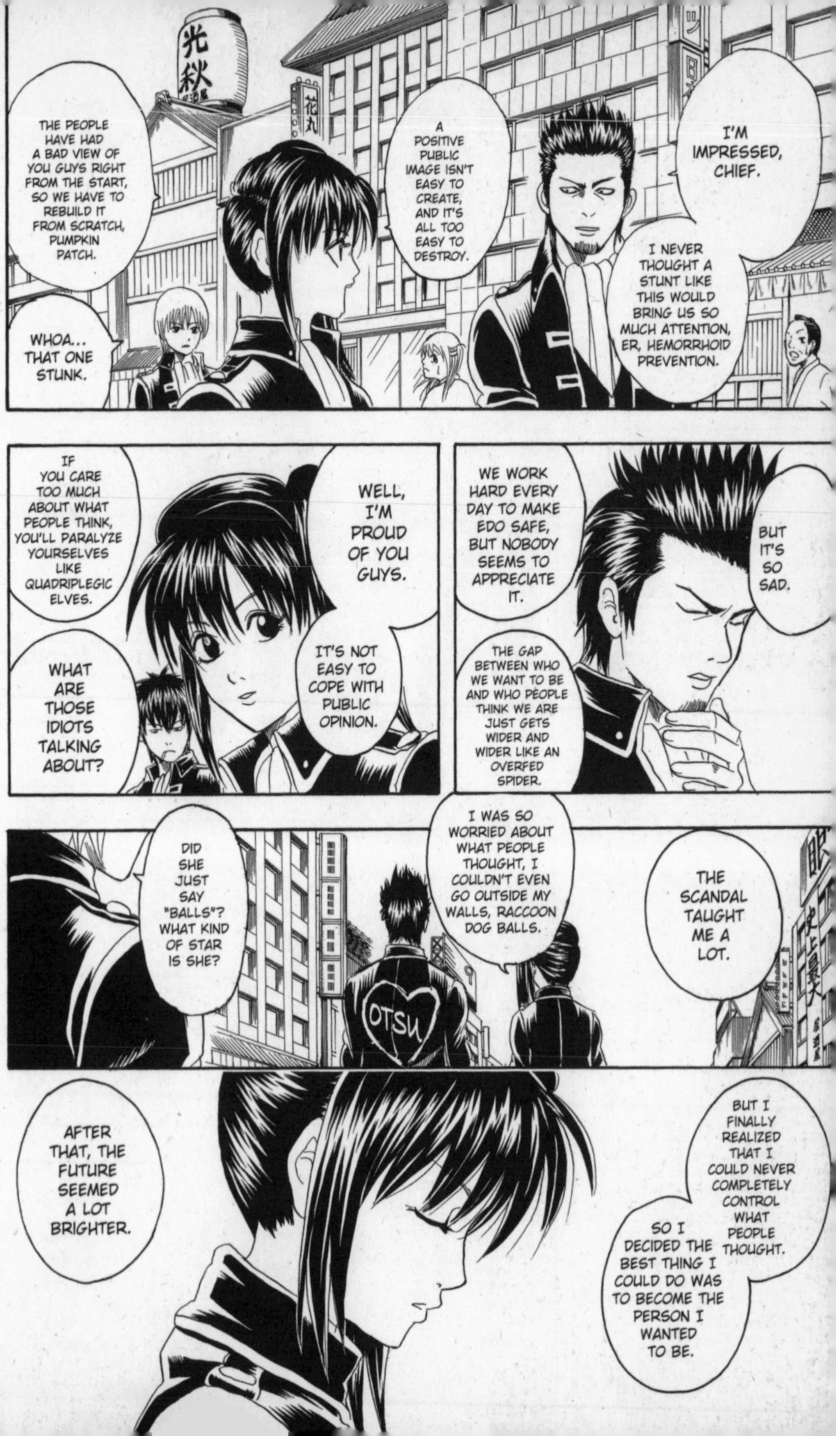
I'M IMPRESSED, CHIEF.
I NEVER THOUGHT A STUNT LIKE THIS WOULD BRING US SO MUCH ATTENTION, ER, HEMORRHOID PREVENTION.
A POSITIVE PUBLIC IMAGE ISN'T EASY TO CREATE, AND IT'S ALL TOO EASY TO DESTROY.
THE PEOPLE HAVE HAD A BAD VIEW OF YOU GUYS RIGHT FROM THE START, SO WE HAVE TO REBUILD IT FROM SCRATCH, PUMPKIN PATCH.
WHOA... THAT ONE STUNK.
BUT IT'S SO SAD.
WE WORK HARD EVERY DAY TO MAKE EDO SAFE, BUT NOBODY SEEMS TO APPRECIATE IT.
THE GAP BETWEEN WHO WE WANT TO BE AND WHO PEOPLE THINK WE ARE JUST GETS WIDER AND WIDER LIKE AN OVERFED SPIDER.
WELL, I'M PROUD OF YOU GUYS.
IT'S NOT EASY TO COPE WITH PUBLIC OPINION.
IF YOU CARE TOO MUCH ABOUT WHAT PEOPLE THINK, YOU'LL PARALYZE YOURSELVES LIKE QUADRIPLEGIC ELVES.
WHAT ARE THOSE IDIOTS TALKING ABOUT?
THE SCANDAL TAUGHT ME A LOT.
I WAS SO WORRIED ABOUT WHAT PEOPLE THOUGHT, I COULDN'T EVEN GO OUTSIDE MY WALLS, RACCOON DOG BALLS.
DID SHE JUST SAY "BALLS"? WHAT KIND OF STAR IS SHE?
OTSU
BUT I FINALLY REALIZED THAT I COULD NEVER COMPLETELY CONTROL WHAT PEOPLE THOUGHT.
SO I DECIDED THE BEST THING I COULD DO WAS TO BECOME THE PERSON I WANTED TO BE.
AFTER THAT, THE FUTURE SEEMED A LOT BRIGHTER.

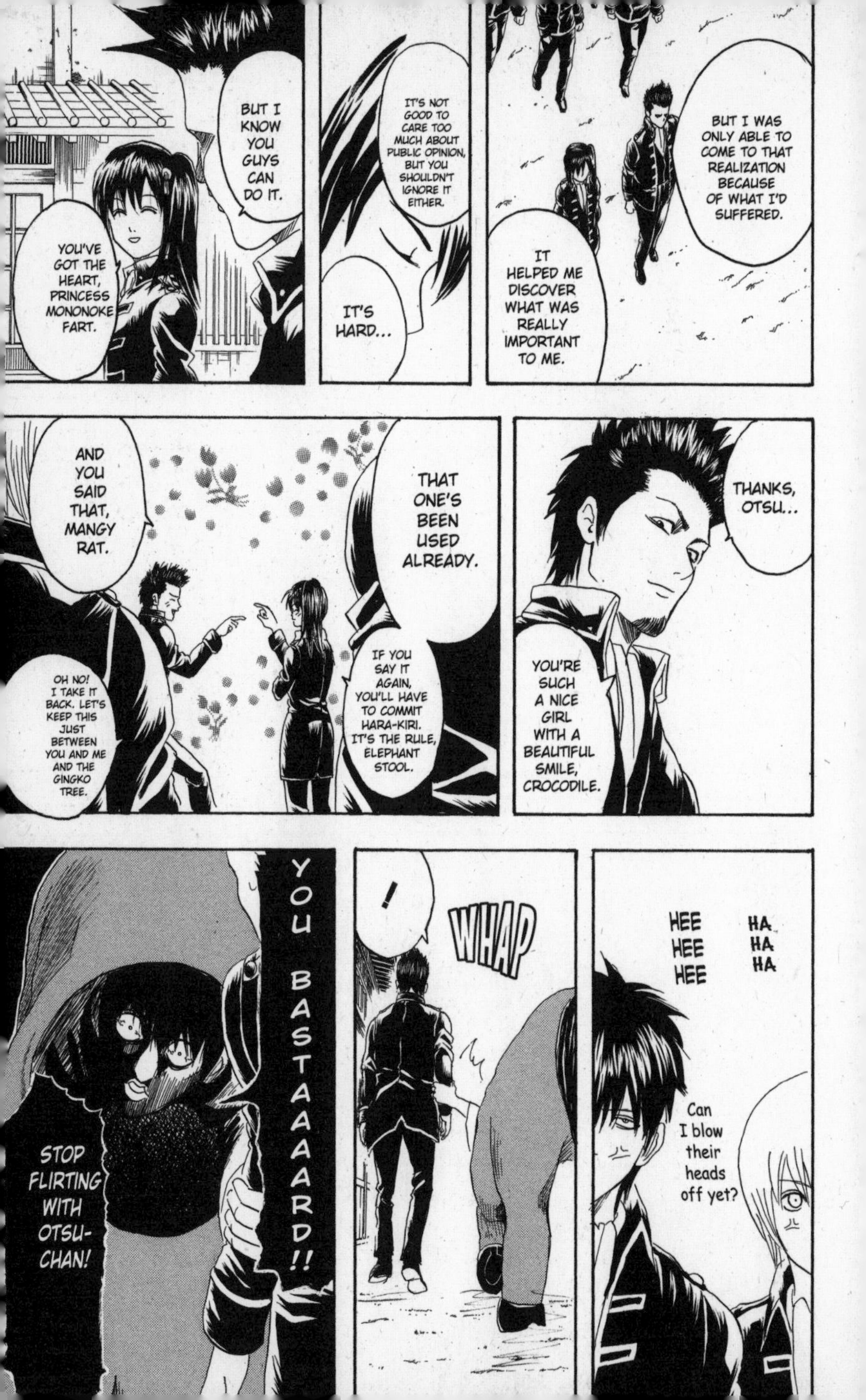
BUT I WAS ONLY ABLE TO COME TO THAT REALIZATION BECAUSE OF WHAT I'D SUFFERED.
IT HELPED ME DISCOVER WHAT WAS REALLY IMPORTANT TO ME.
IT'S NOT GOOD TO CARE TOO MUCH ABOUT PUBLIC OPINION, BUT YOU SHOULDN'T IGNORE IT EITHER.
IT'S HARD...
BUT I KNOW YOU GUYS CAN DO IT.
YOU'VE GOT THE HEART, PRINCESS MONONOKE FART.
THANKS, OTSU...
YOU'RE SUCH A NICE GIRL WITH A BEAUTIFUL SMILE, CROCODILE.
THAT ONE'S BEEN USED ALREADY.
AND YOU SAID THAT, MANGY RAT.
IF YOU SAY IT AGAIN, YOU'LL HAVE TO COMMIT HARA-KIRI. IT'S THE RULE, ELEPHANT STOOL.
OH NO! I TAKE IT BACK. LET'S KEEP THIS JUST BETWEEN YOU AND ME AND THE GINGKO TREE.
HEE HEE HEE
HA HA HA
Can I blow their heads off yet?
!
WHAP
YOU BASTAAAAARD!!
STOP FLIRTING WITH OTSU-CHAN!

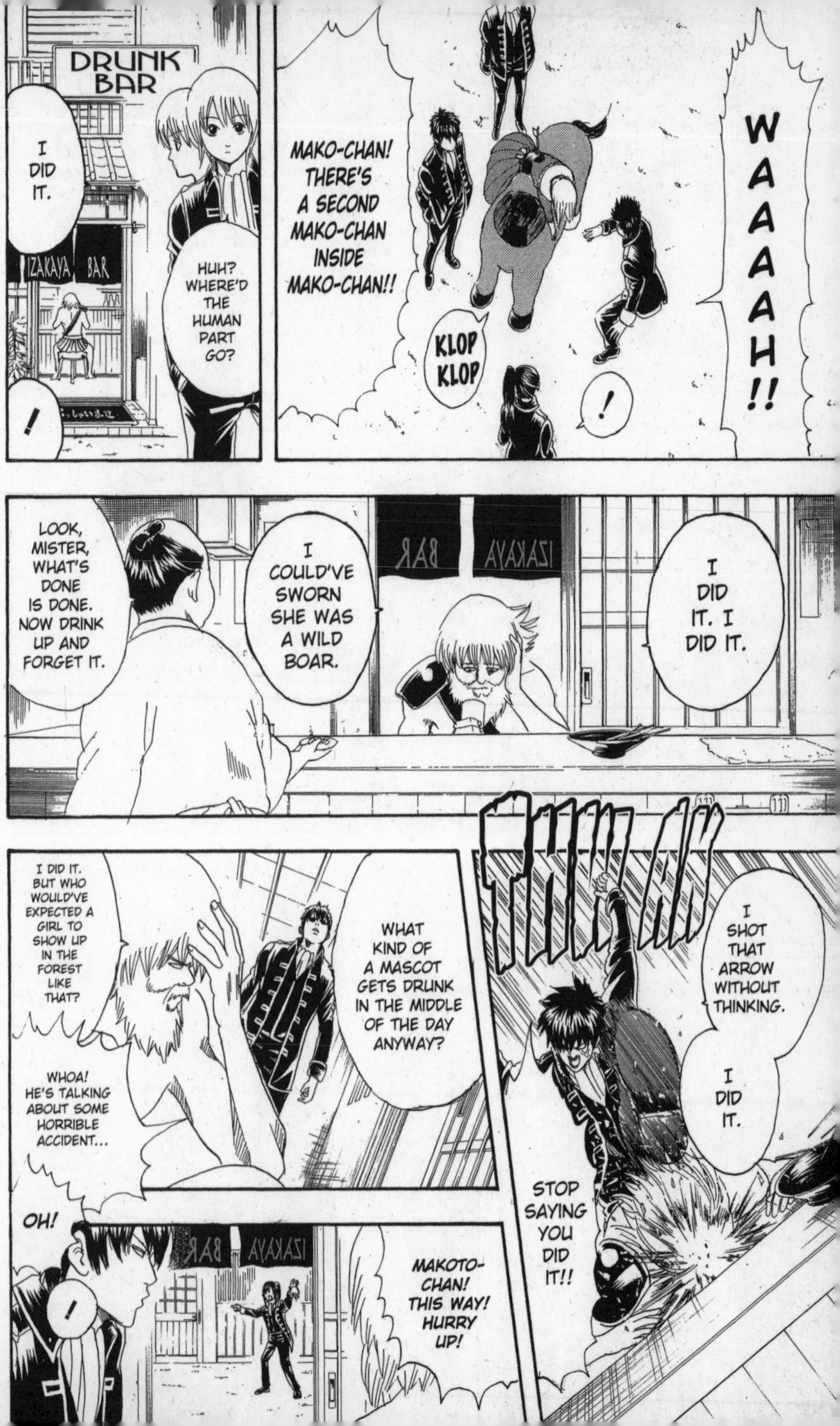
WAAAAAH!!
MAKO-CHAN! THERE'S A SECOND MAKO-CHAN INSIDE MAKO-CHAN!!
!
KLOP KLOP
DRUNK BAR
HUH? WHERE'D THE HUMAN PART GO?
I DID IT.
IZAKAYA BAR
!
I DID IT. I DID IT.
I COULD'VE SWORN SHE WAS A WILD BOAR.
IZAKAYA BAR
LOOK, MISTER, WHAT'S DONE IS DONE. NOW DRINK UP AND FORGET IT.
I SHOT THAT ARROW WITHOUT THINKING.
I DID IT.
STOP SAYING YOU DID IT!!
WHAT KIND OF A MASCOT GETS DRUNK IN THE MIDDLE OF THE DAY ANYWAY?
I DID IT. BUT WHO WOULD'VE EXPECTED A GIRL TO SHOW UP IN THE FOREST LIKE THAT?
WHOA! HE'S TALKING ABOUT SOME HORRIBLE ACCIDENT...
MAKOTO-CHAN! THIS WAY! HURRY UP!
IZAKAYA BAR
OH!
!

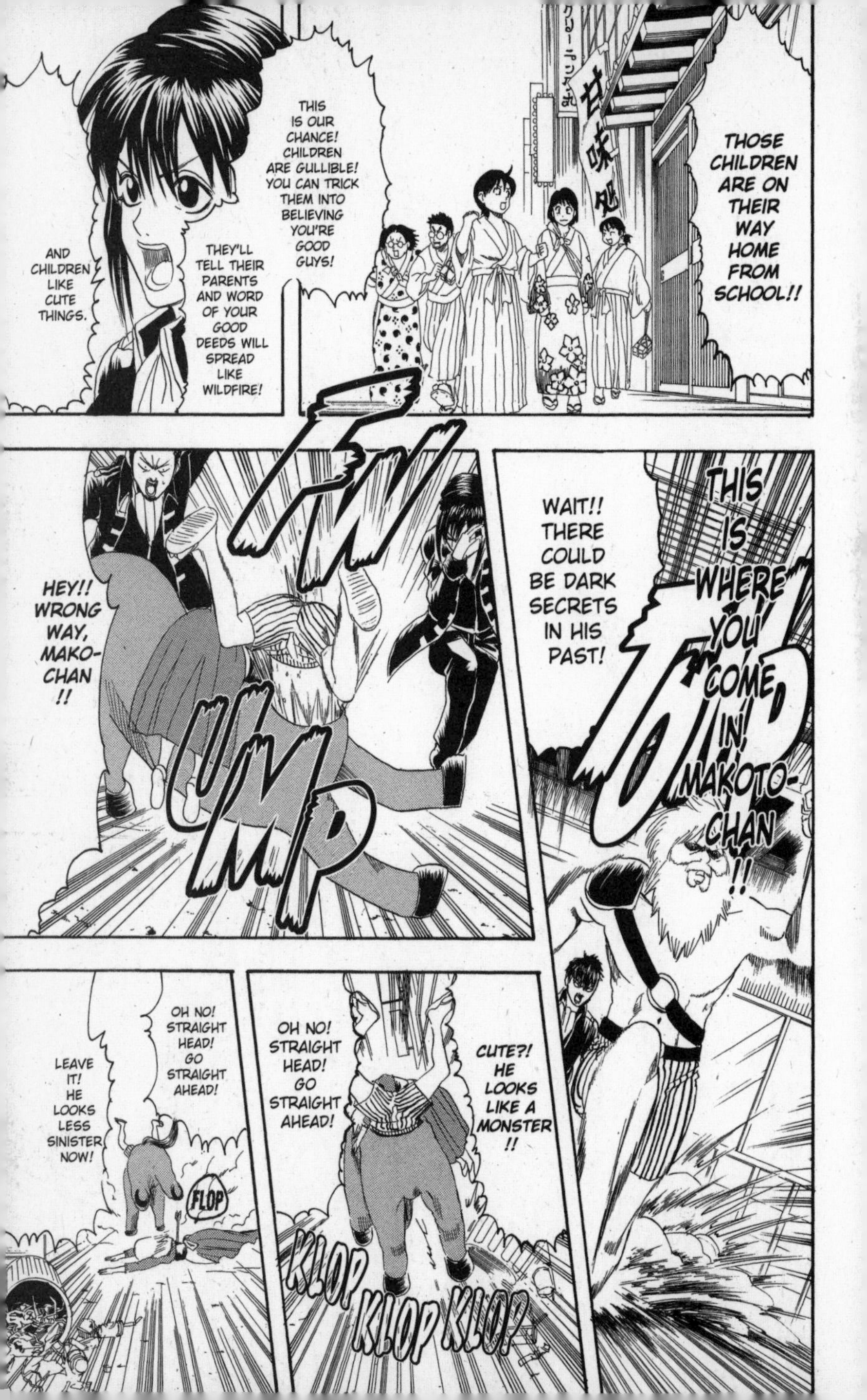
THOSE CHILDREN ARE ON THEIR WAY HOME FROM SCHOOL!!
甘味処
THIS IS OUR CHANCE! CHILDREN ARE GULLIBLE! YOU CAN TRICK THEM INTO BELIEVING YOU'RE GOOD GUYS!
THEY'LL TELL THEIR PARENTS AND WORD OF YOUR GOOD DEEDS WILL SPREAD LIKE WILDFIRE!
AND CHILDREN LIKE CUTE THINGS.
THIS IS WHERE YOU COME IN! MAKOTO-CHAN!!
WAIT!! THERE COULD BE DARK SECRETS IN HIS PAST!
FWUMP
HEY!! WRONG WAY, MAKO-CHAN!!
CUTE?! HE LOOKS LIKE A MONSTER!!
OH NO! STRAIGHT HEAD! GO STRAIGHT AHEAD!
KLOP KLOP KLOP
OH NO! STRAIGHT HEAD! GO STRAIGHT AHEAD!
LEAVE IT! HE LOOKS LESS SINISTER NOW!
FLOP

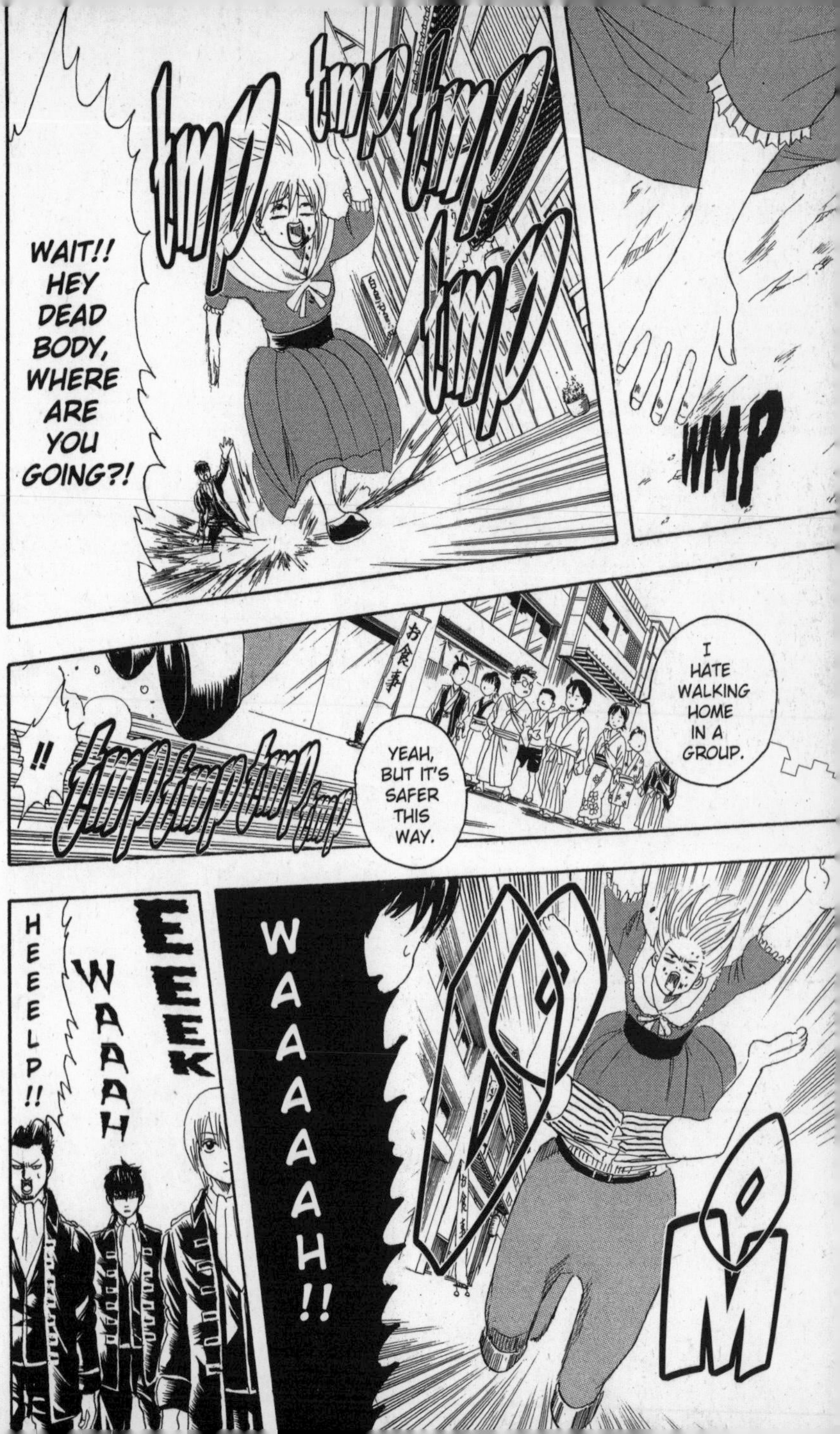

WMP
tmp tmp tmp tmp tmp
WAIT!! HEY DEAD BODY, WHERE ARE YOU GOING?!
I HATE WALKING HOME IN A GROUP.
YEAH, BUT IT'S SAFER THIS WAY.
お食事
tmp tmp tmp tmp
!!
WAAAAAAH!!
EEEK
WAAAH
HEEELP!!

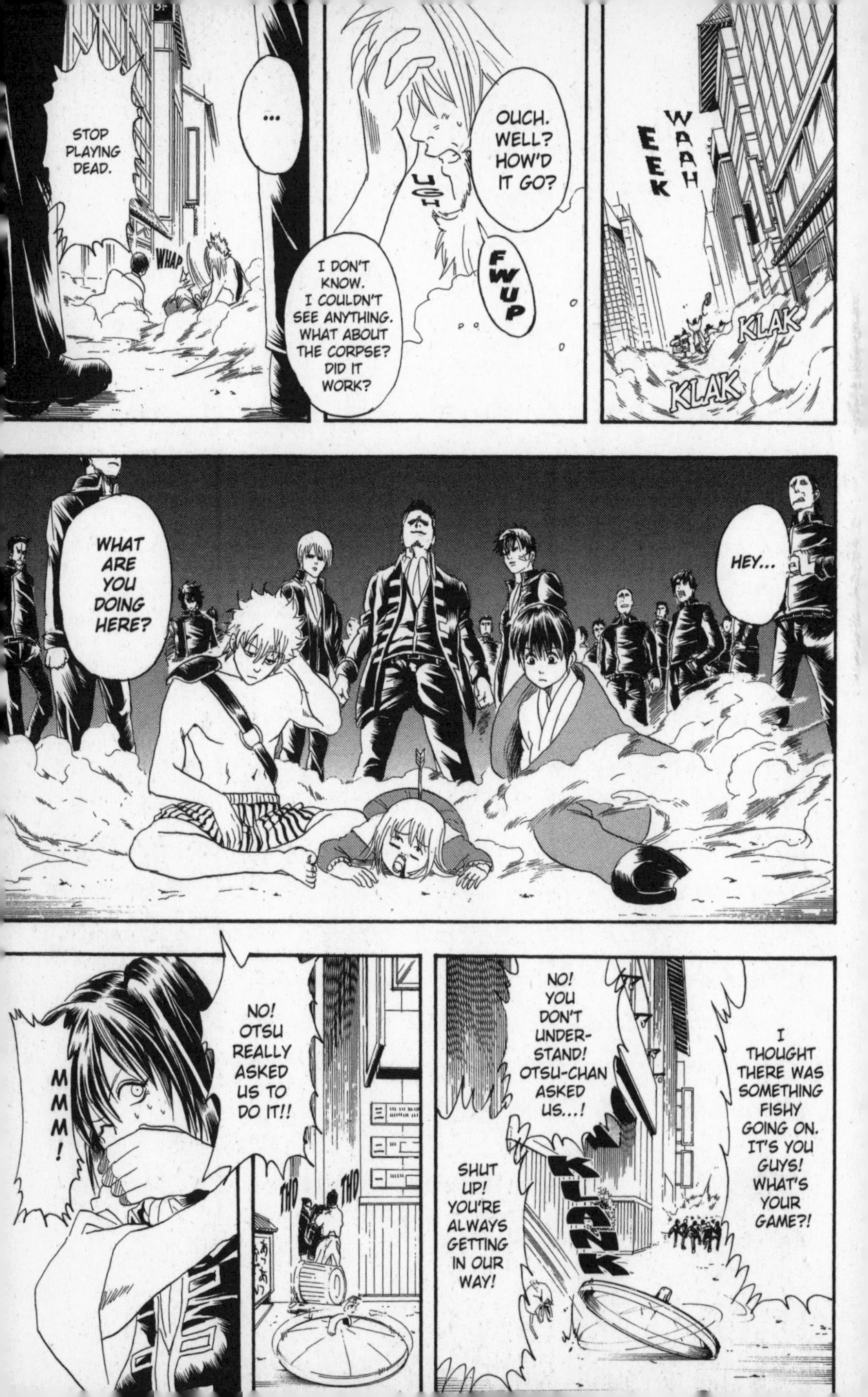

WAAH
EEK
KLAK
KLAK
OUCH. WELL? HOW'D IT GO?
UGH
FWUP
I DON'T KNOW. I COULDN'T SEE ANYTHING. WHAT ABOUT THE CORPSE? DID IT WORK?
...
STOP PLAYING DEAD.
WHAP
HEY...
WHAT ARE YOU DOING HERE?
I THOUGHT THERE WAS SOMETHING FISHY GOING ON. IT'S YOU GUYS! WHAT'S YOUR GAME?!
NO! YOU DON'T UNDER-STAND! OTSU-CHAN ASKED US...!
KLANK
SHUT UP! YOU'RE ALWAYS GETTING IN OUR WAY!
NO! OTSU REALLY ASKED US TO DO IT!!
THO
THO
MMM!

Okay, that's it for volume 12. Before I began *Gin Tama* and was still living with my parents, I found a hair growing out of my back. It really grossed me out and I wanted to pluck it, but my mother told me not to because it was good luck. So I left it, but the other day I looked at my back for the first time in years, and there were black hairs all over the place! Now I'm really disgusted! Mommy! Am I all right? I don't want to die when I finish *Gin Tama*. I have a lot of years ahead of me, so I want to spread my luck out evenly. But it seems like my back hairs are running wild. It's like we all agreed to run together in a school marathon race, but once the race began, they started running at full speed and got way ahead of me. "Hey, slow down! You'll poop out in the second half!" But when they cross the finish line in last place, I'd appreciate it if you gave them a warm applause. So let's all keep running together into the future.

VIZ Media
ATTN: Mike Montesa, Gin Tama Editor
295 Bay Street
San Francisco, CA
94133

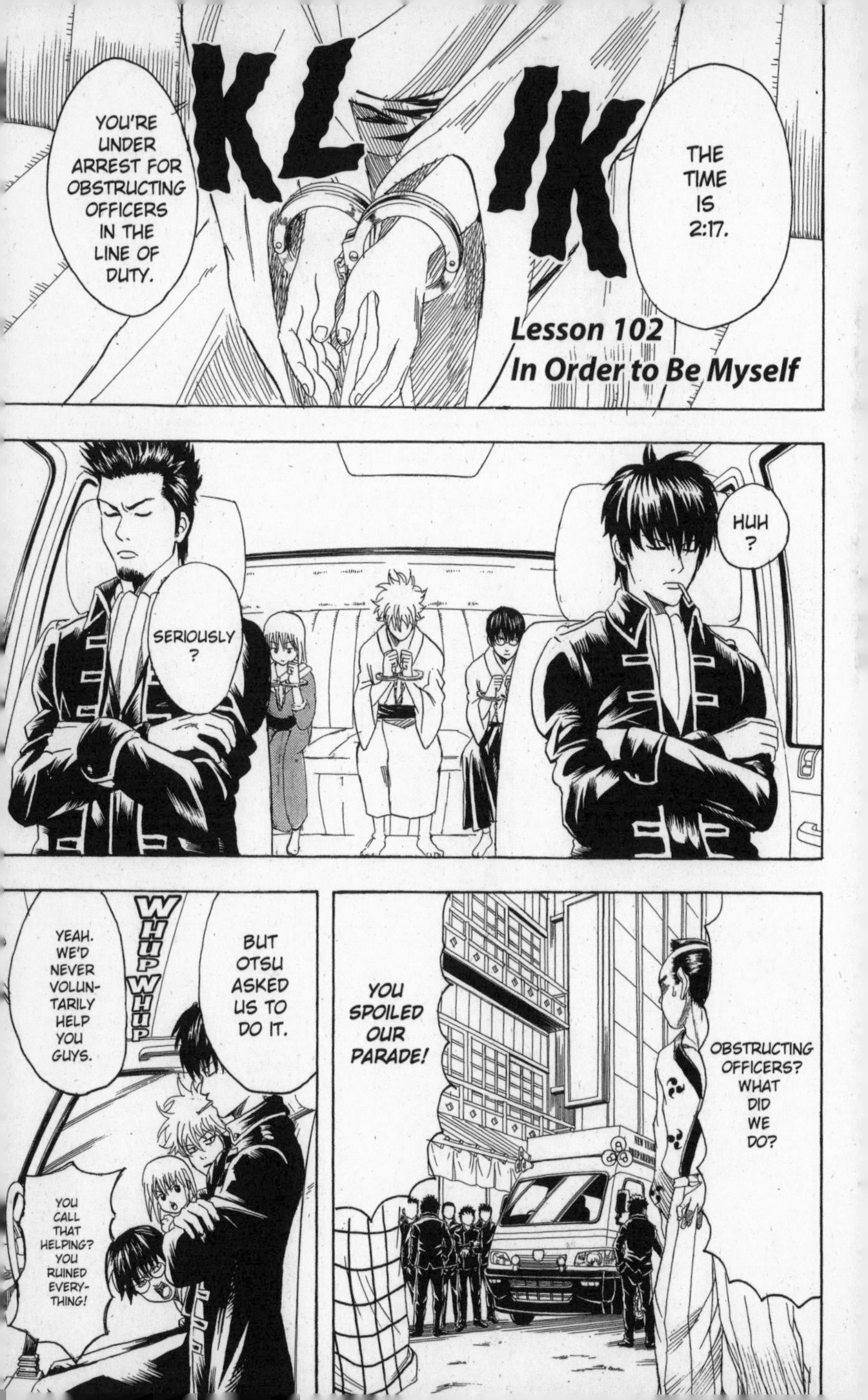
KLIK
THE TIME IS 2:17.
YOU'RE UNDER ARREST FOR OBSTRUCTING OFFICERS IN THE LINE OF DUTY.
Lesson 102
In Order to Be Myself
HUH ?
SERIOUSLY ?
OBSTRUCTING OFFICERS? WHAT DID WE DO?
YOU SPOILED OUR PARADE!
BUT OTSU ASKED US TO DO IT.
WHUP WHUP
YEAH. WE'D NEVER VOLUN-TARILY HELP YOU GUYS.
YOU CALL THAT HELPING? YOU RUINED EVERY-THING!

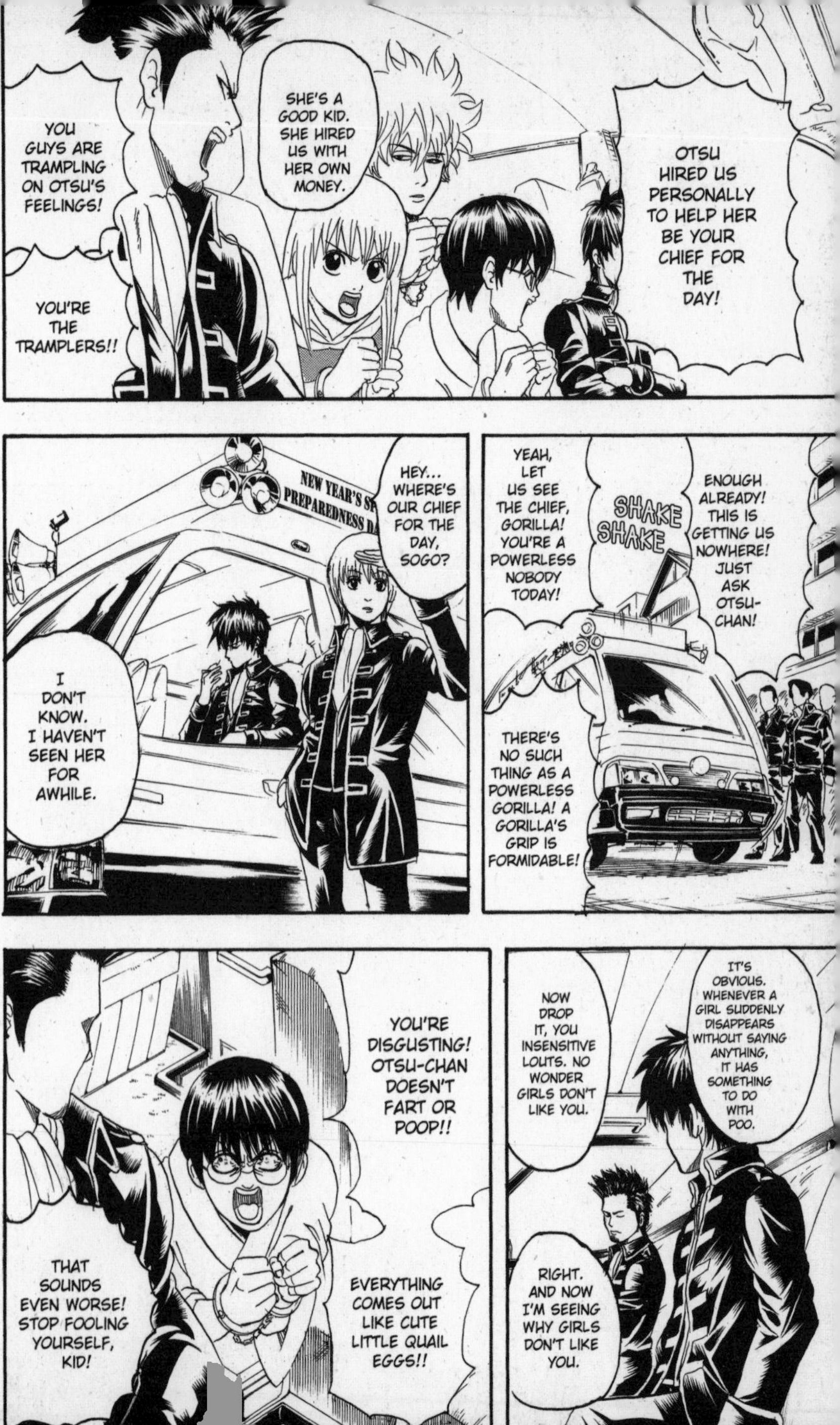
OTSU HIRED US PERSONALLY TO HELP HER BE YOUR CHIEF FOR THE DAY!
SHE'S A GOOD KID. SHE HIRED US WITH HER OWN MONEY.
YOU GUYS ARE TRAMPLING ON OTSU'S FEELINGS!
YOU'RE THE TRAMPLERS!!
ENOUGH ALREADY! THIS IS GETTING US NOWHERE! JUST ASK OTSU-CHAN!
SHAKE SHAKE
YEAH, LET US SEE THE CHIEF, GORILLA! YOU'RE A POWERLESS NOBODY TODAY!
THERE'S NO SUCH THING AS A POWERLESS GORILLA! A GORILLA'S GRIP IS FORMIDABLE!
NEW YEAR'S SP PREPAREDNESS DA
HEY... WHERE'S OUR CHIEF FOR THE DAY, SOGO?
I DON'T KNOW. I HAVEN'T SEEN HER FOR AWHILE.
IT'S OBVIOUS. WHENEVER A GIRL SUDDENLY DISAPPEARS WITHOUT SAYING ANYTHING, IT HAS SOMETHING TO DO WITH POO.
NOW DROP IT, YOU INSENSITIVE LOUTS. NO WONDER GIRLS DON'T LIKE YOU.
RIGHT. AND NOW I'M SEEING WHY GIRLS DON'T LIKE YOU.
YOU'RE DISGUSTING! OTSU-CHAN DOESN'T FART OR POOP!!
EVERYTHING COMES OUT LIKE CUTE LITTLE QUAIL EGGS!!
THAT SOUNDS EVEN WORSE! STOP FOOLING YOURSELF, KID!

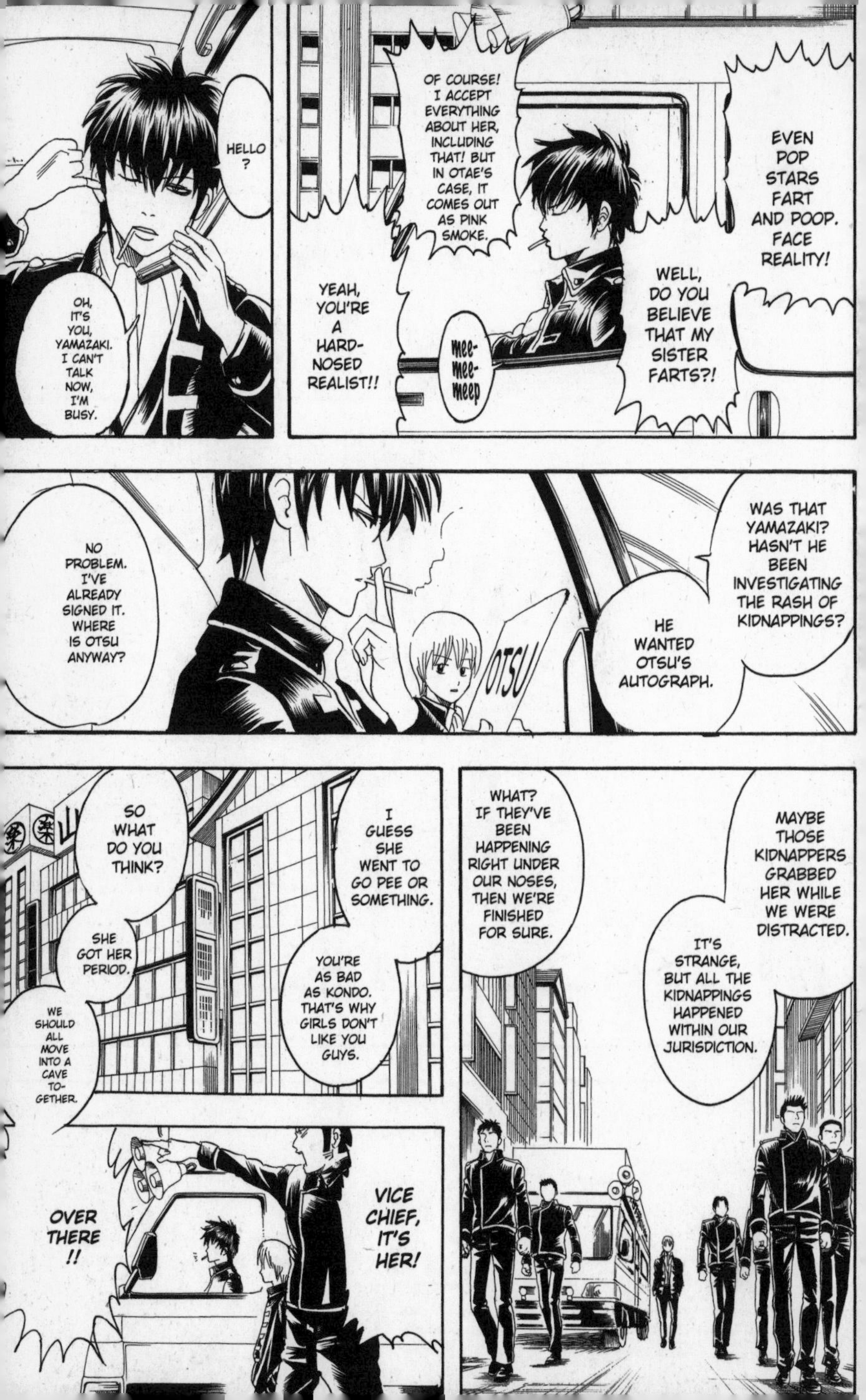
EVEN POP STARS FART AND POOP. FACE REALITY!
WELL, DO YOU BELIEVE THAT MY SISTER FARTS?!
OF COURSE! I ACCEPT EVERYTHING ABOUT HER, INCLUDING THAT! BUT IN OTAE'S CASE, IT COMES OUT AS PINK SMOKE.
YEAH, YOU'RE A HARD-NOSED REALIST!!
mee-mee-meep
HELLO?
OH, IT'S YOU, YAMAZAKI. I CAN'T TALK NOW, I'M BUSY.
WAS THAT YAMAZAKI? HASN'T HE BEEN INVESTIGATING THE RASH OF KIDNAPPINGS?
HE WANTED OTSU'S AUTOGRAPH.
OTSU
NO PROBLEM. I'VE ALREADY SIGNED IT. WHERE IS OTSU ANYWAY?
MAYBE THOSE KIDNAPPERS GRABBED HER WHILE WE WERE DISTRACTED.
IT'S STRANGE, BUT ALL THE KIDNAPPINGS HAPPENED WITHIN OUR JURISDICTION.
WHAT? IF THEY'VE BEEN HAPPENING RIGHT UNDER OUR NOSES, THEN WE'RE FINISHED FOR SURE.
SO WHAT DO YOU THINK?
I GUESS SHE WENT TO GO PEE OR SOMETHING.
YOU'RE AS BAD AS KONDO. THAT'S WHY GIRLS DON'T LIKE YOU GUYS.
SHE GOT HER PERIOD.
WE SHOULD ALL MOVE INTO A CAVE TO-GETHER.
VICE CHIEF, IT'S HER!
OVER THERE!!

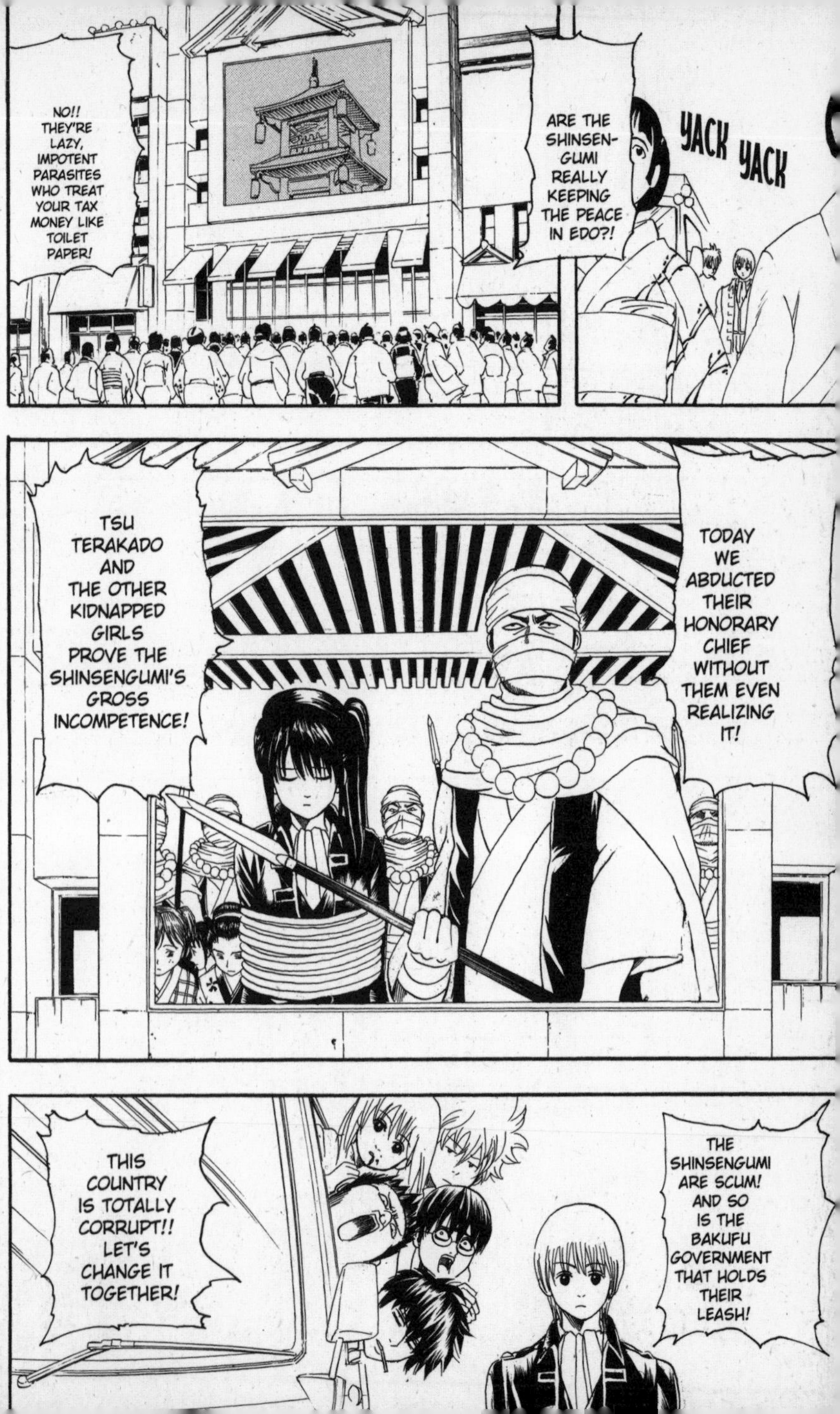
ARE THE SHINSENGUMI REALLY KEEPING THE PEACE IN EDO?!
YACK YACK
NO!! THEY'RE LAZY, IMPOTENT PARASITES WHO TREAT YOUR TAX MONEY LIKE TOILET PAPER!
TODAY WE ABDUCTED THEIR HONORARY CHIEF WITHOUT THEM EVEN REALIZING IT!
TSU TERAKADO AND THE OTHER KIDNAPPED GIRLS PROVE THE SHINSENGUMI'S GROSS INCOMPETENCE!
THE SHINSENGUMI ARE SCUM! AND SO IS THE BAKUFU GOVERNMENT THAT HOLDS THEIR LEASH!
THIS COUNTRY IS TOTALLY CORRUPT!! LET'S CHANGE IT TOGETHER!

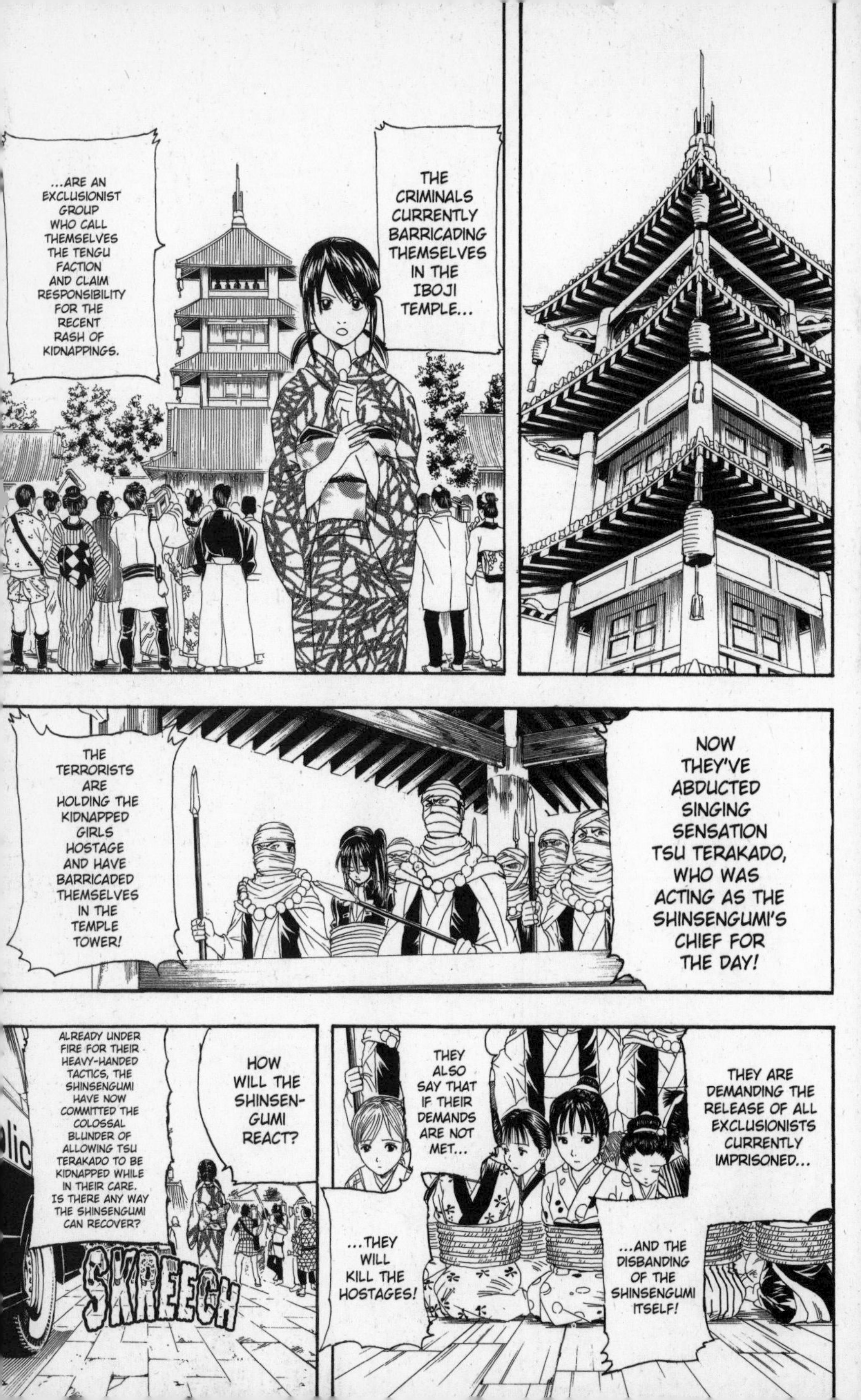

THE CRIMINALS CURRENTLY BARRICADING THEMSELVES IN THE IBOJI TEMPLE...
...ARE AN EXCLUSIONIST GROUP WHO CALL THEMSELVES THE TENGU FACTION AND CLAIM RESPONSIBILITY FOR THE RECENT RASH OF KIDNAPPINGS.
NOW THEY'VE ABDUCTED SINGING SENSATION TSU TERAKADO, WHO WAS ACTING AS THE SHINSENGUMI'S CHIEF FOR THE DAY!
THE TERRORISTS ARE HOLDING THE KIDNAPPED GIRLS HOSTAGE AND HAVE BARRICADED THEMSELVES IN THE TEMPLE TOWER!
THEY ARE DEMANDING THE RELEASE OF ALL EXCLUSIONISTS CURRENTLY IMPRISONED...
...AND THE DISBANDING OF THE SHINSENGUMI ITSELF!
THEY ALSO SAY THAT IF THEIR DEMANDS ARE NOT MET...
...THEY WILL KILL THE HOSTAGES!
HOW WILL THE SHINSEN-GUMI REACT?
ALREADY UNDER FIRE FOR THEIR HEAVY-HANDED TACTICS, THE SHINSENGUMI HAVE NOW COMMITTED THE COLOSSAL BLUNDER OF ALLOWING TSU TERAKADO TO BE KIDNAPPED WHILE IN THEIR CARE. IS THERE ANY WAY THE SHINSENGUMI CAN RECOVER?
SKREECH

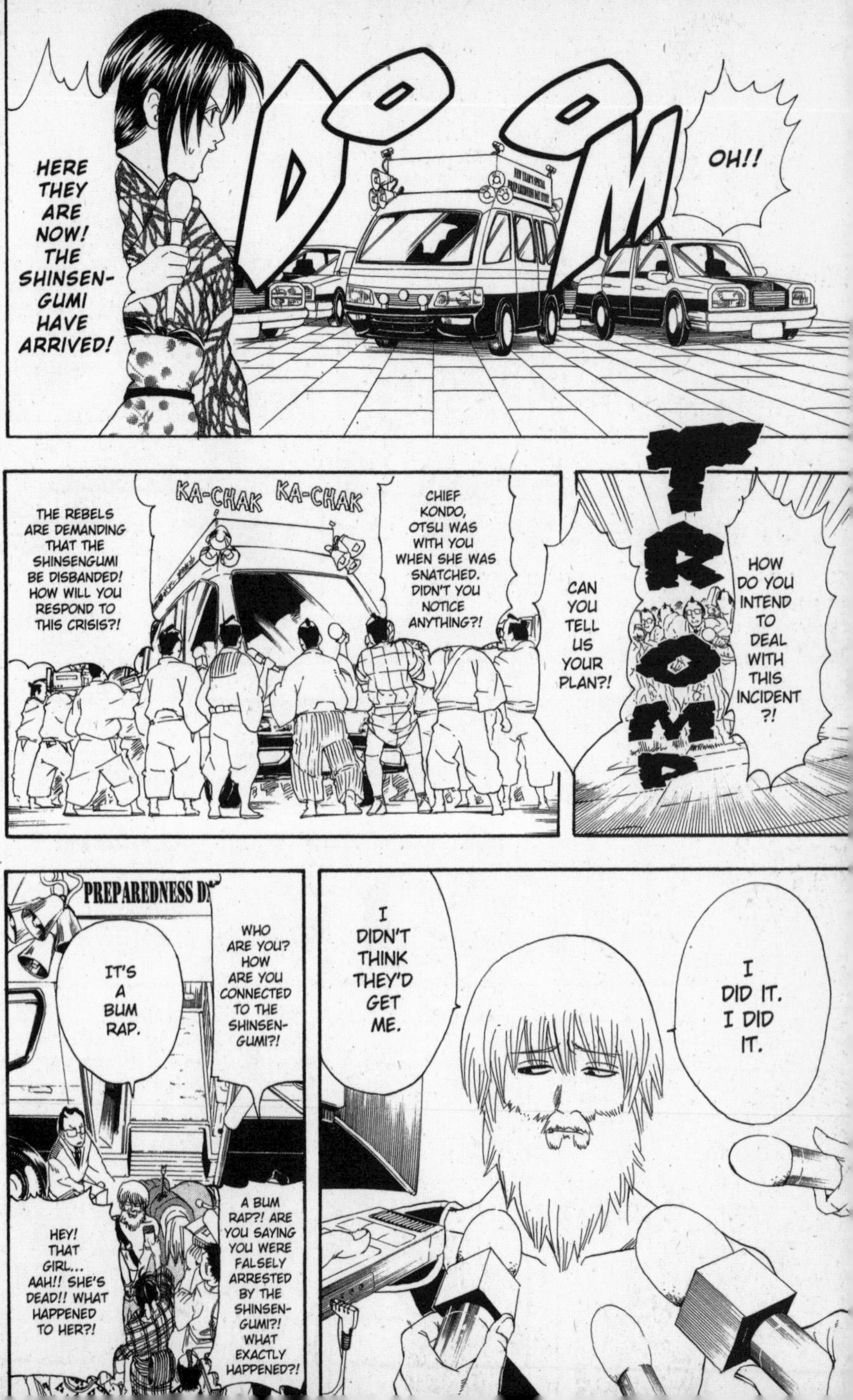
OH!!
DOOM
HERE THEY ARE NOW! THE SHINSEN-GUMI HAVE ARRIVED!
HOW DO YOU INTEND TO DEAL WITH THIS INCIDENT?!
CAN YOU TELL US YOUR PLAN?!
TROMP
CHIEF KONDO, OTSU WAS WITH YOU WHEN SHE WAS SNATCHED. DIDN'T YOU NOTICE ANYTHING?!
KA-CHAK KA-CHAK
THE REBELS ARE DEMANDING THAT THE SHINSENGUMI BE DISBANDED! HOW WILL YOU RESPOND TO THIS CRISIS?!
I DID IT. I DID IT.
I DIDN'T THINK THEY'D GET ME.
PREPAREDNESS D
WHO ARE YOU? HOW ARE YOU CONNECTED TO THE SHINSEN-GUMI?!
IT'S A BUM RAP.
A BUM RAP?! ARE YOU SAYING YOU WERE FALSELY ARRESTED BY THE SHINSEN-GUMI?! WHAT EXACTLY HAPPENED?!
HEY! THAT GIRL... AAH!! SHE'S DEAD!! WHAT HAPPENED TO HER?!

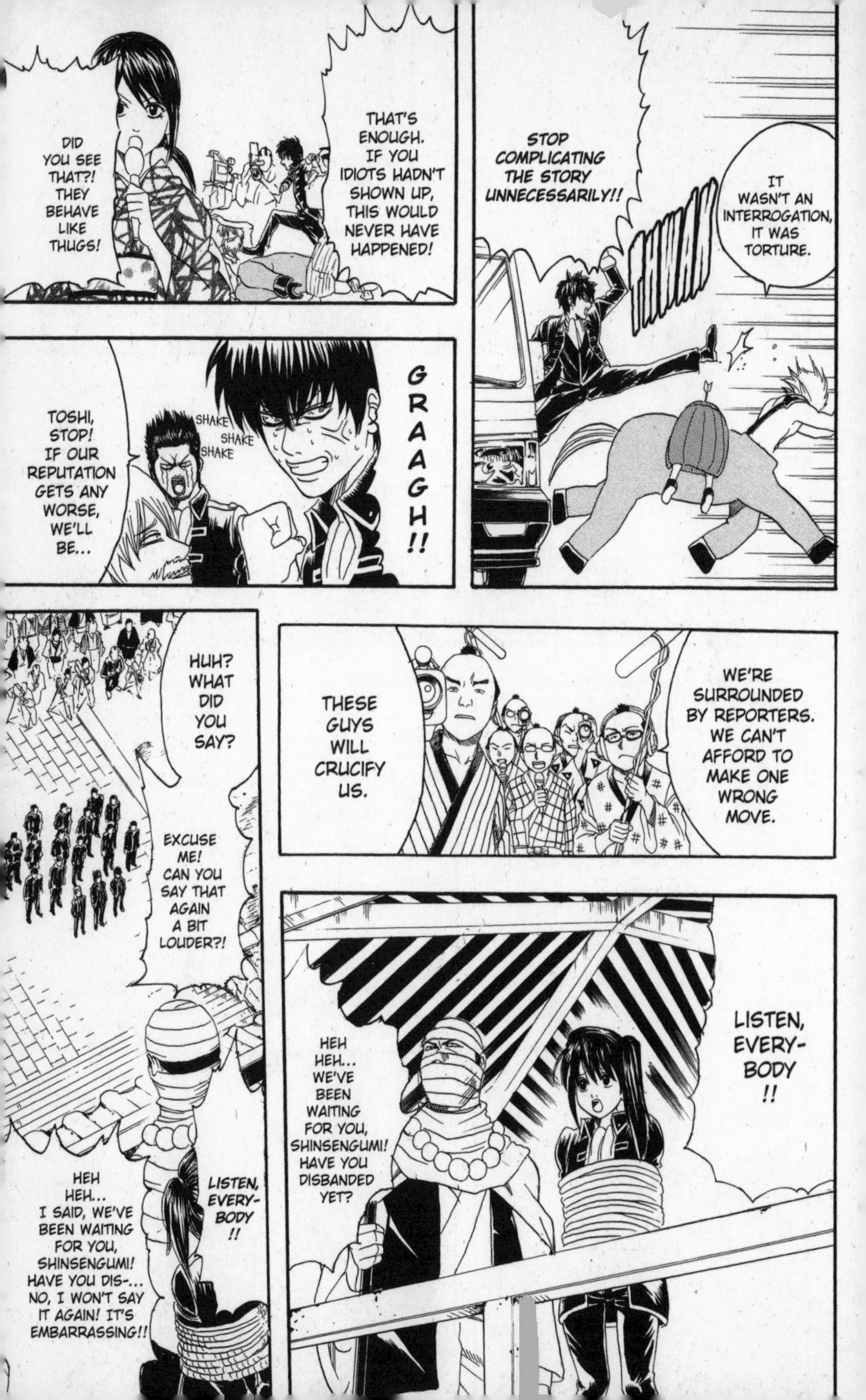
IT WASN'T AN INTERROGATION, IT WAS TORTURE.
STOP COMPLICATING THE STORY UNNECESSARILY!!
THWAK
THAT'S ENOUGH. IF YOU IDIOTS HADN'T SHOWN UP, THIS WOULD NEVER HAVE HAPPENED!
DID YOU SEE THAT?! THEY BEHAVE LIKE THUGS!
GRAAGH!!
SHAKE SHAKE SHAKE
TOSHI, STOP! IF OUR REPUTATION GETS ANY WORSE, WE'LL BE...
WE'RE SURROUNDED BY REPORTERS. WE CAN'T AFFORD TO MAKE ONE WRONG MOVE.
THESE GUYS WILL CRUCIFY US.
LISTEN, EVERY-BODY!!
HEH HEH... WE'VE BEEN WAITING FOR YOU, SHINSENGUMI! HAVE YOU DISBANDED YET?
HUH? WHAT DID YOU SAY?
EXCUSE ME! CAN YOU SAY THAT AGAIN A BIT LOUDER?!
LISTEN, EVERY-BODY!!
HEH HEH... I SAID, WE'VE BEEN WAITING FOR YOU, SHINSENGUMI! HAVE YOU DIS-... NO, I WON'T SAY IT AGAIN! IT'S EMBARRASSING!!

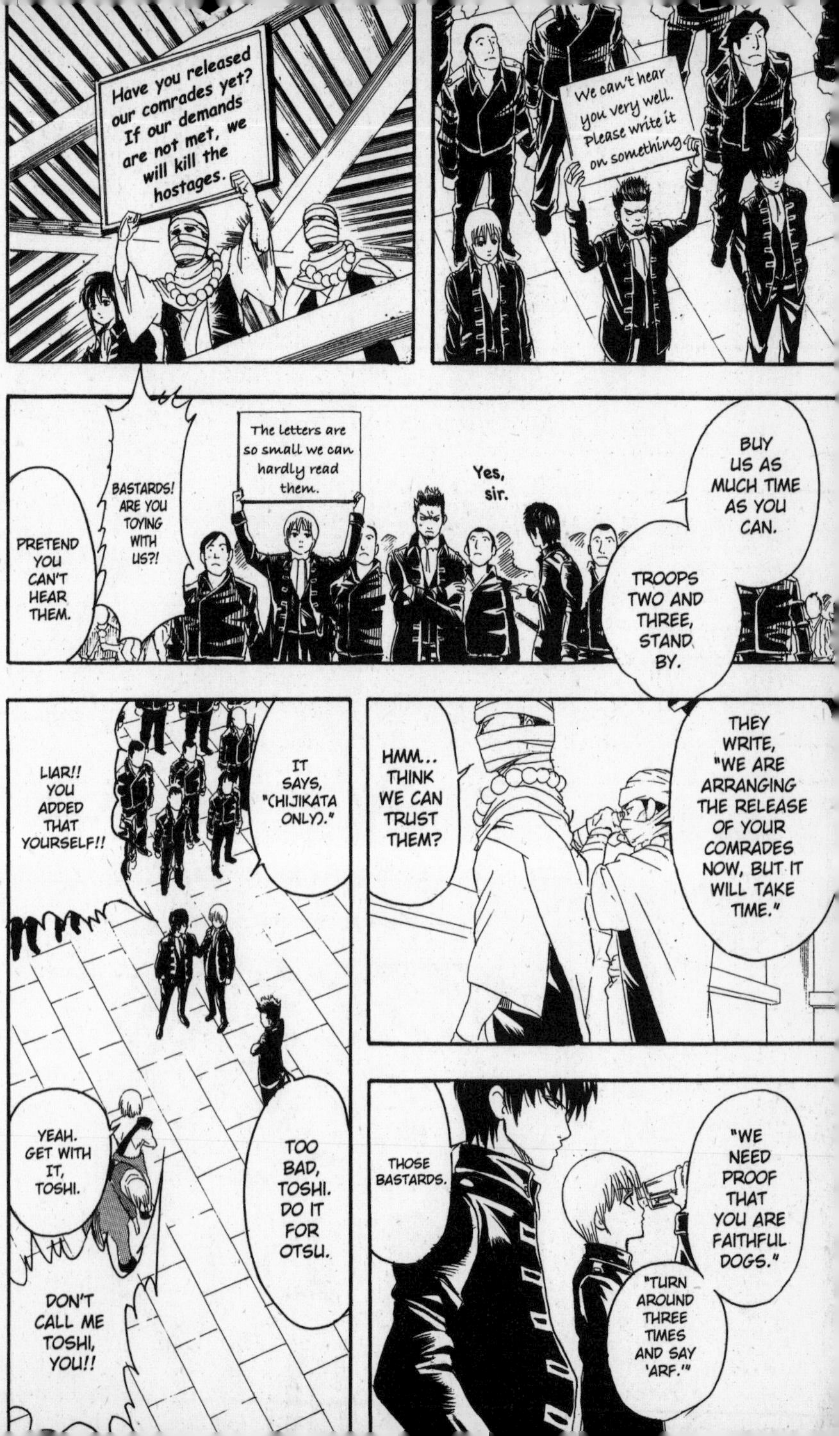
Have you released our comrades yet? If our demands are not met, we will kill the hostages.
We can't hear you very well. Please write it on something.
BASTARDS! ARE YOU TOYING WITH US?!
PRETEND YOU CAN'T HEAR THEM.
The letters are so small we can hardly read them.
Yes, sir.
BUY US AS MUCH TIME AS YOU CAN.
TROOPS TWO AND THREE, STAND BY.
THEY WRITE, "WE ARE ARRANGING THE RELEASE OF YOUR COMRADES NOW, BUT IT WILL TAKE TIME."
HMM... THINK WE CAN TRUST THEM?
"WE NEED PROOF THAT YOU ARE FAITHFUL DOGS."
"TURN AROUND THREE TIMES AND SAY 'ARF.'"
THOSE BASTARDS.
IT SAYS, "(HIJIKATA ONLY)."
LIAR!! YOU ADDED THAT YOURSELF!!
TOO BAD, TOSHI. DO IT FOR OTSU.
YEAH. GET WITH IT, TOSHI.
DON'T CALL ME TOSHI, YOU!!

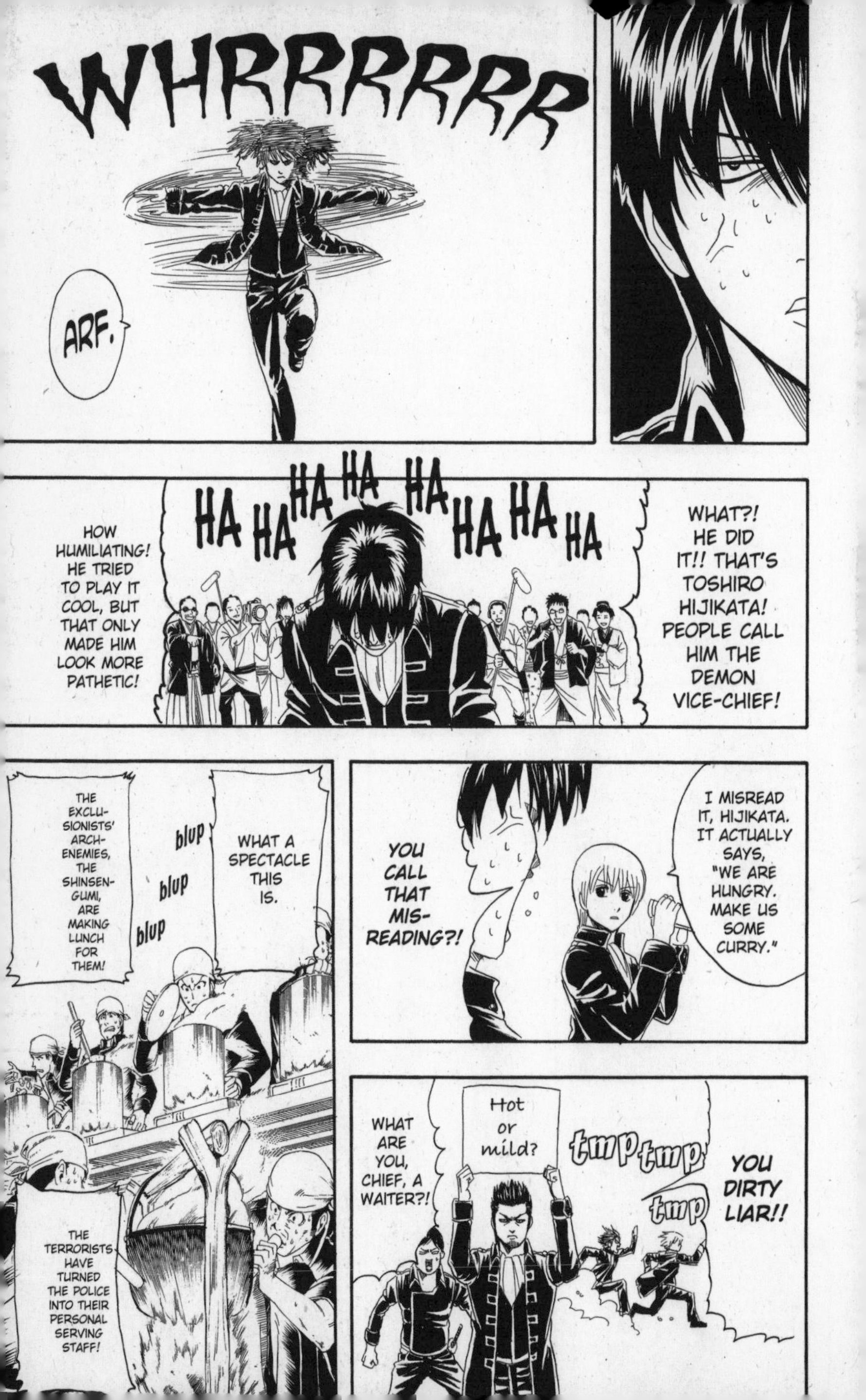
WHRRRRRRR
ARF.
WHAT?! HE DID IT!! THAT'S TOSHIRO HIJIKATA! PEOPLE CALL HIM THE DEMON VICE-CHIEF!
HA HA HA HA HA HA HA HA HA
HOW HUMILIATING! HE TRIED TO PLAY IT COOL, BUT THAT ONLY MADE HIM LOOK MORE PATHETIC!
I MISREAD IT, HIJIKATA. IT ACTUALLY SAYS, "WE ARE HUNGRY. MAKE US SOME CURRY."
YOU CALL THAT MIS-READING?!
YOU DIRTY LIAR!!
tmp tmp
tmp
Hot or mild?
WHAT ARE YOU, CHIEF, A WAITER?!
WHAT A SPECTACLE THIS IS.
THE EXCLUSIONISTS' ARCH-ENEMIES, THE SHINSEN-GUMI, ARE MAKING LUNCH FOR THEM!
blup
blup
blup
THE TERRORISTS HAVE TURNED THE POLICE INTO THEIR PERSONAL SERVING STAFF!

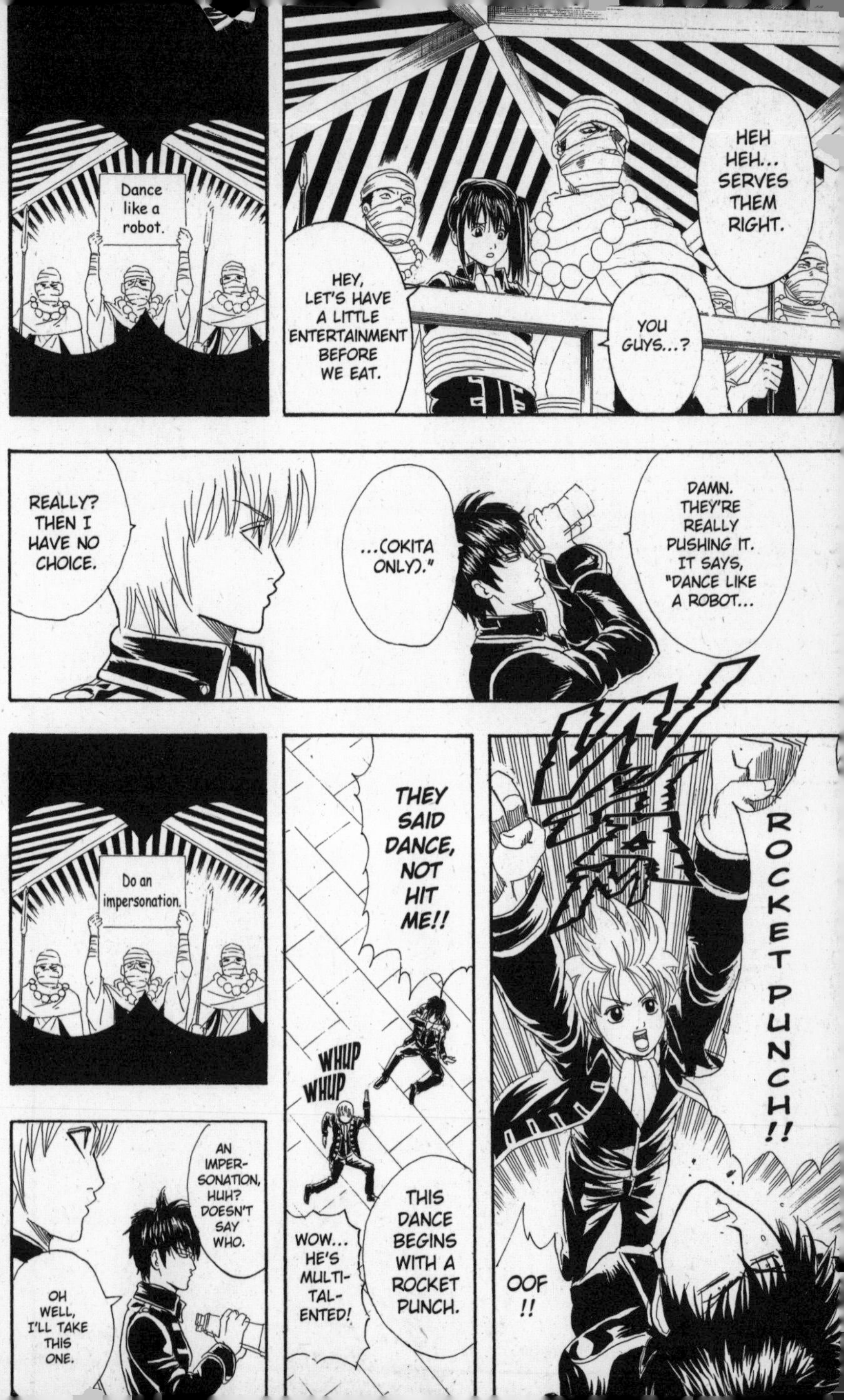
HEH HEH... SERVES THEM RIGHT.
YOU GUYS...?
HEY, LET'S HAVE A LITTLE ENTERTAINMENT BEFORE WE EAT.
Dance like a robot.
DAMN. THEY'RE REALLY PUSHING IT. IT SAYS, "DANCE LIKE A ROBOT...
...(OKITA ONLY)."
REALLY? THEN I HAVE NO CHOICE.
ROCKET PUNCH!!
OOF !!
THEY SAID DANCE, NOT HIT ME!!
WHUP WHUP
THIS DANCE BEGINS WITH A ROCKET PUNCH.
WOW... HE'S MULTI-TALENTED!
Do an impersonation.
AN IMPERSONATION, HUH? DOESN'T SAY WHO.
OH WELL, I'LL TAKE THIS ONE.

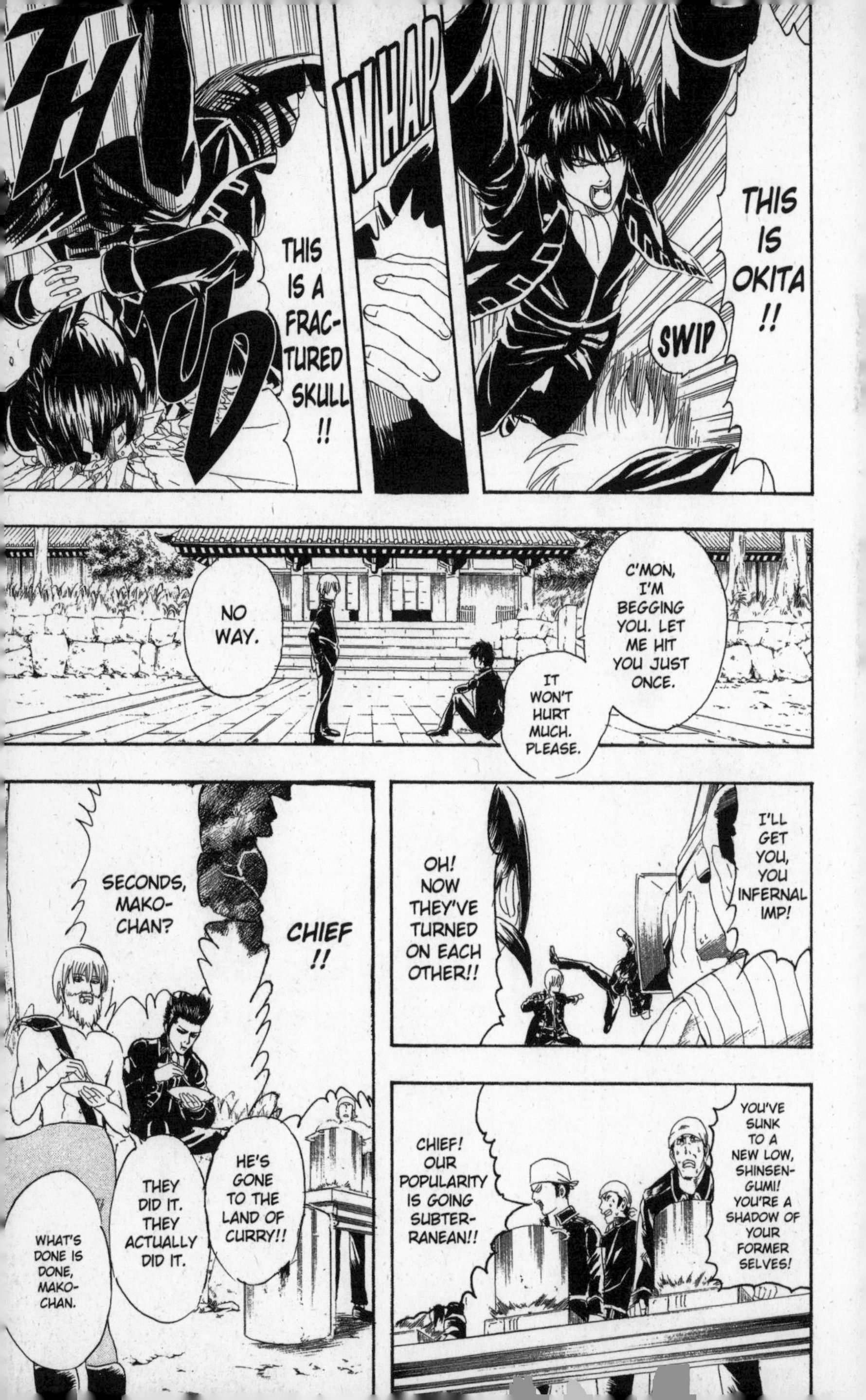
THIS IS OKITA!!
SWIP
WHAP
THIS IS A FRACTURED SKULL!!
C'MON, I'M BEGGING YOU. LET ME HIT YOU JUST ONCE.
IT WON'T HURT MUCH. PLEASE.
NO WAY.
I'LL GET YOU, YOU INFERNAL IMP!
OH! NOW THEY'VE TURNED ON EACH OTHER!!
YOU'VE SUNK TO A NEW LOW, SHINSENGUMI! YOU'RE A SHADOW OF YOUR FORMER SELVES!
CHIEF! OUR POPULARITY IS GOING SUBTERRANEAN!!
CHIEF!!
SECONDS, MAKO-CHAN?
HE'S GONE TO THE LAND OF CURRY!!
THEY DID IT. THEY ACTUALLY DID IT.
WHAT'S DONE IS DONE, MAKO-CHAN.

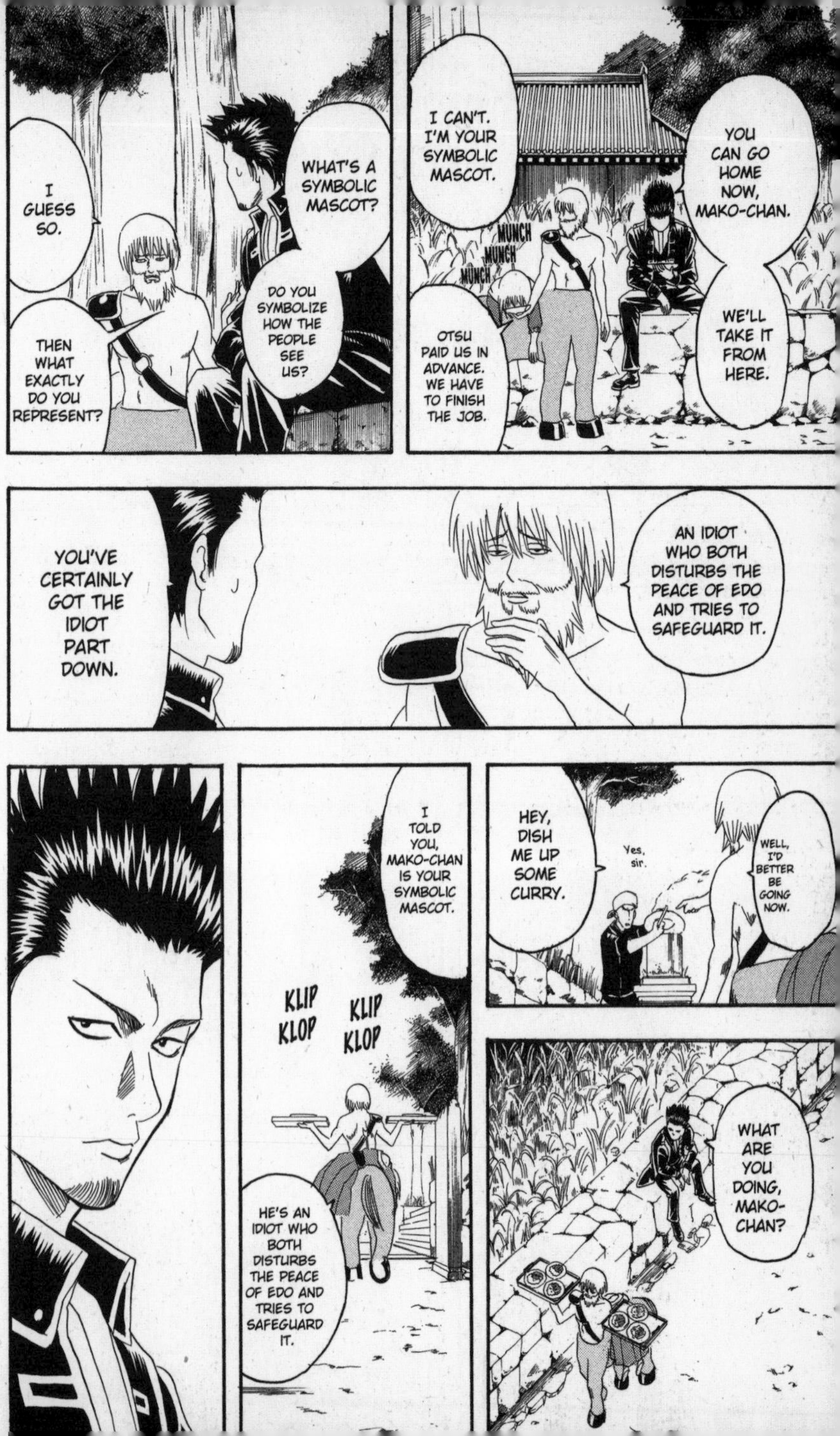
YOU CAN GO HOME NOW, MAKO-CHAN.
WE'LL TAKE IT FROM HERE.
I CAN'T. I'M YOUR SYMBOLIC MASCOT.
MUNCH
MUNCH
MUNCH
OTSU PAID US IN ADVANCE. WE HAVE TO FINISH THE JOB.
WHAT'S A SYMBOLIC MASCOT?
DO YOU SYMBOLIZE HOW THE PEOPLE SEE US?
I GUESS SO.
THEN WHAT EXACTLY DO YOU REPRESENT?
AN IDIOT WHO BOTH DISTURBS THE PEACE OF EDO AND TRIES TO SAFEGUARD IT.
YOU'VE CERTAINLY GOT THE IDIOT PART DOWN.
WELL, I'D BETTER BE GOING NOW.
Yes, sir.
HEY, DISH ME UP SOME CURRY.
WHAT ARE YOU DOING, MAKO-CHAN?
I TOLD YOU, MAKO-CHAN IS YOUR SYMBOLIC MASCOT.
KLIP KLOP
KLIP KLOP
HE'S AN IDIOT WHO BOTH DISTURBS THE PEACE OF EDO AND TRIES TO SAFEGUARD IT.

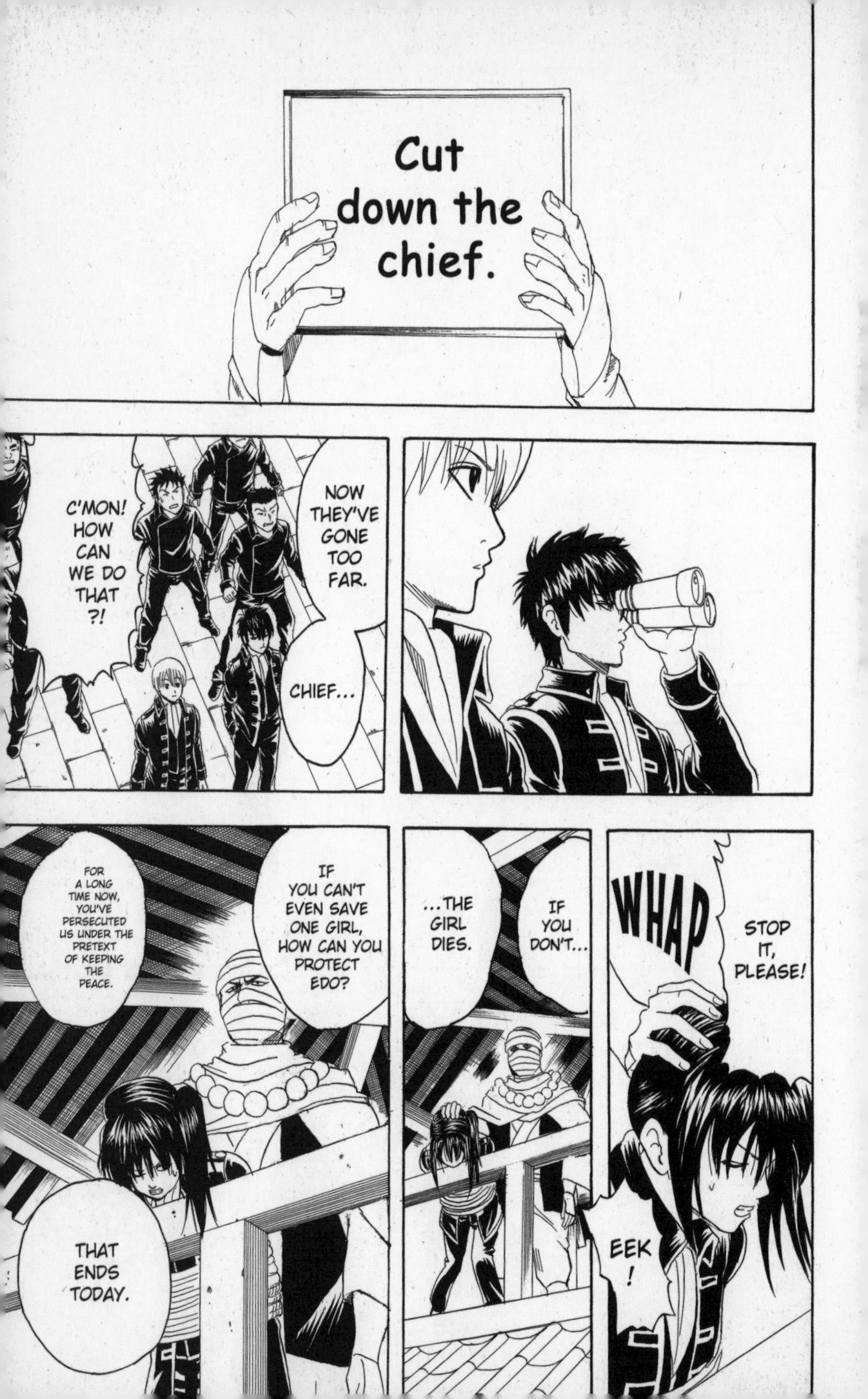
Cut down the chief.
NOW THEY'VE GONE TOO FAR.
C'MON! HOW CAN WE DO THAT?!
CHIEF...
WHAP
STOP IT, PLEASE!
EEK!
IF YOU DON'T...
...THE GIRL DIES.
IF YOU CAN'T EVEN SAVE ONE GIRL, HOW CAN YOU PROTECT EDO?
FOR A LONG TIME NOW, YOU'VE PERSECUTED US UNDER THE PRETEXT OF KEEPING THE PEACE.
THAT ENDS TODAY.

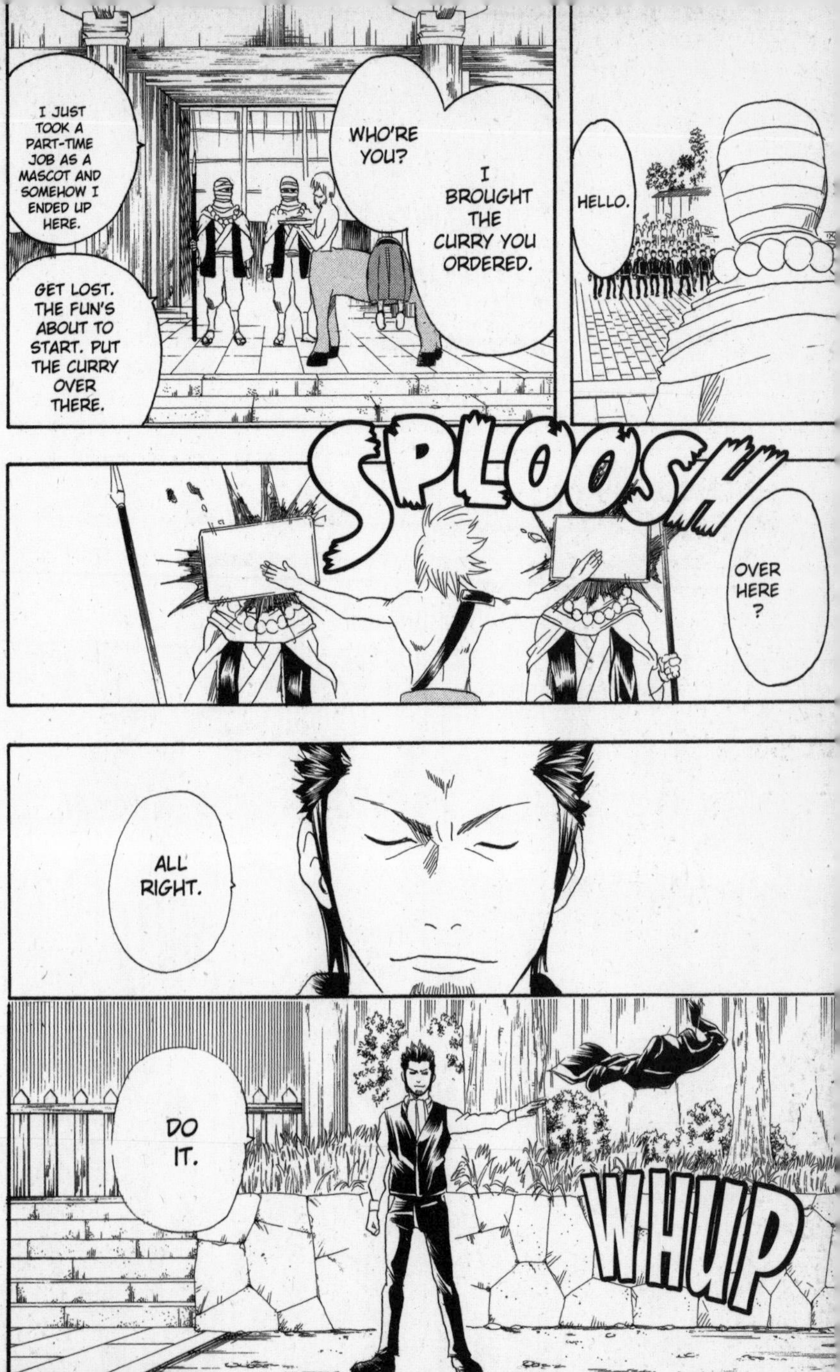
HELLO.
WHO'RE YOU?
I BROUGHT THE CURRY YOU ORDERED.
I JUST TOOK A PART-TIME JOB AS A MASCOT AND SOMEHOW I ENDED UP HERE.
GET LOST. THE FUN'S ABOUT TO START. PUT THE CURRY OVER THERE.
OVER HERE?
SPLOOSH
ALL RIGHT.
WHUP
DO IT.

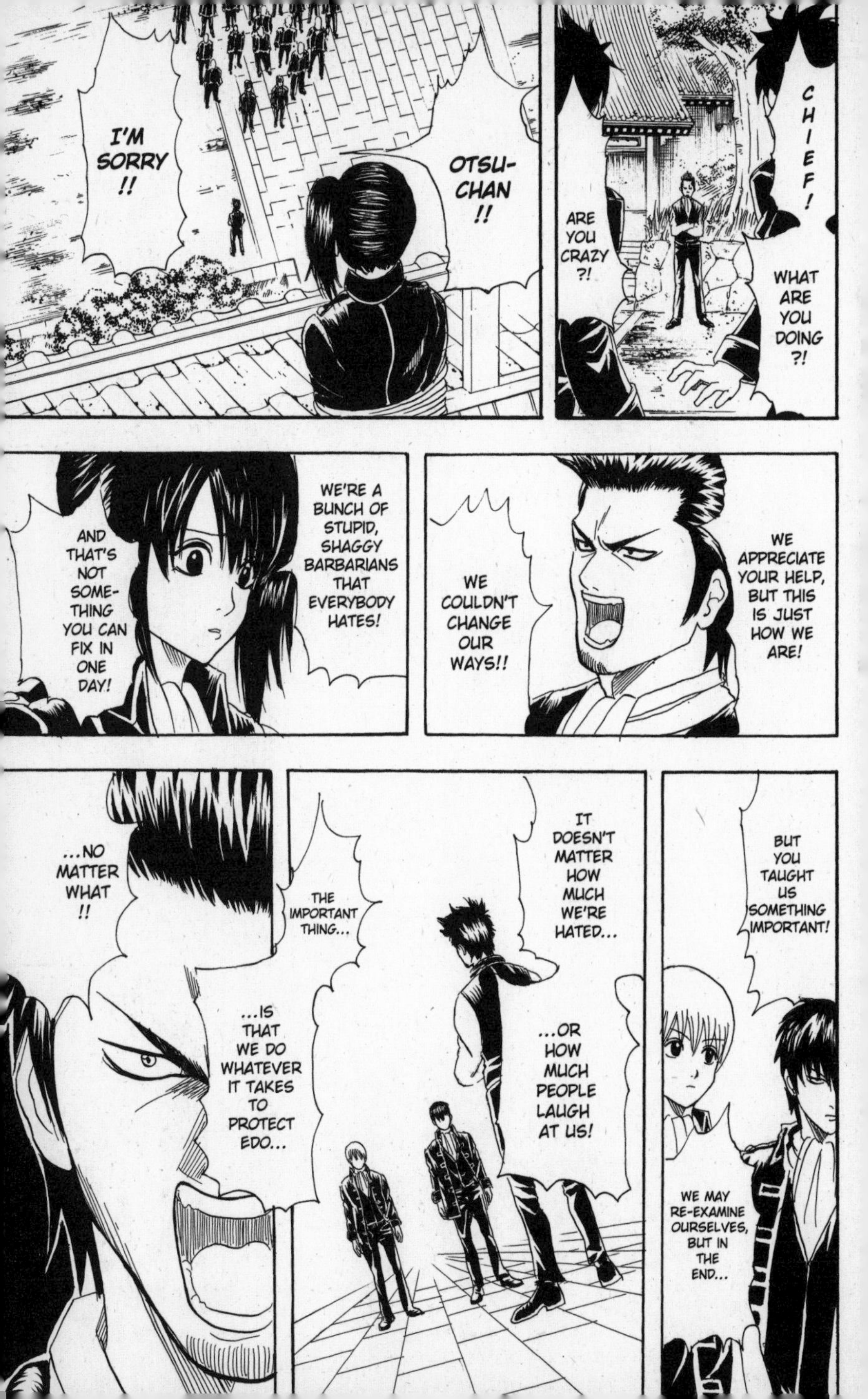
CHIEF!
WHAT ARE YOU DOING?!
ARE YOU CRAZY?!
OTSU-CHAN!!
I'M SORRY!!
WE APPRECIATE YOUR HELP, BUT THIS IS JUST HOW WE ARE!
WE COULDN'T CHANGE OUR WAYS!!
WE'RE A BUNCH OF STUPID, SHAGGY BARBARIANS THAT EVERYBODY HATES!
AND THAT'S NOT SOMETHING YOU CAN FIX IN ONE DAY!
BUT YOU TAUGHT US SOMETHING IMPORTANT!
WE MAY RE-EXAMINE OURSELVES, BUT IN THE END...
IT DOESN'T MATTER HOW MUCH WE'RE HATED...
...OR HOW MUCH PEOPLE LAUGH AT US!
THE IMPORTANT THING...
...IS THAT WE DO WHATEVER IT TAKES TO PROTECT EDO...
...NO MATTER WHAT!!

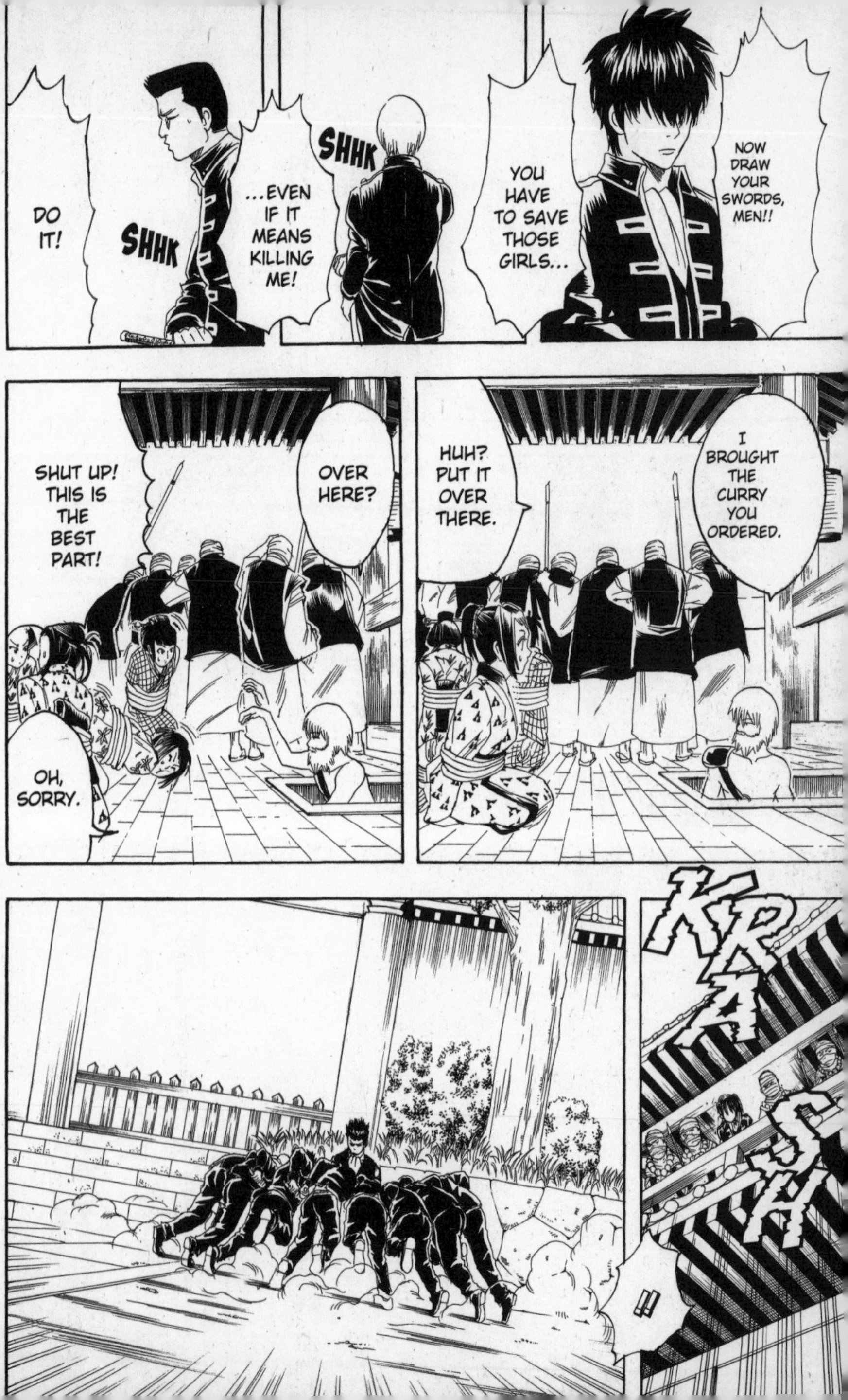
NOW DRAW YOUR SWORDS, MEN!!
YOU HAVE TO SAVE THOSE GIRLS...
SHHK
...EVEN IF IT MEANS KILLING ME!
SHHK
DO IT!
I BROUGHT THE CURRY YOU ORDERED.
HUH? PUT IT OVER THERE.
OVER HERE?
SHUT UP! THIS IS THE BEST PART!
OH, SORRY.
KRA
!!

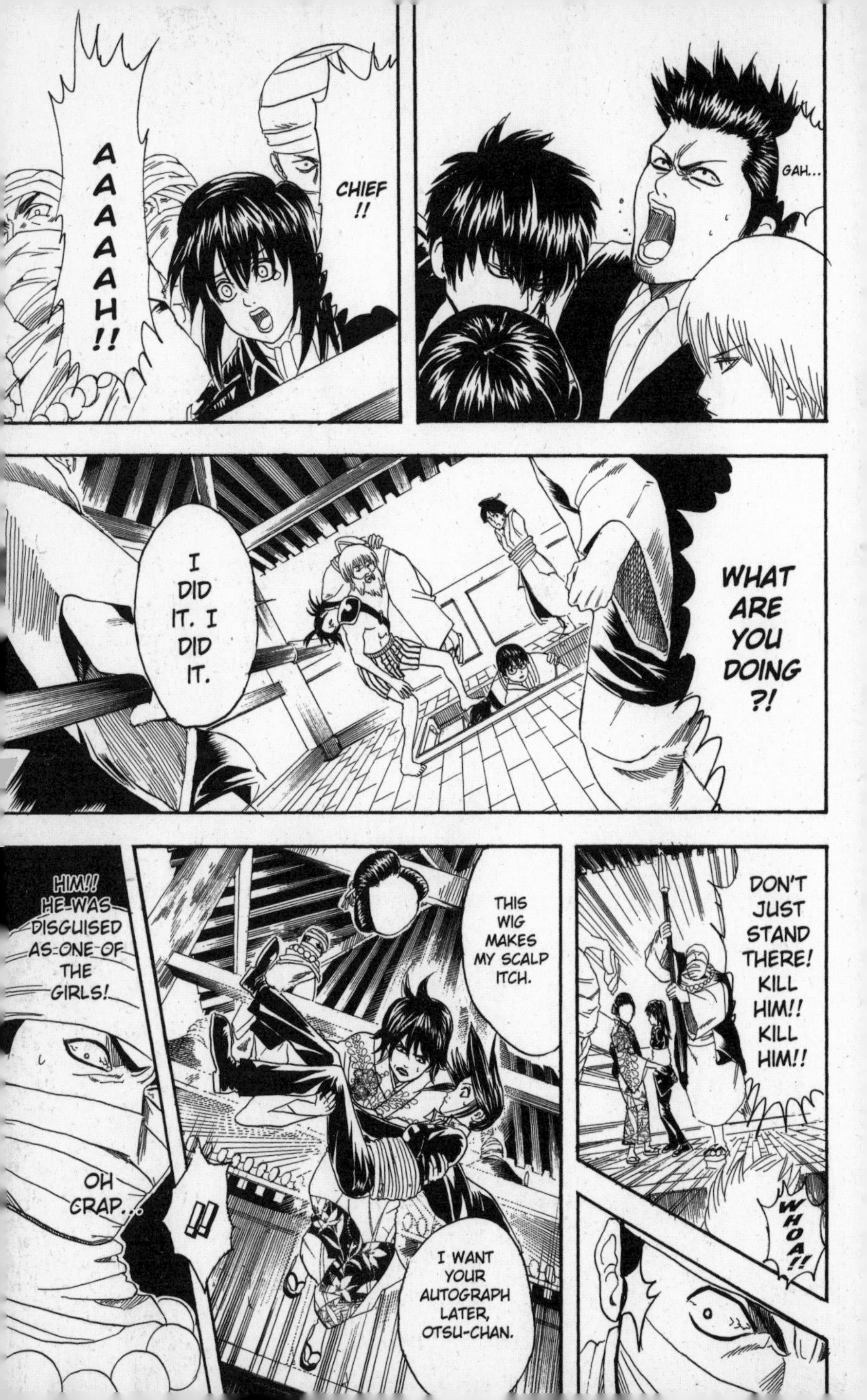
GAH...
CHIEF !!
AAAAAAH!!
WHAT ARE YOU DOING ?!
I DID IT. I DID IT.
DON'T JUST STAND THERE! KILL HIM!! KILL HIM!!
WHOA!!
THIS WIG MAKES MY SCALP ITCH.
I WANT YOUR AUTOGRAPH LATER, OTSU-CHAN.
HIM!! HE WAS DISGUISED AS ONE OF THE GIRLS!
!!
OH CRAP...

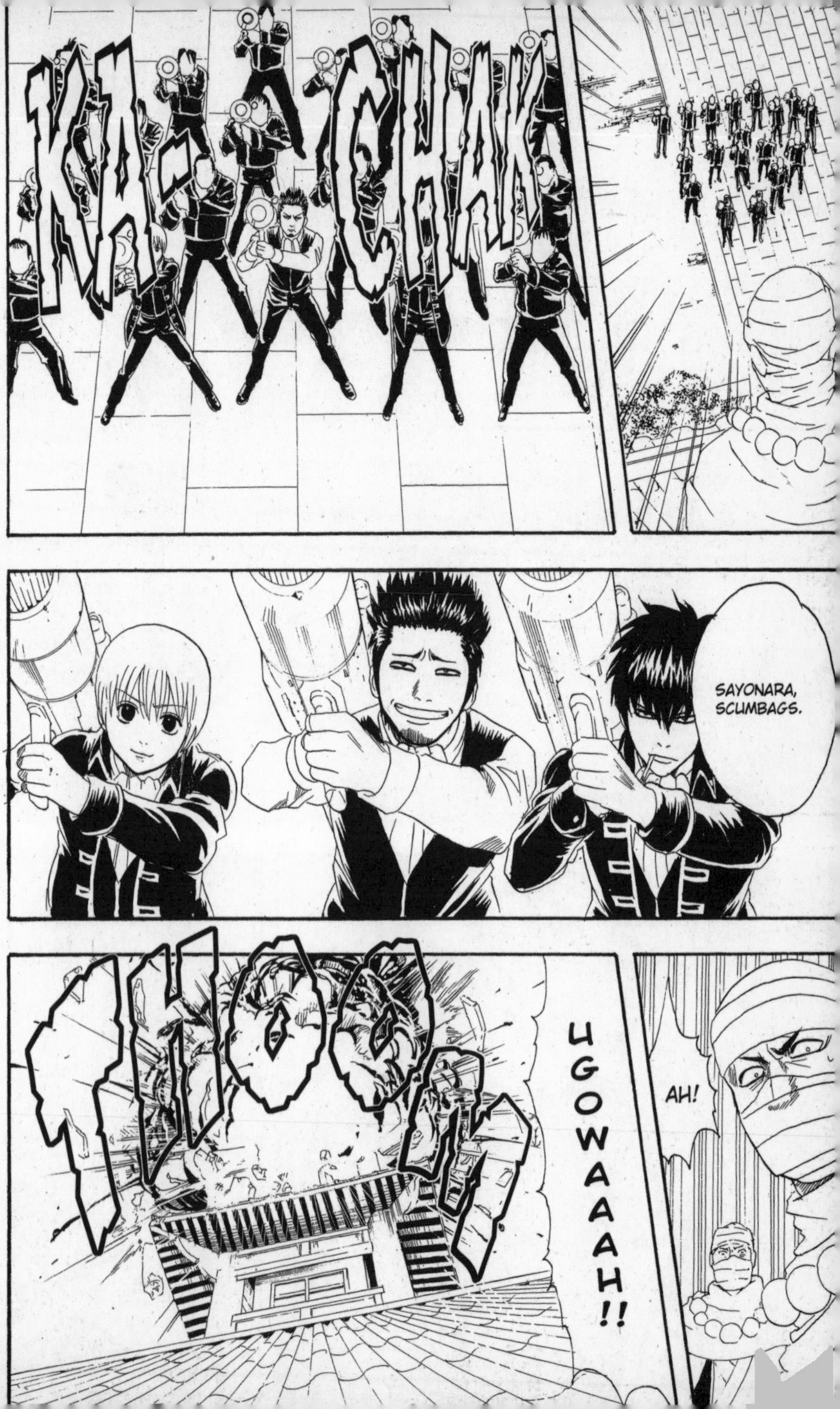
KA-CHAK
SAYONARA, SCUMBAGS.
AH!
UGOWAAAAH!!

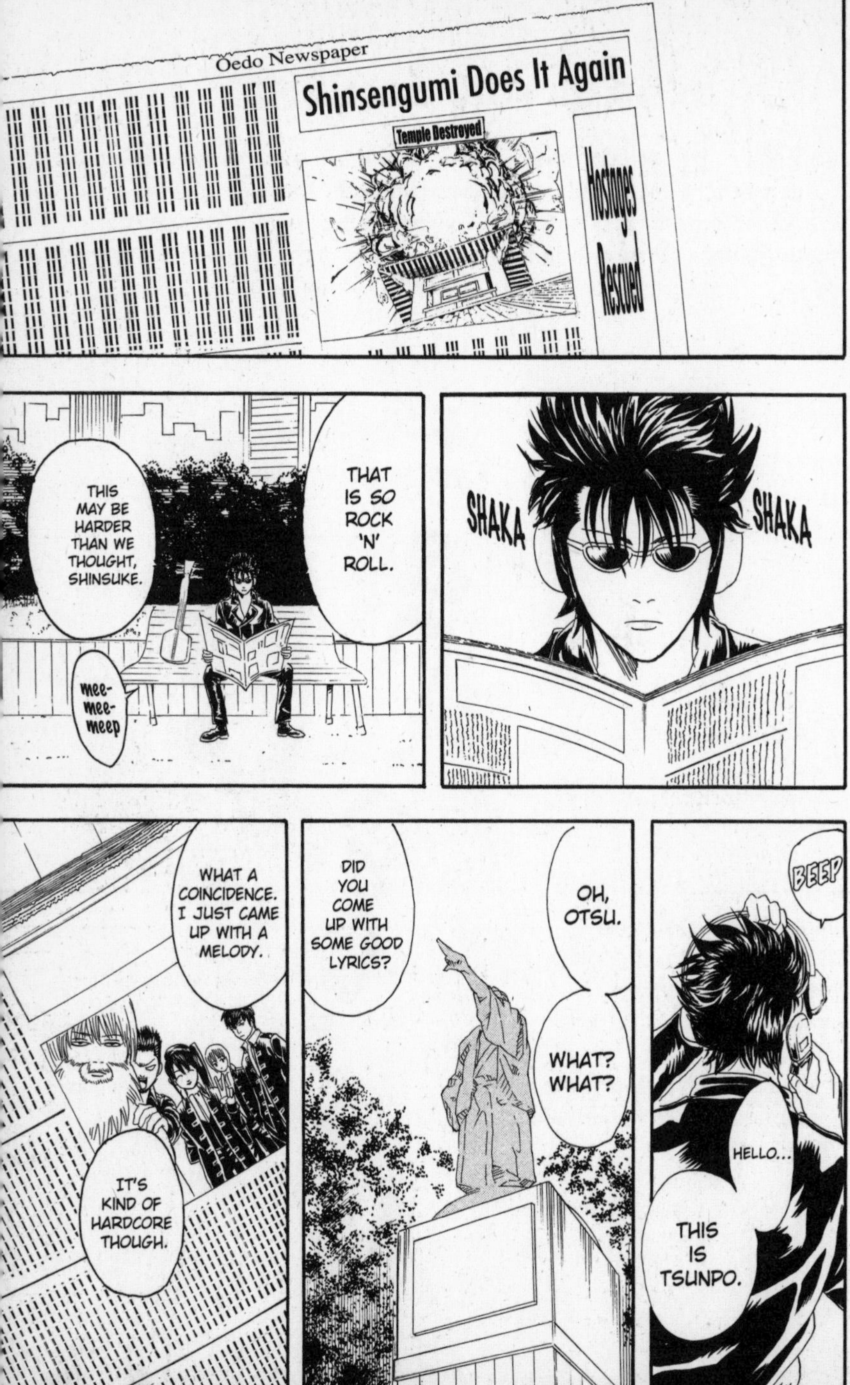
Oedo Newspaper
Shinsengumi Does It Again
Temple Destroyed
Hostages Rescued
SHAKA
SHAKA
THAT IS SO ROCK 'N' ROLL.
THIS MAY BE HARDER THAN WE THOUGHT, SHINSUKE.
mee-mee-meep
BEEP
HELLO...
THIS IS TSUNPO.
OH, OTSU.
WHAT? WHAT?
DID YOU COME UP WITH SOME GOOD LYRICS?
WHAT A COINCIDENCE. I JUST CAME UP WITH A MELODY.
IT'S KIND OF HARDCORE THOUGH.

Send us your Fan Art!

We'd like to give you, our loyal *Gin Tama* readers, a chance to show off
your artistic talents! Send us your drawings of the Yorozuya crew or
your other favorite characters from *Gin Tama*! If they're good enough to
impress Granny Otose (which ain't easy), you just might see them in the
pages of future VIZ Media volumes of *Gin Tama*!

Send your fan art to:

VIZ Media
Attn: Mike Montesa, Editor
295 Bay St.
San Francisco, CA 94133

Be sure to include the signed
release form available here:
http://www.shonenjump.com/
fanart/Fan_Art_Release.pdf
Submissions will not be returned.
Submissions without a signed
release form will be fed to the
Amanto sea lions at Fisherman's
Wharf…

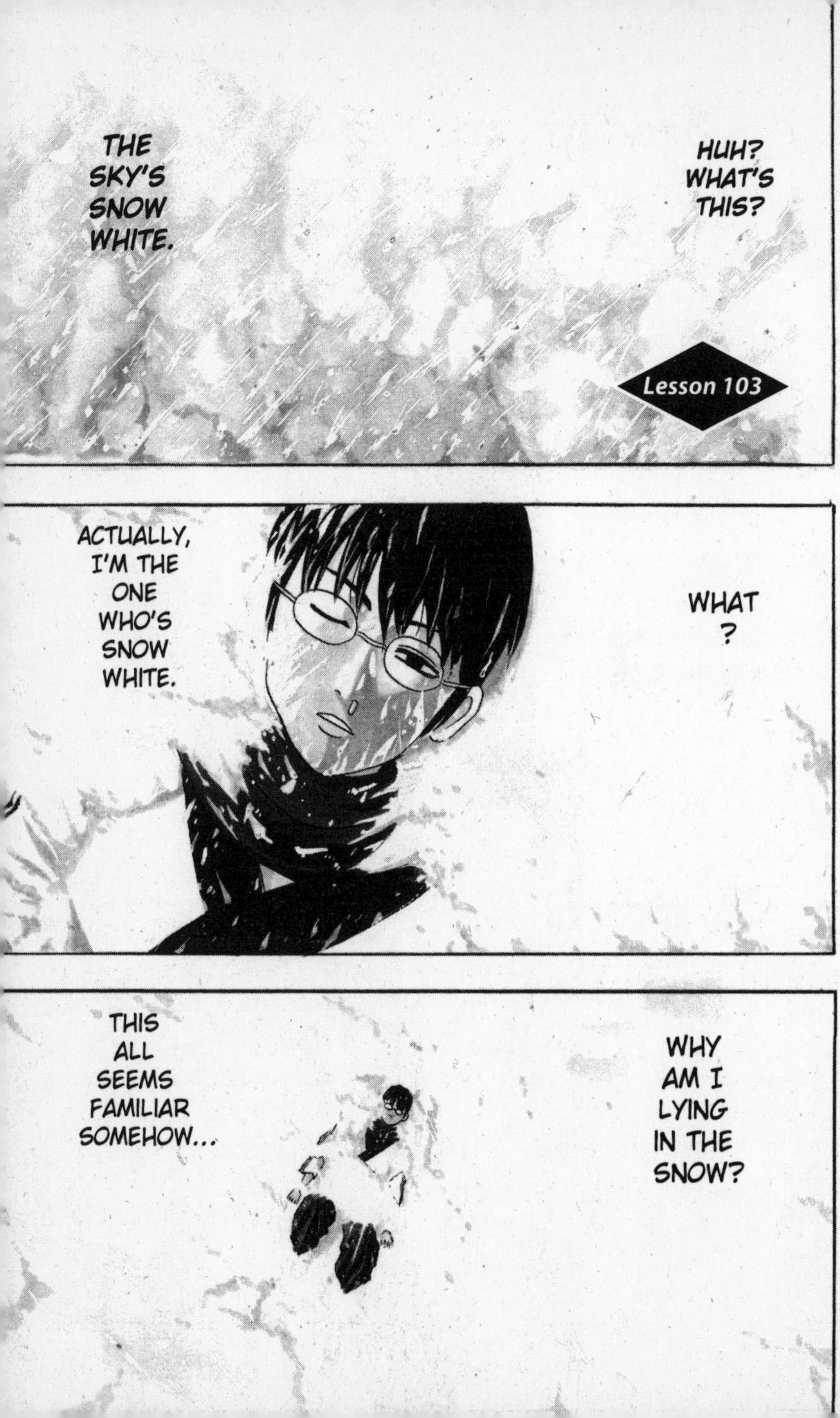
HUH? WHAT'S THIS?
THE SKY'S SNOW WHITE.
Lesson 103
WHAT ?
ACTUALLY, I'M THE ONE WHO'S SNOW WHITE.
WHY AM I LYING IN THE SNOW?
THIS ALL SEEMS FAMILIAR SOMEHOW...

Only Children Play in the Snow

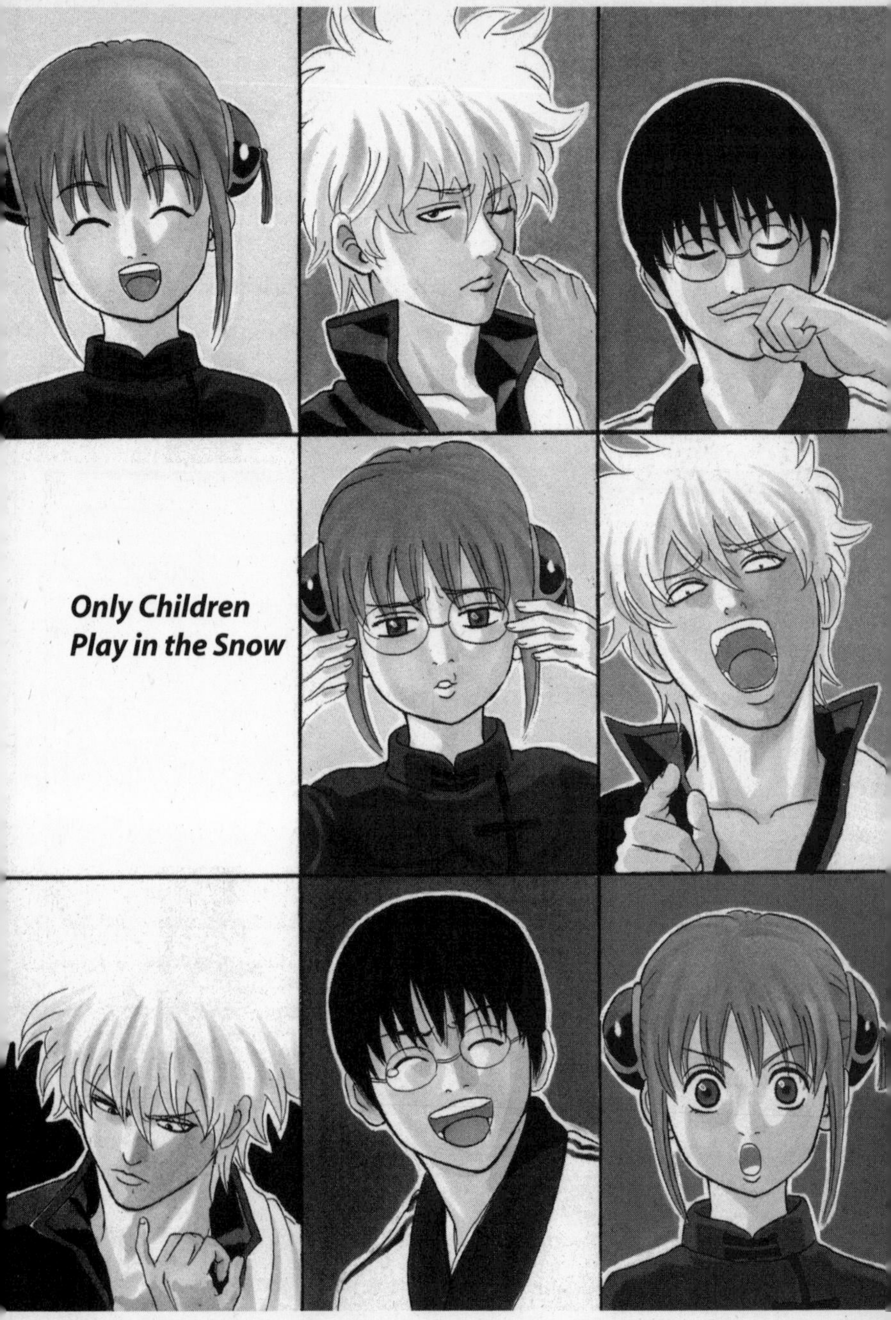

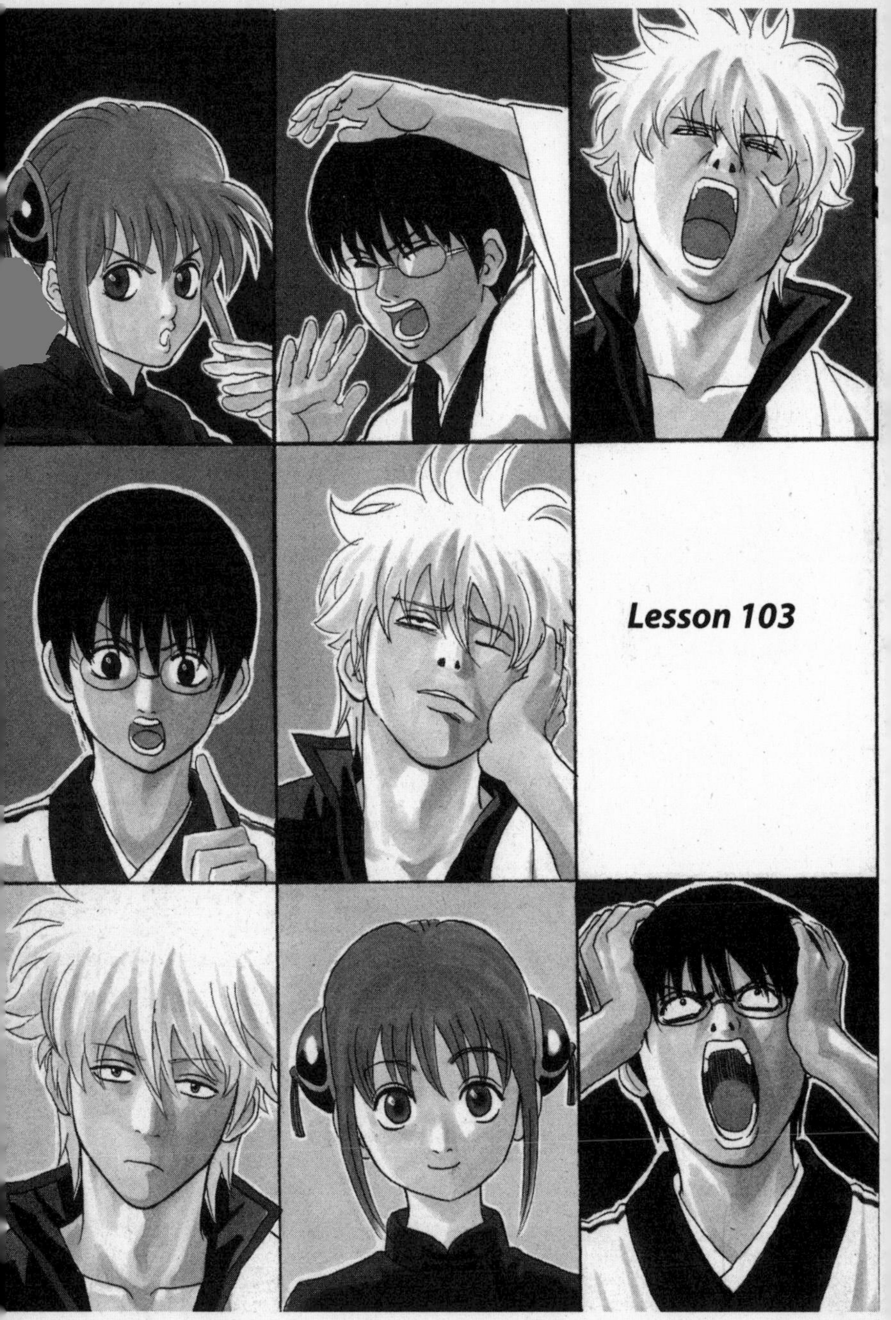
Lesson 103

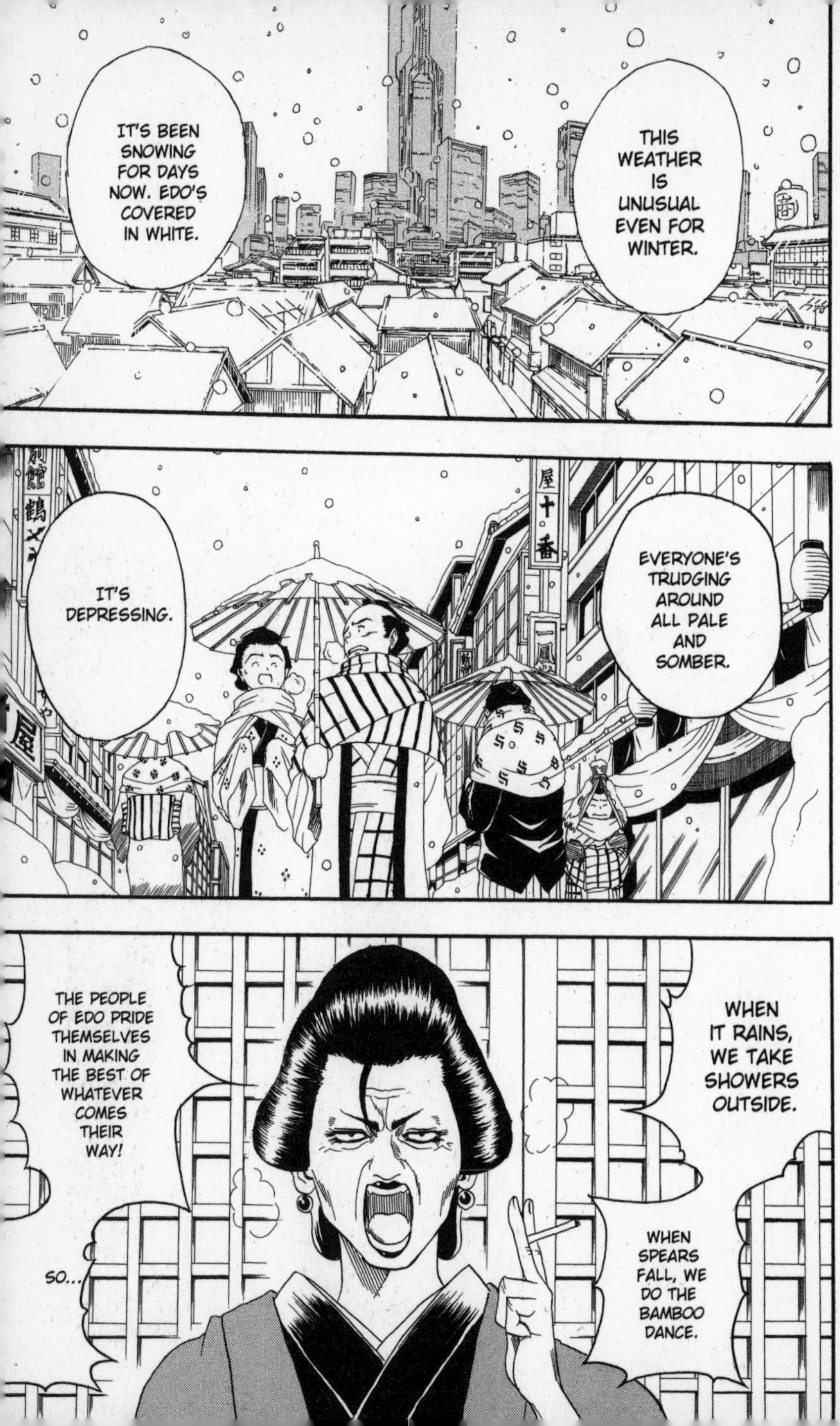
THIS WEATHER IS UNUSUAL EVEN FOR WINTER.
IT'S BEEN SNOWING FOR DAYS NOW. EDO'S COVERED IN WHITE.
EVERYONE'S TRUDGING AROUND ALL PALE AND SOMBER.
IT'S DEPRESSING.
WHEN IT RAINS, WE TAKE SHOWERS OUTSIDE.
THE PEOPLE OF EDO PRIDE THEMSELVES IN MAKING THE BEST OF WHATEVER COMES THEIR WAY!
WHEN SPEARS FALL, WE DO THE BAMBOO DANCE.
SO...

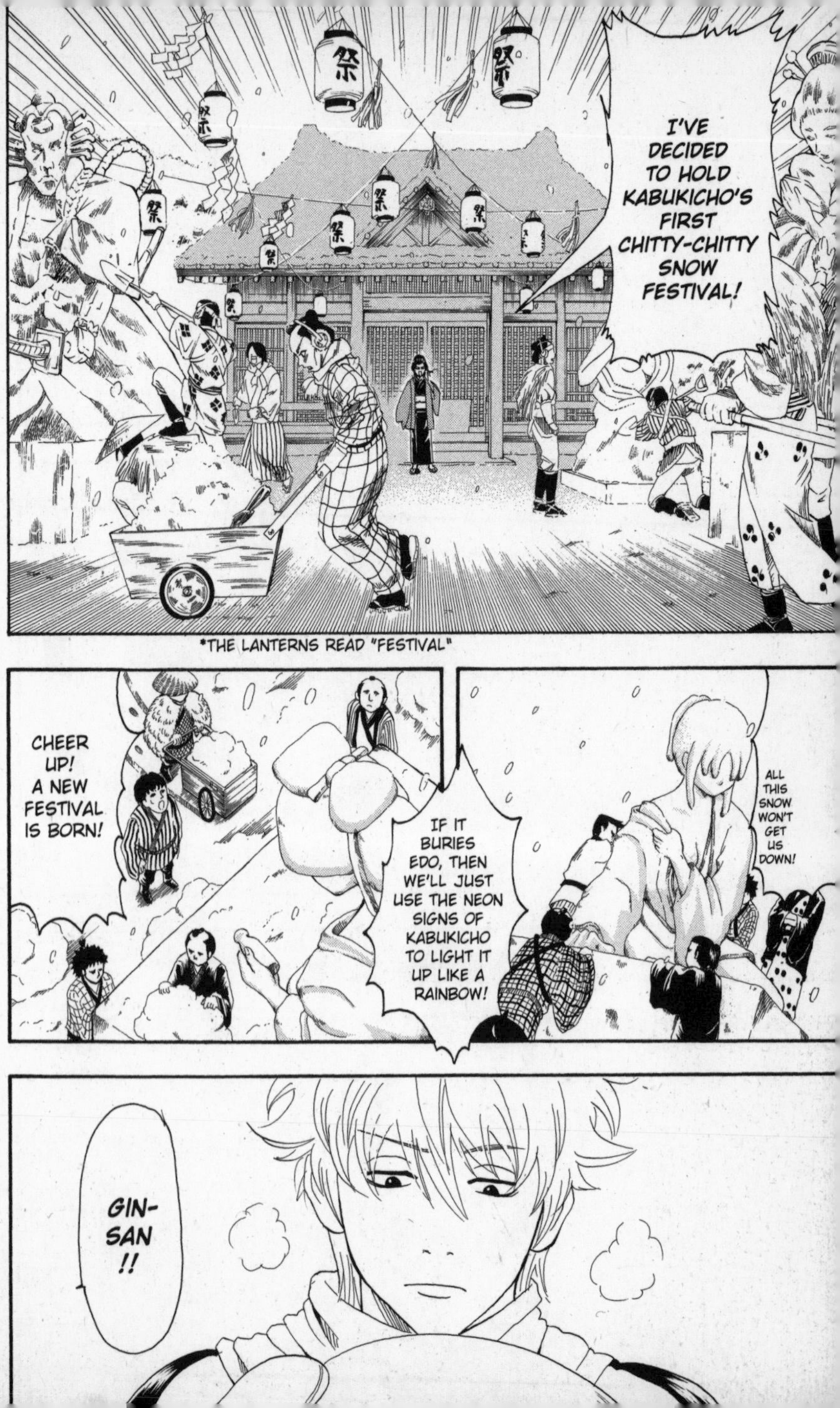
I'VE DECIDED TO HOLD KABUKICHO'S FIRST CHITTY-CHITTY SNOW FESTIVAL!
*THE LANTERNS READ "FESTIVAL"
ALL THIS SNOW WON'T GET US DOWN!
IF IT BURIES EDO, THEN WE'LL JUST USE THE NEON SIGNS OF KABUKICHO TO LIGHT IT UP LIKE A RAINBOW!
CHEER UP! A NEW FESTIVAL IS BORN!
GIN-SAN!!

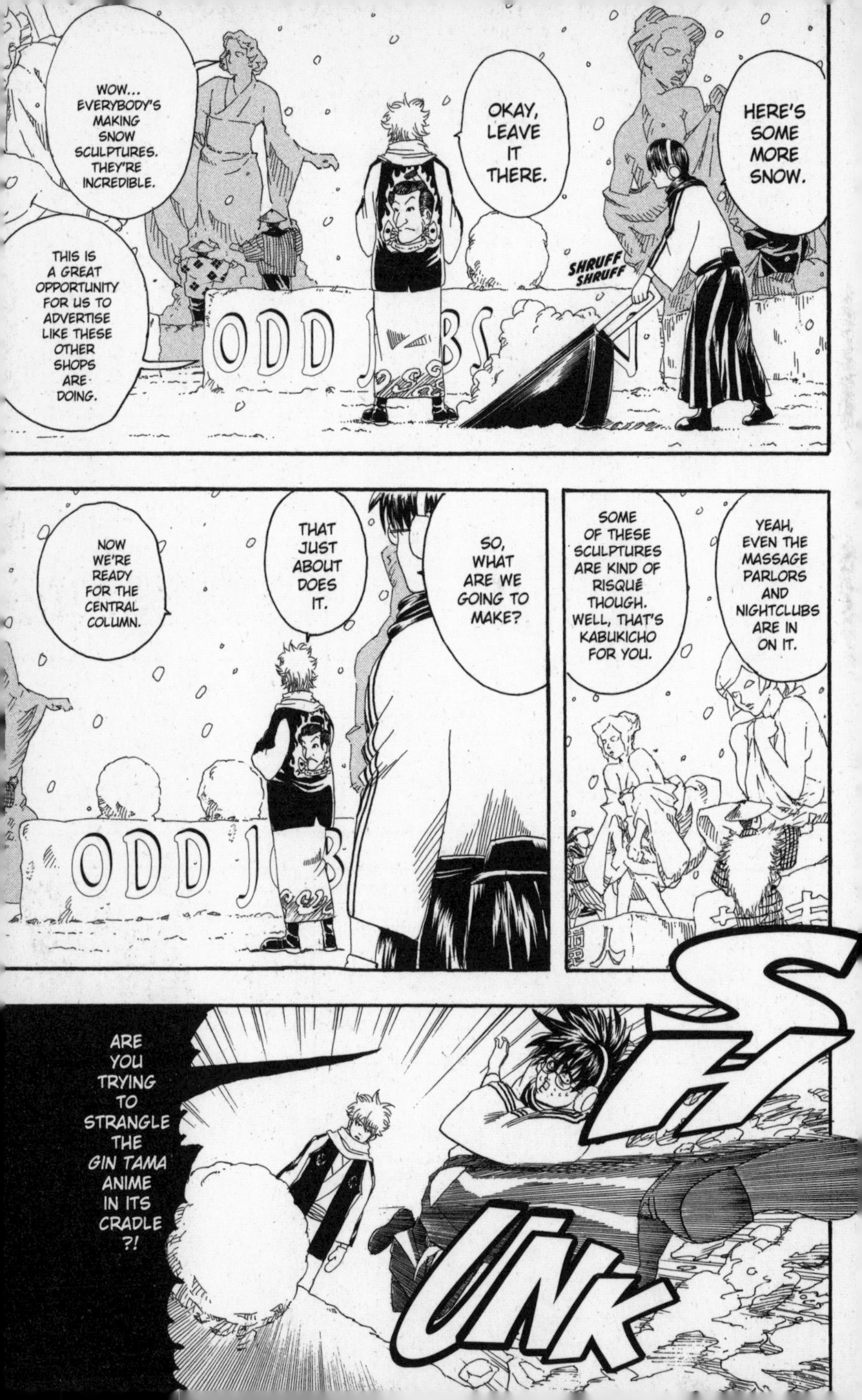
HERE'S SOME MORE SNOW.
SHRUFF SHRUFF
OKAY, LEAVE IT THERE.
WOW... EVERYBODY'S MAKING SNOW SCULPTURES. THEY'RE INCREDIBLE.
THIS IS A GREAT OPPORTUNITY FOR US TO ADVERTISE LIKE THESE OTHER SHOPS ARE DOING.
YEAH, EVEN THE MASSAGE PARLORS AND NIGHTCLUBS ARE IN ON IT.
SOME OF THESE SCULPTURES ARE KIND OF RISQUÉ THOUGH. WELL, THAT'S KABUKICHO FOR YOU.
SO, WHAT ARE WE GOING TO MAKE?
THAT JUST ABOUT DOES IT.
NOW WE'RE READY FOR THE CENTRAL COLUMN.
SHUNK
ARE YOU TRYING TO STRANGLE THE GIN TAMA ANIME IN ITS CRADLE?!

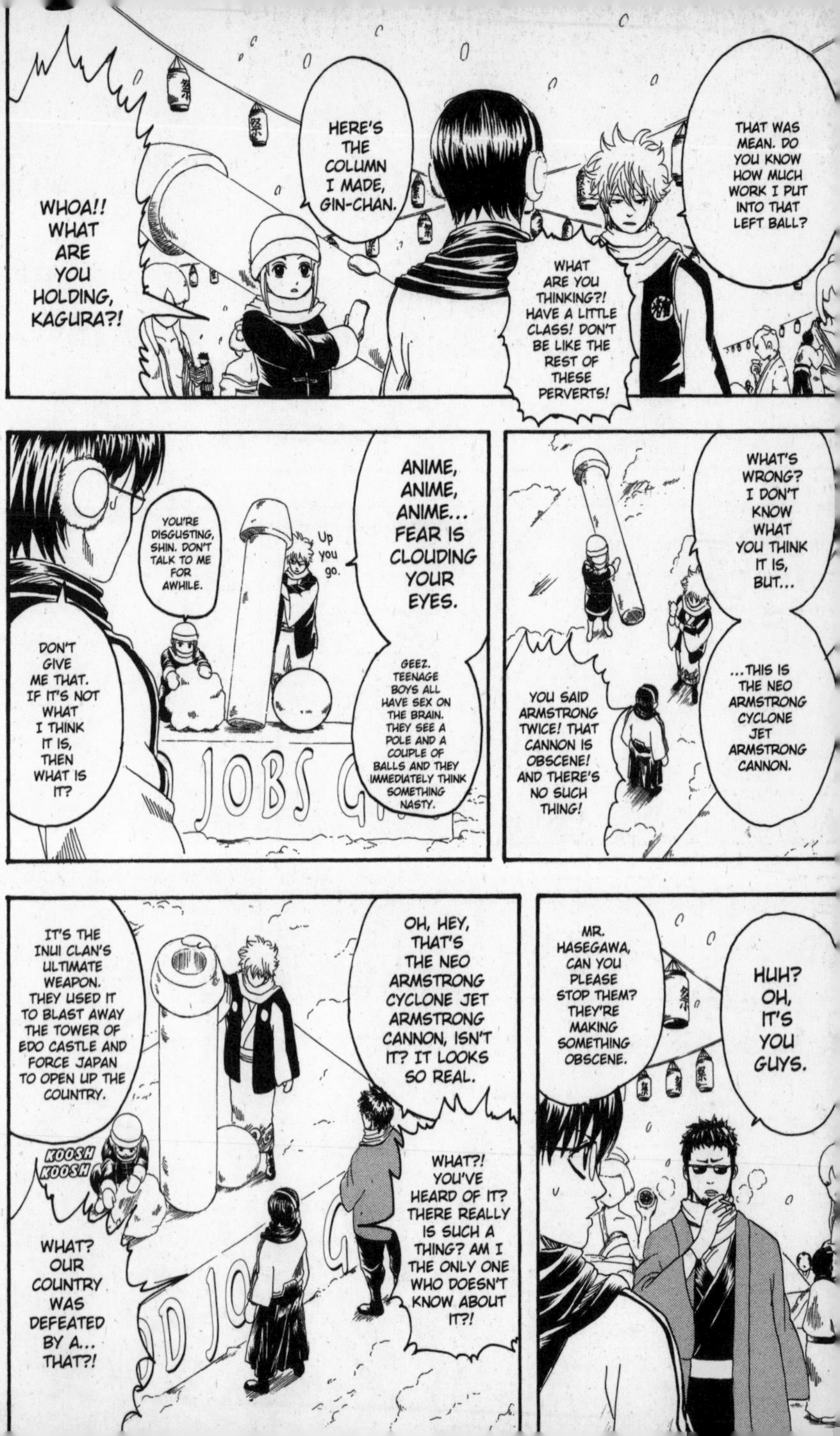
THAT WAS MEAN. DO YOU KNOW HOW MUCH WORK I PUT INTO THAT LEFT BALL?
WHAT ARE YOU THINKING?! HAVE A LITTLE CLASS! DON'T BE LIKE THE REST OF THESE PERVERTS!
HERE'S THE COLUMN I MADE, GIN-CHAN.
WHOA!! WHAT ARE YOU HOLDING, KAGURA?!
WHAT'S WRONG? I DON'T KNOW WHAT YOU THINK IT IS, BUT...
...THIS IS THE NEO ARMSTRONG CYCLONE JET ARMSTRONG CANNON.
YOU SAID ARMSTRONG TWICE! THAT CANNON IS OBSCENE! AND THERE'S NO SUCH THING!
ANIME, ANIME, ANIME... FEAR IS CLOUDING YOUR EYES.
Up you go.
YOU'RE DISGUSTING, SHIN. DON'T TALK TO ME FOR AWHILE.
GEEZ. TEENAGE BOYS ALL HAVE SEX ON THE BRAIN. THEY SEE A POLE AND A COUPLE OF BALLS AND THEY IMMEDIATELY THINK SOMETHING NASTY.
DON'T GIVE ME THAT. IF IT'S NOT WHAT I THINK IT IS, THEN WHAT IS IT?
HUH? OH, IT'S YOU GUYS.
MR. HASEGAWA, CAN YOU PLEASE STOP THEM? THEY'RE MAKING SOMETHING OBSCENE.
OH, HEY, THAT'S THE NEO ARMSTRONG CYCLONE JET ARMSTRONG CANNON, ISN'T IT? IT LOOKS SO REAL.
IT'S THE INUI CLAN'S ULTIMATE WEAPON. THEY USED IT TO BLAST AWAY THE TOWER OF EDO CASTLE AND FORCE JAPAN TO OPEN UP THE COUNTRY.
WHAT?! YOU'VE HEARD OF IT? THERE REALLY IS SUCH A THING? AM I THE ONLY ONE WHO DOESN'T KNOW ABOUT IT?!
KOOSH KOOSH
WHAT? OUR COUNTRY WAS DEFEATED BY A... THAT?!

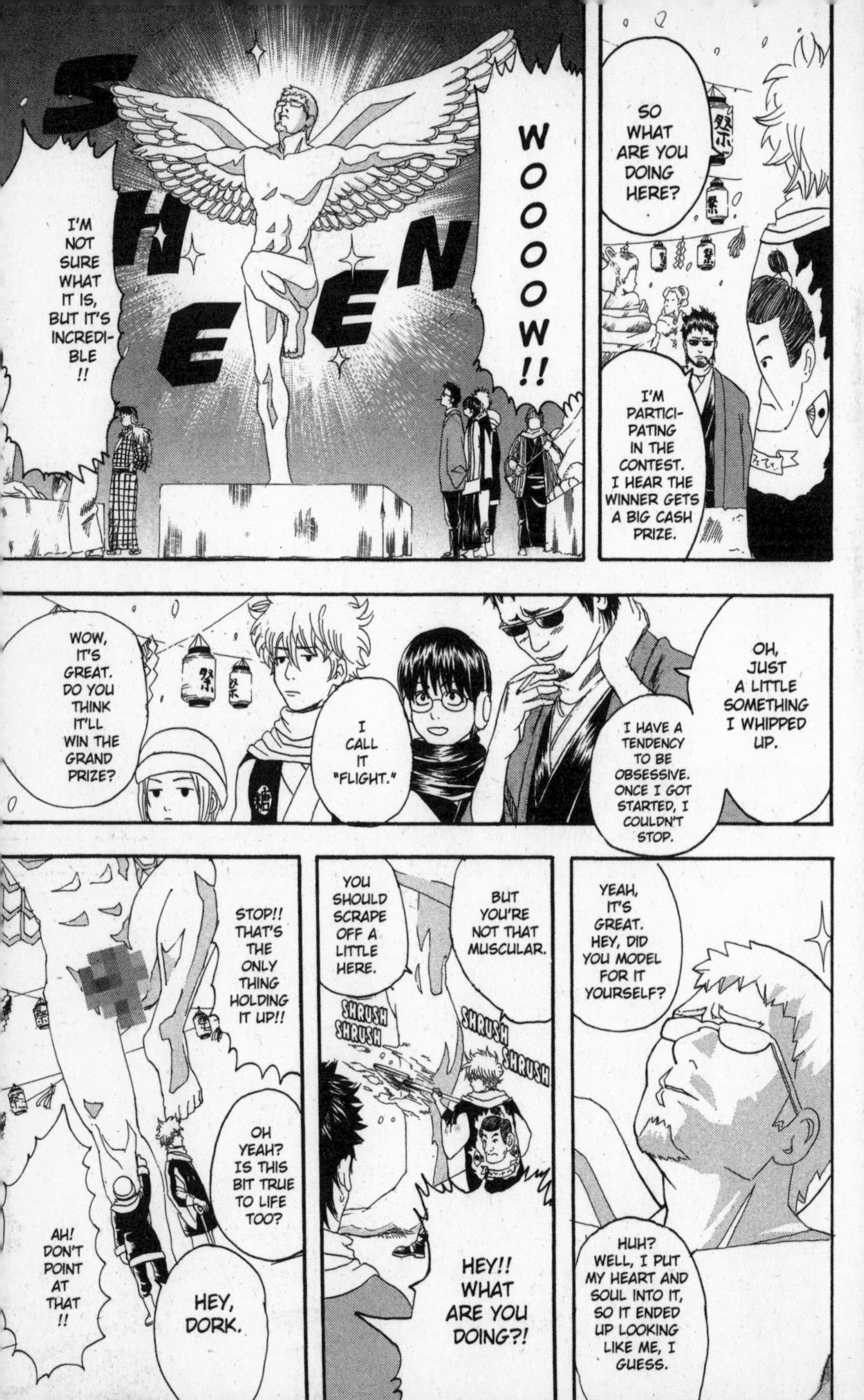

SO WHAT ARE YOU DOING HERE?
I'M PARTICIPATING IN THE CONTEST. I HEAR THE WINNER GETS A BIG CASH PRIZE.
WOOOOOW!!
SHEEN
I'M NOT SURE WHAT IT IS, BUT IT'S INCREDIBLE!!
OH, JUST A LITTLE SOMETHING I WHIPPED UP.
I HAVE A TENDENCY TO BE OBSESSIVE. ONCE I GOT STARTED, I COULDN'T STOP.
I CALL IT "FLIGHT."
WOW, IT'S GREAT. DO YOU THINK IT'LL WIN THE GRAND PRIZE?
YEAH, IT'S GREAT. HEY, DID YOU MODEL FOR IT YOURSELF?
HUH? WELL, I PUT MY HEART AND SOUL INTO IT, SO IT ENDED UP LOOKING LIKE ME, I GUESS.
BUT YOU'RE NOT THAT MUSCULAR.
YOU SHOULD SCRAPE OFF A LITTLE HERE.
SHRUSH SHRUSH
SHRUSH SHRUSH
HEY!! WHAT ARE YOU DOING?!
STOP!! THAT'S THE ONLY THING HOLDING IT UP!!
OH YEAH? IS THIS BIT TRUE TO LIFE TOO?
AH! DON'T POINT AT THAT!!
HEY, DORK.

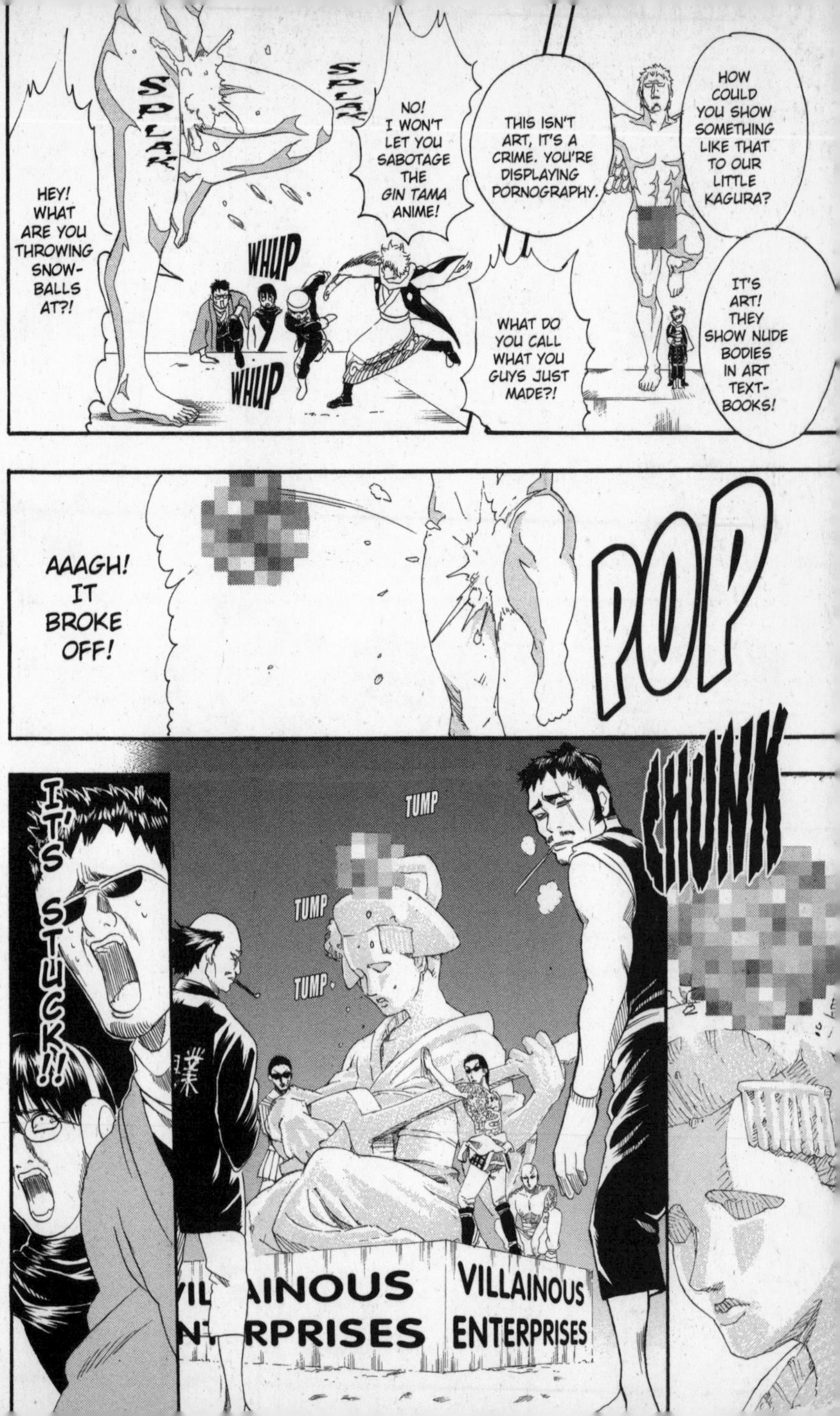
HOW COULD YOU SHOW SOMETHING LIKE THAT TO OUR LITTLE KAGURA?
IT'S ART! THEY SHOW NUDE BODIES IN ART TEXT-BOOKS!
THIS ISN'T ART, IT'S A CRIME. YOU'RE DISPLAYING PORNOGRAPHY.
WHAT DO YOU CALL WHAT YOU GUYS JUST MADE?!
SPLAK
NO! I WON'T LET YOU SABOTAGE THE GIN TAMA ANIME!
SPLAK
WHUP
WHUP
HEY! WHAT ARE YOU THROWING SNOW-BALLS AT?!
POP
AAAGH! IT BROKE OFF!
CHUNK
TUMP
TUMP
TUMP
VILLAINOUS ENTERPRISES
VIL AINOUS NT RPRISES
IT'S STUCK!!

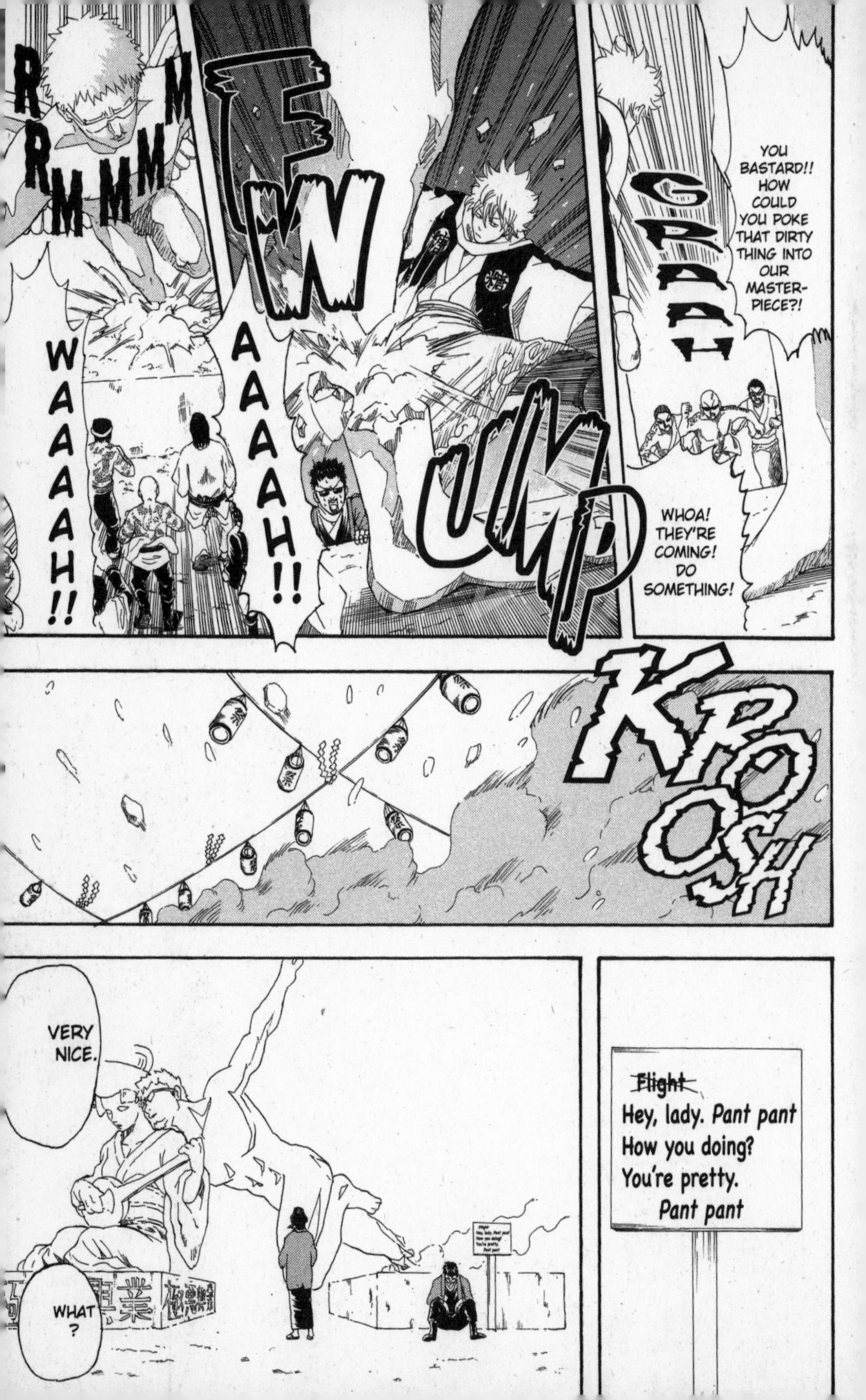
YOU BASTARD!! HOW COULD YOU POKE THAT DIRTY THING INTO OUR MASTER-PIECE?!
GRAAH
WHOA! THEY'RE COMING! DO SOMETHING!
FWUMP
AAAAAH!!
RRMMMMMM
WAAAAAH!!
KROOSH
~~Flight~~
Hey, lady. *Pant pant*
How you doing?
You're pretty.
Pant pant
VERY NICE.
WHAT?

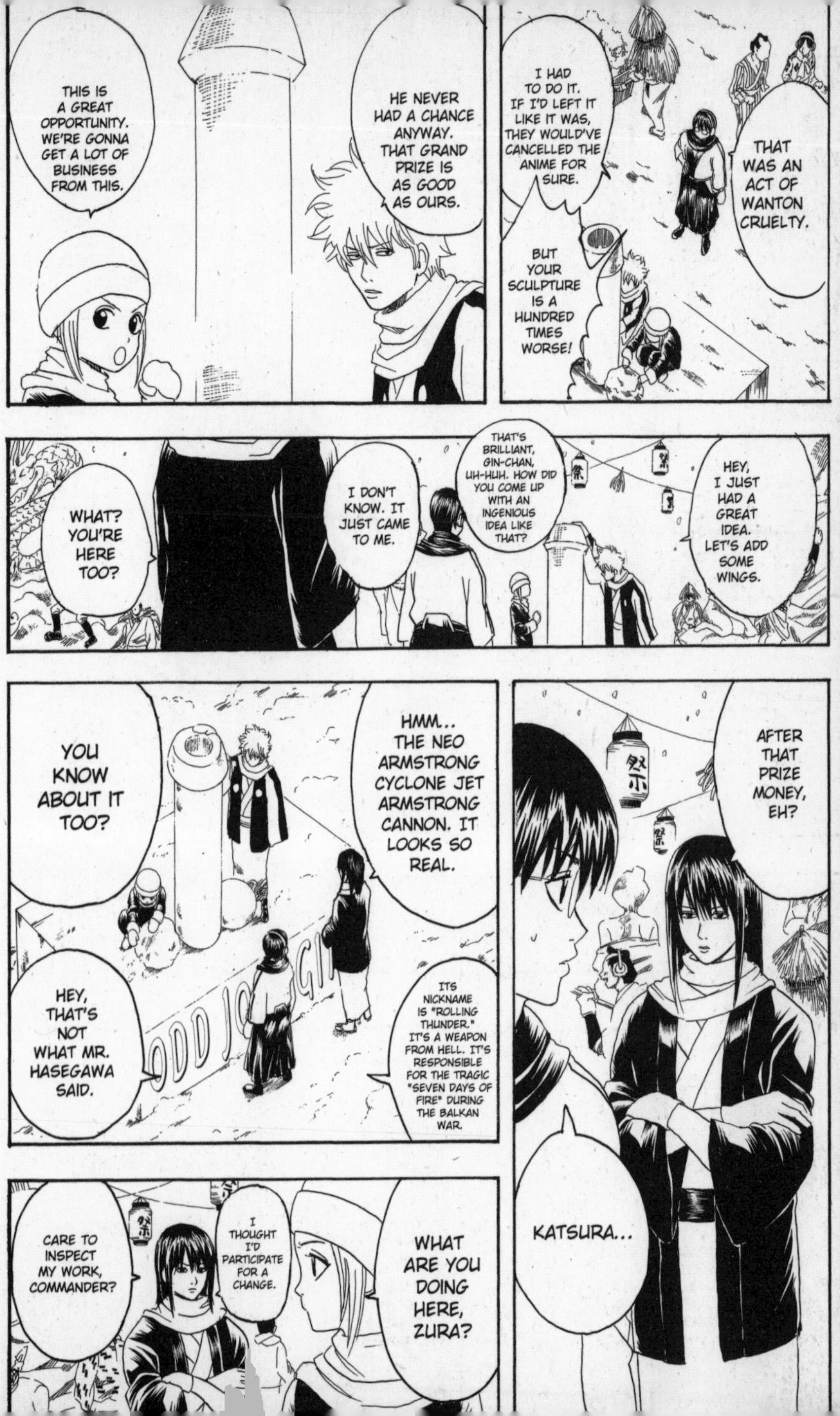
THAT WAS AN ACT OF WANTON CRUELTY.
I HAD TO DO IT. IF I'D LEFT IT LIKE IT WAS, THEY WOULD'VE CANCELLED THE ANIME FOR SURE.
BUT YOUR SCULPTURE IS A HUNDRED TIMES WORSE!
HE NEVER HAD A CHANCE ANYWAY. THAT GRAND PRIZE IS AS GOOD AS OURS.
THIS IS A GREAT OPPORTUNITY. WE'RE GONNA GET A LOT OF BUSINESS FROM THIS.
HEY, I JUST HAD A GREAT IDEA. LET'S ADD SOME WINGS.
THAT'S BRILLIANT, GIN-CHAN, UH-HUH. HOW DID YOU COME UP WITH AN INGENIOUS IDEA LIKE THAT?
I DON'T KNOW. IT JUST CAME TO ME.
WHAT? YOU'RE HERE TOO?
AFTER THAT PRIZE MONEY, EH?
KATSURA...
HMM... THE NEO ARMSTRONG CYCLONE JET ARMSTRONG CANNON. IT LOOKS SO REAL.
YOU KNOW ABOUT IT TOO?
ITS NICKNAME IS "ROLLING THUNDER." IT'S A WEAPON FROM HELL. IT'S RESPONSIBLE FOR THE TRAGIC "SEVEN DAYS OF FIRE" DURING THE BALKAN WAR.
HEY, THAT'S NOT WHAT MR. HASEGAWA SAID.
WHAT ARE YOU DOING HERE, ZURA?
I THOUGHT I'D PARTICIPATE FOR A CHANGE.
CARE TO INSPECT MY WORK, COMMANDER?

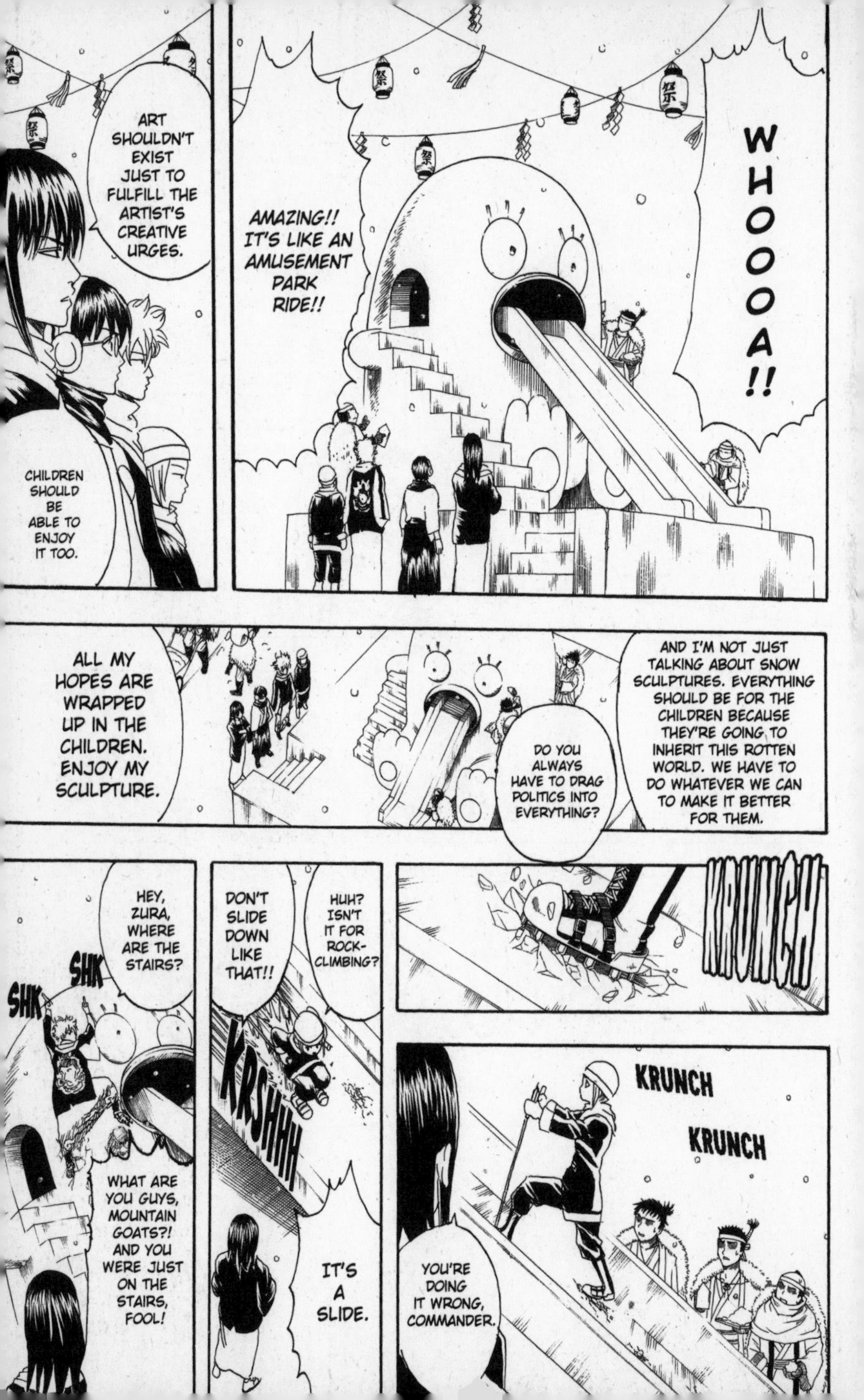
WHOOOA!!
AMAZING!! IT'S LIKE AN AMUSEMENT PARK RIDE!!
ART SHOULDN'T EXIST JUST TO FULFILL THE ARTIST'S CREATIVE URGES.
CHILDREN SHOULD BE ABLE TO ENJOY IT TOO.
AND I'M NOT JUST TALKING ABOUT SNOW SCULPTURES. EVERYTHING SHOULD BE FOR THE CHILDREN BECAUSE THEY'RE GOING TO INHERIT THIS ROTTEN WORLD. WE HAVE TO DO WHATEVER WE CAN TO MAKE IT BETTER FOR THEM.
DO YOU ALWAYS HAVE TO DRAG POLITICS INTO EVERYTHING?
ALL MY HOPES ARE WRAPPED UP IN THE CHILDREN. ENJOY MY SCULPTURE.
KRUNCH
KRUNCH
KRUNCH
YOU'RE DOING IT WRONG, COMMANDER.
HUH? ISN'T IT FOR ROCK-CLIMBING?
DON'T SLIDE DOWN LIKE THAT!!
KRSHHH
IT'S A SLIDE.
HEY, ZURA, WHERE ARE THE STAIRS?
SHK
SHK
WHAT ARE YOU GUYS, MOUNTAIN GOATS?! AND YOU WERE JUST ON THE STAIRS, FOOL!

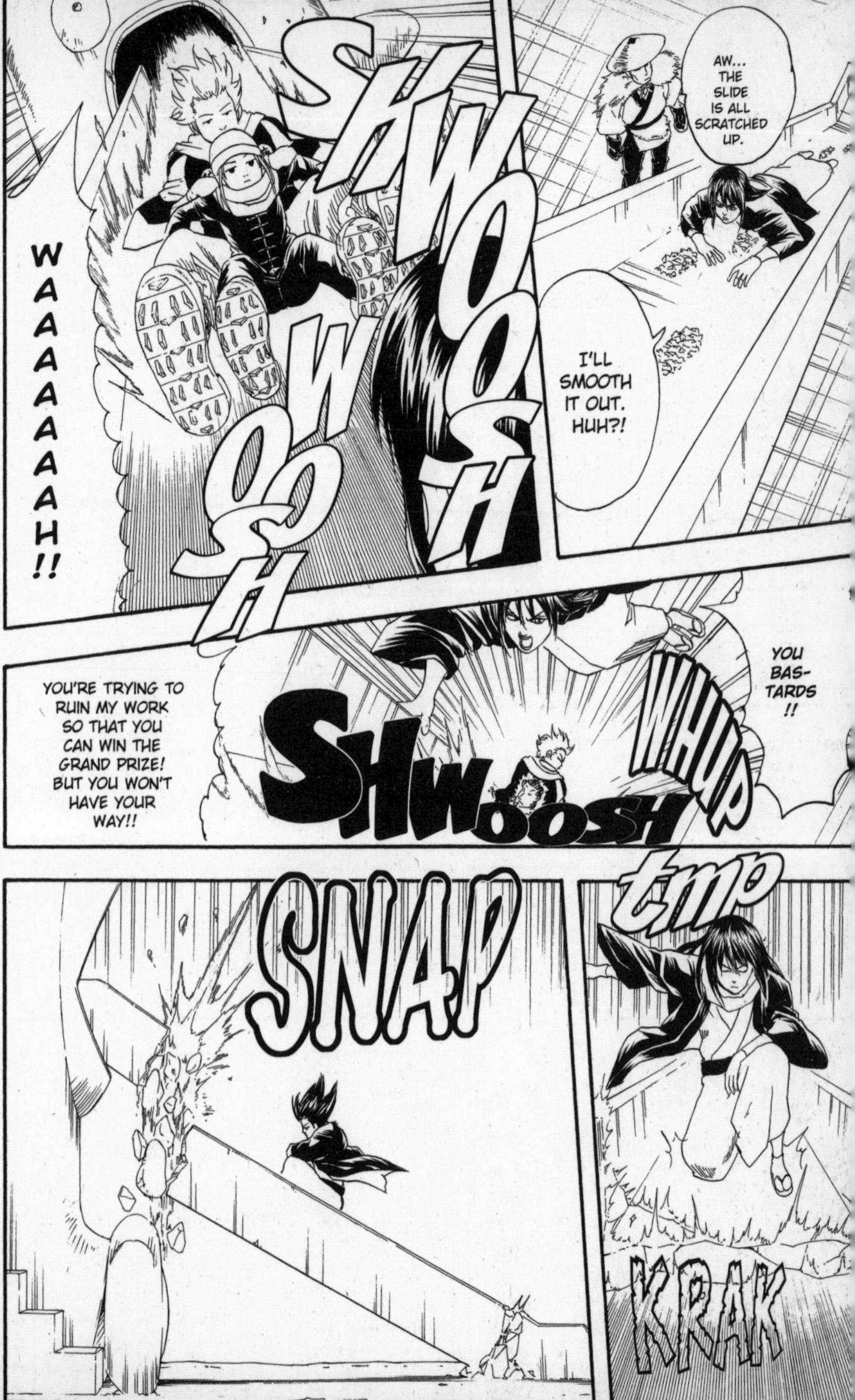
AW... THE SLIDE IS ALL SCRATCHED UP.
I'LL SMOOTH IT OUT. HUH?!
SHWOOSH
SWOOSH
WAAAAAAAH!!
YOU BASTARDS!!
WHUP
SHWOOSH
YOU'RE TRYING TO RUIN MY WORK SO THAT YOU CAN WIN THE GRAND PRIZE! BUT YOU WON'T HAVE YOUR WAY!!
tmp
KRAK
SNAP

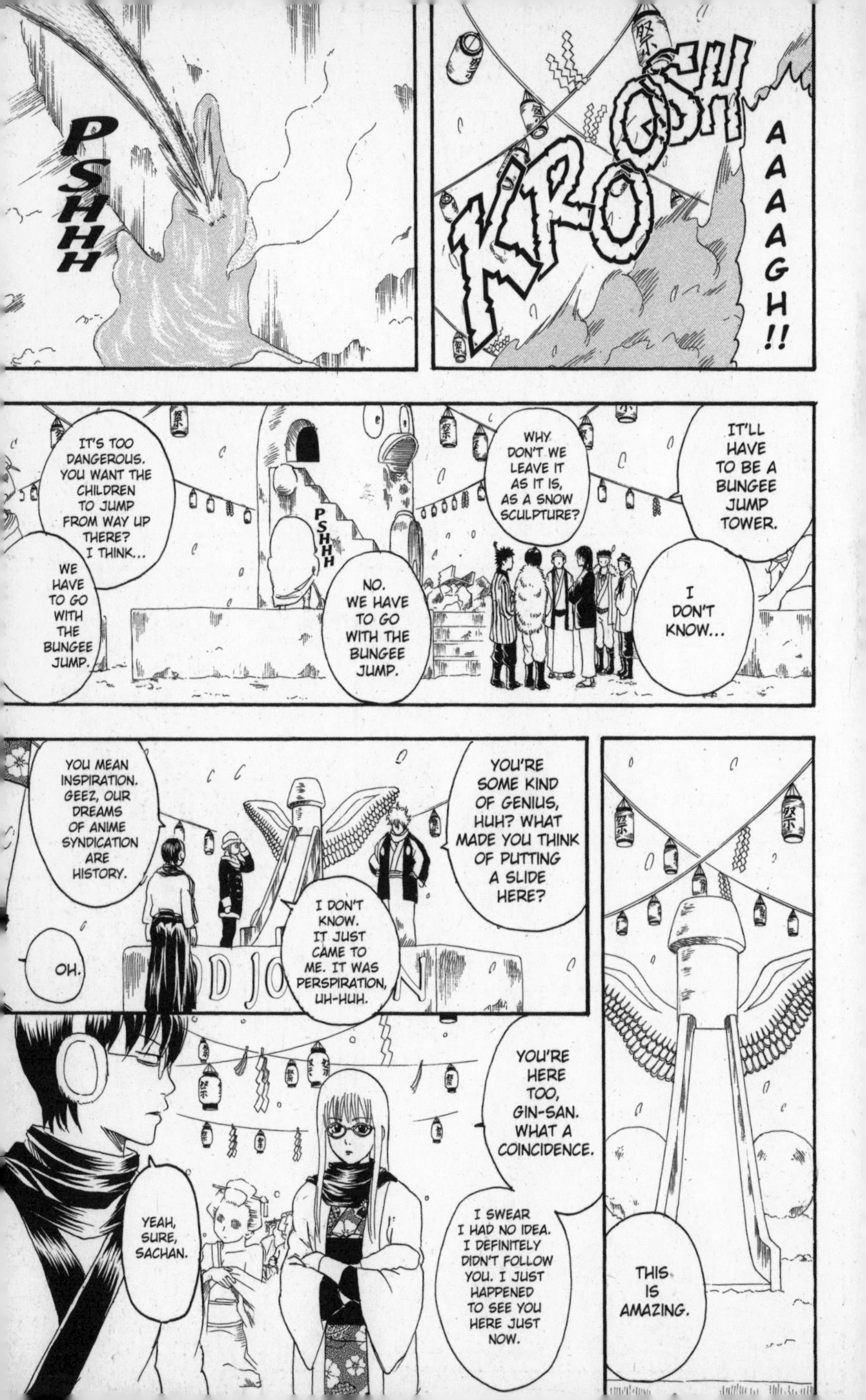
KROOSH
AAAAAGH!!
PSHHH
IT'LL HAVE TO BE A BUNGEE JUMP TOWER.
I DON'T KNOW...
WHY DON'T WE LEAVE IT AS IT IS, AS A SNOW SCULPTURE?
NO. WE HAVE TO GO WITH THE BUNGEE JUMP.
PSHHH
IT'S TOO DANGEROUS. YOU WANT THE CHILDREN TO JUMP FROM WAY UP THERE? I THINK...
WE HAVE TO GO WITH THE BUNGEE JUMP.
THIS IS AMAZING.
YOU'RE SOME KIND OF GENIUS, HUH? WHAT MADE YOU THINK OF PUTTING A SLIDE HERE?
I DON'T KNOW. IT JUST CAME TO ME. IT WAS PERSPIRATION, UH-HUH.
YOU MEAN INSPIRATION. GEEZ, OUR DREAMS OF ANIME SYNDICATION ARE HISTORY.
OH.
YOU'RE HERE TOO, GIN-SAN. WHAT A COINCIDENCE.
I SWEAR I HAD NO IDEA. I DEFINITELY DIDN'T FOLLOW YOU. I JUST HAPPENED TO SEE YOU HERE JUST NOW.
YEAH, SURE, SACHAN.

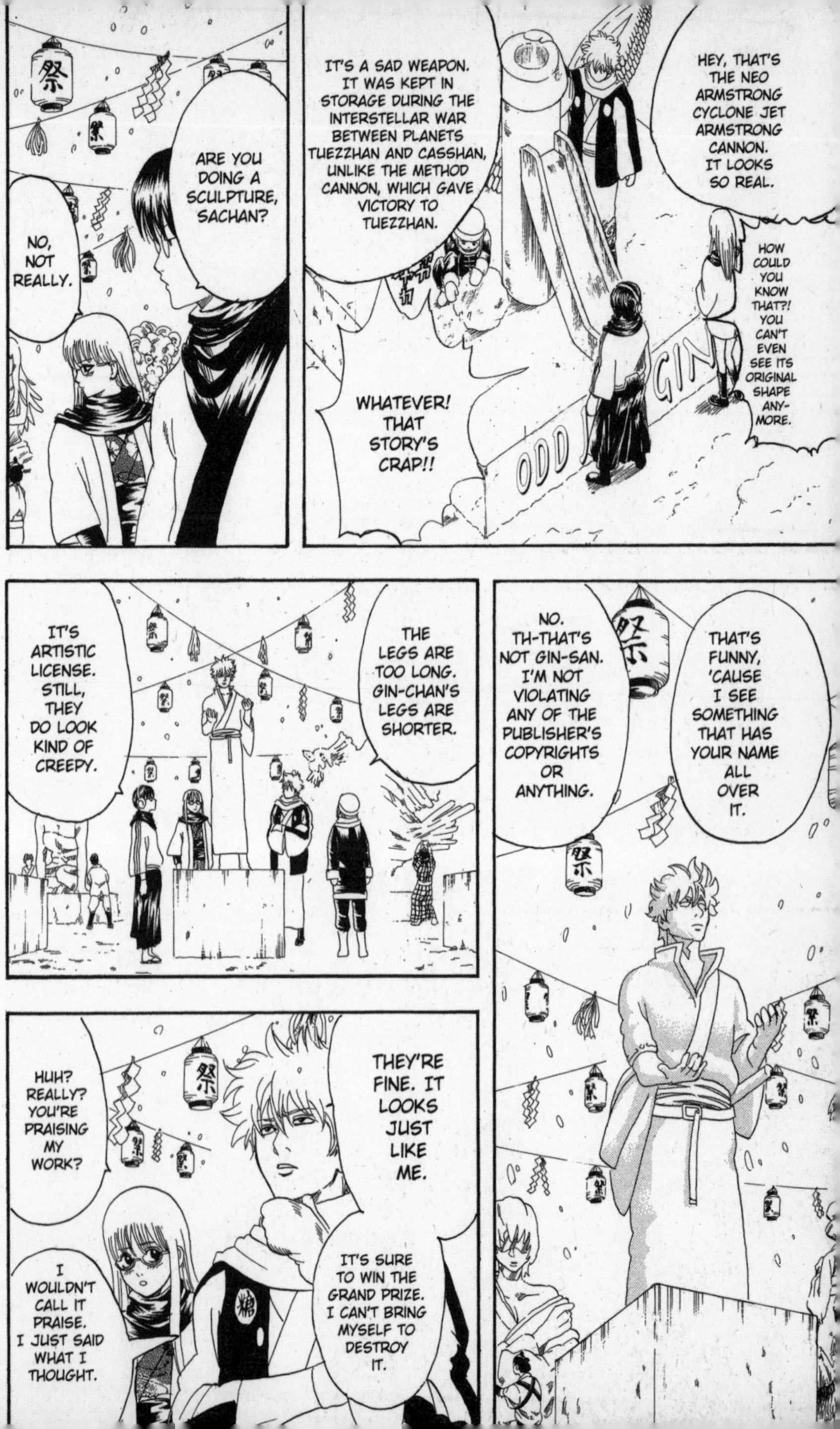
HEY, THAT'S THE NEO ARMSTRONG CYCLONE JET ARMSTRONG CANNON. IT LOOKS SO REAL.
IT'S A SAD WEAPON. IT WAS KEPT IN STORAGE DURING THE INTERSTELLAR WAR BETWEEN PLANETS TUEZZHAN AND CASSHAN, UNLIKE THE METHOD CANNON, WHICH GAVE VICTORY TO TUEZZHAN.
HOW COULD YOU KNOW THAT?! YOU CAN'T EVEN SEE ITS ORIGINAL SHAPE ANY-MORE.
WHATEVER! THAT STORY'S CRAP!!
ODD GIN
ARE YOU DOING A SCULPTURE, SACHAN?
NO, NOT REALLY.
THAT'S FUNNY, 'CAUSE I SEE SOMETHING THAT HAS YOUR NAME ALL OVER IT.
NO. TH-THAT'S NOT GIN-SAN. I'M NOT VIOLATING ANY OF THE PUBLISHER'S COPYRIGHTS OR ANYTHING.
THE LEGS ARE TOO LONG. GIN-CHAN'S LEGS ARE SHORTER.
IT'S ARTISTIC LICENSE. STILL, THEY DO LOOK KIND OF CREEPY.
THEY'RE FINE. IT LOOKS JUST LIKE ME.
HUH? REALLY? YOU'RE PRAISING MY WORK?
IT'S SURE TO WIN THE GRAND PRIZE. I CAN'T BRING MYSELF TO DESTROY IT.
I WOULDN'T CALL IT PRAISE. I JUST SAID WHAT I THOUGHT.

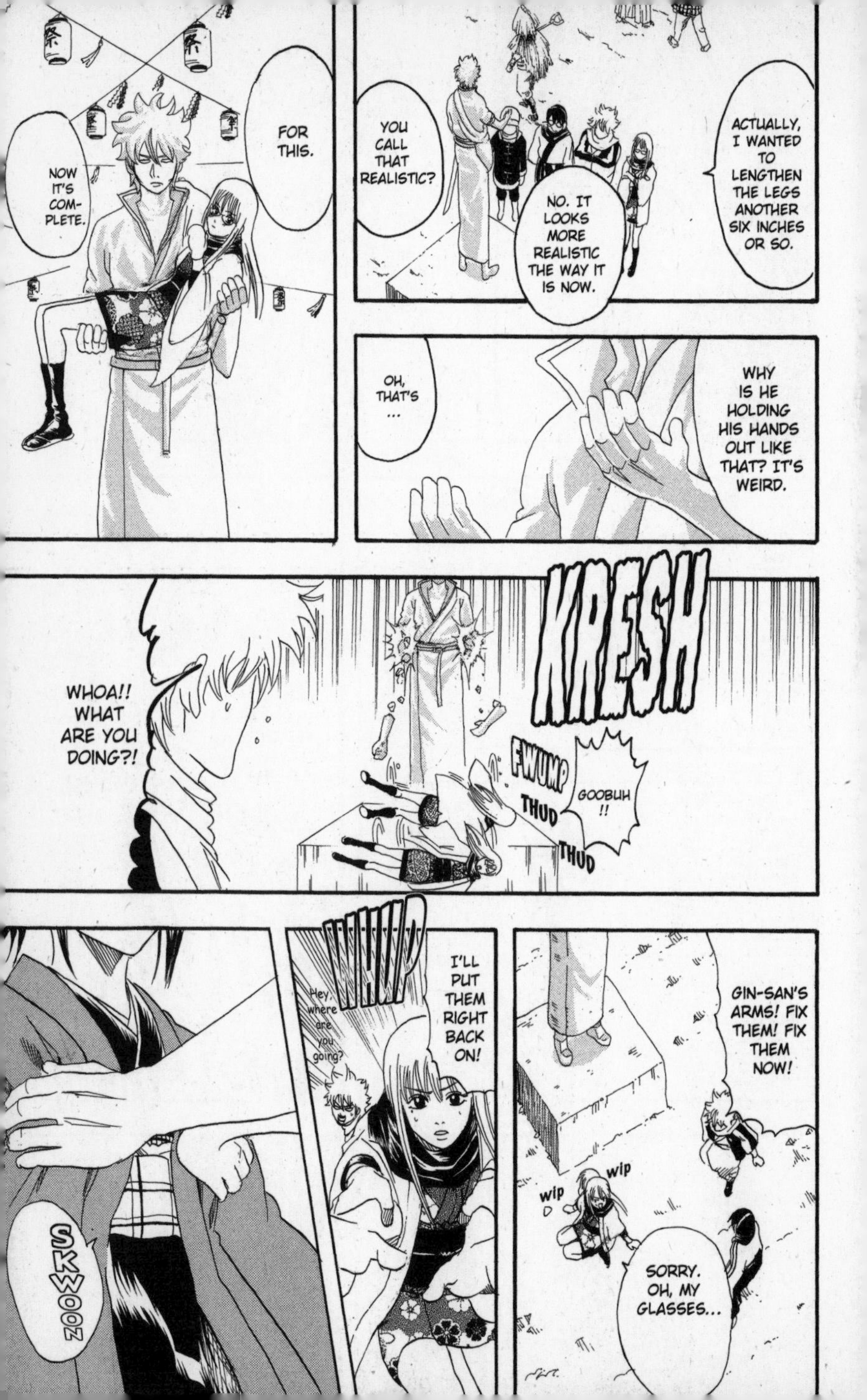
ACTUALLY, I WANTED TO LENGTHEN THE LEGS ANOTHER SIX INCHES OR SO.
NO. IT LOOKS MORE REALISTIC THE WAY IT IS NOW.
YOU CALL THAT REALISTIC?
WHY IS HE HOLDING HIS HANDS OUT LIKE THAT? IT'S WEIRD.
OH, THAT'S ...
FOR THIS.
NOW IT'S COM-PLETE.
KRESH
FWUMP
GOOBUH !!
THUD
THUD
WHOA!! WHAT ARE YOU DOING?!
GIN-SAN'S ARMS! FIX THEM! FIX THEM NOW!
wip
wip
SORRY. OH, MY GLASSES...
WHIP
I'LL PUT THEM RIGHT BACK ON!
Hey, where are you going?
SKWOON

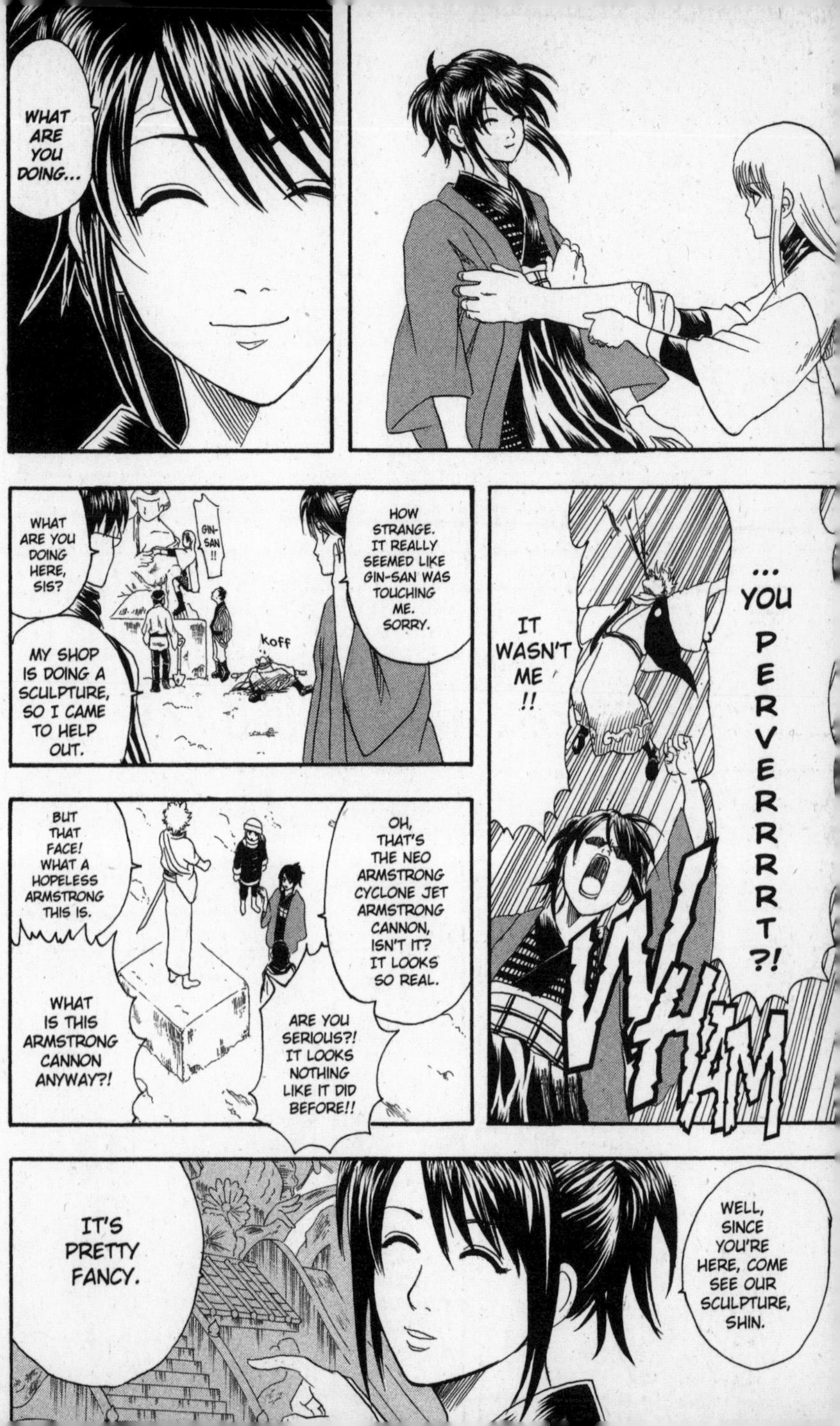
WHAT ARE YOU DOING...
... YOU PERVERRRRT?!
IT WASN'T ME!!
WHAM
HOW STRANGE. IT REALLY SEEMED LIKE GIN-SAN WAS TOUCHING ME. SORRY.
GIN-SAN!!
koff
WHAT ARE YOU DOING HERE, SIS?
MY SHOP IS DOING A SCULPTURE, SO I CAME TO HELP OUT.
OH, THAT'S THE NEO ARMSTRONG CYCLONE JET ARMSTRONG CANNON, ISN'T IT? IT LOOKS SO REAL.
BUT THAT FACE! WHAT A HOPELESS ARMSTRONG THIS IS.
ARE YOU SERIOUS?! IT LOOKS NOTHING LIKE IT DID BEFORE!!
WHAT IS THIS ARMSTRONG CANNON ANYWAY?!
WELL, SINCE YOU'RE HERE, COME SEE OUR SCULPTURE, SHIN.
IT'S PRETTY FANCY.

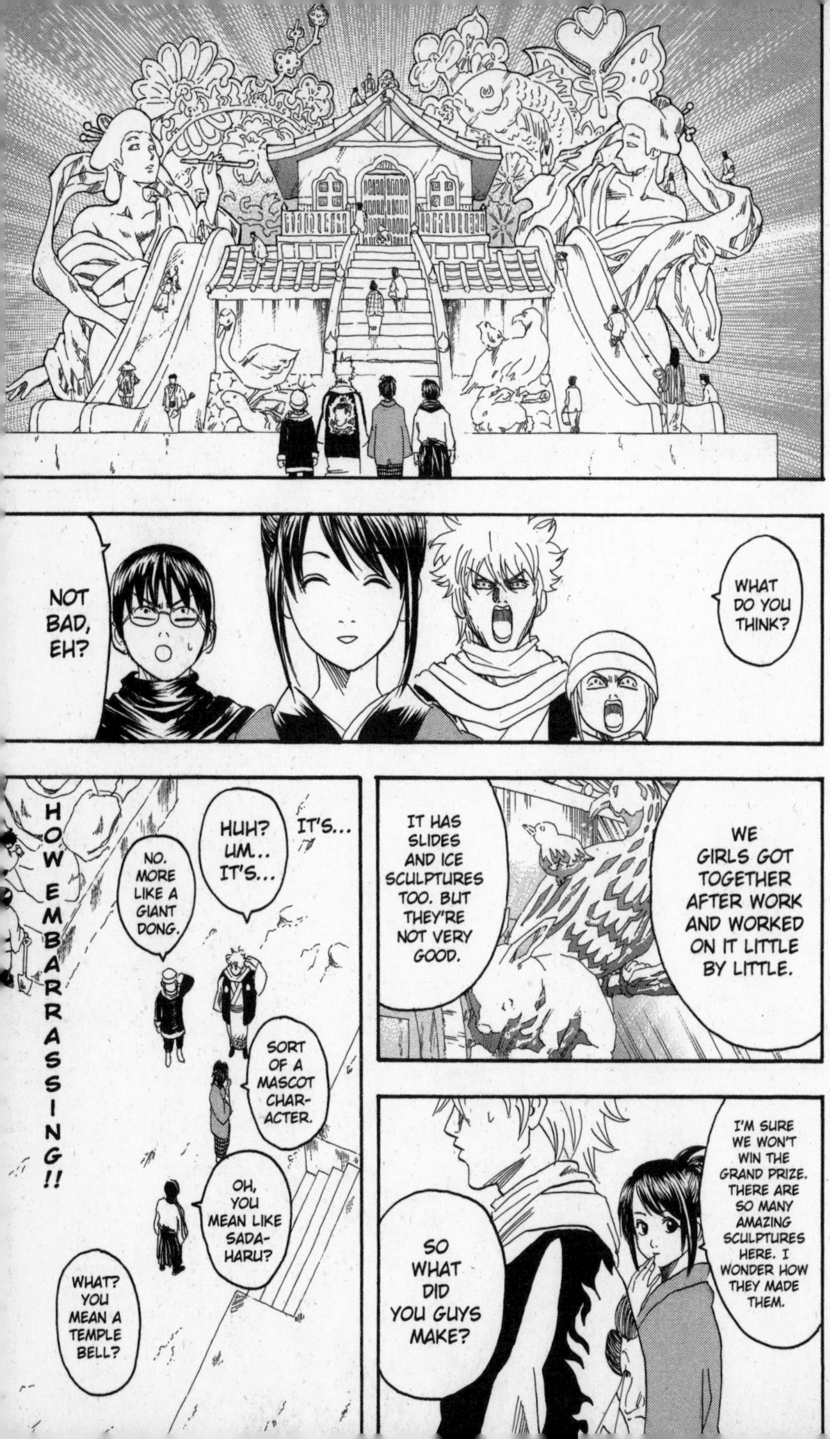
WHAT DO YOU THINK?
NOT BAD, EH?
WE GIRLS GOT TOGETHER AFTER WORK AND WORKED ON IT LITTLE BY LITTLE.
IT HAS SLIDES AND ICE SCULPTURES TOO. BUT THEY'RE NOT VERY GOOD.
I'M SURE WE WON'T WIN THE GRAND PRIZE. THERE ARE SO MANY AMAZING SCULPTURES HERE. I WONDER HOW THEY MADE THEM.
SO WHAT DID YOU GUYS MAKE?
IT'S...
HUH? UM... IT'S...
NO. MORE LIKE A GIANT DONG.
HOW EMBARRASSING!!
SORT OF A MASCOT CHARACTER.
OH, YOU MEAN LIKE SADAHARU?
WHAT? YOU MEAN A TEMPLE BELL?

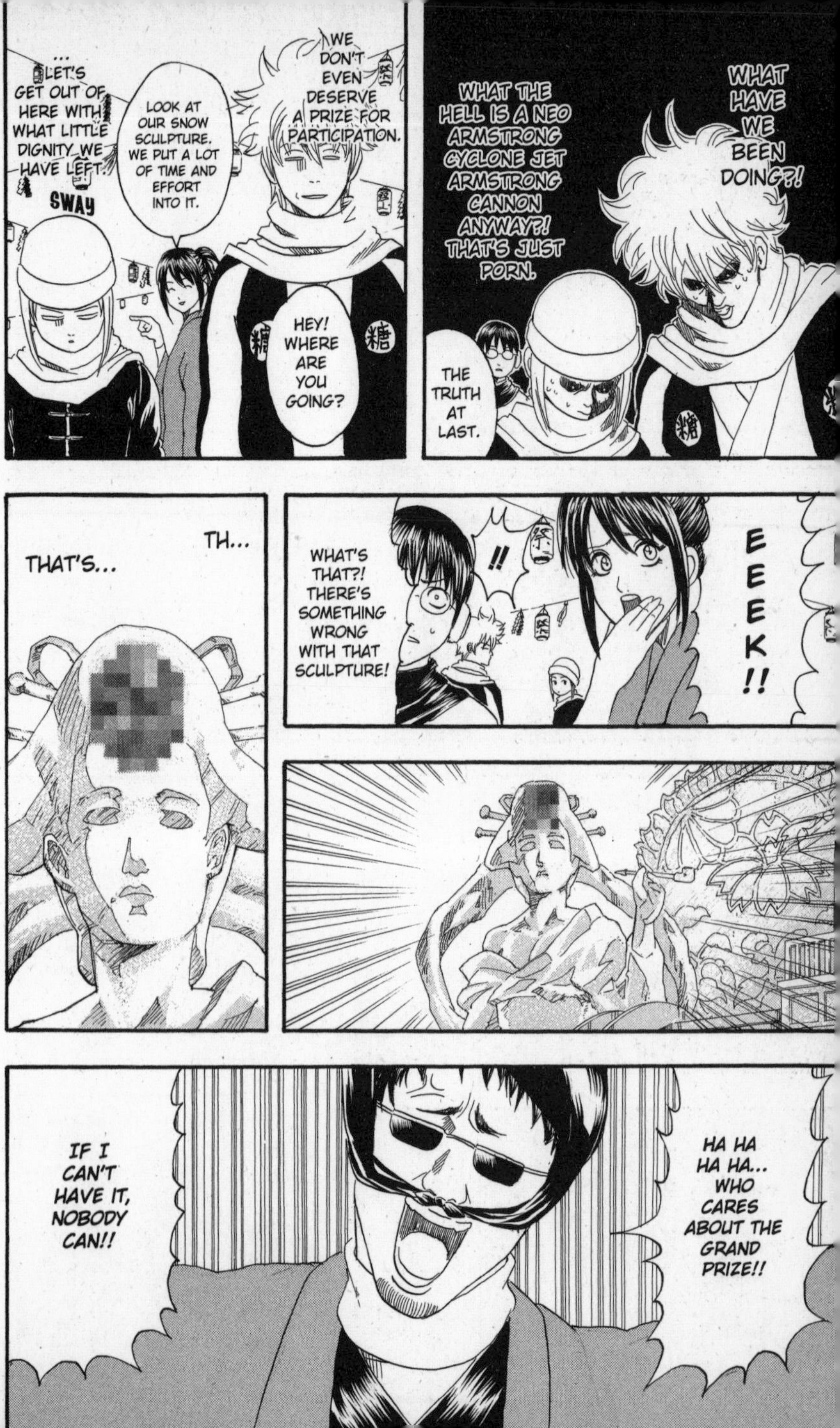
WHAT HAVE WE BEEN DOING?!
WHAT THE HELL IS A NEO ARMSTRONG CYCLONE JET ARMSTRONG CANNON ANYWAY?! THAT'S JUST PORN.
THE TRUTH AT LAST.
WE DON'T EVEN DESERVE A PRIZE FOR PARTICIPATION.
LOOK AT OUR SNOW SCULPTURE. WE PUT A LOT OF TIME AND EFFORT INTO IT.
... LET'S GET OUT OF HERE WITH WHAT LITTLE DIGNITY WE HAVE LEFT.
SWAY
HEY! WHERE ARE YOU GOING?
EEEK!!
!!
WHAT'S THAT?! THERE'S SOMETHING WRONG WITH THAT SCULPTURE!
TH...
THAT'S...
HA HA HA HA... WHO CARES ABOUT THE GRAND PRIZE!!
IF I CAN'T HAVE IT, NOBODY CAN!!

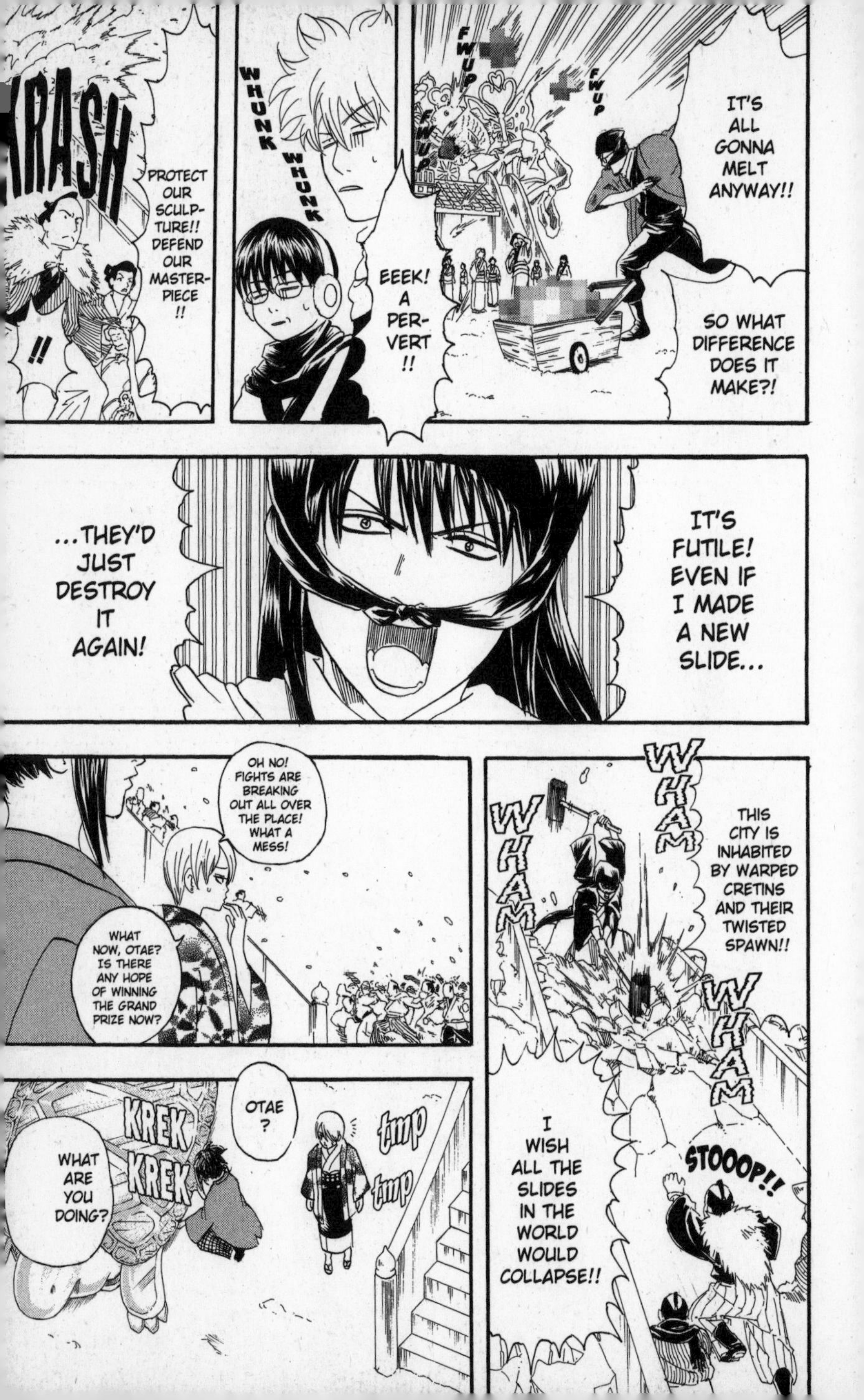
FWUP
FWUP
FWUP
FWUP
IT'S ALL GONNA MELT ANYWAY!!
SO WHAT DIFFERENCE DOES IT MAKE?!
WHUNK
WHUNK
EEEK! A PER-VERT!!
KRASH
PROTECT OUR SCULP-TURE!! DEFEND OUR MASTER-PIECE!!
!!
IT'S FUTILE! EVEN IF I MADE A NEW SLIDE...
...THEY'D JUST DESTROY IT AGAIN!
WHAM
WHAM
THIS CITY IS INHABITED BY WARPED CRETINS AND THEIR TWISTED SPAWN!!
WHAM
I WISH ALL THE SLIDES IN THE WORLD WOULD COLLAPSE!!
STOOOP!!
OH NO! FIGHTS ARE BREAKING OUT ALL OVER THE PLACE! WHAT A MESS!
WHAT NOW, OTAE? IS THERE ANY HOPE OF WINNING THE GRAND PRIZE NOW?
tmp
tmp
OTAE?
KREK
KREK
WHAT ARE YOU DOING?

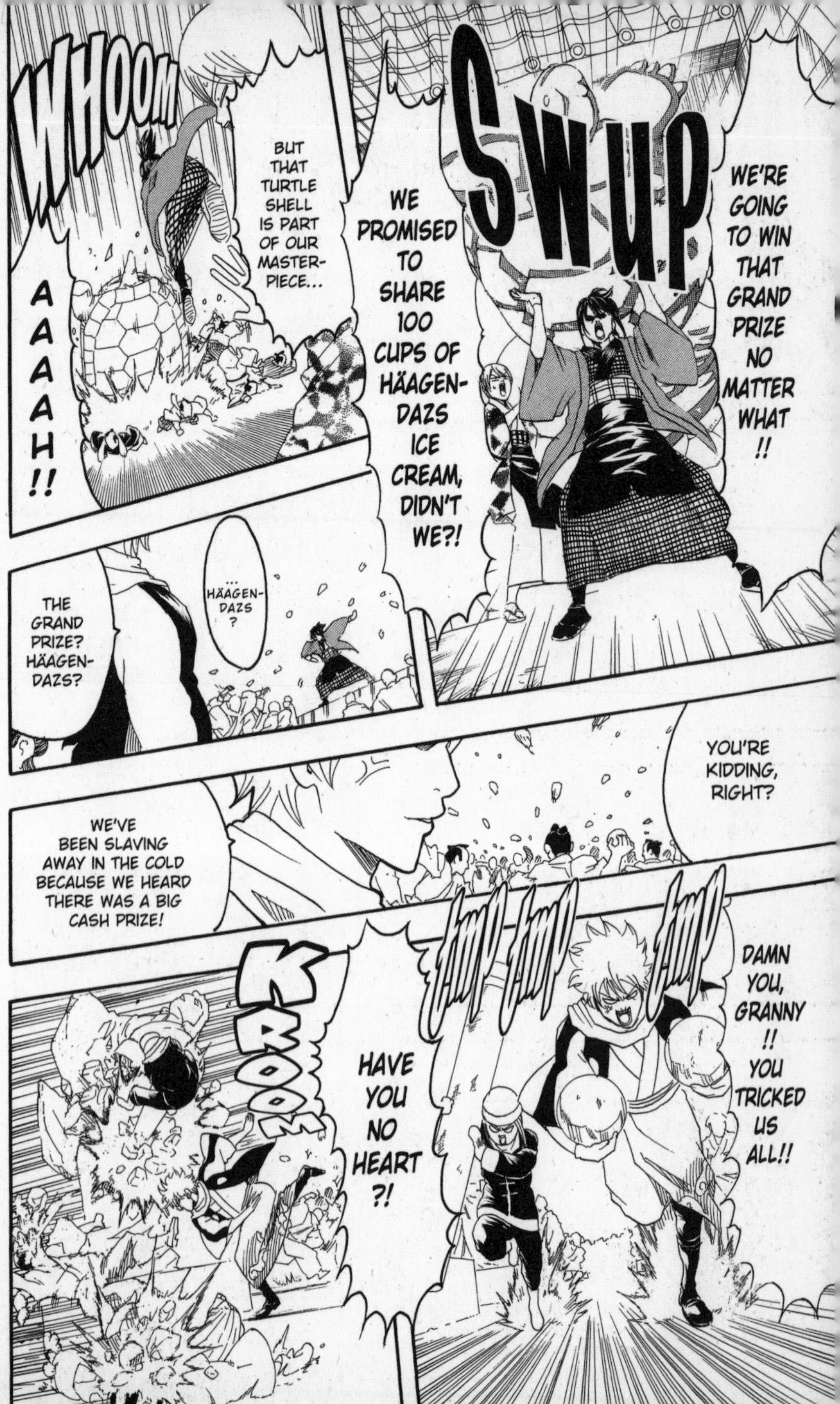
SWUP
WE'RE GOING TO WIN THAT GRAND PRIZE NO MATTER WHAT!!
WE PROMISED TO SHARE 100 CUPS OF HÄAGEN-DAZS ICE CREAM, DIDN'T WE?!
WHOOM
BUT THAT TURTLE SHELL IS PART OF OUR MASTER-PIECE...
AAAAAH!!
... HÄAGEN-DAZS ?
THE GRAND PRIZE? HÄAGEN-DAZS?
YOU'RE KIDDING, RIGHT?
WE'VE BEEN SLAVING AWAY IN THE COLD BECAUSE WE HEARD THERE WAS A BIG CASH PRIZE!
DAMN YOU, GRANNY!! YOU TRICKED US ALL!!
HAVE YOU NO HEART?!

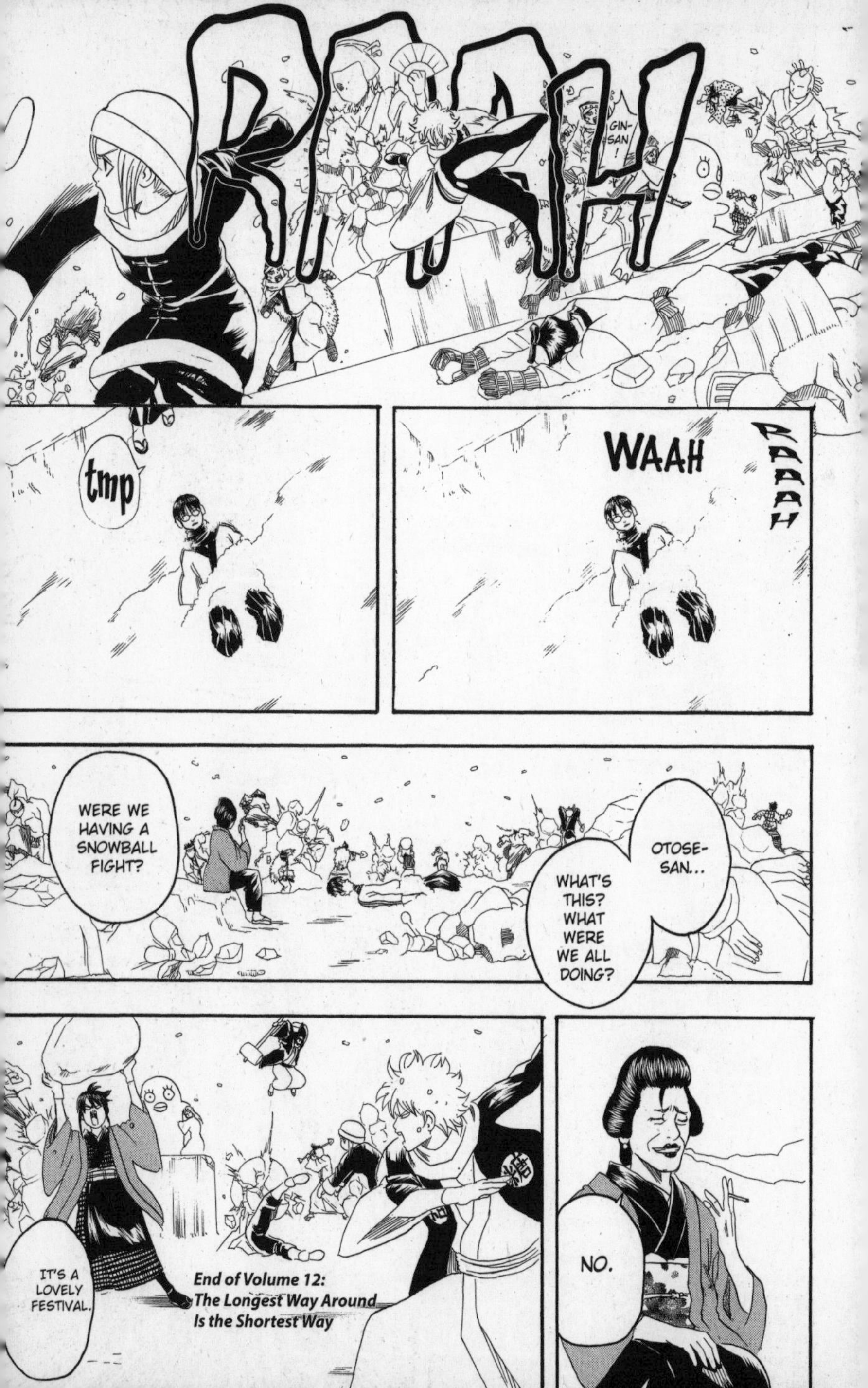
RAAH
GIN-SAN!
RAAAH
WAAH
tmp
OTOSE-SAN... WHAT'S THIS? WHAT WERE WE ALL DOING?
WERE WE HAVING A SNOWBALL FIGHT?
NO.
IT'S A LOVELY FESTIVAL.
End of Volume 12: The Longest Way Around Is the Shortest Way

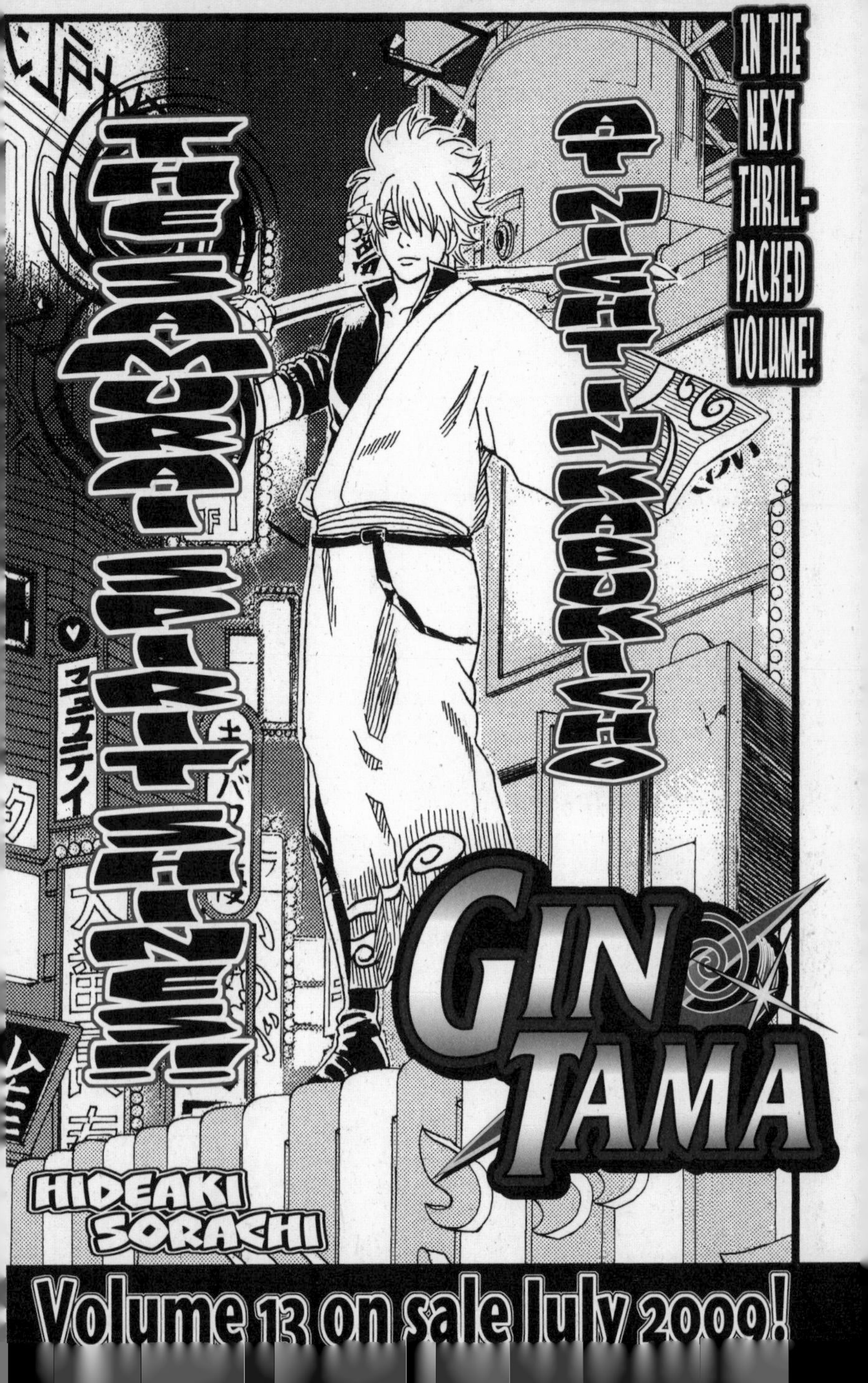
IN THE NEXT THRILL-PACKED VOLUME!
GIN TAMA
HIDEAKI SORACHI
Volume 13 on sale July 2009!

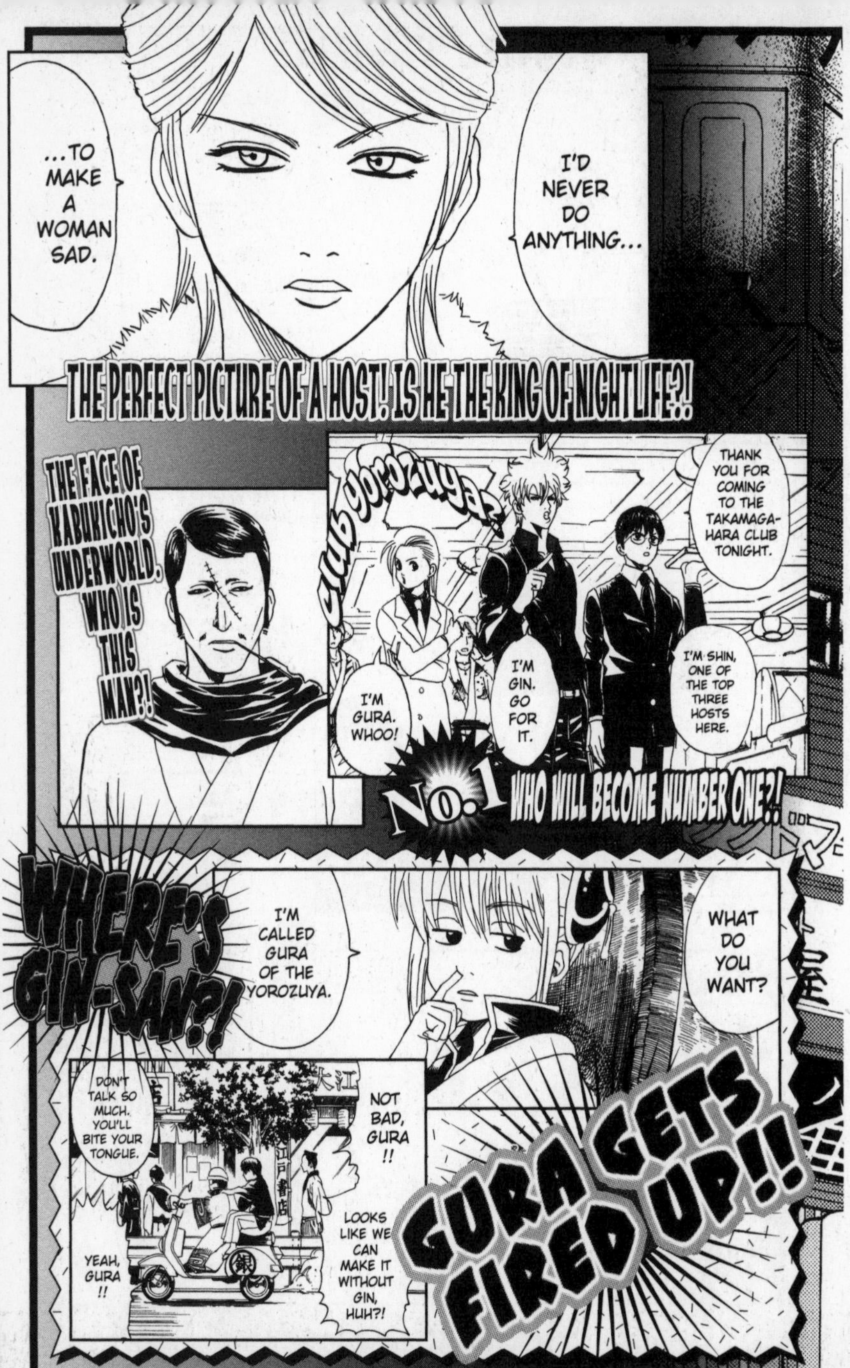
I'D NEVER DO ANYTHING...
...TO MAKE A WOMAN SAD.
THE PERFECT PICTURE OF A HOST! IS HE THE KING OF NIGHTLIFE?!
CLUB YOROZUYA?
THANK YOU FOR COMING TO THE TAKAMAGA-HARA CLUB TONIGHT.
I'M SHIN, ONE OF THE TOP THREE HOSTS HERE.
I'M GIN. GO FOR IT.
I'M GURA. WHOO!
No.1 WHO WILL BECOME NUMBER ONE?!
THE FACE OF KABUKICHO'S UNDERWORLD. WHO IS THIS MAN?!
WHAT DO YOU WANT?
I'M CALLED GURA OF THE YOROZUYA.
WHERE'S GIN-SAN?!
GURA GETS FIRED UP!!
NOT BAD, GURA !!
DON'T TALK SO MUCH. YOU'LL BITE YOUR TONGUE.
LOOKS LIKE WE CAN MAKE IT WITHOUT GIN, HUH?!
YEAH, GURA !!

Gorilla Thrilla!

Gin's Street Fighting Lessons Learned (Top 5)

1. Frontal wedgies are extremely effective.
2. Girls hit a lot harder the more innocent they look (unless they are alien gorillas).
3. Only morons start fights in the Ninja Bar. Yeah, only morons…
4. Using a bazooka is cheating (but it sure settles things quickly).
5. No one hits harder than Shinpachi's sister Otae when she's riled.

COMING JULY 2009